PESSIMISM

PESSIMISM

PHILOSOPHY, ETHIC, SPIRIT

Joshua Foa Dienstag

PRINCETON UNIVERSITY PRESS

PRINCETON AND OXFORD

KH

Library of Congress Cataloging-in-Publication Data

Dienstag, Joshua Foa, 1965–

Pessimism : philosophy, ethic, spirit / Joshua Foa Dienstag.

p.   cm.

Includes bibliographical references and index.

ISBN-13: 978-0-691-12552-7 (cloth : alk. paper)

ISBN-10: 0-691-12552-X (cloth : alk. paper)

1. Pessimism.   2. Pessimism—Political aspects.   I. Title.

B829.D54   2006

149'.6—dc22   2005056513

British Library Cataloging-in-Publication Data is available

This book has been composed in Sabon Typeface

Printed on acid-free paper. ∞

pup.princeton.edu

Printed in the United States of America

1   3   5   7   9   10   8   6   4   2

2/7/08

for Jenn

All the tragedies which we can imagine
return in the end to the one and only tragedy:
the passage of time.

—SIMONE WEIL

CONTENTS

Preface   ix

Acknowledgments   xv

Abbreviations   xvii

PART I

CHAPTER ONE
The Anatomy of Pessimism   3

PART II

CHAPTER TWO
"A Philosophy That Is Grievous but True": Cultural Pessimism
in Rousseau and Leopardi   49

CHAPTER THREE
"The Evils of the World Honestly Admitted": Metaphysical
Pessimism in Schopenhauer and Freud   84

CHAPTER FOUR
"Consciousness Is a Disease": Existential Pessimism
in Camus, Unamuno, and Cioran   118

PART III

CHAPTER FIVE
Nietzsche's Dionysian Pessimism   161

CHAPTER SIX
Cervantes as Educator: *Don Quixote* and the Practice
of Pessimism   201

CHAPTER SEVEN
Aphorisms and Pessimisms   226

CHAPTER EIGHT
Pessimism and Freedom (The Pessimist Speaks)   244

Afterword   265

Bibliography   273

Index   283

PREFACE

PERHAPS I should get the most difficult matter—to some no doubt the most shocking matter—out of the way first: namely, that this book on the pessimistic spirit is not an attack on that spirit but, instead, an appraisal and, indeed, an endorsement of it, at least in a certain form. That this will strike most readers as perverse cannot be helped. Indeed, it is my first request of readers that they take this reaction, quite common in itself, and examine it. Why is it that pessimism, once a respectable if not popular philosophy, has become so despised in our culture that the word "pessimist" can be used today as a term of political or intellectual abuse? Look in any American newspaper for a few days and one will immediately see that this is true. It is enough to label an idea (or a person) "pessimistic" in order to be allowed to dismiss it (or him) without further discussion as irrational, emotional, indefensible or, worst of all, unpatriotic.

Why should this be? After all, an expectation that things will go badly is not, on the surface, any more or less rational than the expectation that things will go well. An extended examination of the question could well yield a judgment in favor of the one or the other—but the label is used precisely to foreclose such an inquiry. Pessimism is dismissed before serious debate begins, not during or afterward. One might venture that, somehow, the idea of pessimism is so threatening that people decline to consider it seriously because they are afraid of the effects such a consideration might produce. But then this phenomenon itself should be enough of a curiosity to require investigation. While those so fearing might be tempted to stop at this point, I can at least dispute the common perception that pessimism must somehow necessarily issue in behaviors of resignation and withdrawal.

Of course, some pessimisms *might* result in such a posture. But to assume that all pessimists are thus is akin to claiming that all optimists must arrive at the attitude of Dr. Pangloss, who believed that this was the best of all possible worlds. Not every theory of progress is Panglossian and, likewise, not all pessimisms are suicidal or nihilistic. This book does not defend all pessimisms, then, but a more particular one that will emerge in the course of its chapters. One point of my title, however, is to reverse the customary understanding of pessimism as something necessarily dispiriting. In the right hands, pessimism can be—and has been—an energizing and even a liberating philosophy. While it does indeed ask us to limit and eliminate some of our hopes and expectations, it can also provide us with the means to better navigate the bounded universe it describes.

There exists today an entire literature, both scholarly and popular, de-

voted to blaming pessimism for whatever spiritual crisis is thought to occupy us at the moment.[1] Indeed, "pessimism" is such a flexible term of
abuse that it has readily been applied to almost every nonliberal political
theory that has appeared in this century. Existentialism, psychoanalysis,
critical theory, and postmodernism are all routinely labeled pessimistic, as
if that were enough to discredit them. While the term is more appropriate in some of these cases than others, thought should be given to the question of why this word functions so well as a gesture of dismissal. In part,
this is a case of killing the messenger: philosophers who have written in
these traditions have often presented a bleak picture of human existence
and thereby offended modern sensibilities. But of course the authors of
these images do not *celebrate* such a situation; they simply consider it their
duty to call attention to it. Critics have often mistaken a depiction of the
world for a *choice* about our future, as if philosophers had rejoiced at the
decline or decay that they described. But this is like deriding scientists who
warn of global warming because their models give apocalyptic predictions. Do we normally assume that such scientists want their predictions
to come true? Miguel de Unamuno once complained about a style of the-
ology that always attacked the "baneful consequences" of opposing
views: "the baneful consequences of a doctrine may prove, at best, that
the doctrine is baneful, but not that it is false" (*TSL* 104). Rather than address the threats to happiness that the world provides on a daily basis,
critics of pessimism have focused on the bearers of ill tidings and hoped
that silencing them would abolish the "baneful consequences" as well. Yet
despite the abuse they attract pessimists keep appearing—and this should
not be surprising since the world keeps delivering bad news.

Instead of blaming pessimism, perhaps we can learn from it. Rather
than hiding from the ugliness of the world, perhaps we can discover how
best to withstand it. As I noted above, pessimism's critics have often assumed that it must issue in some sort of depression or resignation. But this
assumption says more about the critics than about their targets. Who is
it, exactly, that cannot bear a story unless guaranteed a happy ending?
Pessimists themselves have often been anything but resigned. Indeed, they
have taken it as their task to find a way to live with the conclusions they
have arrived at, and to live well, sometimes even joyfully. If this cannot
be true for all of us, it is not the pessimists who are to blame, but the problems they grapple with.

---

[1] Some representative titles: *The Future and Its Enemies* by Virginia Postrel; *Enough of Pessimism* by Philip Abelson; *Enemies of Hope: A Critique of Contemporary Pessimism* by Raymond Tallis; *The Idea of Decline in Western History* by Arthur Herman; and *Sweet Violence* by Terry Eagleton. This list could be longer, but even apart from books devoted to the subject, my concern is as much with the routine use of 'pessimist' and its cognates as a casual intellectual put-down.

The pessimism that is offered here is neither a theory of history nor (as I will emphasize below) an emotional complex. Instead, it is what used to be called an "ethic" and what today might be called a "technique of the self" or a "form of life." More modestly, pessimism is a philosophical sensibility from which political practices can be derived. It is a proposed stance from which to grapple with a world that we now recognize as disordered and disenchanted. It includes judgments about history and the possible course of our civilization, but it is not really a detailed set of predictions about future politics or economics. As such, pessimism stands opposed to a modern optimism that has taken many forms. Most, if not all, political writers today are ready to recognize and reject the historical utopianism found in the philosophical descendants of Hegel. Pessimism, however, is equally critical both of that tradition and of the less flamboyant but, from its perspective, similarly progressive liberalism found in the descendants of Locke, Kant, Mill, and Dewey. Indeed, one of the intellectual benefits of reviving the tradition of pessimism is the way that it causes us to reassess the theoretical debates of the last three centuries so that we see more clearly how the various forms of optimism have been allied. From this perspective, the great divide in modern political theory is not between the English-speaking and the Continental schools, but between an optimism that has had representatives in both of these camps and a pessimism whose very existence those representatives have sought to suppress.

Recently there has been a great deal said about reviving the philosophy of the self—as if none had been written since late antiquity. It is my contention here that philosophies of the self have remained with us all along, often unremarked as such, and often under the name of pessimism. Like the Stoics and Epicureans, the pessimists have been concerned to locate the best path toward freedom in a political environment that presents the individual with a landscape whose basic features are well beyond his or her control—a vast, disordered, and dangerous terrain that confronts us as La Mancha confronted Don Quixote.

For centuries, much philosophy, both Anglo-American and Continental, has been premised on the idea (not always explicitly defended) of a gradual improvement in the human condition. But what if we grapple with the possibility that such a melioration cannot be expected, that we must make do with who and what we are? Pessimism is the philosophy that accepts this challenge. It does not preach inevitable gloom. In a relentlessly optimistic world, it is enough to give up the *promise* of happiness to be considered a pessimist. Pessimism's goal is not to depress us, but to edify us about our condition and to fortify us for the life that lies ahead. To build proper fortifications, one must have a proper sense of the enemy and his weapons. For the pessimists, it is fundamentally our time-bound condition that threatens us. But this presents a special problem since it is also our existence within time, and our consciousness of time, that makes possible many of the most excellent and glorious of human attributes, not least of which is the reason that allows us to philosophize at all. So pessimism must suggest a kind of fortification of the self against an enemy that is already inside the gates of the soul.

In such a situation, there can be no impregnable barrier that, once perfected, would obviate the need for further attention to the threat. Consequently, the pessimists, like ancient philosophers of the self, often suggest and describe a perpetual wrestling within one's own psyche, as Jacob wrestled on the mountain-top, with a foe he could barely make out, in order to learn his own name. It is a struggle with the self that never ends, but can productively define us. And it is never the same, because, for everything we do, time flows out ahead of us, relentlessly changing ourselves and our circumstances. Pessimism is a philosophy of self-conduct; it suggests an approach to a universal problem that any individual will have to modify in the course of taking it up. We can even learn, as Jacob did, to find a blessing in such a struggle.

Many of the greatest pessimists (e.g., Arthur Schopenhauer, Giacomo Leopardi, Friedrich Nietzsche, E. M. Cioran) have also been aphorists and this overlap is not accidental. I suggest instead that so many pessimists have chosen to employ aphorism because its very form suggests and represents the dissonance and disorder that pessimism sees in the world. The rareness of aphorism today is perhaps one more reflection of the unpopularity of pessimism itself. My attempt to revive interest in the aphoristic form is part and parcel of an attempt to reexplore pessimism—*not*, I repeat, out of a desire to depress and stupefy my readers, but rather with the goal of stimulating them to the critical energy that has always been the best outcome of the writings of previous aphorists. "Aphorism" is from the Greek *ap-horeizen*, to set a boundary or a horizon. Aphoristic writing, when it works, draws one's attention away from the everyday to the farthest frontier of vision. Such a vista may be jarring, but it is surely better to live with a clear view of the world than to remain optimistic by averting one's gaze from its fearful and terrible moments.

My goal in writing this book is thus twofold: first, to introduce my readers to pessimism and to persuade them to see it as an important tradition in the history of political thought (like liberalism, republicanism, Marxism, pragmatism, et cetera) even if they do not find it appealing. I undertook this project, however, because I consider pessimism to be far more than a historical curiosity. It is my claim that the field of political philosophy, and more importantly, the very lives that we lead, have been diminished by the suppression and dismissal of pessimism that has taken place in the last hundred years. So my second task is to explain the appeal that I find in pessimism and to recreate it, insofar as is possible, in the minds of my readers. These two tasks are not fully separable, of course—but I would rest satisfied if, after reading this book, pessimism (distinguished from such traditions, or pseudotraditions, as nihilism, skepticism, and cynicism, with which it is too often willingly confused) remains on my readers' horizons as a challenge, even if they are displeased to find it there.

To survive a violent stream, you can chart its eddies and swirls in ever more detailed complexity and thoroughness—or you can build a stronger boat. The drawback of the second method: some of the most adaptable boats, kayaks for example, are built to the contours of their owners' bodies—you cannot share them as you share navigation charts. You can *lend* your boat to someone, but it may not *fit* others nearly as well. This, too, is part of the predicament that pessimists face. The burden of time strikes every human differently and a technique or fortification fitted to one person may not sit so well on another. The problem is both universal and infinitely individualized; the solutions on offer partial, temporary, and always in need of revision, as a ship tacking into the wind must constantly alter its course to continue its journey.

So we beat on, boats against the current, borne back ceaselessly into the past.[2]

---

[2] Fitzgerald 1991, 152.

ACKNOWLEDGMENTS

AMONG those who have read and commented helpfully on some portion of the manuscript are Lawrie Balfour, Jane Bennett, Aurelian Criatu, Aurelian Demars, Jason Frank, Matthew Goldfeder, Amy Gutmann, George Kateb, Charles Matthews, Sara Monoson, Alexander Nehamas, Andrew Norris, Bernard Reginster, Sophie Rosenfeld, Kelly Ann Sarabyn, Dana Villa, and Stephen White. I owe special thanks to those who read and offered detailed comments on a nearly complete draft of the whole: Allan Megill, Robyn Marasco, Melissa Orlie, Verity Smith, Annie Stilz, and an anonymous reviewer for Princeton University Press. I also want to note a special debt to the late Ilinca Zarifopol-Johnston for discussions about E. M. Cioran that were especially helpful and encouraging. My apologies if I have forgotten anyone.

The University of Virginia and the American Council of Learned Societies supported the leave time during which much of the writing took place. Northwestern University and the Harvard Law School graciously provided office space and library access that was useful at, respectively, the very beginning and the very end of this project. I would also like to thank the panelists and audience members at various conferences and university colloquia for stimulating feedback when I presented segments of this book. Likewise the students, graduate and undergraduate, in my pessimism-themed seminars endured many preliminary formulations of the theses offered here and helped to improve them. Ian Malcolm, of Princeton University Press, stewarded the manuscript through the editorial process, and offered advice as well, for which I am extremely grateful. Jon Munk preformed an excellent copyedit, and the index was prepared by Jim Curtis.

An earlier version of chapter 5 appeared in the *American Political Science Review*. I thank the editors for permission to reproduce it.

My parents witnessed the long gestation of this project with their usual good humor and sage advice, my children with their unusual good humor and cheerful, blessed ignorance.

The dedication of this book cannot begin to reflect the debt I owe to my wife, Jennifer Mnookin, for support of a degree and kind that it would be useless to attempt to catalog.

ABBREVIATIONS

Q UOTATIONS are followed by the abbreviation and a page number
or, if noted below, another reference number. For works not listed
here, I follow a modified MLA citation style. Full details for cited texts
can be found in the bibliography.

Works by Albert Camus

MS	*The Myth of Sisyphus*
R	*The Rebel*
RRD	*Resistance, Rebellion, and Death*

Works by Miguel de Cervantes

DQ	*The Ingenious Hidalgo Don Quixote de la Mancha* (cited by volume and chapter)

Works by E. M. Cioran

AA	*Anathemas and Admirations*
AGD	*All Gall Is Divided*
DAQ	*Drawn and Quartered*
FT	*The Fall into Time*
HU	*History and Utopia*
NG	*The New Gods*
O	*Oeuvres*
OHD	*On the Heights of Despair*
SHD	*A Short History of Decay*
TBB	*The Trouble with Being Born*
TE	*The Temptation to Exist*
TS	*Tears and Saints*

Works by Sigmund Freud

BPP	*Beyond the Pleasure Principle*
CD	*Civilization and Its Discontents*

CP   *Collected Papers*
EI   *The Ego and the Id*
ID   *The Interpretation of Dreams*

Works by Giacomo Leopardi

OM   *The Moral Essays (Operette Morali)*
P   *Thoughts (Pensieri)*

Works by Friedrich Nietzsche
(all cited by numbered section when available)

AC   *The Anti-Christ*
AOM   *Assorted Opinions and Maxims*
BGE   *Beyond Good and Evil*
BT   *The Birth of Tragedy*
CW   *The Case of Wagner*
D   *Daybreak*
EH   *Ecce Homo*
HH   *Human, All-Too-Human*
GS   *The Gay Science*
GM   *On the Genealogy of Morals*
KGW   *Werke: Kritische Gesamtausgabe* (cited by volume, book, and
          page)
PTG   *Philosophy in the Tragic Age of the Greeks*
TI   *Twilight of the Idols*
UM   *Untimely Meditations*
WP   *The Will to Power*
Z   *Thus Spoke Zarathustra*

Works by Jean-Jacques Rousseau

E   *Émile*
ES   *Émile and Sophie*
FD   *Discourse on the Sciences and Arts (First Discourse)*
LD   *Letter to M. d'Alembert on the Theatre*
OL   *Essay on the Origin of Languages*
RSW   *Reveries of the Solitary Walker*
SC   *On the Social Contract*

SD   *Discourse on the Origin and the Foundations of Inequality*
          (Second Discourse)

Works by Arthur Schopenhauer

EA   *Essays and Aphorisms*
PP   *Parerga and Paralipomena*
WWR   *The World as Will and Representation*

Works by Miguel de Unamuno

OLDQ   *Our Lord Don Quixote*
TSL   *The Tragic Sense of Life in Men and Nations*

PART I

Chapter One

THE ANATOMY OF PESSIMISM

The idea that a pessimistic philosophy is necessarily
one of discouragement is a puerile idea, but
one that needs too long a refutation.
—ALBERT CAMUS

CAN IT really be the case that an entire tradition of thought has gone
missing from our standard histories of political theory? A claim like
this sounds extravagant on first hearing. In some sense, perhaps, it is extravagant—but not in the way that immediately comes to mind. In attempting to reframe the history of political thought so that pessimism becomes one of its major strands, I will not be arguing for paying attention
to a series of writers who have hitherto been wholly unknown. While
there certainly are authors, important to identify, who have been unjustly
neglected on account of their pessimism, that is not the only, or even the
main, story. Instead, I argue that while many of the pessimists are well-
known, the nature of their common project (indeed, the very idea that
they have a common project) has been obscured. Since pessimism is perceived more as a disposition than as a theory, pessimists are seen primarily as dissenters from whatever the prevailing consensus of their time happens to be, rather than as constituting a continuous alternative. The result
is that each seems disconnected from the mainstream of the history of political thought. They appear as voices in the wilderness, to put it politely—
or to put it less politely, as cranks. While they are often admired for their
style, or respected for the critiques they offer, their apparent lack of a
"positive project" is made to appear as a badge of second-rank philosophical status. They interest us; but, it is believed, they cannot possibly
orient us.

With greater or lesser degrees of respect, then, pessimists have in many
cases been dismissed from the upper reaches of the canon of political
thought. Or when they are admitted, as in the case of a figure like Nietzsche, they are taken to be radically isolated from other elements in that
canon. Nietzsche's philosophy *is* highly distinctive, of course, but this
should not blind us to the ways in which he, like many of the other figures to be discussed here, remains part of a tradition that has itself been
rendered invisible. Even as, in recent decades, the traditional list of great
works has been strenuously attacked, stretched, revised, and reconsid-

ered, the idea of a pessimistic political theory has not been seriously entertained. There are several reasons for this—but none of them are really barriers to a reconsideration of pessimism. First, as I mentioned above, pessimism is often taken to be a state of mind, rather than a philosophy or philosophical orientation. This is perfectly understandable; there are, of course, happy and unhappy people and they do tend to have different attitudes about the world. But just as theories of progress are not the same thing as a cheerful attitude toward life, neither should pessimism be equated with a foul disposition. Nor is it even true that these attitudes and philosophies are regularly correlated in individuals. John Stuart Mill, for example, was famously optimistic in his belief about the long-term growth of mankind through the continuous application of reason, and he was just as famously depressive and dyspeptic. Schopenhauer, it is often claimed, was pessimistic in both the psychological and philosophical senses. But even were this claim true, Schopenhauer is not the whole of pessimism (though he is often mistaken for it) and, were one to proceed in this way, one could find just as many happy pessimists as sad ones. But I will not be examining the relative cheerfulness of the philosophical pessimists in any detail; nor would I suggest that anyone should do so on behalf of theorists of progress. It will, I hope, be enough to point out here that philosophy and disposition should simply not be confused with one another. The real question is whether I can demonstrate that a pessimistic *philosophy*, as such, exists. If I do, I hope that its distinctness from depressive attitudes will be granted as a matter of course.

A second reason that pessimistic theory has not been recognized as such is that it is often lumped together with nihilism, cynicism, skepticism, and other like philosophies. Few writers, of course, adopt the label of "nihilist" or "cynic" for themselves (though there are many self-proclaimed skeptics). But these schools of thought are nonetheless named and studied by their critics, usually for their deleterious effects on the species.[1] Without getting into these debates in any detail, I think it is fair to say that, in discussions such as these, the word "pessimistic" is one of a list of adjectives used very loosely to describe any "negative" philosophy, that is, any philosophy opposed to traditional attempts at system-building or the defense of some concrete political order. While pessimism is a negative philosophy, in this sense, with the goal only of fortifying us in a limited existence, it is otherwise not directly related to skepticism or nihilism,

---

[1] Tallis is fairly typical here: "[T]he contemporary attack on Enlightenment values carries great dangers. . . . [I]t is part of a process by which contemporary humanity is talking itself into a terminal state of despair, self-disgust and impotence." (Tallis 1999, xiv). Likewise Herman: "the sowing of despair and self-doubt has become so pervasive that we accept it as normal intellectual stance." "Modern pessimism . . . has managed to wreck our faith in the idea of civilization itself" (Herman 1997, 10, 450).

which are generally the true objects of attack by those suspicious of negative philosophy. That is to say, insofar as pessimism has been considered at all, it has been rendered an adjunct to skepticism or nihilism. If, therefore, my description of pessimism shows it to be something genuinely distinct from these, then it will have to be considered anew, even by those still inclined to be critical of it.

Finally, the dismissal of pessimism reflects the continuing grip that ideas of progress retain on contemporary consciousness. Though supposedly slain many times (Lewis Mumford called it the "deadest of dead ideas" in 1932), this beast continues to rise from the ashes for the simple reasons that, first, it helps us to make sense of the linear time of our calendar and, second, there is no easy substitute for it.[2] However much it may be denied in principle, in practice the idea of progress is difficult to displace. And from this perspective, pessimism is especially bewildering. Precisely because it asks us to rethink our sense of time, pessimism is an idea that challenges our notions of order and meaning in dramatic ways. Though it may not seem, on the surface, to be an especially political doctrine (it often appears, and is assumed to be, antipolitical), pessimism attacks the roots of modern political orders by denying their sense of time. Pessimism *is* a substitute for progress, but it is not a painless one. In suggesting that we look at time and history differently, it asks us to alter radically our opinion both of ourselves and of what we can expect from politics. It does not simply tell us to expect less. It tells us, in fact, to expect nothing. This posture, I argue below, while difficult, is not impossible and not suicidal either. It is neither skeptical (knowing nothing) nor nihilistic (wanting nothing). It is a distinct account of the human condition that has developed in the shadow of progress—alongside it, as it were—with its own political stance.

Pessimism, I have been saying, has been hiding in plain sight. Its exemplars could be said to include, among others: Rousseau, Leopardi, Schopenhauer, Nietzsche, Weber, Unamuno, Ortega y Gasset, Freud, Camus, Adorno, Foucault, and Cioran—to name just a few in what could become a very long list. It could be said to have precursors in figures like Mon-

---

[2] Christopher Lasch helpfully distinguishes the belief in progress from the less common, though also modern, utopianism: "not the promise of a secular utopia that would bring history to a happy ending but the promise of steady improvement with no foreseeable ending at all." (1991, 47). His book surveys the irrepressibility of the idea of progress in Anglo-American thought in the last two centuries. For a longer view, focused more on Europe, see Kumar 1978. The classic account is J. B. Bury's *The Idea of Progress* (1923). Even such apparently radical contemporary theorists as Derrida proclaim themselves "progressists": "So we have to change the law, improve the law, and there is an infinite progress to be performed, to be achieved in that respect. . . . [P]eople would like to oppose . . . deconstruction to the Enlightenment. No, I am for the Enlightenment, I'm for progress, I'm a 'progressist'" (Derrida 2001, § 31).

taigne, Lichtenburg, Pascal, and La Rochefoucauld. And it could be said to have close associates in writers like Sartre, Arendt, Benjamin, Wittgenstein, and Weil. The list would grow considerably longer, of course, if one included poets and fiction writers (e.g., Dostoevsky, Thomas Mann, et al.) but here (with one notable exception) we will confine ourselves to works drawn from the philosophical tradition. For whatever reason, the idea of a pessimistic novelist has never been as illegitimate as the idea of a pessimistic philosopher. (It would be an interesting project to determine just why this is so, but one I cannot pursue here.) The former has been as prominent as the latter has been invisible; and so it is only the latter whose existence I am concerned to vindicate.[3]

Nonetheless, I should be clear about the nature of the endeavor undertaken here. In saying that these various philosophers—all modern and

---

[3] Though the term is used in a casual way with great frequency, there was almost no sustained attention, in the last century, to pessimism as a tradition in intellectual history or political philosophy. Apart from occasional essays usually focused on a single figure or books about Schopenhauer, the best (virtually the only) twentieth-century work, is Henry Vyverberg's *Historical Pessimism in the French Enlightenment* (1958). As its title indicates, it is restricted in scope, but it does have the virtue of arguing that "progress was neither the exclusive focus nor the one logical consummation of Enlightened French philosophy, . . . historical pessimism too had its roots deep in the 'philosophical' movement" (1). While the book contains much useful information, and I refer to it below, it covers such a variety of figures that none are really given sustained attention and it is more concerned with episodes of hesitation and doubt among optimists than with establishing a true countertradition. Historians of the idea of progress, such as Bury, do acknowledge the presence of pessimists such as Rousseau, but they are characterized as outliers or vestigials, rather than as part of an alternate modern line of reasoning (Bury 1923, ch. 9). Bury is updated, in the American context, by Chambers 1958, which also reviews those who seconded Bury's thesis (197).

In the nineteenth century, on the other hand, Schopenhauer's prominence and the short-lived existence of a recognized school of pessimism inspired a number of critical works, especially in German but also in English (see, e.g., Sully 1891 and Saltus 1885, the former of which contains an extensive bibliography of contemporary works on the subject, as does Hübscher 1989, 496–97). For the most part, these analyses are fairly simplistic and often conceive pessimism as merely positing an excess of pain over pleasure in life, a misconception I deal with below. However, some of these works do note the existence of a pessimistic tradition and place more emphasis on, for example, figures like Leopardi who are utterly ignored in the twentieth century.

Inspired by the work of Raymond Williams, two recent works of political sociology, Joe Bailey's *Pessimism* (1988) and Oliver Bennett's *Cultural Pessimism* (2001) seek to explore pessimism as a "structure of feeling." But both are exclusively concerned with public discourse of the post–World War II period, largely in the United Kingdom. Williams's framework blurs the distinction between pessimism as emotion and as theory in a way that I believe is counterproductive for understanding the philosophical lineage I explore here.

The antipessimistic tracts I mentioned in the preface are for the most part journalistic polemics and I do not consider them further. Even the best of them (Tallis 1999 and Herman 1997) are haphazard briefs for the prosecution. They implicate pessimism or decline willy-nilly in every political ideology to which they object, however tenuous the connection. In what follows, I hope to provide a more balanced assessment.

European but nonetheless drawn from several centuries and countries—should be collectively understood as pessimists, I shall not attempt to demonstrate that they share a single idea (e.g., that "life is suffering"). That, in any case, is not really a good test for the existence of a school of thought. One would be hard-pressed, I think, to name the *single* thought shared by, say, all liberal political philosophers or all republicans. Even where a school is said to derive from a single figure (as, say, with Platonists), there is no reason for there to be a single proposition on which all members agree. We are better off, I believe, if we utilize here Wittgenstein's notion of "family resemblance"—his term for a situation in which there is no one element in common but rather "a complicated network of similarities overlapping and criss-crossing" (Wittgenstein 1958, 32). The various members of a family may all be visibly related to one another without there being a single feature they all share. But, Wittgenstein argues, that does not mean we are mistaken to call them by a single name. In fact, we do this all the time; it is only when we reflect on the practice that we mistakenly demand that each name correspond to a single feature rather than a network of overlapping similarities. Furthermore, he argues, one cannot say exactly where one family ends and another begins. Instead, Wittgenstein suggests the idea of a strand composed of many overlapping filaments: "the strength of the thread does not reside in the fact that some one fibre runs through the whole length, but in the overlapping of many fibres" (Wittgenstein 1958, 32). Likewise, I shall be arguing that pessimism is a strand that has been woven through the history of modern political thought, where many overlapping elements comprise a single trajectory. But this is not meant to set pessimism off from other sorts of political philosophy—modern political thought (to continue the metaphor) is, on this view, just a fabric of many such similarly constituted fibers. In the second half of this chapter, I will elaborate a series of propositions that, I claim, are characteristic of pessimism. Perhaps no pessimist subscribes to all of them, but in order to be a pessimist one must subscribe to several of them. If there is, throughout, an implicit attempt to harmonize these various propositions into a whole, this should be understood as my own effort at a sort of fusion of various horizons. It is not proposed as an interpretation of any of the pessimists in particular, but rather as an attempt to say what the thread of pessimism, built up from a variety of fibers, amounts to.

But pessimism *is* set off from other modern schools of philosophy (though not all of them) by something else. As I granted above, pessimists generally do not set out a scheme of ideal government structure or principles of justice. Theirs is (for the most part) a philosophy of personal conduct, rather than public order. Since such schemes or principles are, to some, the very essence of a political philosophy, this fact, by itself, has been enough to disqualify the pessimists from serious consideration in some quarters. Recently however, there have been a variety of attempts to rehabilitate such non-system-building philosophy (for it has a long history) under a variety of rubrics. In the first place, there has been renewed interest in those later Hellenistic philosophers grouped under such names as Stoics, Cynics, Epicureans, and Skeptics. These philosophers, it is generally agreed, practiced a sort of philosophy that focused much more on the individual's approach to life than on the structure of the state within which she lived. The very titles of recent works such as Pierre Hadot's *Philosophy as a Way of Life* and Martha Nussbaum's *The Therapy of Desire* betray a renewed interest in this style of reasoning while insisting that it is no less a part of the philosophical tradition. Although both Nussbaum and Hadot have been critical of Foucault's attempts, in his late works, to use these same writers in the service of redefining philosophy as a "technique of the self," all parties to these disputes would have to agree that our understanding of political philosophy is wrongly narrowed if we limit it to that which systematizes.[4] In a related development, recent interpretations of Nietzsche have focused on the idea that what is suggested to us in his books is an "art of living" in which we are directed, not to act in a particular way, but to view our actions in the light of criteria both historical and, for lack of a better word, aesthetic.[5] This, in turn, has given rise to varieties of feminism and postmodernism that show a renewed concern with personal conduct, as opposed to government structure.[6] Now, with the exception of Nietzsche himself, very little of this writing is, to my mind, pessimistic. So, if pessimism is indeed, by the very nature of its concerns, set off from such traditional schools of philosophy as liberalism, Marxism, republicanism, and so forth, it is certainly not *alone* in being so distinguished. Indeed, it is in part the renewed attention being paid to this style of philosophy that makes it easier for us now to recognize the pessimistic tradition in philosophy.

As an antisystematic philosophy, pessimism still needs to be distinguished from other such philosophies, especially such premodern ones as Stoicism and Epicureanism. As will become clear as we proceed, it undoubtedly shares certain elements with these perspectives and is in some sense a descendant of them. Nonetheless, there is a reasonably sharp divide between such earlier philosophies of the self and pessimism, marked out by their different attitudes toward time. Like the idea of progress, and the various philosophies to which it gave rise, pessimism is a modern phe-

---

[4] See Hadot 1995, 206–13; Nussbaum 1994, 5–6; Foucault 1986, 37–68.
    [5] Some exemplary texts in this tradition are Strong 1988, Nehamas 1985, Rorty 1989, Theile 1990, and Honig 1993.
    [6] See Orlie 1997 and Butler 1990, 1997.

nomenon. The word "pessimism" itself (from the Latin *pessimus*—the worst) came into widespread use only in the nineteenth century.[7] Although the philosophical tradition I will be examining is considerably older than that, it does have an identifiable beginning. Like optimism, pessimism relies on an underlying linear concept of time, a concept that only became a force in Western thinking in the early modern period.

My argument here relies on the fairly common idea (still contested in some quarters) that a transformation in the time-consciousness of Europe sharply distinguishes the modern era from previous ones. While it is surely an oversimplification to say that ancient notions of time were simply "cyclical" while modern ones are purely "linear," it is nonetheless true that there was a change in Western ideas of time that had a profound effect on nearly every element of society, philosophy included. Though there were a variety of ancient views on time (as on any subject), the cyclical view, in different forms, was by far the dominant one. Pythagoras, for example, taught that "events recur in cycles, and that nothing is ever absolutely new" (Kirk, Raven, and Schofield 1983, 238). Stoic cosmology held that "time is passing just as we say the year passes, on a larger circuit," and the world was perpetually destroyed and recreated such that "after the conflagration of the cosmos everything will again come to be in numerical order, until every specific quality too will return to its original state, just as it was before and came to be in that cosmos" (Sambursky 1959, 107; 1956, 201–2). Even Aristotle's more measured discussion of time links it fundamentally to motion, and since the revolution of the heavens is the fundamental motion of the universe, "all other things are discriminated by time, and end and begin as though conforming to a cycle" (*Physics* 223b27–28).[8] Ancient political theory relied on these

---

[7] Leibniz first used the term "optimum," as a correlate to "maximum" and "minimum" in his *Théodicée* of 1710. French writers then began to refer to his doctrine as one of *optimisme*. The international popularity of Voltaire's *Candide ou l'Optimisme* of 1759 apparently propelled the term into English, but also provoked Voltaire's Jesuit critics in the *Revue de Trévoux* to accuse him of "*pessimisme*" (I thank M. Aurelian Demars for this information). Lichtenberg uses the term "*pessimismus*" in 1766; in 1789 a satirical French play entitled *Le pessimiste ou l'homme méconte de tout* appeared; and the first known printed appearance of "pessimism" in English follows shortly thereafter, although the context seems to indicate that the term was already in use. The French Academy admitted the word "*optimisme*" in 1762 but "*pessimisme*" only in 1878 (See Hübscher 1989, 259–60)!

[8] Plato's views on time are more obscure, appearing only in the highly rhetorical *Timaeus*. Nevertheless, he too appears there to subscribe to the idea, common in the ancient world, that the cycle of time is marked out by a Great Year, that is, the period of time in which the solar and lunar cycles (and, in the case of Plato, the cycles of the other major heavenly bodies) perfectly coincide: "the perfect number of time brings to completion the perfect year at that moment when the relative speeds of all eight periods have been completed together and, measured by the circle of the Same that moves uniformly, have achieved their consummation" (39d; the solar-lunar year is approximately thirty-three standard years, but the Great

views in its descriptions of historical patterns—and of the place of human beings within those patterns. As a result, progress, decline, or even an endless but linear accumulation of experience, played little part in ancient philosophy.[9] Modernity, by contrast (as discussed in greater detail below) has been marked out from the start by a belief in linear time and noncyclical historical narrative.

Although this commonplace of modern historiography has had its critics, most attempts to refute this idea have only addressed it in an extreme form, as if by employing the notion of cyclical time one contends that ancient cultures all believed in some kind of reincarnation or the eternal return of the same. Some members of the Old Stoa, like Chrysippus, may have tended toward this view, but this is clearly not the case in general.[10] When ancient writers like Polybius or Aristotle spoke of a cycle of regime-types, for example, they meant only that the same sort of governments could be expected to reappear on a regular basis, as one expects the springtime every year, without thinking that this spring will be identical to the last one. What is significant about such an idea is not that it predicts a recurrence of events, but that it limits the potential for innovation within the system. When Aristotle gave an inventory of the various possible political regimes, he did not expect that new ones might appear in the future, as someone who lists the four seasons does not expect to learn of a fifth.

It is also true, however, that no society has ever possessed a time-consciousness that is purely linear or purely cyclical. Even today, when we meticulously count the seconds and years in a linear fashion, great portions of our lives are governed by daily, weekly, and yearly cycles that would change very little if we gave up the progressive numbering of our annual calendar. We continue to use expressions like the "cycle of life" or "to every thing there is a season" in a perfectly comfortable way. Similarly, even when other cultures have a view of history that is nonlinear, or even have a language without a future tense, this has hardly prevented

---

Year that Plato describes would be many times the length of a human life and, hence, unobservable to a given individual. See Turetzky 1998; Borst 1993; Samuel 1972). In general, ancient philosophers connected time to movement and thus to spatial measures—which, given their cosmology, led inevitably to circular patterns. Modern physicists, by contrast, posit the existence of an "absolute" time that is unrelated to the movements of heavenly bodies or anything else. See n. 15, below.

[9] A partial exception should be made here for some later Roman historians, such as Tacitus, who were concerned with decline. However, this concern was more civic than historical and could easily be accommodated within a larger cyclical narrative. I do not want to deny, however, that there is a certain incipient modernism in some of the later Romans that might well have developed into something recognizable as a modern historical consciousness if not for the collapse of the Western Empire.

[10] See Turetzky 1998, chap. 3, and Voytko 1994.

them from making plans for tomorrow, or next week, much as we do. Yet even in Arnaldo Momigliano's heroic attempts to work these plain facts up into a refutation of the thesis of a change in time-consciousness, he makes an exception for philosophers who, he acknowledges, did indeed have a circular conception of time in ancient Greece, which later philosophy abandoned.[11]

While many intellectual historians have agreed that a change in time-consciousness marks the end of the Middle Ages and the beginning of the modern period, there is less agreement as to the exact nature of the shift, its timing and causes. Reinhart Koselleck, in his influential book *Futures Past*, focuses largely on the emergence of ideas of progress in the fourteenth and fifteenth centuries, and attributes these ideas to the appearance of new technologies that made material progress visible in the course of a single lifetime, something that had not happened before (Koselleck 1985, 267–88). In a similar vein, Hans Blumenberg emphasizes developments in astronomy in the sixteenth century, where comparisons between ancient and modern data gave rise to the thought of cosmic changes over long periods of time (Blumenberg 1974, 18ff.). By contrast, J.G.A. Pocock contends that it was the historical ideas of the Italian Renaissance that were crucial since "the Christian world-view . . . was based on the exclusion from consideration of temporal and secular history, and [] the emergence of historical modes of explanation had much to do with the supersession of that world-view by one more temporal and secular" (Pocock 1975, 8).

Despite Pocock's claims, it must nonetheless be recognized that the decline of European paganism and its replacement with the biblical faiths had something to do with the changes in western time-consciousness. A long tradition of classical scholarship has insisted that it is the history of the Old Testament, stretching from Creation to the Prophets (and only spread to the West, but not essentially modified, by Christianity) that forms the basis for the modern view of time.[12] Other scholars have ar-

---

[11] Momigliano 1966, 7. Momigliano's real target, in this essay, is the idea that cycles are "Greek" while linearity is "Hebrew," especially insofar as the distinction grounded a kind of lingering antisemitism in postwar classical studies. About this conclusion, I have no qualms, but it seems to me that Momigliano, in seeking to erase this distinction, tends too strongly in the direction of asserting that no significant differences in time-consciousness have ever existed.

[12] Momigliano (1966, 1–8) discusses the prevalence of this view, while criticizing it. Blumenberg (1983) also criticizes it as an element of the "secularization" thesis of Löwith (1949); Löwith had written that modern historical consciousness "is as Christian by derivation as it is non-Christian by consequence" (197). That is, the modern sense of history should be understood as a "secularization" of biblical eschatology—so the structure of history remains parallel to the biblical while the "meaning" of that structure is transformed from something sacred to something mundane. Blumenberg's arguments parallel those of

gued that it is Christianity proper that provokes the change. G. J. Whitrow, for example, focuses on the uniqueness of Christ's Incarnation and argues that "the non-repeatability of events was the very essence of Christianity" (Whitrow 1972, 17). In any case, it is clear enough that Augustine, writing in the fourth century CE, produced an account of time that is notably linear—focusing as it does on the relation between past, present, and future—and that did not subordinate time to motion (Augustine 1960, 285ff).

For my purposes, the timing and nature of the change, and its diffusion into the world of politics, are ultimately more important than the exact causes that brought it about. While it seems clear that we can only speak, at best, of a growing emphasis on linearity in time-consciousness (rather than, say, a radical paradigm-shift), there are good reasons to think that such a change did occur in that period of several centuries that we now consider either late medieval or early modern. The most prominent markers of this change were the sudden ubiquity of mechanical clocks in the fourteenth century and the less sudden, but broadly coincident and ultimately very widespread agreement on, and use of, a common calendar that marked the years in an unbroken, ascending fashion.

In his acclaimed *History of the Hour*, Gerhard Dohrn-van Rossum describes the appearance of the mechanical clock and its radical effect on almost every element of European culture.[13] It is difficult for us now to register just how differently daily life was navigated in the absence of reliable time-telling devices. Before the mechanical clock was invented (the exact date and location of the invention are unknown, but it almost certainly occurred in northern Italy around 1300), the hours were generally not of fixed length but waxed and waned with the seasons so that there were twelve hours from dusk to dawn and twelve from dawn to dusk. Insofar as time was kept at all, it was done with sundials (useless in cloudy weather) and waterclocks (very unreliable, labor-intensive, and useless when temperatures were below freezing), and the hours marked were those of the monastery (Prime, Tierce, Nones, Compline, et cetera).[14]

Koselleck in placing the emphasis instead on intellectual developments of the late medieval period, though he stresses those that are internal to scholasticism as well as outside it. For an alternative view on the evolution of modern temporality, see George Poulet's *Studies in Human Time* (1956, chap. 1); Poulet's account is marvelously suggestive but, to my judgment, ultimately contrived and unreliable.

[13] Most of the material in this paragraph and the next is drawn from this remarkable book (Dohrn-van Rossum 1996), along with Borst 1993, Poole 1998, and Toulmin and Goodfield 1965. In condensing so much material, I have had to simplify somewhat the very complex, and still-debated, story of the emergence of modern time-telling devices. But I hope to have done no real violence to its main features.

[14] Monasteries had the greatest need for accurate time-keeping since the rules that governed the monks' lives (starting with the original Benedictine rule) prescribed particular ac-

Minutes and seconds were something measured only by astronomers; the degrees of precision we take for granted in ordinary conversation ("Meet me in half an hour . . ." "I'll be back in five minutes . . .") were far from routine. Short periods of time were often measured by repetitions of the Lord's Prayer.

The first reliable mechanical clocks began to appear in the belltowers of northern Italian towns in the early fourteenth century. Inaccurate by our standards, they nonetheless functioned regardless of weather and provided the first common, public measures of time. Although these clocks only marked a cycle of hours, they altered time-consciousness in such a way as to clearly foreshadow modern, linear understandings. First, of course, clocks had the effect of divorcing the measure of time from nature, and made it into a matter of mechanical regularity. The day no longer began or ended according to the sun, but according to the clock.[15] Second, by making the hours (and, eventually, minutes and seconds) into units of fixed length, rather than something that varied with the seasons, they reinforced the idea that time was a succession of identical units.[16] Augustine's linear time, by contrast, had been highly subjective (he emphasized how our individual perceptions of time could differ and contrasted these with the more substantial timeless eternity where God dwelled), and thus offered astronomers and historians no fixed temporal structure by which to measure events.

The effects of these changes on science were obviously profound; but the cultural changes were likewise radical. In becoming measurable and calculable, time became less like the seasons and more like a commodity. A minor, but telling, detail mentioned by Dohrn-van Rossum gives us some sense of what this meant: after the emergence of the clock, hourglasses began to appear regularly in Renaissance paintings and in personal

---

tivities at particular hours. They often maintained elaborate water-clocks for this purpose, with mixed results. Our word "noon" derives from the Latin "nones," originally, the ninth hour after dawn, which ought to be around 2 PM (but may have been moved up to accommodate hungry monks, who were forbidden to eat before that hour).

[15] Hence the expression "o'clock" meaning "of the clock" rather than by the sun. Depending on the time of year, ten o'clock could be a somewhat different point than "ten" measured in the variable hours of the old system. While it would take several centuries for clock-time to fully replace sun-time, especially outside of cities, it is also clear that the very *idea* of clock time had a profoundly transformative effect on daily life, even before everyone wore a wristwatch. See Stephens 2002.

[16] This divorce is encapsulated by Newton's statement of 1686: "Absolute, true and mathematical time flows into itself, and by its own nature, equably, without reference to anything external; . . . Relative, visible and ordinary time is a perceptible and external measurement of duration by means of motion, be it exact or inequable, which one ordinarily makes use of in place of true time (n.b.), for example the hour, the month, the year" (Cited in Poole 1998, 20).

inventories, apparently because they came into more common use. As a technology, of course, hourglasses did not depend on the existence of clocks—but it was only at this point, after the appearance of mechanical clocks, that people began to find it necessary to frequently measure exact periods of time. And the concept of time as the flowing of an endless stream of identical grains is obviously congruent with a more linear view of it. In these paintings, the hourglass is also a symbol of mortality and the fleetingness of existence. As Lichtenberg put it in 1772, "Hour-glasses remind us, not only of how time flies, but at the same time of the dust into which we shall one day decay" (Lichtenberg 1990, 42). It is surely no co-incidence, then, that the very time and place where Pocock sees modern concepts of history emerging (north-central Italy of the fourteenth century) is the same time and place where the mechanical clock first appeared. As time became less a matter of heavenly revolutions and more a matter of secular sequences, the idea of a long-term direction or trend to human history became increasingly conceivable.

Compounding this process were the effects of the Gregorian calender reform of 1582, which confirmed and universalized the system of year-numbering with which we are now familiar, with its constant upward march. Remembered today largely for skipping eleven days to correct for the errors that had crept into the Julian calendar over fifteen centuries, this reform signaled something else as well—a common measure of historical time in Europe. In the pre-Christian era, most cities kept their own calendars, tied to local religious or political rituals. These were sometimes cyclical, but often unnumbered, with years simply being denoted by the names of the most prominent officeholders. Roman rule unified the calendar, but years were still commonly denoted by the name of the consuls or the emperor.[17] With the collapse of the empire, control over the calendar reverted to local authorities. The Roman legacy meant that there was a certain commonality to these calendars, but over the centuries they began to diverge. New Year's was celebrated in some places on January 1, but in others on the day after Christmas, and in still others on March 1 or 25. The numbering system we use today was only proposed in the sixth century by a Scythian monk, then spread slowly within the Church,

---

[17] That is, by "year of the consulship of X" or "third year of the reign of X". In the later empire, of course, the Romans also possessed a calendar that measured the years in a linear fashion from the founding of Rome (*ab urbe condita* = AUC). But this calendar (originated by Varro in the first century BC) was apparently not in wide use. The consular or regnal year was the normal designation—but it was also a common habit to note the years with reference to iterations of a fifteen-year tax cycle (the "indiction" cycle), much as the Greeks had earlier used the cycle of the Olympiad to track historical time. That this latter system survived the empire and remained in use in certain parts of Europe for nearly 1500 years is strong evidence that it, rather than the AUC numbering, was the more common one.

and was not common, outside of church documents, before the eleventh century. Local authorities generally had little use for this numbering scheme and regnal reckonings (e.g., "the tenth year of the reign of X") were simpler to use for many purposes (Poole 1918).[18] Though the Gregorian reform was largely motivated by a desire to celebrate Easter at the right time (and to reenforce the church's control of that celebration), the effect of the reform, eventually adopted by both Catholic and Protestant countries (England held out until 1752, Sweden until 1753) was to unify the count of years across Europe and to ensure the authority of astronomers and mathematicians in any future reforms. The calendar, then, seemed less like a local convenience and more like a universal, natural measure of time—a measure that was linear and open-ended.

It is this cluster of changes from the fourteenth to the sixteenth century that, in my judgment, undermines the view that Christianity (with or without Judaism) is the crucial factor in creating the modern linear notion of time. Although Augustine, for example, may well have contributed to the intellectual climate that was ultimately amenable to linearity, his reflections on time were attributed greater importance in the modern period (e.g., by Jansenism) than by his contemporaries. Augustine's main preoccupation in his writing on time is to distinguish the human experience of temporality from eternity, wherein God abides. The result is that all human temporality, in his analysis, takes on an air of unreality—the linearity he describes is ultimately understood as an artifact of the (flawed, human) mind (Augustine 1960, 290, 301). Thus, despite Augustine's great contemporary influence, it is several centuries before the church (almost accidentally) composes a linear calendar, and centuries more before that calendar has notable influence, even within the church itself.[19] More importantly, perhaps, Augustine's analysis produces no great interest (either in himself or in his successors in the church) in questions of historical theodicy—this too is something that appears only in modern times. From this perspective, Pocock's judgment that the church's denigration of the secular and temporal was a hindrance to modern concepts of time and history seems strongly supported. If it were otherwise, then one would ex-

[18] "If we suppose a traveler to set out from Venice on March 1, 1245, the first day of the Venetian year, he would find himself in 1244 when he reached Florence; and if after a short stay he went on to Pisa, the year 1246 would have already begun there. Continuing his journey westward, he would find himself again in 1245 when he entered Provence, and on arriving in France before Easter he would be once more in 1244. This seems a bewildering tangle of dates. But, in fact, our traveler would not think of the year; he would note his movements by the month and day" (Poole 1918, 47).

[19] More important within the church in the early medieval period were the liturgical and monastic times that emphasized daily and yearly cycles as well as the ecstatic "already/not yet" suspension of time that saw human beings as awaiting an endtime that had, in some sense, already begun. I thank Alison Dickie for a very helpful conversation on this point.

pect the gap from an Augustine to a Newton to be something less than the ten centuries it, in fact, was.

The modern changes in time-consciousness did not, of course, force philosophers and historians to alter their views. But they did provide an underlying mental structure that *allowed* new ideas about human history and the human experience of time to be built atop it, and which made those new ideas feel more plausible once proposed. It has been said many times that the idea of progress is something modern. To this truth, two points should be added. First, the widespread acceptance of this idea would not have come about without the foundation laid by the overall change in time-consciousness that occurred in the late medieval/early modern period. Second, and more importantly from our perspective, this change in time-consciousness did not *only* authorize the idea of progress. Pessimism too is one of its progeny, the hidden twin (or perhaps the *doppelgänger*) of progress in modern political thought. What is surprising in standard intellectual histories is how rapidly the idea of linearity is assimilated to the idea of progress, as if progress and stasis were the only two choices available to human thought and the first is straightforwardly the result of linear time while the latter is the direct issue of cyclicality. Montaigne complained of a similar conclusion when he wrote, "The philosophers . . . always have this dilemma in their mouths to console us for our mortal condition: 'The soul is either mortal or immortal. If mortal, it will be without pain; if immortal, it will go on improving.' They never touch the other branch: 'What if it goes on getting worse?'" (Montaigne 1958, 413).

My proposal is that we should think of pessimism as equally descended from the modern notion of linear time, and hence, as equally a conceptual child of modernity. "Not a freak, a sport, but an authentically organic growth" (Vyverberg 1958, 6). If it were simply a matter of thinking through the meaning of linear time, one might imagine pessimism as equally plausible as progress. But if pessimism is indeed a child of modernity, it would have to be considered a prodigal—one rarely seen and, when seen, often ill-recognized, and often diagnosed as an ailment rather than a philosophy. While professional historians may, in principle, dismiss the idea of progress, to be a pessimist is still to be, at best, an oddball and, at worst, someone with an unpleasant character; "pessimist" is still a term of abuse. But as the idea of progress becomes more questionable to us, we have greater reason to turn to the unappreciated history of pessimism. If we find it impossible to return to a circular or cyclical view of the past, and if narratives of progress seem equally mythical, then we ought to reflect more on the nonprogressive, linear accounts of time that remain—and this means pessimism. As the alternatives decline in plausibility, the value of pessimism must be reconsidered.

As a first step in this reconsideration, we must learn to avoid thinking of pessimism as a psychological disposition somehow linked to depression or contrariness. However late the term itself appeared in our language, it clearly names a persistent thought, or set of thoughts, that have recurred often in social and political theory since the Enlightenment. Treating pessimism as a disposition robs it of its seriousness and transforms it into a mere complaint, one with which some people are mysteriously and unfortunately stricken. Yet while it would be recognized as absurd to treat the optimistic conclusions of Mill and Marx in terms of their authors' sunny dispositions (especially since they did not have them), such analyses of the pessimists that exist routinely take a biographical tack and, for example, attribute Schopenhauer's pessimism to some condition of genetic unhappiness or childhood trauma.[20] We must divorce the concept of pessimism from that of unhappiness as thoroughly as we separate theories of progress from happiness. Happiness and unhappiness, it ought to go without saying, have existed forever. But pessimism, like progress, is a modern idea.

What is it, then, to be a philosophical pessimist? Many people will say, after all, that they are optimistic about some things and pessimistic about others. Even if we specify that, since we are dealing with political philosophy, the things in question must be important social and political processes or institutions or values, the terms "optimist" and "pessimist" will still strike some as too imprecise to be of real use. John Dewey, for example, once said that he was "very skeptical about things in particular but [had] an enormous faith in things in general."[21] And while it is perfectly possible to understand what he meant, it is nonetheless my contention that most modern political theory, in response to the linearization and historicization of Western time-consciousness, has some fundamental answer to the question of whether the human condition is meliorable or not. There are many different ways, of course, in which one could imagine the human condition improved—moral, political, material, technological, et cetera. Yet most political theorists will have a position on which of these categories is most important, and it is along this line, whatever it may be, that one is justified in calling them "optimistic" or "pessimistic." Although Dewey may have been pessimistic about American political prospects, he had no doubt that the functioning of human intelligence, over time, was bound to bring about a freer, morally and materially ad-

[20] See, for example, R. J. Hollingdale's extensive introduction to the Penguin edition of Schopenhauer's essays, Schopenhauer (1970, 9–38). But pick up almost *any* account of Schopenhauer and one is likely to be greeted by preliminary ruminations (usually wildly speculative and ungrounded) about his character, temperament, and moods.

[21] Letter to Scudder Klyce, April 16, 1915. Quoted in Rockefeller (1991, 328). I thank Alan Ryan for calling my attention to this passage.

vanced society. On the other hand, a pessimist such as Rousseau, for example, may grant that the material conditions of society have greatly improved over the centuries and are likely to continue improving. But this does not weaken his contention (indeed, as we shall see, it strengthens it) that at the same time the species has been degenerating morally. And since this moral degeneration is, for him, the crucial issue, it is appropriate to characterize his philosophy as pessimistic[22] just as it is appropriate to call Dewey an optimist. "Optimism," as I shall use this term, thus encompasses a broader variety of modern political thought than pessimism, which names a relatively discrete group of theorists. The optimistic account of the human condition is both linear and progressive. Liberalism, socialism, and pragmatism may all be termed optimistic in the sense that they are all premised on the idea that the application of reason to human social and political conditions will ultimately result in the melioration of these conditions. Pessimism, while retaining a linear account of time and history, denies this premise, or (more cautiously) finds no evidence for it and asks us to philosophize in its absence.[23]

One point that deserves emphasis here is the non-equation of pessimism with theories of decline. While pessimists *may* posit a decline, it is the denial of progress, not an insistence on some eventual doom, that marks out modern pessimism. Pessimism, to put it precisely, is the negation, and not the opposite, of theories of progress. This may immediately strike some readers as a fudge, but consider: most of those thinkers whom we could agree without argument to call pessimists, like Schopenhauer, did not profess a belief in any permanent downward historical trend. Schopenhauer posits no long-term historical trends at all, merely a constantly regrettable human condition burdened (as I discuss below) by linear time. In fact, belief in a permanent decline of the human condition is relatively rare in political theory (Horkheimer and Adorno's wartime *Dialectic of Enlightenment* comes to mind, and Rousseau's first two *Discourses*, but little else). But it is not by accident that writers such as Schopenhauer are known as pessimists—for the nonprogressive yet linear view of human existence is indeed profoundly discomfiting. Unlike a cyclical account, where the pattern of history is essentially pregiven, pessimism is historical in the modern sense: change occurs, human nature and society may be profoundly altered over time, just not permanently for the better. Although pessimism does not *issue* from black moods, it could indeed inspire them. But

---

[22] Especially in the case of such a contradictory figure as Rousseau, this is a characterization to be made with great hesitancy. In chapter 2, I will discuss the reasons for this judgment in more detail.

[23] This dichotomy, of course, does not capture every element of modern political thought perfectly. One might argue, for example, that Hobbes's theory, in its purely spatial, geometric approach seeks to avoid the question of temporality entirely. But I cannot deal with such exceptional cases here.

even this, as we shall see, is not the regular conclusion of pessimistic philosophies.

. . . . .

What does a pessimist believe and on what basis? In the rest of this chapter, I shall try to answer these questions. I remind the reader again that, in setting out a series of propositions as the central claims of pessimism, I do not insist that everyone I describe as a pessimist subscribes to all of them. I should add as well that, even when they do reach similar conclusions, the means they employ to arrive at them can be very different. What they share is something more than a sensibility, but less than a doctrine. It might be best to say that they share a problematic—their thoughts all emerge from the question posed to them by the modern problems of time and history—that issues in a certain approach to traditional questions of political theory.[24] While I could provide a series of portraits of each thinker, it will be more effective, and more likely to demonstrate their common endeavor, to proceed through a series of propositions that pessimists subscribe to in greater or less degrees. These propositions, which to some extent build on one another, are, in their bluntest form, as follows: that time is a burden; that the course of history is in some sense ironic; that freedom and happiness are incompatible; and that human existence is absurd. Finally, there is a divide between those pessimists, like Schopenhauer, who suggest that the only reasonable response to these propositions is a kind of resignation, and those, like Nietzsche, who reject resignation in favor of a more life-affirming ethic of individualism and spontaneity.[25]

The Burden of Time

What does it mean to think of time as a burden? One way to get at this question is to look at what the pessimists have to say about the difference

---

[24] Two important recent books which attempt to reexamine the history of political thought from the perspective of its central problems, and which share many of the thematic concerns of this volume, are Susan Neiman's *Evil in Modern Thought: An Alternative History of Philosophy* (2002) and J. Peter Euben's *The Tragedy of Political Theory: The Road Not Taken* (1990). While not fully in agreement with either, I admire both for their willingness to insist that political philosophy is first and foremost a study of human limitations, provoked not by our utopian dreams but by our tragic experiences. Because of this, they are far more helpful than any of the critical literature on pessimism.

[25] The concept of "resignation" has itself been recently complicated, in a useful way, by Thomas Dumm (1998). Although Dumm finds affirmative possibilities in resignation that deserve consideration, I use "resignation" here, as I have throughout, in what I take to be the commonplace sense of a paralyzing despair or purposeful withdrawal from all activity.

between human beings and animals. The distinction between humans and animals is one repeatedly drawn in the pessimistic tradition and one that centers on the consciousness of time. At the beginning of his essay "On the Uses and Disadvantages of History for Life," Nietzsche famously compares human beings, with their keen sense of history, to animals (specifically, in this case, cows) who are "contained in the present" (*UM* 61). Animals, to Nietzsche, live "unhistorically" in the sense that they can form no concept of past or future. They respond to stimuli in the present in a routine and automatic way, as their natures dictate, but are unable, on the one hand, to form plans or hopes about the future, and on the other, to have regrets or satisfactions about the past. The animal, as Schopenhauer puts it, "is the present incarnate" (*EA* 45). To be human, on the other hand, is to have, for better or worse, a linear sense of time. Human existence, in Nietzsche's words, is "an imperfect tense that can never become a perfect one."

However unobjectionable this distinction may seem (at least as rough description), it is not one that has always been made. Thomas Aquinas, for example, explicitly maintained that higher animals have the capacity for hope and, therefore, a sense of past and future, even if more limited than that in humans.[26] By itself, this disagreement would mean very little if it were not connected to certain vital issues. To Aquinas, the animals' capacity for hope is one of a series of traits that connects them to humans in a common createdness. To the pessimists, however, the human condition is existentially unique—its uniqueness consisting precisely in the capacity for time-consciousness. In Rousseau's *Discourse on the Origin and Foundations of Inequality* (*Second Discourse*), the difference is put between earlier, animalistic humans and the conscious beings we have become. The savage's soul "yields itself wholly to the sentiment of its present existence, with no idea of the future, however near it may be, and his projects, as narrow as his views, hardly extend to the close of the day" (*SD* 151). More importantly, perhaps, "an animal will never know what it is to die, and the knowledge of death and of its terrors was one of man's first acquisitions on moving away from the animal condition" (*SD* 150).[27]

There are several points here worth emphasizing. The first is the close identification that pessimism makes between time-consciousness and consciousness per se. If self-consciousness means a sense of self as a continu-

---

[26] See Aquinas 1981, II-I, 40, 3, 1; 760ff.). I thank Jennie Donnellon for her conversations and papers on the question of Aquinas's belief about the sense of time in animals.

[27] Rousseau is not responding directly to Aquinas, of course, but has in mind such figures as Shaftesbury and some of the *philosophes* who, in positing a natural sociability in humans, emphasized the continuity between human and animal constitutions (see Hulliung 1994, chap. 2). I thank Annie Stilz for her conversations and papers on Shaftesbury and the question of natural sociability.

ous being over time, then obviously the animals cannot be in possession of it if they have no sense of time at all. In this sense, *self-consciousness is time-consciousness* to the pessimist in the sense that consciousness of time is the fundamental, indispensable attribute of self-consciousness. Human beings are separated from the animals, and even from their earlier animal selves, by their conscious existence within time. I use the phrase "conscious existence within time" here to cover a variety of views on whether the human recognition of time is itself valid. To Schopenhauer, for example, linear time (as I explain in more detail in chapter 3) is in some sense an illusion, or more properly, a delusion from which death will release us. To Rousseau, in contrast, our emergence into time-consciousness is a genuine intellectual advance, even if it dooms us to unhappiness. But whatever disagreement there may be on this question, it is the common currency of pessimism that humans are marked out from the animals by their sense of time. The timelessness of animal existence, whether seen as an Eden or as an infancy, is something we have left behind and can never recover, except perhaps in occasional moments of reverie or transcendence.[28]

To say that human existence is defined by time-consciousness is also, for the pessimist, to say that it is burdened. Pessimists depict this burden in a variety of ways, none more important than the one mentioned above in the passage by Rousseau: consciousness of time means consciousness of death. Human beings are unique among the animals in having foreknowledge of their own death and this conditions the life they lead. Rousseau simply calls this knowledge one of the many "terrors" of consciousness. Perhaps it is enough to say here that many will find the prospect of their eventual nonexistence to be terrifying. Even apart from the suffering that often precedes death, the prospect of the end of life is not one on which human beings are apt to dwell. But the threat of death is also linked to a whole series of other conditions that, to the pessimists, threaten to drain even the days we have left of meaning and purpose. The first of these is colorfully illustrated in the "Dialogue of Fashion and Death" by Giacomo Leopardi. In it, the goddess Fashion catches up with Death, "the mortal foe of memory," to remind her that they are both

---

[28] Insofar as possible, I attempt to remain agnostic here about the question of time's true nature, a fascinating topic that a book like this cannot hope to resolve. As a result, I must also leave to one side here the depiction of time in modern physics. However, it may be useful for readers to realize that the Newtonian postulate of a natural absolute linear time, after dominating for three centuries, is now open to question from within the field of physics itself. Einstein's theory first made time less than absolute, but did not question its linear character. However, in the wake of quantum theory, some physicists are now willing to speak of the fundamental unreality of time in a language that sounds positively Schopenhauerian (see Greene 2004).

"daughters of Decay." Though Death at first denies the relationship, Fashion points out how much they have in common: "I know that both of us equally aim continually to destroy and change all things here below, although you achieve this by one road and I by another" (*OM* 51). As a daughter of Decay, Death not only represents the final end of life, but also defines the *path* of life. Every moment of our lives, we are on our way to death, whether we recognize this or not. Governed indirectly by Death or directly by Fashion, "the greater part of life is a wilting away" (*OM* 173). Other pessimists put the point more plainly. Freud just says, "the aim of all life is death," while Don Quixote declares that he was "born to live dying" (*BPP* 46; *DQ* 2:59).

This sentiment—of the constant presence of death in our lives—is one both central to the pessimistic tradition and also central to misunderstandings of it. Critics have often used this sort of material to accuse the pessimists of teaching resignation or nihilism. But this is usually (though not always) a mistake. It is not the pessimists, but their opponents, who draw the conclusion that the acknowledgment of death must lead to inactivity or helplessness. This is hardly ever the conclusion of the pessimists themselves. To say that our lives are always on the way to death is not at all to say that they are pointless, but simply to set out the parameters of possibility for our existence. Pessimism may warn us to acknowledge our limitations—but it does not urge us to collapse in the face of them. Death is merely the ultimate reminder that we do not control the conditions of our existence and are not ever likely to. And from her kinship with Fashion, we know that these conditions include relentless, unpredictable change.

This constant change is something else that the pessimist takes to be a burden of temporal existence. To live within the flow of time means that whatever exists now is always rushing into the nonexistence of the past. Schopenhauer puts this point in its most extreme form when he laments "*Time* and that *perishability* of all things existing in time that time itself brings about. . . . Time is that by virtue of which everything becomes nothingness in our hands and loses all real value" (*EA* 51). He refers to this phenomenon as the "vanity of existence"—meaning thereby the older sense of "vanity" as a nothing or nullity. The change of fashions that Leopardi describes is thus emblematic to the pessimist of the ordinary nature of temporal, nonprogressive existence: constant change to no particular effect.

For pessimism, the fleetingness of existence has a series of related implications. First is the sense of unreality that it brings to human life. Since every moment disappears into the past as it occurs, it can be hard to take anything too seriously. Nothing is so solid that it will not melt into air, if not in this moment, then in one soon to come. For someone like Schopenhauer, the implication of this is that all human striving is in some sense futile. Whatever one sets as one's goal in life, even if one can achieve it, will disappear the moment it arrives. Nothing is permanent, and we suffer most from the lack of permanence in the people and things that we most care about it. Indeed, the more we care, the more we suffer. Even if one rejects his conclusion that withdrawal from existence is the best course, Schopenhauer's reasoning on the intensification of suffering by time-consciousness remains powerful:

> Yet how much stronger are the emotions aroused in [man] than those aroused in the animal! How incomparably more profound and vehement are his passions! . . . This arises first and foremost because with him everything is powerfully intensified by thinking about absent and future things, and this is in fact the origin of care, fear and hope, which once they have been aroused, make a far stronger impression on men than do actual present pleasures or sufferings, to which the animal is limited. For, since it lacks the faculty of reflection, joys and sorrows cannot accumulate in the animal as they do in man through memory and anticipation. With the animal, present suffering, even if repeated countless times, remains what it was the first time: it cannot sum itself up. (*EA* 44)

Animals, like humans, lose whatever it is they possess every moment. But only humans feel the pain of that loss, since only human consciousness retains a sense of these things as past. Nor is our capacity for hope, or anticipation of the future, a compensation for this condition. Indeed, it compounds our situation, since most of our hopes are bound to be disappointed, and those that are fulfilled are disfulfilled in the next moment as the objects of our hopes slip into the past. All in all, time-consciousness is a bad deal from the perspective of human happiness.

Of course, happiness is not the only metric that can be applied to human existence. Time-consciousness does offer other compensations to human beings. The primary benefit is simply that of consciousness itself—the intellectual capacity for higher thought that accompanies the emergence from animal status. Enlightenment figures such as Locke termed this the capacity for "reflection"—a word which, for Rousseau, perfectly captures the connection that pessimism draws between time-consciousness and what we call reason. For Rousseau, the essence of reasoning is the ability to make comparisons between different conditions. The animal can never compare his present condition to that of his past (or potential future) because it lacks the requisite sense of continuity over time. One can think of this as an incapacity to recognize one's own reflection in a mirror. A mirror always displays an image of a self that is removed from the conscious mind by an infinitesimally small moment. The ability to see this image as an image *of oneself* is thus the simplest marker of a sense of continuity over time. To reflect is thus the core of higher thought in the sense that it is our capacity to reflect ourselves to ourselves that marks us out as thinking beings.

But Rousseau had little patience with the idea that this capacity was simply of benefit to us: "the state of reflection is a state against Nature, and the man who meditates a depraved animal" (SD 145). The natural condition, as the multitude of animals demonstrates, is to be timeless and happy. Whether we abandoned this condition by choice or an unfortunate series of accidents or an act of Providence is beside the point. Once abandoned it can never be returned to; reflection produces knowledge and knowledge, secured by our newly founded memory, accumulates. In the state of nature, "there was neither education nor progress, generations multiplied uselessly; and as each one of them always started at the same point, centuries went by in all the crudeness of the first ages, the species had already grown old, and man remained ever a child" (SD 166). Emerging from this state, we gain knowledge, but only at considerable cost. In language that anticipates the passage from Schopenhauer quoted above, Rousseau writes: "Reflection . . . causes him to regret past benefits and keeps him from enjoying the present: it shows him a happy future, so that his imagination might seduce and his desires torment him, and it shows him an unhappy future so that he might experience it ahead of time" (FD 107). Unamuno made the same point rather more pungently: "Consciousness," he wrote, "is a disease" (TSL 22).

To this point, I have not been clear about whether it is the thought of time or the thought of death that is primary in pessimistic thinking. Rousseau's way of putting things, however, makes clear that it is the former that precedes the latter. We do not, after all, acquire an image of death by experiencing it, either in ourselves or through others. An animal can witness the death of fellow-members of its species and still have no anticipation of its own death. How is it, then, that the pessimists conclude that we come to anticipate and fear death? Rousseau's sense of self-consciousness as reflection answers this question. If coming to consciousness means having a sense of oneself as continuous over time, then it is only on this basis that we can come to imagine an end to such a continuity. That is, it is only when we understand ourselves as continuous with our past that we can imagine ourselves projected into the future *and also not projected into the future.* So if knowledge of death was "one of man's first acquisitions on moving away from the animal condition," it was not the very first. The idea that, at some point in the future, we might not exist (just as the idea that, at some point in the past, we *did* not exist) is only available once we have a sense of our existence over time. Birth and death are not meaningful concepts to the timeless. Knowledge of death may be terrible—but it is *knowledge*, something acquired through the conscious reflection made possible by time-consciousness. All our experience of death as animals never endowed us with a consciousness of it.

Like Schopenhauer, then, Rousseau argues that time-consciousness, by itself, leads to human suffering. Or to be more precise, time-consciousness magnifies the trifling sufferings of animal existence into something much greater. This point is central to the entire pessimistic tradition and appears, I believe, in every author discussed in this book in one form or another. But Rousseau's account points to something else that is less developed in some later writers. In leaving the state of Nature, human beings become, not just temporal, but *historical* creatures as well. The implications of this historicality form the second major heading under which I have grouped the conclusions of pessimism.

The Irony of History

The pessimist finds that man has emerged from a timeless animality or infancy into an adulthood of linear time. Some of the effects of this emergence, those outlined above, are felt nearly instantaneously. But others only emerge later. That we are aware of the temporal dimension of existence means, for the first time, that our experiences can accumulate and multiply and interact. This is what it means for humans to be historical animals. While most pessimists do not doubt that time, as such, has always proceeded in a linear fashion, it is only when humans become conscious of this fact, even in a primitive way, that history begins to have an effect on us as individuals. Of course an historical optimist, no less than a pessimist, believes in this process. The difference between the two lies in how they interpret the effects of the accumulation of experience and the resulting development of reason. While much philosophy has taken it for granted that these effects are (or in the long run will always be) positive, pessimism has found little ground for this confidence and much evidence for the reverse conclusion.

Pessimists do not deny the existence of "progress" in certain areas—they do not deny that technologies have improved or that the powers of science have increased. Instead, they ask whether these improvements are inseparably related to a greater set of costs that often go unperceived. Or they ask whether these changes have really resulted in a fundamental melioration of the human condition. This often results, as my title for this section suggests, in a conception of history as following an ironic path, one that appears, on the surface, to be getting better when in fact it is getting worse (or, on the whole, no better). Again, the reasoning that supports this view varies among the pessimists, but not so greatly as to obscure the common sentiment.

It was the contention of Plato, and many philosophers following him, that true knowledge and true happiness must be coterminous. In the myth that concludes the *Gorgias*, for example, it is the philosopher himself who is judged, not just the most virtuous, but also the happiest of men, both in this world and the next (526c, 527c). To the pessimists, this is a fundamental mistake on the part of the philosophical tradition, one it is largely too late to set right. Reason has its benefits but, from a pessimistic perspective, happiness is simply not among them. Indeed, in its destruction of illusions, reason is actually productive of unhappiness.

It is this destructiveness that makes reason cumulatively (as opposed to instantaneously) harmful to human felicity. When humans became self-conscious, they had taken a great leap from the animal condition, but they were still relatively ignorant creatures. Now, however, they would not remain so. Little by little, illusions and mistakes are overcome by reason. Leopardi narrates this process in the bleakly comic "History of the Human Race": Jove creates human beings and continually strives to make them happy. But humans remain perpetually dissatisfied with mortal existence despite the god's efforts to make it pleasant. Finally, Jove becomes exasperated with their demands and resolves "to set all mercy aside and to punish the human species for ever, condemning it for all future ages to a wretchedness far worse than that of the past. For this purpose [Jove] decided not only to send Truth down among them for a while, as they asked, but to give her eternal abode among them; and removing those lovely phantoms which he had placed here below, to make her alone the perpetual moderator and mistress of the human race."

At this point, the other gods protest, since this act will surely make the humans too god-like. But Jove reassures the other gods that the reign of Truth will only increase the distance between mortal and immortal:

> Jove disabused them of this opinion by pointing out that . . . whereas [Truth] was wont to show the immortals their beatitude, to men she would entirely reveal and continually hold before their eyes their own wretchedness. . . . Nothing will seem truer to them than the falsity of all mortal things; and nothing solid, but the emptiness of all but their own griefs. For these reasons they will be deprived even of hope; with which, from the very beginning until the present day, more than any other pleasure or comfort, they have sustained their lives. And hoping for nothing, nor seeing any worthwhile end to all their toils and endeavors, they will fall into such neglect and abomination of all industrious, not to say magnanimous works, that the usual habits of the living will scarcely differ from those of the dead and buried. But in this loss and despair they will not be able to prevent that craving for immense happiness, innate in their spirits, from stinging and cruciating them as much worse than before as it will be the less impeded and distracted by the variety of their concerns and the impetus of action. (*OM* 41–42)

This convinces the other gods who now find Jove's punishment to be, if anything, too cruel. For creatures condemned to an earthly existence, the acquisition of knowledge about their fate does not, as Plato thought, arrive as a gift, but as a terrible penalty.

Leopardi's parable shows the burden of time compounding itself over the course of history: if humans were happier as animals than as conscious beings, then as primitive, ignorant conscious beings they remain happier than as more developed and civilized ones. Since the reality of temporal existence is transience, decay, and death, happiness is found in illusion. The piercing of illusion may be counted as a philosophical, and even a moral, advance. But if we knew of the consequences beforehand and cared about our happiness, such insight would not be pursued. The growth of reason, however, once initiated cannot be frozen at any point. Knowledge cannot draw a limit to itself since the knowing mind finds it nearly impossible to value ignorance.

A parallel kind of reasoning (in a very different vocabulary, of course) appears in Freud's account of the displacement of hallucination with ratiocination in the course of human history. Dreams, Freud says, are a piece of childhood preserved in the adult, but "behind this childhood of the individual we are promised a picture of a phylogenetic childhood" so that "the analysis of dreams will lead us to a knowledge of man's archaic heritage" (*ID* 587–88). Initially, Freud says, our entire mental life was like that of our dreams today. What Leopardi calls our capacity to fulfill our longings through "imagination," Freud calls hallucination and he posits that "there was a primitive state . . . in which wishing ended in hallucinating" (*ID* 605). That is, when our thoughts were unimpeded by any notion of fidelity to a true understanding of the world, our every desire could be fulfilled by means of self-created illusions. What Leopardi calls the descent of Truth from Heaven, Freud calls, in *The Interpretation of Dreams*, "the bitter experience of life" and later, the supplanting of the pleasure principle with the reality principle. As we come to be more knowledgeable, reason destroys not just particular illusions, but our capacity for self-delusion, and thus self-satisfaction, more generally. Our infantile dreaming is replaced by adult thinking: "Thought is after all nothing but a substitute for a hallucinatory wish" (*ID* 606). As in Leopardi, coming to know the world better reduces our capacity to be happy within it. While Freud, valuing knowledge over happiness, does not regret this transformation in the same manner as Leopardi, his account of the costs involved is no different. The illusions dismantled by knowledge were a source of childhood delight for which the development of science and philosophy make a poor substitute, no matter how many creature comforts they provide.

Both of these accounts have a fundamentally ironic structure: what appears from one perspective to be an advance is, from another, in equal measure, a diminishment. Every step away from our animal condition is a step closer to misery; the path toward enlightenment and the path to hell are one and the same. Nor is this trajectory reversible. Reason, once engaged, has its own logic, and we can no more ignore its conclusions than we can consciously decide to become unconscious. Leopardi does not hesitate to draw the conclusion that the optimistic faith that philosophy has placed in itself is unfounded:

> Therefore they greatly deceive themselves, who declare and preach that the perfection of man consists in knowledge of the truth, and that all his woes proceed from false opinions and ignorance, and that the human race will at last be happy, when all or most people come to know the truth, and solely on the grounds of that, arrange and govern their lives. And these things are said by not far short of all philosophers both ancient and modern. . . . I am not unaware that the ultimate conclusion to be drawn from true and perfect philosophy is that we need not philosophize. From which we infer that, in the first place, philosophy is useless, for in order to refrain from philosophizing, there is no need to be a philosopher; in the second place it is exceedingly harmful, for the ultimate conclusion is not learned except at one's own costs, and once learned, cannot be put into effect; as it is not in the power of man to forget the truths they know, and it is easier to rid oneself of any habit before that of philosophizing. Philosophy in short, hoping and promising at the beginning to cure our ills, is in the end reduced to a longing in vain to heal itself. (*OM* 186–187)

In this indictment of philosophy, Leopardi is developing a line of reasoning largely initiated by Rousseau. As is well-known, Rousseau became famous for arguing that the development of reason in general, and the Enlightenment in particular, was responsible for a pernicious decline in the moral character of the species. In the *Discourses*, he traces several paths by which progress is transmuted or refracted into its opposite. These stories combine to create a nearly mathematical certainty that "our souls have become corrupted in proportion as our Sciences and our Arts have advanced toward perfection" (*FD* 7).[29] The decline of morals, rather than resulting from weakness, evil character, or a philosophical error that further learning could alleviate, is instead seen to derive directly from mental growth: "It is reason that engenders vanity, and reflection that reinforces it; It is what turns man back upon himself; . . . It is Philosophy that isolates him" (*SD* 162). Again, the sense of human thought as "reflection" is important: for humans to "reflect" means that they dwell more upon

---

[29] In the *First Discourse*, the primary story concerns the spread of luxury; in the *Second Discourse*, the focus is on property and inequality. These will be discussed in more detail in chapter 2.

themselves. They become more individuated and thus more interesting to themselves: "his first look at himself aroused the first movement of pride in him" (*SD* 172). Concomitantly, their identification with others declines and with it their sense of moral obligation. Thus while human reason is "perfected," the species is "deteriorating" (*SD* 168). Each intellectual accomplishment, though individually admirable, only fuels Rousseau's pessimism about humanity as a whole. No philosophy, however moral or ascetic, could cure the disease of Philosophy itself. This, then, is the result for Rousseau of everything that modern society has called "progress." Intellectual development and moral sturdiness are locked in a zero-sum struggle, which the latter is bound to lose, for the former accumulates steadily as time passes while the forces of the latter are fixed in, and by, timeless, unchanging nature.

Rousseau's argument here has become known as the "auto-critique of the Enlightenment,"[30] but this term, though apt in some respects, is misleading if it is taken to imply that human development before the Enlightenment is not equally placed under suspicion. Although recent times, for Rousseau, may be especially dubious in their celebration of reason, it is the entire path of human history, from the dawn of reflection onward, that is the subject of his concern. This point is amplified in philosophical descendants like Heidegger who are explicit about the dangers of reason from the moment of its first arrival on the scene. Heidegger's essay "The Question Concerning Technology," for example, can be usefully read as a complement to Rousseau's *First Discourse*. In it, Heidegger depicts us as increasingly unfree, enslaved to a technology that we only think we control. His concern that we see nature only as the object of our desires parallels Rousseau's depiction of philosophical humans as increasingly vain and self-interested. Just as humans, in Rousseau, lose their natural sympathy toward others and instinctive attachment to the world, so for Heidegger do we come to view the world as "standing-reserve," a collection of resources that exists for our potential benefit. Heidegger, like Rousseau, does not contest the technological improvements of the last few centuries; rather he argues, again like Rousseau, that these accomplishments have been dehumanizing and denaturalizing—literally, depraving. Although the technological tendency has, for Heidegger, become ever more dominant since the Enlightenment, he, like Leopardi, traces its roots back to Athenian philosophy, contrasting this with the earlier approach of the pre-Socratics. But Rousseau's theme of the "tyranny of reason" and its historical development has also resonated with writers on the other end of the political spectrum from Heidegger, for example in Horkheimer and Adorno's *Dialectic of Enlightenment*. What all these diverse authors

---

[30] See Hulliung 1994, chap. 2.

(and others discussed in later chapters) share is an apprehension about the accumulating effects of reason, and the ironic development whereby what appears to be mankind's greatest tool and achievement becomes, in Heidegger's words, "the supreme danger" (Heidegger 1977, 26).

Finally, there is another historical concern expressed, not by all pessimists, but nearly exclusively by pessimists: boredom. An emotion we often view with contempt (as the privilege of the adolescent or idle rich), boredom, to the pessimists, is a particularly modern contagion, one of the long-term effects of linear time.[31] It is easy to see why this is so. The situation is encapsulated in modern dramas like Beckett's *Waiting for Godot* or Sartre's *No Exit*. If history neither repeats itself nor goes on improving, what else is left? While some pessimists, like Rousseau, envision decline, most simply see a kind of earthly purgatory where nothing changes but nonetheless that same nothing lasts forever. Human beings often manage to distract themselves from this underlying reality, but when they do not, or their distractions fail, boredom is the inevitable result. According to the pessimists, then, we are not juvenile or lazy if we feel bored; we are instead simply cognizant of a fundamental element of the human condition.

It is perhaps Schopenhauer who is best known for this view, but in fact he was preceded in this theme by Leopardi. Boredom is one of the main concerns of the *Moral Essays* and the effects of boredom are there depicted in the most dramatic terms. Boredom, like laughter, is one of those characteristics that separates humans from animals. But again, it is not so much that we have a special capacity for tedium, but rather that we are able to feel our continuous existence in time; boredom is simply one of the consequences of this. Since boredom springs from this fundamental attribute of self-consciousness, it is effectively the baseline mental condition from which we can only be distracted, either by pain or by relentless activity. This latter does not bring happiness, exactly, but at least it is neither pain nor tedium, the two most common conditions. So, for example, Leopardi puts into the mouth of Columbus, a figure he greatly admires, the following speech:

> if at this moment you and I, and all our companions, were not aboard these
> ships, in the midst of the sea, in this unknown solitude, in a condition as un-

---

[31] Patricia Meyer Spacks (1995) argues that the concept of boredom did not really exist, as such, before the eighteenth century. Although the French word *ennui* is very old, the English verb "to bore" did not exist until the second half of the eighteenth century and noun "boredom" not until the nineteenth. Spacks is more interested in describing the evolution of the concept than in explaining its emergence but speculates that it has to do with the collapse of the Christian worldview, with its sense of responsibility, thus allowing the sin of *acedia* (sloth) to become the condition of boredom (11).

certain and risky as you please; what other situation in life would we find ourselves in? What would we be doing? How would we be spending these days? Do you think, more happily? Or would we not rather be in some greater trouble or anxiety, or else full of boredom? What does one mean by a condition free of uncertainty and danger? If content and happy, that is to be preferred to any other; if tedious and wretched, I cannot see what other state is not to be preferred to it. . . . Even if we gain no other benefit from this voyage, it seems to me that it is most profitable to us, in that for a while it keeps us free of boredom, renders life dear to us, and makes us value many things that we would not otherwise take into account. (*OM* 161)

But the condition of happiness, which Columbus apparently believes in, is withdrawn as a possibility by Leopardi's larger philosophy. Nor is boredom a neutral state, halfway between happiness and unhappiness. Rather, boredom is our normal condition of unfulfillment, lacking only an active pain. This unfulfillment is caused simply by the length of our conscious existence coupled with our loss of the animal ability to be satisfied in the moment. So human beings, for the most part, alternate between pain and boredom, with only the exceptional figure, like Columbus, able to banish both temporarily through vigorous action: "I truly believe that by tedium we should understand none other than the pure longing for happiness; not assuaged by pleasure, and not overtly afflicted by distress. But this craving, as we agreed not long ago, is never gratified; and real pleasure is never to be found. So that human life, so to speak, is composed and interwoven, partly of pain and partly tedium; and is never at rest from one of these passions without falling into the other" (*OM* 96).

Schopenhauer, like Leopardi, connects the prevalence of boredom to the absence of true pleasure in life. We are, he argues, compelled by needs that are hard to satisfy. But even when we do satisfy them, "their satisfaction achieves nothing but a painless condition in which [man] is only given over to boredom . . . and that boredom is direct proof that existence is in itself valueless, for boredom is nothing other than the sensation of the emptiness of existence. For if life . . . possessed in itself a positive value and real content, there would be no such thing as boredom: mere existence would fulfill and satisfy us. As things are, we take no pleasure in existence except when we are striving after something (*EA* 53–54)." Boredom, then, is not so much a problem in itself as it is a marker for time-boundedness. Our condition is one of linear extension and yet that extension has no pattern (progress), goal (telos), or end (eschaton). It is the bare condition of temporality, with nothing given to distract us from its endlessness and meaninglessness. Unless we can divert ourselves with self-imposed tasks, as Columbus did in Leopardi's fable, boredom is the best we can hope for. A disenchanted universe offers us nothing else.

Insofar as we value this knowledge, we can consider boredom, as Leopardi sometimes did, as "in some ways the most sublime of human feelings" (*P* 48), the key to an understanding of our predicament. But it is perhaps more likely that we will take the perspective that E. M. Cioran encapsulates in a simple exchange: "'What do you do from morning to night?' 'I endure myself.'" (*TBB* 36).

Whether viewed as a source of disillusion or boredom, then, the historicity of human experience is something that pessimism views as a lamentable consequence of time-consciousness. We cannot, the pessimists argue, separate the material and intellectual achievements that the accumulation of experience makes possible from the costs such an accumulation imposes. What optimistic philosophies depict simply as a growth of ability and power is, to all the pessimists, the cause of much human suffering and, to some of them, the source of a certain moral decrepitude as well. While we should again recognize how simplistic it would be to evaluate the conditions of our life merely in terms of pain and pleasure, part of the pessimists point here is to reveal how just such a hedonism underlies the position of their opponents: it is the optimists who claim that the increase in human mental and technological abilities will inevitably produce a society of happier, freer individuals. (Indeed, stripped of this claim, it would be hard to know what their philosophy amounted to.) To the pessimists, whether this assertion is made in a Platonic form with regard to philosophy itself, on in an Enlightenment form where philosophy is said to be allied with science, it is a false promise, one without foundation in experience or theory. Without denying the increase in cerebral agility that we have attained, a full account of both historicity and the human beings who endure it cannot, the pessimists claim, be made in a mood of celebration. Indeed, insofar as we have mistaken the instruments of suffering for those of self-betterment, only an ironic tone can capture the situation accurately. While we need not conclude, with Leopardi, that the *only* solution for the philosopher is not to philosophize, it is the more general conclusion of pessimism that any philosopher who truly wishes her work to be of some aid to her species must, at the least, recognize the limitations of her instrument and the burdens that historicity imposes alongside its better-known benefits. While these are indeed serious restrictions, it should again be noted that it is only the critics of pessimism, and not the pessimists themselves, who find them paralyzing.

The Absurdity of Existence

Thus far, I have described pessimism as an investigation into the effects of temporality on the human condition. This it certainly is, but it is also a judgment of these effects and a recommendation for how to respond to them. This section will deal with the first of these topics, the next with the second. The simplest way to characterize the pessimistic reaction to the human condition is with words like "absurd" or "contradictory." Absurdity of existence is illustrated by the persistent mismatch between human purposes and the means available to achieve them: or again, between our desire for happiness and our capacity to encounter or sustain it. Different generations put the point in different ways, of course, but the enduring thought is not a complicated one. To my mind, it is contained in the view that freedom and happiness, both difficult to obtain, are furthermore incompatible with one another.

The germ of this idea is found in Rousseau's contention, cited above, that our condition of consciousness is one "against Nature." Even after Nature ceases to function as a regulative ideal for later pessimists, the sense that a thinking being must be in permanent tension with his or her environment is a continuing one. "Human life," Schopenhauer writes, "must be some kind of mistake" (*EA* 53). The mistake consists in the poor fit between the aims that human beings share and the world in which they are settled to pursue those aims. Since we are nonetheless taught, by the false optimism that predominates in modern society, to believe that our goals are achievable, "life presents itself as a continual deception, in small matters as well as great" (*WWR* 2:573). We are thus constantly subject to what Schopenhauer calls (in English) "disappointment," the sensation of finding that the world has once again let us down (*EA* 47). Freud puts a similar point in a more scientific-sounding language: "the purpose of life is simply the programme of the pleasure principle . . . and yet its programme is at loggerheads with the whole world . . . all the regulations of the universe run counter to it" (*CD* 24–25). Camus, in introducing the concept of "the absurd" to philosophical discourse, speaks of the "divorce between man and his life, the actor and his setting" as "properly the feeling of absurdity" (*MS* 6).

While pessimism is a philosophy rather than a disposition, it is, of course, concerned with dispositions in the limited sense that most pessimists view human beings as largely unhappy and largely fated to remain so. Pessimism, as a theory, is interested in the prevalence of human unhappiness. In some cases, as for example with Freud, a pessimist may even offer an account of this condition that is itself primarily rooted in psychology. But this is of course very different from the theory itself having its origin in a particular disposition within its authors. Indeed, fundamentally, the pessimistic account of the origin of unhappiness (even, I would maintain, in Freud) has little to do with psychology itself but with a claim of ontological misalignment between human beings and the world they inhabit. Furthermore it is not so much the prevalence of unhappiness that pessimism condemns (though it certainly does deplore it) as the use-lessness and aimlessness of such suffering—along with the deception constantly being perpetrated on us that our suffering is unnecessary, temporary or the result of individual misfortune. Thus Leopardi has Nature identify the mistake of one who complains of our perpetual distress: "Did you perhaps imagine that the world was made for your benefit?" (*OM* 102).

A crucial element of this deception is the contention made by optimistic philosophy that our capacity to reason is something that gives us power over the world and thus a means of alleviating our suffering. In order for this to be true, the world would in some sense have to be aligned with or amenable to the force of reason when, to the pessimists, it simply is not. Thus, to Nietzsche, the "optimism" of Socrates is contained in "his faith that the nature of things can be fathomed, [he] ascribes to knowledge and insight the power of a panacea" (*BT* 97). But to Nietzsche, as to Leopardi, the world was made neither for our benefit nor our understanding. This is not to deny that reason exists or that it has certain powers; but in order to know *in advance* that our powers of reason could ensure our happiness (that is, in advance of the day, yet to arrive, when it actually did so), we would also have to make assumptions about the nature of the world in which reason finds itself. This, Nietzsche contends, was the leap that Socrates made, without foundation, and that through Plato was transmitted to the rest of the philosophical tradition in the West. But beginning at least with Rousseau, the pessimists have been concerned that the opposite might be the case: that in abandoning the condition of animals for one of reason, we only distance ourselves from the world and make it less likely that we will be at home in it. Thus Camus cries: "This ridiculous reason is what sets me in opposition to all creation" (*MS* 51).

Put another way, we can say that there is a kind of pragmatism buried so deeply in Western philosophy that it is almost impossible to root out. This is the notion that there *must be* an answer to our fundamental questions, even if we have not found it yet, and that this answer will deliver us from suffering. That is, there must be a way for human beings to live free and happy. Socrates' constant attempts to discern the superior modes of human life are pragmatic in the sense that they assume that such questions are *problems* that can be rationally solved, that there is some plane on which philosophy intersects with life, or rather that philosophy itself is something capable of providing answers. Such a question-answer vision is still clearly visible, for example, in Hegel's reading of history—where Oriental civilization is seen as posing a riddle the Greeks first solve, with the solution then being improved upon by subsequent civilizations. Human life, in this allegory, is a riddle awaiting an Oedipus with a rational answer. But the pessimistic critique helps to make visible how widely such a pragmatism is shared. Even modern liberalism, which offers no grand narrative like Hegel's, assumes that justice is the achievable object of political philosophy and that the patient application of reason to human society will result in political structures that increasingly approach such a condition. This is even true of a theorist as seemingly atemporal as Hobbes, who is often (and quite wrongly) described as a pessimist because of his bleak description of natural man. For whatever the perils of the state of nature, Hobbes has no doubt that the political and social difficulties he describes can be cured by the proper set of institutions. There are obstacles to doing so, but none of them are immovable. Once properly delineated, he maintained, the problem he describes is readily grasped by the mind and defeated. And for no other liberal is the problem even as formidable as it is for Hobbes.

It is this widely shared model of a universe predisposed to being subdued by the proper dialectic that pessimism objects to via the language of the "absurd." Pessimism differs from other modern philosophies, then, not because of a recommendation of lassitude but because of a diagnosis of the human condition that finds no basis for the faith in progressive reason that these varieties of optimism share. Seemingly opposed, Anglo-American and Continental optimism are in fact equally based in the Socratic rationalism, transplanted into and multiplied by modern time-consciousness, that pessimism identifies as the taproot of so much disappointment in modern politics.

To the pessimists, human existence is not a riddle waiting to be solved by philosophy; human existence merely is. Freedom and happiness do not exist as the solution to a problem. Rather, starting with Rousseau's contention that reasoning is against Nature, pessimists have asserted, contra the optimistic Socrates and his descendants, that freedom and happiness are in a fundamental tension with one another as a result of the ontological "divorce" between the time-conscious being full of desires, goals, and memories and the time-bound universe that constantly destroys the objects of its inhabitants' desires. The concept of freedom that the pessimists have in mind here is not one distinct to them, but rather one widely shared in modern philosophy, namely, that freedom is something that can only be obtained by a conscious being. The capacity of reflective, reasoning beings to be self-directed—that is, to choose their own goals and to direct their efforts over time toward such goals—is the property we honor with the name of freedom. But since, for the pessimists, the more we strive to develop our (time-)conscious capacities, the more we will increase our discomfort in the world, the struggle for freedom must always have an ironic consequence for the goal of happiness. Socrates has it exactly backwards; it is only release from the burdens of consciousness, which ultimately means time-consciousness, that could purchase our happiness. But we are no longer in a position to strike such a bargain, even if reason could be convinced to, in effect, commit suicide.

The absurdity of existence to the pessimist is thus contained in the idea that freedom and happiness oppose one another. Political philosophy therefore cannot be framed as a search for the terms upon which both can be obtained. Rather, it should start from the predicament of their mutual contradictoriness. There is no question that reflection on this predicament can lead pessimism to the edge of the darkest thoughts. Leopardi puts the following words in the mouth of the fictional Filippo Ottonieri: "Asked for what purpose men are born, he replied in jest: to learn how much more expedient it is, not to be born" (*OM* 145). And what Leopardi writes as a sort-of joke, is taken up in deadly earnest by later pessimists. Schopenhauer writes, "There is only one inborn error, and that is the notion that we exist in order to be happy . . . everything in life is certainly calculated to bring us back from that original error, and to convince us that the purpose of our existence is not to be happy" (*WWR* 2:634–35). This we may regard as the final irony to the pessimist's history—that what life teaches us is not to want it. But this is only one element of the pessimist's response to the absurdity of existence and not the last word.

Resignation or Its Opposite

Camus famously begins his essay "The Myth of Sisyphus" with the proclamation that "there is but one truly serious philosophical problem, and that is suicide. Judging whether life is or is not worth living amounts to answering the fundamental question of philosophy" (*MS* 3). This sentiment, I would claim, marks out a particular feature of pessimistic philosophy, namely, its willingness to contend with the possibility that ordinary human life is so full of misery that it is perfectly sensible—rational even—to consider giving it up. In a philosophy that focuses on death as the inevitable limit of life and that considers us fundamentally out of place in the cosmos, this is not surprising. It is more surprising, perhaps, that so few nonpessimists have taken on Camus' challenge to justify human life, as it were, from the ground up.[32] Is it because the challenge is too

---

[32] One prior exception to this generalization is William James's early essay *Is Life Worth Living?* Its contents might give pause even to the most convinced optimists. While James shows a subtle appreciation for pessimistic literature (including a generous assessment of Leopardi), he appeals ultimately to a sphere of the unknown, which, he claims, we ought to affirm as the ground of meaningfulness, while acknowledging our ignorance of it. It is his analogy for this situation that is disturbing and that gives a sense of how far optimists have been willing to go at times to preserve the grounds for their optimism: he likens ordinary human life to that of a dog undergoing vivisection for the purpose of medical instruc-

great? If so, that, in a way, admits pessimism's insight. But even if there are other, better reasons for the evasion of this question by so much modern philosophy, there is perhaps some comfort to be taken in the fact that even the pessimists, in acknowledging the force of the question, do not simply give way to it. No pessimist recommends suicide (though Leopardi comes close on various occasions). Several do recommend something similar: a withdrawal from life into a hermitage of inactivity and (depending on the writer) pure thought or pure sensation. But others, Camus prominent among them, have found that their pessimism issues in an embrace of a vigorous and active life, one committed to political participation. While it will be left for later chapters to describe the reasons behind these choices in more detail, here I will try to indicate the texture of the various responses.[33]

One way to conceive the divide is as follows: given that pessimists agree that our existence is to be principally one of suffering, one can then ask, should we or should we not desire to escape this suffering? There is no question of masochism here—all things being equal, suffering is something all pessimists regret. The question is, are the human properties that are concomitant with suffering such that we should endure what is necessary on their behalf? Or are these properties, valuable as they may be, simply an insufficient compensation? Notice here that there is also no question of hedonism—no pessimist simply adds up the pains and pleasures of life in deciding whether to go on with it.[34] All of them weigh pain and suffering against various other life-qualities. But while writers like Camus, Nietzsche, Unamuno, and Leopardi end up affirming life, others, like Rousseau and Schopenhauer, advocate a kind of retreat, if not into

---

tion. If, he argues, the dog could understand that its suffering served a higher educative purpose, "all that is heroic in him would religiously acquiesce"[!] (James 1896, 54). It is hard to know what to make of the idea that comparing our life-experience to an uncomprehended vivisection gives us grounds for affirming it. Indeed, James reconsidered his answer and when he returned to the topic in a later essay, *What Makes a Life Significant?* (1912), in which he gives much more ground to the pessimists than he did at first. (See also the fine, if brief, reflection on the question in Harries 1991.)

[33] It might be objected here that only those who embrace resignation are truly deserving of the label "pessimist." But this objection is, again, akin to insisting that every optimist is a Dr. Pangloss. There are varieties of pessimism as there are varieties of hopefulness. One would in any case still have to deal with the presence of a tradition that rejects progress while remaining focused on the effects of linear time, whether one called it pessimism or something else.

[34] To this generalization, alas, I must make one exception: Nietzsche abuses the pessimist Eduard von Hartmann precisely because he *does* make this pleasure/pain calculation against life. Hartmann, greatly influenced by Schopenhauer, was well-known in the late nineteenth century for his *Philosophy of the Unconscious* (1869) and other works on pessimism, but is today largely forgotten. Nietzsche's criticisms of Hartmann will be discussed further in chapter 5.

death then into a highly detached simulacrum of it where suffering is min-imized by means of self-isolation.

The tenor of the first response can be seen in Leopardi's "Dialogue of Nature and a Soul" in which the former says simply to the latter: "Live, and be great and unhappy." When the Soul inquires whether these two qualities are bound together, Nature replies that "the two things are more or less the same: for the excellence of souls brings greater urgency to [men's] lives; which in turn brings a greater feeling of their own unhap-piness; which is as much as to say greater unhappiness" (*OM* 66). Nature does not shape things this way out of malice; indeed, she has nothing but benevolence towards the soul. The joke of the dialogue is that the Soul is not enamored of this benevolence and is far from eager to embrace life on these conditions—Nature must try to talk her into it. But it is clearly Leopardi's view that we *should* allow ourselves to be talked into it, though there is no overpowering reason that *must* convince us. Full of pain though human life may be, it has possibilities for achievement that are not available to any other form of life. To retreat from it is to allow oneself to be governed simply by pain and pleasure, like an animal. To choose a life "great and unhappy," moreover, is not to make a calculation that somehow one's quantity of greatness outweighs one's quantity of unhap-piness (these quantities, in any case, could not be known in advance). It is rather to judge that the qualities unique to human existence, achieved in whatever degree, are worth striving for—they do not simply outweigh pain, they outrank it. Unchosen though human life may be initially, in our rejection of suicide or its surrogates we embrace human existence for its unique possibilities—in effect, for its unknown future—and leave behind all "economic" calculations, which ever show us the losers. Unamuno's similar analysis ends with the bare assertion: "I will not resign from life; I must be dismissed" (*TSL* 144).

Unamuno's defiance can also be read as a direct reply to Schopenhauer, who wrote: "Resignation . . . is like the inherited estate; it frees its owner from all care and anxiety for ever" (*WWR* 1:390). Schopenhauer's defense of resignation is doubtless the most famous of the second sort of response to pessimism. The suffering of this life, he contends, has no aim or pur-pose beyond that of teaching us not to want life. Consciousness is no compensation for suffering because all the projects of consciousness are themselves swept away by the continuous passage of time. While suicide solves nothing (it too is another futile attempt to seize happiness by pos-itive action), we can minimize our suffering if we imitate the detachment from existence taught by various Eastern religions, above all Buddhism. The central attribute of Buddhism, for Schopenhauer, is its focus on self-denial, or more specifically, on denial of the will. Just as Leopardi argued that suffering is magnified by striving, so Schopenhauer believes that we minimize suffering by stifling our own will. And as the stories of the Christian saints tell us, this is not something we can achieve once and for all, but something to be continuously labored at: "We therefore find in the lives of saintly persons that peace and bliss we have described, only as the blossom resulting from the constant overcoming of the will . . . for on earth no one can have lasting peace" (*WWR* 1:391). We already have something that approaches this practice, Schopenhauer believes, in the act of contemplating art, which removes us from the stream of life and puts us in touch with the timeless. Art recreates us as "will-less subject . . . i.e., a pure intelligence without aims or intentions" (*EA* 155). The feelings of pleasure that are associated with experiences of beauty are thus nothing positive in themselves, but simply a release from the suffering created by our willfulness.

From another perspective, one can view the divide within pessimism in terms of the question, is the suffering that comes with time-consciousness in any sense *justified*? This is what separates Schopenhauer from Nietzsche. For Schopenhauer, the pains of time-consciousness are a just punishment for our evil natures. Though he disdains religion, the story of the Fall does, to him, contain an eternal truth. Human misery is a fitting reward for our greedy, selfish constitution. That this reward is imposed automatically by an unconscious universe rather than by a knowing, vengeful God is of little concern to him. Indeed, it is better this way. In a passage that likely inspired Kafka's parable *The Penal Colony*, for example, he wrote:

> As a reliable compass for orienting yourself in life nothing is more useful than to accustom yourself to regarding this world as a place of atonement, a sort of penal colony. When you have done this you will order your expectations of life according to the nature of things and no longer regard the calamities, sufferings, torments and miseries of life as something irregular and not to be expected but will find them entirely in order, well knowing that each of us is here being punished for his existence and each in his own particular way. (*EA* 49)

In contrast, Nietzsche, who saw the world no less than did Schopenhauer as a place of continuous suffering, took the opposite tack: "You ought to learn the art of this-worldly comfort first; you ought to learn to laugh, my young friends, if you are hell-bent on remaining pessimists. Then perhaps, as laughers, you may someday dispatch all metaphysical comforts to the devil—metaphysics in front" (*BT* 26).

In Nietzsche's approach, we come to value existence neither because it constitutes progress nor because it constitutes an appropriate punishment for our failings. Indeed, the very idea of a metaphysical "justification" for existence—Nietzsche calls it a "comfort"—is rejected. But just on account of the constant transformation, the continual reappearance of novelty, that is the consequence, along with constant decay and death, of a temporal existence—just on this basis we can find a way to embrace life. Hannah Arendt used the term "natality" (the property of being born, as opposed to "mortality") to mark out this special attribute of the human condition. If human beings, among all the animals, are the only ones capable of appreciating the significance of death, above all their own death, it is equally true that they are the only animals capable of appreciating the significance of birth, above all their own birth. Each human being represents a new beginning, a new set of possibilities. As mortality marks our whole lives and not just the moment of our death, so too does natality continue to inspirit us apart from the moment of birth. While nothing that humans do will endure forever, the very fact of their newness is, in Arendt's term, a "miracle" that can be appreciated by itself, apart from any consequences it may bring. It is just such an appreciation that Nietzsche had in mind, I believe, as a "this-worldly comfort" that could be learned. We may even be moved by it, as Nietzsche suggests, to the point of laughter. But laughing at our existence is not an overcoming of pessimism. It is in fact the embrace of it.

A pessimist might initially seem like someone who bears the burden of expectations too thoroughly. But in reality the opposite is the case. *The pessimist expects nothing*—thus he or she is more truly open to every possibility as it presents itself. A pessimist can recognize and delight in the fact that we live in a world of surprises—surprises that can only strike the optimist as accidents and mishaps, disturbing as they do a preordered image of the world's continuous improvement. This openness to the music of chance lends to the pessimist an equanimity that might strike an outsider as callous. The optimist, on the other hand, must suffer through a life of disappointment, where a chaotic world constantly disturbs the upward path he feels entitled to tread.

These, then, are the two poles of response available to a pessimistic diagnosis: resignation, on the one hand, and what I will call spontaneity, or futurity, on the other. The latter, I should be clear, is *not* a last-minute rejection of pessimism—not a back-door optimism that a dishonest theory leaves open for itself. Rather, it is a form of self-conduct that values the life we are given in spite of the pessimistic diagnosis of its condition. It is also, for that reason, the final proof that pessimism is not by itself to be equated with resignation or depression or cynicism or nihilism. In the face of great suffering, this kind of pessimist—what Nietzsche called a "Dionysian pessimist"—does not retreat, but rather advances willingly into hostile territory, not to die gloriously but instead to "live dangerously" and to die necessarily. Or, as Leopardi put it (with perhaps a bit too much self-importance), "I have the courage . . . to gaze intrepidly on the desert of life . . . and to accept all the consequences of a philosophy that is grievous, but true" (*OM* 219).

This pessimistic spirit is a restless one, unlikely to be enamored of the status quo. Still, there remains the question of whether, or how far, the activity that such a pessimism stimulates can be properly called political. Does pessimism, in teaching limitations, so reduce the possibility for acting in concert with others or engaging in public projects that it effectively forecloses the political space? Here, I think, the answer is that it need not—but that this certainly has been a temptation that all of the pessimists have faced and to which some have given in. It will be the burden of chapter 4, and especially its pages on Camus, to combat the idea that pessimism must lead to political quietism. As I argue there, Camus was keen to point out the ways in which pessimism motivates and energizes political participation.[35]

Just as importantly, pessimism helps us to rethink concepts of central concern to any political theory, most significantly freedom and individuality. Over the course of the book, and especially in the later chapters, I hope to articulate a concept of freedom (and an idea of the sort of individual who can experience that freedom) that, while rooted in the widely shared elements noted above, is unique to pessimism. It is a freedom that is not easily described by the vocabularies that currently dominate either political or philosophical discourses. Pessimistic freedom is not tied to historical outcomes—neither to national projects nor to personal life-plans. Nor can it be tied to institutional arrangements of noninterference or nondomination. Rather, pessimism envisions a democracy of moments for an individual who can neither escape time but is not imprisoned by it either. Freedom for the pessimists is not merely a status but an experience that a time-bound person can aspire to through a certain approach to life. As I will elaborate later, the pessimists have tended to see this approach exemplified in questing figures like Columbus or Don Quixote.

Optimism is to time what metaphysics is to space. It projects perfection elsewhere or, more properly, elsewhen. It teaches one to despise the here and now, which ultimately means to despise oneself. Most philosophy today, on the Left and the Right, considers itself to be postmetaphysical— that is, it abstains from condemning what exists from the standpoint of a transcendental realm of perfection. But if Nietzsche's diagnosis of the ori-

---

[35] Camus is not alone in taking this position. Besides the figures discussed in this book, Arendt, Foucault and Adorno, I believe, also hold it. But the issue itself can be adequately addressed through a discussion of Camus. Though undertaken from a very different perspective, Dana Villa's *Socratic Citizenship* (2001) is likewise concerned with revealing the political dimension to a life-practice often taken to be antipolitical; I am indebted to his example.

gin of metaphysics in *ressentiment* is correct, optimism must be understood as one more refuge for the tendency to revenge and self-hatred that authorized metaphysics. "The future," Camus wrote, "is the only transcendental value for men without God" (*R* 166). Finally it is optimism, rather than pessimism, which is best understood as a negative emotion or disposition (resentment of the present or of time itself). The realm of perfection metaphysical philosophies projected onto a transcendental plane is projected by optimistic philosophies onto an ever-receding future. If we understand the move to postmetaphysical philosophy as a reflection of our growing humanism, we cannot consider this humanism complete until our thinking is postoptimistic as well—beyond the "idolatry of tomorrow," as Cioran called it (*FT* 47). This is the path the pessimistic tradition has quietly explored for the last 250 years.

Three Kinds of Pessimism

The rest of this book will offer the reader a *tour d'horizon* of the pessimistic tradition. As I said above, although there are several propositions around which pessimists tend to converge, they arrive at these conclusions from a variety of perspectives. As a rough typology I divide pessimism into three basic sorts, which I call *cultural*, *metaphysical*, and *existential* pessimism, respectively. Although all these pessimisms ultimately derive from the problematic of linear time, we should not blind ourselves to the different avenues by which this problematic can be articulated. What is at issue here is not so much disagreements between different pessimists (although these, of course, occur) as the different *levels of explanation* they characteristically employ. In the succeeding chapters, I explore each type of pessimism in turn. For each chapter, I have chosen to focus on two or three figures. I do this both to show that the types I propose do not merely generalize from a single case as well as to explore the different responses, especially on the question of resignation, available to a pessimistic diagnosis.

As exemplars of cultural pessimism, I have chosen Rousseau and Leopardi. Their pessimism is cultural in the sense that, for them, the burdens of time appear particularly in the realms of mores and behaviors. Human society, in their conception, has necessarily developed along a negative historical dynamic that can be described and understood but not altered—because the tools we use to describe and understand it are the very engines of social decay itself. These authors do not, as is sometimes thought, simply assess the flaws of human nature nor, on the other hand, do they lament timeless facts about the universe. The misfortune of our species derives from something that occurs within historical time and that can only be understood through historical consciousness. But the "history" with which they concern themselves is, I think, best described as cultural (or, perhaps, social). It has to do neither with particular events nor with individuals nor nations, but rather with the development of human mores and forms of consciousness.

In the chapter on metaphysical pessimism, I focus on Schopenhauer and Freud. Here the problem of time is closer to the surface. Both philosophers identified time as a fundamental structure of human experience and described it as a problem. History, by contrast, understood as the development of the species within time, although not entirely absent, is relatively unimportant. It is the relationship of the individual to the universal-metaphysical that is crucial. The burdens of a temporal existence fall nearly as heavily on the first humans as on the most recent, though, to be sure, our species was not really human until it became amenable to these burdens. Although there may be, to these pessimists, some particularities of our culture that accentuate our susceptibility to suffering, the sources of that suffering are such that all are subject to them. Human beings inhabit a universe that they would be justified in calling malevolent if it could be shown to have an author (which, to them, it does not).

The existential pessimists I discuss—Camus, Cioran, and Unamuno—occupy a position that is, in some ways, intermediate between these earlier two types—or rather, they combine elements from the preceding pessimisms into a distinct position. On the one hand, they reject the kind of metaphysical determinism to be found in the second group. They are concerned with the accumulation of experience within human history, yet their explanations aspire to a kind of universality that is more general than those proposed by the cultural pessimists. They see that our experience of time is something that itself has a history—but a history that we do not escape simply by taking notice of it. Thus to the question of whether the difficulties that pessimism points out are universal or modern, they answer "yes" in both cases. And this is just one of the many ironies or "contradictions" (understood here in a manner quite different from Marxism) with which, they suggest, it is necessary to make our peace.

Although these chapters will give some evidence for the recognition, by the later pessimists, of their kinship with the earlier ones, I will not lay a great deal of stress on this point. While it is important to know that Leopardi, for example, was consciously indebted to Rousseau and that Schopenhauer and Nietzsche in turn were similarly indebted to Leopardi, it is not my aim here to trace out such a history of influence. That would require a very different sort of book. In speaking of pessimism as a "tradition" I mean to indicate a series of authors who wrote on similar topics in a similar vein. Establishing the precise degree of influence they had on one another is a different question (a less important one, I think) than establishing the conceptual content of what we can (retrospectively) see as their common project. When this common project is acknowledged, others can then explore the question of to what degree the pessimistic tradition was a self-conscious one.[36]

It will not have escaped the reader's notice, at this point, that there is also a rough periodization that could be placed atop the typology I have proposed, where the three pessimisms succeed each other chronologically. To some extent, I think such a periodization is valid—there is, after all, a sense in which different forms of reason (or, if you like, styles of argument) have come in and out of fashion in philosophy generally. Thus, although a very gross generalization, it is not inaccurate to say that for pessimists and nonpessimists alike, the dominant style of philosophy in the eighteenth century was cultural, in the nineteenth century metaphysical, and in the twentieth century postmetaphysical. However, not only does this generalization misdescribe many important figures, in the case of the pessimists it is also to some extent an artifact of the figures I have chosen to focus on. If one expanded the list of pessimists, the chronology could be broken down rather quickly—but I believe the typology remains useful. For example, twentieth-century figures like Foucault and Heidegger (all their protestations aside) would probably best be characterized as cultural and metaphysical pessimists, respectively.

In any case, the typology is only proposed as a tool of organization and understanding. Personally, I find the similarities among the pessimists to be more important than the differences. But I should not hide, in all of this, that I do find some versions of pessimism more edifying than others, and that I find Nietzsche's the most edifying of all. For this reason, although I would group Nietzsche with the existentials, I have chosen to let his own name for his pessimism, "Dionysian pessimism" stand—and to discuss it in a separate chapter. Because Nietzsche was, to such a high degree, in dialogue with Schopenhauer, this chapter will also serve to describe some of the ways in which existential pessimism arose out of its predecessors. Following the Nietzsche chapter is one on Cervantes, which suggests that in *Don Quixote* we have an example of the sort of pessimistic world and pessimistic exemplar Nietzsche had in mind.

Finally, there are two further chapters: one on aphoristic writing in the

---

[36] This would be a very complicated and interesting question where one would have to weigh carefully the authors' own declarations against their patterns of admitting to influence and evidence of their education, reading habits, et cetera. Schopenhauer, for example, was happy to acknowledge that his pessimism continued that of earlier authors, although he claimed to be the first to perfect it philosophically. Nietzsche, on the other hand, was wont to disparage his indebtedness to previous figures in proportion to their standing. He thus emphasized his differences with Schopenhauer and maligned Rousseau while praising Leopardi, who was lesser-known and then primarily as a poet.

history of pessimism and another on pessimistic freedom that attempts to synthesize and focus some of what the preceding pages have set out. I will simply note here again that it can be no accident that so many pessimists have chosen to employ an aphoristic form of writing. As a preliminary matter, we can say that this style of composition is well-suited to harmonize with the antisystematic approach that pessimists largely adopt—but there is more than this to be learned from the form of aphorism, which is distinct from the maxim and epigram, on the one hand, and from the fragment and short essay on the other. Aphorisms are a literary form that aims to capture a particular human experience that I will describe at more length below. My effort to revive the pessimistic spirit and to give voice to its particular idea of freedom would have felt incomplete without attention to this subject. While it would have overtaxed my talents as a prosaist to have composed this entire book in aphoristic form—as I once considered doing—I hope that these pages will indicate why I do not view the study of pessimism as a mere historical expedition but as an encounter with a tradition as vital, more vital really, as any written about today.[37]

Camus was doubtless correct in both the idea that it is wrong to link pessimism to discouragement—and that any refutation of this linkage would take too long. I hope not to have exceeded the reader's patience with this extended introduction. But the barriers (historical, philosophical, and psychological) to taking pessimism seriously are so many and so varied in nature that I thought it necessary to proceed as I have. Even so, I feel it is necessary to point out to my readers that, in what has come and what follows, I discuss many periods, thinkers, and texts in a relatively brief book, and will therefore undoubtedly fail to do justice to the subtleties of each and to the secondary literatures that have grown up around them. I can only beg the forbearance of specialists here and repeat that the task I have set myself is primarily inductive and synthetic, rather than deductive or analytic. Having failed to internalize the virtues of brevity exemplified by the aphorists and pessimists I discuss, I can only hope to have faithfully translated a portion of their wisdom.

---

[37] I believe this to be true even in the American context. Although, as I mentioned in the preface, pessimism is often particularly derided in the United States, I think it could easily be shown that there is a long tradition of American pessimism (including such figures as Herman Melville, Mark Twain, Henry Adams, George Santayana, Lewis Mumford, and W.E.B. Du Bois, to name a few) that has as much claim on the cultural history of the nation as any other. I regret that I have not been able to pursue this thread of American intellectual history here and hope to do so at a later time.

PART II

Chapter Two

"A PHILOSOPHY THAT IS GRIEVOUS BUT TRUE"

CULTURAL PESSIMISM IN ROUSSEAU

AND LEOPARDI

IF PESSIMISM can be said to have an identifiable starting point in the philosophical tradition, it must be found in the contradictory figure of Jean-Jacques Rousseau. This is not to say, of course, that Rousseau's pessimism is without precursors and influences. In earlier French authors such as Montaigne and Pascal, one can trace an increasing concern with inwardness and psychological depth; in Machiavelli and other Florentine writers, there is a developing interest in historical time; and in critics such as Vauvenargues, La Rochefoucauld, and Montesquieu, one can find a growing suspicion that the increase of knowledge and civilization since the Renaissance have created a society of excessive pride, hypocrisy, and decadence.[1] But Rousseau welded these themes (and many others) into something genuinely novel. As far as I can determine, the constellation of arguments that I outlined in the previous chapter and labeled "pessimism" come together in his writings for the first time. This is also not to say that such a multifarious and protean figure as Rousseau (a musician, novelist, and botanist as well as a political theorist) can be captured in a single word. His complexities have inspired a series of learned interpretations far more detailed and comprehensive than I can hope to offer here.[2] Pessimism may not ultimately define Rousseau—but it is no mistake to call him, as has been done, "the patriarch of pessimism" (*OLDQ* xxxiii).[3] Rousseau's pessimism, whether or not it was his last word, has been the

---

[1] See, especially, Vyverberg 1958, chaps. 2, 6, 11, 21. Notwithstanding the author's doubtful conclusion that Rousseau is an historical optimist, Vyverberg's book provides much evidence for the roots of Rousseau's thoughts on decadence in French writers of the seventeenth century.

[2] Two of the most important for the themes developed here are Starobinski 1988 and Philonenko 1984. Although it is not a principal theme, Starobinski refers more than once to Rousseau's "pessimism," writing that, for Rousseau, "history is essentially decay. . . . he recoils in horror from the danger, but also from the fecundity, of temporal existence" (302). Philonenko's very title, *Jean-Jacques Rousseau et La Pensée du Malheur*, gives a sense of his orientation. Most English-language commentary has taken little notice of Rousseau's pessimism. Cladis 1995 is an exception.

[3] Walter Starkie offers this characterization in his extended introduction to Unamuno's text on *Don Quixote*.

germ that gave flower to many others. This is what will be examined below. At the very least, I will claim, pessimism defines Rousseau's early phase as a political theorist and marks the *First* and *Second Discourses* as well as the *Letter to M. D'Alembert On the Theatre* and the *Essay on the Origin of Languages*. But I find traces of it continuing into such later works as *On the Social Contract* and the *Reveries of the Solitary Walker*.

While Rousseau's political philosophy has inspired many competing interpretations, Giacomo Leopardi's, at least in the last hundred years, has hardly given rise to any. Although his poetry and notebooks, above all his *Zibaldone*, are read by every Italian schoolchild, his main works of political theory, the *Moral Essays* (*Operette Morali*) of 1827 and the posthumous *Pensieri* have engendered almost no commentary in the last century in any language other than Italian.[4] Among the factors contributing to this, no doubt, is Leopardi's pessimism, which has made it difficult for interpreters to connect him to existing debates. In the nineteenth century, however, pessimism did not disqualify philosophers from obtaining a hearing, as it does today, and Leopardi was widely read and influential. Both Schopenhauer and Nietzsche, as their citations show, were familiar with his writing and held it to be an important forerunner of their philosophies. As this chapter will demonstrate, moreover, Leopardi's pessimism has many similarities to Rousseau's and forms a powerful alternative to it. Both Leopardi and Rousseau gave voice to what I am calling *cultural pessimism*. That is, both centered their concerns about the prospects for human happiness on developments that had taken place over time in society as a whole. While, in each case, they believed that the Enlightenment had accelerated these developments, their arguments cast a much larger historical net and were meant, in some sense, to cover the development of the species from the moment of our emergence into sentience. But Leopardi, although admiring Rousseau, did not merely copy his approach. Where Rousseau's response to the pessimistic diagnosis often involved a fantasy of time's reversal, or a desire to escape the effects of time completely, Leopardi suggested a more active embrace of our conditions of existence. Although in *The Social Contract* Rousseau appeared to celebrate the participatory citizen in an ideal republic, in other texts he often suggested that, in the imperfect world in which we find ourselves, withdrawal from politics is the best alternative.[5] Leopardi, on the other hand, favored engagement in circumstances perfect and imperfect, condi-

---

[4] While there is a large scholarly literature on Leopardi's poetry, some of the few works on his philosophy are: Ferrucci 1989 and Origo 1999, chap. 10.

[5] As I argue below, I believe *On the Social Contract* also represents a withdrawal from the temporal, but that is a more complicated matter.

tions handsome and unhandsome, whether or not one expected one's efforts to succeed.

The Effects of Time

In the fifth of the *Reveries of the Solitary Walker*, composed near the end of his days, Rousseau recalls a brief period, more than a decade earlier, which he now terms "the happiest time of my life." Isolated on the island of St. Pierre on a lake in rural Switzerland, he had spent his mornings in botanical study and his afternoons adrift on the lake that surrounded the island:

> I rowed to the middle of the lake when the water was calm; and there, stretching myself out full-length in the boat, my eyes turned to heaven, I let myself slowly drift back and forth with the water, sometimes for several hours, plunged in a thousand confused, but delightful, reveries which, even without having any well-determined or constant object, were in my opinion a hundred times preferable to the sweetest things I had found in what are called the pleasures of life. (*RSW* 44)

What was it that made these conditions the sine qua non of happiness? A few pages later, Rousseau explains that "everything is in continual flux on earth. Nothing on it retains a constant and static form, and our affections, which are attached to external things, necessarily pass away and change as they do." Our emotions are always "ahead of or behind us, they recall the past which is no longer or foretell the future which often is in no way to be" (*RSW* 46). In other words, the fundamental source of unhappiness for mortals is their insertion into time, combined with the constant churning of people, places, and events that takes place in a time-bound universe. For a sentient being to be happy means for some object to give him or her pleasure, but no object—not even oneself—can be counted on to continue its existence, not even for another moment, much less indefinitely. Likewise, the attempt to attach ourselves to objects future or past is a futile fantasy. The simple Heraclitan knowledge that "everything flows" by itself destroys all security. These thoughts are important enough to Rousseau that he essentially repeats them at the beginning of the ninth section of the book, now drawing the conclusion that "all our plans for felicity in this life are idle fancies" (*RSW* 78). But stretched out in the boat, bobbing gently on the water, Jean-Jacques could have an experience that escaped this condition—or appeared to—where "the present lasts forever . . . without any trace of time's passage" (*RSW* 46). While he knows, of course, that he has not really left the natural world, he can at least imagine what such an emancipation would be like.

As long as such moments last, he says, we are perfectly self-sufficient, "like God." Floating outside of time, we need no "constant object" to sustain our happiness but are, for once, content with ourselves.[6]

The sentiment Rousseau experiences here is not simply that of divinity; it is also, according to the theory that he set out in the *Discourses*, the timelessness of the preconscious human animals that we once were. The animals, while they share the same universe with us, have no experience of time. They age and die, but they have no knowledge of this and, thus do not really change as humans do. As I outlined in the previous chapter, animal existence for Rousseau, though infinitely simpler than our own, is also (indeed for that very reason) infinitely happier. It is ignorance of time that keeps it so. While human beings, capable of comparing their current selves to those of a remembered past or an imagined future, can thus reflect upon themselves and endeavor to improve themselves (the faculty of perfectibility that Rousseau discusses in the *Second Discourse*), an animal rests perfectly content in the identity to which it was born. Human consciousness of time, on the other hand, creates a perpetual dissatisfaction with the self, an endless process of comparison to others and restless striving: "The Savage lives in himself; sociable man, always outside himself" (*SD* 199). While this striving has led to many material improvements in the human condition of which we are justly proud, we are no happier for any of them. Indeed, we are less so. Our cultural development resembles the joke of a malignant deity: the more we strive for happiness, the further it retreats from us. From his earliest to his latest texts, then, Rousseau identifies a problematic of temporality and uses it to express his deepest suspicions about any form of civilized life.

Leopardi's *Moral Essays* follow in this vein and are even more explicit about viewing life as a divine joke. The short works that comprise the book are "essays" in only the loosest sense. Their forms are highly varied: parables, fables, dialogues of fictitious characters, and satires of traditional genres, such as the memorabilia. They are all informed by a darkly comic vision of the world and the efforts of its inhabitants. What

---

[6] These points are well discussed in Poulet 1956, 158–63. The distinction between a divine indifference to time and a human condition in which time appears to be the source of evil leads Starobinski to argue that Rousseau's discussion amounts to a "philosophical *Genesis*" in which the Fall of man is simply retold "in another language" (1964, LII–LIII). I think this view radically oversimplifies, although this is a complicated issue that deserves more attention than I can give it here. It is doubtless true that Rousseau was influenced to a degree by the French Augustinian Jansenists who emphasized the fall into time as a central element of human damnation. However, as I argued in chapter 1, it is not clear whether this view really originates with Augustine or whether it is a modern gloss on Augustine's more ambiguous reflections on temporality. If the latter, then what Starobinski claims as an element of Rousseau's Christianity should be understood instead as an element of his modernism, a modernism he shared with such Christian thinkers as Pascal.

Rousseau finds painful and pathetic, Leopardi often finds funny. But for all that, Rousseau and Leopardi do not view the world so differently, at least in its fundamental form. What I hope to demonstrate in this chapter, among other things, is the manner in which Leopardi's philosophy traces that of Rousseau while nonetheless offering an alternative to the Rousseauian prescription of withdrawal. Although the *Moral Essays* offer many characters who speak in many voices, Leopardi's pessimism can be heard clearly enough through all of them. It offers a philosophy that matches Rousseau in the depth of its despair over the human condition, but prefigures Nietzsche in the active nature of its response.

The parallel between the two begins with Leopardi's articulation of the burdens of temporality. This theme permeates almost all of the *Moral Essays* (as well as Leopardi's poetry) but is particularly vivid in the "Dialogue Between Torquato Tasso and his Guardian Spirit," which imagines the poet Tasso imprisoned and conversing with his ghost about the nature of happiness.[7] The Spirit maintains that pleasure is "a speculative thing, not a real one" (*OM* 94). That is, pleasure is something human beings think about and imagine, but not something they actually experience. We are unable to experience pleasure because our sensory impressions are always subordinated to our hopes and dreams about the future so that "at the very instant of pleasure, . . . you are forever looking forward to a greater and truer enjoyment . . . and always as it were running forward to the future moments of that same pleasure" (*OM* 94). When Tasso protests against this conclusion, the Spirit becomes even more categorical until the mortal submits to its logic:

> SPIRIT: But tell me if at any moment in your life you remember having said in full consciousness and sincerity: I am joyful. Every single day you have said and do say sincerely: I will be joyful; and sometimes, though less sincerely, I have been joyful. So that pleasure is either past or future, but never present.
>
> TASSO: Which is to say it is always nothing. (*OM* 94–95)

Like Rousseau, Leopardi emphasizes how our feeling of the passage of time makes it difficult for us to experience the present directly, as the animals do. The objects of our pleasure consistently elude our grasp as they flow past us in time. And yet, as in Rousseau, this sense of time cannot be easily abandoned, above all because the animals' simplicity is also their ignorance. Knowledge cannot be unlearned —that is why it is at once enduring and poisonous. Animals and human alike are fated to time—our misfortune is to be aware of this fact. And, as in Rousseau, it is tempo-

---

[7] Though the dialogue is entirely fictitious, Tasso, the great Italian poet of the sixteenth century, was imprisoned for madness at one point in his life.

rality's greatest effect to render all things impermanent: "the life of this universe is a perpetual cycle of production and destruction" (*OM* 104). Flux in time is the background condition of existence against which the human desire for happiness must constantly run aground. Nature's "cruelty" is a fundamental ontological circumstance, not a contingent one that could be minimized or altered. We can regret or decry this condition, as Leopardi does on many occasions, but we cannot deny it or adjust our lives to escape its effects.[8]

What is surprising is that we expect things to be otherwise. Yet, Leopardi argues, we often do. "Men are wretched by necessity," he writes, "and determined to believe themselves wretched by accident" (*P* 26). The pessimistic claims about the effects of time would not be so striking if they did not challenge an unspoken presumption that human happiness is

---

[8] There may appear to be a tension here between the "knowledge," as I have called it, of the passage of time and the perpetual destruction that Leopardi and Rousseau claim to be the result of that passage. The supposed contradiction ("If everything changes, how can we know that 'everything changes' is a permanent condition of existence?") is more apparent than real and relies as much on our terminology as it does on the things themselves. A statement such as Rousseau's "everything is in continual flux on earth" is intended as a description of an ontological condition of life grasped through experience; it is not claimed as a certain product of deduction. Nor does Rousseau claim a unique experience—no one would deny the experience of the passage of time; pessimism simply claims that we have not all thought through the implications of that common experience.

As we shall see in chapter 3, Schopenhauer could not stress enough that his epistemology derived from that of Kant, who recognized the concepts of space and time as the organizing ideas of intelligence (a prioris) and not truths that could themselves be established by reasoning. So we are not left in the position of making paradoxical or self-contradictory assertions (e.g., "it is always true that nothing endures"). Such a statement would never be uttered by a pessimist but only by a philosopher of a certain type attempting to render pessimism into a system of propositions. Like Pyrrhonian Skeptics, pessimists do not claim to have established the certainty of their guiding principles—rather, they claim that their principles are those most appropriate to the condition of uncertainty that is ours (a judgment that can itself remain open to debate). It is the optimists, they claim, who rely on a hidden assumption of the certain reality or possibility of progress in the face of all historical evidence to the contrary. Pessimists, of course, make statements that may be well- or poorly supported, like any other philosophers. But pessimism by and large also recognizes what many other philosophies do not, namely that "knowledge is in the end based on acknowledgment." "At some point one has to pass from explanation to mere description" (Wittgenstein 1969, 49, 26).

Might, then, the pessimists be mistaken about flux? Perhaps; and perhaps time will flow backward tomorrow instead of forward, for all that we know. But since certainty is unavailable to us on these fundamental questions, the reasoning of the pessimists on this point is no more poorly secured than that of their opponents and, indeed, insofar as their provisional conclusions are in conformity with our experience, it is considerably stronger. I am at pains to make this point at length because pessimism is so often and so readily held to be self-contradicting. But while one might well take issue with the pessimistic interpretation of the effects of temporal existence, the charge of self-contradiction is baseless. In any case, genuine traditions of human thought and experience should not be dismissed with philosophical quips. My thanks to Annie Stilz for helpful input on this subject.

something normally within our reach, or even owed to us.[9] In insisting on the continuous instability of the time-bound cosmos, Leopardi and Rousseau reject the idea, which they find embedded in Enlightenment optimism, that the universe has a fundamentally rational structure. If this were so, then reason would provide a means of coming to terms with the universe and perhaps of mastering its more deleterious effects. But if the universe has no permanent structure to be the object of our cognition, then reason, no matter how significant as a human achievement, will give us no leverage over it. Or rather, it will only give us leverage in those circumstances where we can reason from firm foundations. In the short run, this might enable great feats of engineering, for example. But in the long run, nothing endures forever. It is not so much that the Enlightenment overestimates the strength of reason as that it underestimates, the pessimists claim, the power of reason's opponent. Just as the individual suffers from the instability of his or her preferred objects, so the species suffers from the refusal of the universe to be a stable object for its reason and (what is the same thing) a source of happiness.

Historical Irony

The direct effects of time on the human soul are, as we shall see, a major theme in the writings of Schopenhauer and Nietzsche. In Rousseau and Leopardi, on the other hand, they are more of a jumping-off point. They lead to a set of reflections that take place in another mode, that of cultural history. Human suffering may emerge primordially from our existential status *in* time, but it also develops *through* time, that is, over the course of human history. Although the first sentient humans may have been less happy than the human animals that preceded them, we moderns are now in a considerably worse position.

Both Leopardi and Rousseau link this development to that which they took the Enlightenment to be celebrating, the progress of human reason.[10] They agreed with the *philosophes* that reason had not emerged fully

[9] Most of the themes of Leopardi's prose are repeated in his poetry (which I do not have the space here to explore in great detail), for example, "That other is not noble / In my belief, but stupid, / Who born to perish and brought up in pain, / Says, I was made for pleasure" (*P* 84).

[10] I phrase things this way because I want to acknowledge the recent scholarship that warns us against the assumption of a univocal "Enlightenment," in which an international clan of philosophers advanced a single purpose across the globe. This is no doubt an oversimplification. However, it seems unlikely that, living within the very period in question, Rousseau and Leopardi were entirely mistaken about what they reacted against: a campaign to replace customs, religions, and traditional authorities with reason and science as the ultimate arbiters in political matters and as the core attributes of the human mind. See Israel 2001 passim.

grown from the forehead of Zeus but had developed in historical time. Only recently had reason at last acquired the dominant position in human society that it had aspired to from the beginning. Leopardi describes this process in terms of the succession of disillusionments that has taken place, each one leaving human beings wiser but worse-off. The first of the *Moral Essays*, the one that sets the stage for all the others, is his short "History of the Human Race." In his telling, we are first created as children and are able to delight in the world around us. But as we grow, the cumulative effects of reason in time take a toll, removing our hopes and eventually bringing us to the point of suicide:

> Seeing that the hopes, which they had until then been putting off from day-to-day, had not yet been realized, it seemed to them that they deserved little trust: while to be content with what they enjoyed in the present . . . did not seem possible to them, especially since the appearance of natural things and every part of their daily lives, either through familiarity or because that first vivacity had waned in their hearts, did not appear to them by any means as delightful and pleasant as in the beginning. . . . Their ill-content increased so much, that they were not yet past their youth before a downright disgust with their very being had universally possessed them. And little by little throughout their manhood, and especially when approaching their declining years, satiety having changed to hatred, some were driven to such desperation that, unable to bear the light and breath of life which at first they had so deeply cherished, in one way or another they of their own accord deprived themselves of it. (*OM* 34)

As Leopardi tells the story, a benevolent Jove deploys many stratagems to reenergize humanity. He makes the Earth larger and more complex, although even he is powerless (against time it seems) to fulfill his charges' main request, that they be returned to the condition of childhood. Nonetheless, the changes he makes succeed in distracting humanity for a period "longer than the first." The effects, unfortunately, are only temporary: "But when with the passing of time all novelty was altogether lacking, while tedium and the contempt for life were reborn and reconfirmed . . . there arose the custom mentioned by historians . . . : that when someone was born, the family and friends gathered round to lament him; and when he died, the day was marked with celebrations and speeches of congratulation addressed to the dead man" (*OM* 36). No quantity of novelty can defeat the unbroken extension of time, and all hopes also founder upon it. All problems give way to boredom, and boredom to necrophilia.

At this point, Jove becomes angered. He decides to offer further "variety" to humanity by introducing disease and active misfortune, previously unknown to us. He also "divide[s] the human race into peoples, nations and tongues, setting strife and discord among them" (*OM* 38). The effect is a stimulating one. Humanity is driven to all manner of activity, both intellectual and physical, to deal with the fresh obstacles that Jove has provided. After an even longer period, of course, the same weariness and boredom with life reappears. But now humanity has a fresh demand. The development of their reason has had an effect of its own and the human race now asks of Jove that he release Truth from the heavens and send it down to dwell among them.

As I recounted in chapter 1, all the other gods object to this since it will raise the status of humans too close to their own. But Jove perceives that humanity will receive Truth as a punishment: "Whereas she was wont to show the immortals their beatitude, to men she would entirely reveal and continually hold before their eyes their own wretchedness" (*OM* 41). Just before he releases Truth, Jove describes the situation he will create thus: "Nothing will seem truer to them than the falsity of all mortal things; and nothing solid, but the emptiness of all but their own griefs. For these reasons they will be deprived even of hope; with which, from the very beginning until the present day, more than any other pleasure or comfort, they have sustained their lives. . . . But in this loss and despair they will not be able to prevent that craving for immense happiness, innate in their spirits, from stinging and cruciating them" (*OM* 41–42).

Leopardi's parable is a masterpiece of historical irony. Initially, the passage of time is itself the source of disillusion. Beginning as children, the disappointment of our childish hopes forces us to use our own reason to provide for our needs. But this sets off a dialectic of enlightenment where each accomplishment only postpones and intensifies our initial desires. Our dissatisfaction multiplies as at each higher plateau of reason we see further and further into an ultimate emptiness. At first, particular hopes are crushed, then ideals, then finally the ideal of hope. As modern human beings, we both know that we are unhappy and (at last we are able to see) that there is no earthly reason to believe this will change. While Leopardi mitigates this situation somewhat in later essays (as he mitigates it in this one by granting that the phantom called Love still occasionally visits Earth), and even provides us with reasons to avoid resignation, this narrative is the basic historical framework within which his philosophy takes place.

What we initially take to be progress is revealed instead to be the development of suffering. Our species constantly seeks after that which injures it the most. Like Oedipus, we pursue the truth only to find that it destroys us. And all this is the product of our historical sense, our sense of time. As children we lived in a simple world and were able to enjoy its simplicity. As adults, we inhabit a complex world where happiness is fugitive and made ever more so by our attempts to attain it. The difference between the two states is marked by nothing more (and nothing less) than our realization that time passes without effect. The world neither repeats itself nor improves, but only stretches onward, offering disappointment and boredom. Leopardi is unclear on whether things can get any worse for human beings or whether, with the destruction of all illusions other than Truth and "not being able either to escape or to rebel against her tyranny" (*OM* 43), we have reached some sort of nadir. But whether the story ends in an endless present or continues, it is our temporal consciousness that has shaped its irony.

.   .   .   .   .

For Rousseau, the details of the story are in important respects different, but the ironic outline is also there. While Leopardi depicts our original condition as that of mythical children, Rousseau counts the entire species as children so long as they are immune from the effects of time: "[In the state of nature] there was neither education nor progress, generations multiplied uselessly; and as each one of them always started at the same point, centuries went by in all the crudeness of the first ages; the species had already grown old, and man remained ever a child" (*SD* 166). As I outlined in the previous chapter, this situation is interrupted by the development of a capacity for "reflection." In the vocabulary of the *Reveries*, we can think of this as the ability of the human mind to have itself as its own object, to see its own reflection and to know that reflection as a representation of itself. Modern psychology would speak of the emergence of the "I," the self-conscious ego.

In the history that Rousseau details in the two *Discourses* and other writings of that period, the appearance of this ability is signaled by two changes. The first is the emergence of language. The second, more or less simultaneous change is the new element of human nature, the faculty of perfectibility. Both of these can be understood as linked to the capacity for reflection, the former as its means and the latter as its principal result. In the *Second Discourse*, Rousseau identifies two principal mental faculties, those of pity and perfectibility—the first is something we share with the animals, the latter distinguishes us from them.[11] Perfectibility is the

[11] Although Rousseau refers to pity as a "principle" and a "natural virtue" (*SD* 160), it is, I believe, a mistake to think of it as a distinct or separable attribute of the human and animal mind, which might or might not exist. If so, its appearance in Rousseau's theory is largely unexplained. It makes more sense to think of pity as our natural openness to the experience of others, a simple epistemological capacity, so to speak—which is then obscured and confined (though not eliminated) in humans by the development of *amour-propre* (vanity), which causes us to reflect upon ourselves to the exclusion of others. In other words, pity appears as a distinct faculty only from our contemporary perspective, where it competes with vanity for control of our attention. Pity, then, is not a tendency to pay *particular* at-

"faculty which, with the aid of circumstance, successively develops all the others . . . it is the faculty which, by dint of time, draws him out of that original condition in which he would spend calm and innocent days . . . which, over the centuries, causes his enlightenment and his errors, his vices and his virtues to arise" (SD 149). In the *Essay on the Origin of Languages*, meanwhile, he argues that the animals have all the physical attributes necessary for the production of language and, indeed, that they may indeed have "natural language" akin to human gestural communication. But, "Conventional language appears only with man. That is why man makes progress in good as well as in evil, and why the animals do not" (OL 65). What, then, is the relation between these two seemingly co-primordial capacities?

In the *Essay*, Rousseau writes both that "reflection is born of ideas compared, and it is their variety that leads to their comparison" and that "the first motives that moved men to speak were passions" (OL 92, 68). As with Leopardi, we are created to a happy condition that we nonetheless reject under the stimulation, so to speak, of our desire for something different.[12] While Rousseau does not speak of the pressures of boredom, the enticements of love play a parallel role such that the first languages are "daughters of pleasure and not of need" (OL 108). We become dissatisfied with ourselves only in the presence of others.[13] Again, as with Leopardi, the first intellectual results of this process are not clear concepts but fantastical tropes and poetry. Our first form of discourse was what, from a later perspective, we would refer to as mythology. But even this was enough to make ourselves into objects of our own cognition and thus to initiate the faculty of perfectibility. Language is the principal means by which we represent ourselves to ourselves; it makes audible and public what was internal and invisible.

---

tention to the suffering of others; it is simply a capacity to notice others in the first place—something that now requires an effort, but initially did not. This reading, I believe, comports better with Rousseau's contention that pity "precedes the exercise of all reflection" (160) as well as his general description of animals as "ingenious machine(s)" governed "by instinct" (148). See Poulet 1956, 158.

12 As others have pointed out, there is a chicken-egg problem here that Rousseau does not (quite) solve, since he appears to maintain both that we need reflection for language and the reverse. But since both of these take place, at first, in tiny baby-steps, we are meant, I believe, to imagine a largely self-bootstrapping process where accidents and coincidences represent the initial, almost infinitesimal, beginnings of a cycle that thereafter feeds on itself and where "the lapse of time makes up for the slight likelihood of events" (SD 169), as a pearl has its origin in a random grain of sand. See Starobinski 1988, 307ff.

13 But others become fully "present" for us only when we can begin to conceive of ourselves as members of a common species, an intellectual development that itself requires some prior reflection. We need to have an image of ourselves in order to compare it with that of others and note the similarities.

"By dint of time" (*à force de temps*), this faculty develops all the others. This phrase may appear incidental in the sentence quoted above, but it is not. In the *Essay*, Rousseau repeatedly points to the changes brought about by "the force of time" (*OL* 73, cf. 89). As I emphasized in the preceding chapter, for Rousseau, self-consciousness and time-consciousness are closely linked, if not identical. The faculty of perfectibility is, first and foremost, a capacity for a certain kind of imagination—an imagination of oneself as different from what one currently is, hence a capacity to conceive of a future (or past) different from the present. Humans become "perfectible," in their own eyes, when they realize that they exist in time and, thus, are capable of being tomorrow what they are not today. Language makes this possible by giving us an arena in which to conceptualize ourselves apart from our direct sensations of existence. But language itself, like everything else in this world, is subject to the pressures of time. And so Rousseau, in the *Essay*, tracks its development and devolution.

What for Leopardi is the malign gift of Jove,[14] the appearance of reason, Rousseau traces in the history of language itself: "The study of philosophy and the progress of reasoning, having perfected grammar, deprived language of its vital and passionate tone that had originally made it so singable" (*OL* 138). The first language, poetic rather than prosaic, more dependent on vowels, tone, accent, and rhythm than on consonants and "articulation" to convey meaning, would be more like music than what we now call talking: "One would sing it rather than speak" (*OL* 71). But the natural beauty of the original language is dependent on the relatively undeveloped state of our reason, which language itself attacks. As our reason develops, our language changes: "It becomes more precise and less passionate; it substitutes ideas for sentiments" (*OL* 73). Simultaneously, its musical nature is diminished: "Voices grow more monotone, consonants increase in number . . . accents erase themselves" (*OL* 73). As our ideas become more regularized, so too does our language. The effect is ultimately to make our speaking, and our thoughts, less individual, since feelings, whatever words we use for them, have a different valence from person to person, which was formerly expressed by emphasis, pronunciation, and accent. Ideas, on the other hand, are held in common and expressed precisely by uninflected words. This change is symbolized by the appearance of written language, where accent and other individual speech patterns are rendered invisible and conceptual clarity is emphasized: "Writing, which might be expected to fix language, is precisely what alters it . . . it substitutes exactitude for expressiveness. One renders one's sentiments in speaking, and one's ideas in writing. In writing, one is forced to use every word in conformity with common meaning" (*OL* 79).

---

[14] But not really, of course. Leopardi blames no one but humanity itself for the development of reason.

In a spiraling process, language and reasoning are each progressively adapted to the other. Language becomes increasingly monotonous and objective; reason, with this more precise tool, is able to achieve greater degrees of distinction (in every sense). And this cycle is nothing other than the process by which man "perfects" himself across the generations. The more we can bring ourselves into focus for ourselves, so to speak, the more we can identify and alter those elements of ourselves that do not meet with our approval. The animal, with no image of itself apart from its bare feeling of existence, lacks this capacity and so its species-character is permanently fixed.

What we might call the increasing objectification of man in language (in the sense of an increasing preoccupation with ourselves as objects) is paralleled, in Rousseau, by our species' increasing preoccupation with physical objects—for example property, our own bodies, and those of others. This is the narrative that dominates the *Second Discourse*. He details the stages by which human beings, originally equal and free of property, arrive at their current condition of alienation, inequality, and unfreedom. This story is too well-known to go over in detail, but it is worth reviewing some of the elements, not always emphasized, that link it with other pessimistic narratives. While Rousseau begins part II of the *Second Discourse* by identifying the establishment of civil society with the appearance of property in land, he immediately reverses ground and claims that this is in fact the "last stage of the State of Nature" and that many other changes must have previously transpired in order to make this one possible (*SD* 170). The attachment to objects that he still speaks of in the *Reveries* develops over the historical time described here, in which he claims to "cover multitudes of centuries in a flash, forced by time running out" (*SD* 173). The first stirrings of language and perfectibility move humanity from an animal condition to a savage, but recognizably social, situation, with primitive tools, dwellings, families and, above all, desires that go beyond natural needs. In this still-peaceful condition, these desires, for objects animate and inanimate, could largely be satisfied. But, in an argument that parallels Leopardi's on boredom and anticipates Schopenhauer's on the prevalence of unhappiness, Rousseau asserts that this "was the first yoke which, without thinking of it, they imposed on themselves . . . since these conveniences, by becoming habitual, had almost entirely ceased to be enjoyable, and at the same time degenerated into true needs, it became much more cruel to be deprived of them than to possess them was sweet, and men were unhappy to lose them without being happy to possess them" (*SD* 174). What is progress and benefit from a material standpoint is burden and loss from a psychic one. The growth of our possessions only multiplies the growth of our needs so that, ever richer, we still lose ground.

Even the name of the faculty that brings all of this about—perfectibility—turns out to be ironic. For what is "in appearance . . . the perfection of the individual" is "in effect . . . the decrepitude of the species" (*SD* 177). "Appearance" is the key term here. Since human souls cannot communicate with one another directly, our sociability is the result of the invention of language. (Pity may be a kind of communication between bodies, but the exercise of animal pity never generates a society.) The evolution of language, however, has its own dynamic that deemphasizes genuine individuality in favor of a more exact, common means of communication. The increasing authority of a single *idea* of man has the effect of suppressing the original diversity of human beings. To Rousseau, this amounts to "exchanging reality for appearance" (*LD* 64). The faculty of language, under the pressure of time, prefers itself to the reality it also represents. So the "perfection" that we pursue is in fact an alienation from our personal identity and a ceaseless, hopeless attempt to assimilate ourselves to the image of humanity that our language stores, projects, and reinforces. The social result is that we can no longer value ourselves without seeing that value reflected somehow in language. We replace our own self-estimations with common ones so that "public esteem acquired a value . . . and this was the first step at once toward inequality and vice" (*SD* 175). Recorded history is then little more than the playing out of this process wherein human beings, with increasing franticness, attempt to buttress their self-image with various objects (physical property, personal adornment, and other people) that continually lose their value as they are acquired.

Finally, one reaches a modern condition where we have literally lost ourselves. Where the Savage lived "in himself," the contemporary human lives entirely "always outside himself" (*SD* 199) and the disinterested observer, were one to exist, can only see "artificial men and factitious passions" (*SD* 198). We have become a society of golems—monsters who seek goals assigned to them by a master—and yet the masters have disappeared and we have forgotten our own role in this transformation. Rousseau sometimes calls this the "last" or "final" stage of human history. But, in his occasional fantasies of time's reversals, he also hints that there may be worse to come:

> There is, I sense, an age at which the individual human being would want to stop; you will seek the age at which you would wish your Species had stopped. Discontent with your present state for reasons that herald even greater discontents for your unhappy Posterity, you might perhaps wish to be able to go back; And this sentiment must serve as the Praise of your first ancestors, the criticism of your contemporaries, and the dread of those who will have the misfortune to live after you. (*SD* 140).

Leopardi and Rousseau both narrate an ironic history of human existence. Our species, once simple and happy, has become learned, complex, and profoundly unhappy. The main culprit in this alteration is our departure from animal obliviousness of time and our insertion into the world of history. Our capacity for reason, which seemed to promise mastery over this new condition, instead compounded its effects. The pessimism of both philosophers is cultural in its preoccupation with the development of human social mores and what we would today call cultural institutions, such as the theater and fashion. Political institutions per se are almost incidental to their accounts and, insofar as they are discussed at all, are described as secondary effects to a broader pattern of development that takes place at the level of language, psyche, and society. Yet both are concerned not simply with a decline in happiness, but also with the loss of freedom over time.

The Illusion of Freedom

With this background, it is unsurprising that Rousseau and Leopardi view contemporary society and politics, the outcome of this history, largely with sadness and despite. An ironic history has produced a society that is itself rife with further ironies: apparently diverse, our condition is instead monotonous; apparently pleasurable, our lives are instead full of self-inflicted pain; apparently free, we are instead shackled. Each of these ironies is worth some exploration, but it is the last that is the greatest concern. While happiness may not be within humanity's grasp, it is a regular refrain of pessimism that a certain kind of freedom could be, if only we were willing to set the futile search for happiness aside. By mistakenly identifying freedom and happiness with one another, and taking reason as the faculty that leads to both, we mislead ourselves into believing them compatible and misdirect our efforts in bringing them about.

The unseen monotony of modern life is a theme Leopardi returns to frequently in the *Moral Essays*. In the "Memorabilia" of the fictitious philosopher Filippo Ottonieri, for example, he laments not simply our loss of individuality, but the loss of our very ability to perceive individuality. Modern senses have been so dulled, it appears, that what we perceive to be extraordinary would hardly have been noticed in earlier times; and what earlier humans perceived as unusual is now beyond our capacity to register.

> He used to say, that the greatest degree of singularity that one can find today in the dress, or the habits, or the actions of any civilized person; compared with that of the men reckoned to be singular by the Ancients, is not only of another kind, but so much less different than that [earlier kind] was from the normal conduct of contemporaries, that however great it may seem to those of today, to the Ancients it would have appeared very little, or nothing at

all. . . . He added that anyone who lived as differently from us as did those
philosophers from the Greeks of their time, would not be taken for singular
man, but in public opinion would be banished, so to speak, from the human
species. (*OM* 139)

Ottonieri goes on to mention Rousseau directly and complains that even
he, an iconoclast by modern standards, would not stand out much in earlier periods.

Rousseau himself dealt with these issues most directly in his *Letter to
M. D'Alembert On the Theatre* of 1758. This text offers more detail than
the *Second Discourse* on the depravity of modern life, exemplified here by
that of Parisian society. Rousseau focuses on the theater, which D'Alembert, at the behest of Voltaire, had suggested introducing to Geneva.[15] To
Rousseau, this would be a calamity because Geneva, modern though it
may have been in some respects, was protected from the worst excesses
of modernity by its simple and egalitarian mores and by the absence of a
theater. Stagecraft, to Rousseau, was little more than an art of illusion and
insincerity. Artistic triumph though it might be, it symbolized the con-
quest of reality by appearances in contemporary social life. "What," he
asks, "is the talent of the actor?"

> It is the art of counterfeiting himself, of putting on another character than
> his own, of appearing different than he is . . . I do not precisely accuse him
> of being a deceiver but of cultivating by profession the talent of deceiving
> men and of becoming adept in habits which can be innocent only in the the-
> atre and can serve everywhere else only for doing harm. . . . In all things the
> temptation to do evil increases with its facility; and actors must be more vir-
> tuous than other men if they are not more corrupt. (*LD* 79–80)

The perfect actor is the person who can exist completely "outside himself," who can *impersonate* some other human being. Modern society
would not produce so many good actors if it did not already have so many
self-alienated people. The institution of the theater incubates this talent
for self-annihilation (*LD* 81) and spreads it to the audience. Though the
theater itself may be innocent of bad intentions, the increasing theatrical-
ity of society that it encourages is an abomination.

Moreover, the variety of emotions that the theater stimulates are themselves only phantoms of the real thing: "The more I think about it, the
more I find that everything that is played in the theatre is not brought
nearer to us but made more distant" (*LD* 25–26). However deeply we
may feel during a theatrical performance, the very artificiality of the situation means that we are otherwise less able to connect these emotions to

---

[15] See Bloom's introduction on the circumstances surrounding the *Letter* (*LD* xv–xvi).

events that occur in real life. The colorful complexity of the theater hides the underlying emotional barrenness of modern life where authentic human relationships are replaced with symbolic affections for well-drawn fictions.

What is symbolized for Rousseau in the modern preoccupation with the theater is exemplified for Leopardi by our attention to fashion. Both, after all, can be called arts that consist in falsifying appearances. We can see these concerns by returning briefly to the "Dialogue of Fashion and Death." In this *operetta*, humanity's increasing preoccupation with fashion is both evidence and explication of what is wrong with modern life. At the beginning of the piece, Death is depicted as constantly in motion such that Fashion, her sister, has to increase her speed to catch up. But catch up she does. The escalating speed with which trends replace one another gives modern life the appearance of diversity and change. But to Leopardi this appearance is illusory in two ways. First, as Fashion commands greater and greater power, it tends, just as language does for Rousseau, to force individuals into common, popular modes of expression. Second, the frequent changes of costume hide a hollowing out of human experience such that we do not even perceive Fashion's kinship with Death, in spite of the tortures it puts us through.[16] While for animals, death is something experienced only at the end of life, we experience Death continually through the medium of Fashion. So Fashion reminds Death that "both of us equally aim continually to destroy and change all things here below" (*OM* 51). Some might think that the changes Fashion ordains are superficial,

> But in fact I have not failed, and do not fail, to play a few tricks that could be compared with yours, as for instance to pierce ears, lips and noses, and to rip them with the knickknacks I hang in the holes; to scorch the flesh of men with the red-hot irons I make them brand themselves with for beauty's sake; to deform the heads of infants with bandages and other contraptions . . . ; to cripple people with narrow boots; to choke their breath and make their eyeballs pop with the use of tight corsets. . . . In fact, generally speaking, I persuade and force all civilized people to put up every day with a thousand difficulties and a thousand discomforts, and often with pain and agony, and some even to die gloriously, for the love they bear me. (*OM* 51)

Here Death represents the effects of time in the long term while Fashion is the short-term effect of time-consciousness. Fashion, while marking our distance from the not-so-distant past, makes us more and more the same in the present, even to the point of reshaping our bodies so that

---

[16] The critique of the modern emphasis on speed has recently been taken up again by, among others, Paul Virilio (1986) and Milan Kundera (1996).

we resemble one another. Moreover, this pursuit is a profoundly unhealthy one, detached as it is from any connection with the natural world. Like the theater in Rousseau's account of it, Fashion replaces a preexistent society of rough, vital individuality with an artificial society that is polished but oppressive in its commonality and phony in its intensity. One does not need to join in Rousseau's admiration of primitive existence to recognize the inversion of priorities created by the pursuit of Fashion: "Little by little, but mostly in recent times, I have assisted you [Death] by consigning to disuse and oblivion those labors and exercises that do good to the body, and introduced or brought into esteem innumerable others that damage the body in a thousand ways, and shorten life" (OM 53). The perpetually changing demands of Fashion do not just occur at random. Some fashions are more fashionable than others and life-denying fashions are the most fashionable of all. What appears to be the pursuit of liveliness (even, one might say, in health and diet "fashions") is, in fact, the opposite; black remains the only permanently fashionable color. Having lost the illusions that helped distract us in earlier stages of our history, we have only the self-disguising of Fashion to ward off the perpetual threat of boredom. But, as with the theater, the frenzy of change that Fashion simulates is a poor cover for the increasing desperation among the mannequins.

Fashion is deceptive as theater is deceptive. By keeping us constantly in motion, it produces a feeling of individuality while in fact it diminishes our differences. It produces the illusion of freedom and self-determination while subjecting us ever more strongly to social pressures. The churning of Fashion represents, in miniature, the process of constant suffering and loss that we subject ourselves to when we exit the timeless condition of animals. It is modern existence distilled out of those elements of premodern life that still cling to us like talismans from a happier time.

Just as the appearance of diversity in modern life is mere appearance, so the appearance of happiness is equally illusory. Both Leopardi and Rousseau mock contemporary claims to satisfaction, as well as the science and philosophy that claim to produce them. In the first place, they hold, it is a mistake to compare earlier humans with contemporary ones. We have been so changed by the process of history that Leopardi, at least, is prepared to speak of a second human nature that has wholly replaced the first: "That primal nature of ancient man, and of the savage and uncivilized peoples, is no longer our nature; but habituation and reason have created in us a different nature; which we have, and will have forever, in the place of the first. It was not in the beginning natural for man to procure death voluntarily: but nor was it natural to desire it. Today both things are natural; that is, in conformity with our new nature" (OM 208–9). Rousseau does not speak of a second nature, but merely of our hav ing lost our first nature and replaced it with something wholly unnatural. In either case, the effects are the same. Where earlier humans had simple desires that could be satisfied by material objects like food and shelter, our desires are multiplied and made immaterial by the development of language and reason, which we wrongly imagine are simply tools for the satisfaction of desire.

As I discussed in chapter 1, Leopardi pursues this claim through an attack on Socrates and on the Socratic dictum that knowledge is the foundation for virtue and happiness. The problem is not just that this idea is mistaken. Its universal acceptance ("these things are said by not far short of all philosophers both ancient and modern") has warped our approach to life: "Therefore they greatly deceive themselves, who declare and preach that the perfection of man consists in knowledge of the truth, and that all his woes proceed from false opinions and ignorance, and that the human race will at last be happy, when all or most people come to know the truth, and solely on the grounds of that, arrange and govern their lives" (*OM* 186). But having "arranged and governed" our lives on this basis for many generations, we are no longer in a position to do anything else. Even if we revise our philosophy to embrace a pessimistic conclusion, we cannot erase our second nature: "it is not in the power of man to forget the truths they know, and it is easier to rid oneself of any habit before that of philosophizing" (*OM* 186–87).

Whatever power philosophy may give us over the world, it does not include the power to reverse time, which is the one thing that would be necessary to avoid the pernicious effects of philosophy itself. In Leopardi's mythological universe, even the gods do not have the ability to reverse time. It is for this reason that the effects of knowledge are permanent. However much we may admire the "ancient errors" and their beneficial effects for earlier human beings, they are "impossible to bring back to life" (*OM* 187). Modern unhappiness, then, is not ultimately predicated on the inherent evils of philosophy but on the unalterable unidirectionality of time. Indeed, apart from his blanket condemnations, in other places Leopardi sometimes reserves judgment on the effects of philosophy on the ancient philosophers themselves. So, for example, when Filippo Ottonieri reads in the *Lives of the Philosophers* by Diogenes Laertius "how Socrates affirmed that there was only one good in the world, and that this was knowledge; and a sole evil, and that this was ignorance," he responds carefully: "I cannot speak for the knowledge and ignorance of the ancients; but today I would reverse this judgment" (*OM* 154). Reason does not do the damage by itself; it is the fact that reason, like every other human faculty, is subject to time that ensures our modern unhappiness in the guise of achievement. It is the cumulative cultural effects of philosophizing that have driven us, now, to a death-like existence (Leopardi proposes that the nineteenth century be called "the century of death" [*OM* 53]). He summarizes this ironic trajectory in a passage that can only remind us of Foucault: "With us, for a very long time now, education has not deigned to think of the body, a thing altogether too base and abject: it thinks of the spirit: and by its very desire to cultivate the spirit, ruins the body: without realizing that in ruining this, it also in turn ruins the spirit" (*OM* 220).

For Rousseau as well, modern life is ruinous for both spirit and body. In the *Letter to M. D'Alembert*, this point is made through a comparison of the modern theater with that of the ancient Greeks. The pleasures of the modern theater are, to Rousseau, quite intense—but our need for such intense, artificial joys bespeaks a degeneration of the species. Our very capacity for pleasure has been dulled. However successful classical plays may have been in their own time, "Who doubts that the best play of Sophocles would fall flat in our theater?" (*LD* 19). Theater, which was once a diversion, has become a need and it is only "discontent with one's self, the burden of idleness," and other modern conditions that create this need. Where we were once satisfied with the emotions that our own relationships generated, these are now too weak to satisfy us. They need supplementation. "I do not like the need to occupy the heart constantly with the stage as if it were ill at ease inside of us" (*LD* 16). Thus the very great theatrical powers Rousseau pays tribute to, above all in the work of Molière, in a sense, condemn themselves. Or rather, they condemn the age that celebrates them. Only a modern man would need such strong liquor to get drunk.

In the *Second Discourse*, Rousseau writes that "savage man and civilized man differ so much in their inmost heart and inclinations that what constitutes the supreme happiness of the one would reduce the other to despair." The former wants only "to live and to remain idle" while the latter can only "be happy and satisfied with themselves on the testimony of others" (*SD* 198). The happiness of earlier humans was unsophisticated, but it was at least present. Moderns pursue happiness rather than possessing it; happiness itself remains fugitive. Though we regularly proclaim how our scientific advances have liberated us from Nature, rich and poor alike are in fact "subjugated by a multitude of new needs to the whole of Nature . . . whose slave he in a sense becomes" (*SD* 180).

Here Rousseau emphasizes that our need to manipulate and control Nature is driven by the fact that, in its raw form, it no longer brings us satisfaction. Our need for the regard of others forces us to extract from Nature much more than it originally provided. As animals, our bare physical needs were capable of being satisfied by what was ready-to-hand in the world. Today, we want "iron and wheat" and must mine and farm for it. Our resulting expertise in metallurgy and agriculture, which seems like mastery over Nature and a source of security and happiness is, like

Molière's plays, only evidence that what ought to make us happy no longer suffices. They are both reactions to a suffering we have inflicted on ourselves.

Rousseau's language of subjugation and slavery here is carefully chosen. To him, the illusions of variety and happiness are subthemes of a larger concern—the deceptive nature of modern political institutions that only institute servitude in the guise of freedom. To put the point another way: the arts and sciences, or philosophy, have wrongly promised us that their own development will promote both freedom and happiness. While happiness of a certain kind was within the grasp of our animalistic ancestors, it is no longer available to us. Rousseau deplores this loss but considers it irreversible. Freedom, on the other hand, is a capacity for self-direction that we have *developed* while losing that for happiness. So the absence of freedom from modern life is deplorable in a different way. Rousseau does speak of earlier humans as "free and independent" (*SD* 180). But he also contrasts this early freedom (the absence of constraint and the absence of desire for the esteem of others), with a truer freedom, the freedom of citizens in the various republics of his fantasies, who are conscious and self-determined, without being subject to the fluctuating regard of other individuals. These citizens are not happy; rather they are fortified against the worst of modern unhappiness. Civilized humans, through the development of their minds, have a capacity for autonomy that animal humans (driven by instincts) did not. What we lack are political structures that would allow this autonomy to function; instead, we have social and cultural institutions that undermine it.

As with the other ironies that mark the modern human condition, our loss of freedom is something that we have succeeded in hiding from ourselves. So, Rousseau says, contemporary civilized people "incessantly boast of the peace and quiet they enjoy in their chains" (*SD* 187). But our subjugation to the opinion of others paves the way for direct political subjugation. The natural equality of the state of nature is destroyed, and inequality creates a need, particularly among the rich, to secure their status through law. With our powers of reason still only weakly developed, the "specious reasons" the powerful invent for institutions that preserve distinctions are found to be persuasive and "all ran toward their chains in the belief that they were securing their freedom" (*SD* 183).

This is the ultimate price that we humans pay for our loss of animal timelessness. Rousseau pauses to contrast "animals born free and abhorring captivity [who] smash their heads against the bars of their prison" with modern men who meekly accept the yoke of a despot who "dispenses grace when he lets them live" (*SD* 187–88). The institutions initially accepted by primitive humans are only further developed by time; distinctions increase and "the People . . . consented to let their servitude increase in order to secure their tranquility" (*SD* 193). The narrative of the *Second Discourse* traces this process and culminates in a grim assessment of the present. From the simple capacity for reflection introduced by time-consciousness have grown the political differences that issue in a society of "Master and Slave" bathed in an illusion of freedom.

Even those who possess political power are not free in any important sense. Rousseau begins *The Social Contract* with the observation that "those who think themselves the masters of others are indeed greater slaves than they" (*SC* 49). Why, one might ask, did Rousseau put things this way? If he had meant to indicate that neither rich nor poor are free in a system of political inequality, he could have said that they equally lacked freedom. In order to understand how masters are "greater slaves" than the slaves, we must look back to the core of Rousseau's pessimism. Since he holds that slavery originates in the condition of living outside oneself, it follows that those who live more outside themselves are more enslaved. But Rousseau also speaks of us as bound to the opinion of others to whatever degree one is esteemed by them. He does not speak of higher and lower esteem but simply of *more* or *less* (that is, he measures esteem by quantity rather than by rank). Those who gain the most esteem are therefore further outside themselves than those who earn no esteem at all in the social sphere. The most despised need no one else to maintain their situation (they receive, so to speak, zero esteem), while the most respected are in constant need of others. The illusion of freedom is thus at its most intense among those who are at the farthest remove from it: "Even domination is servile when it is connected with opinion, for you depend on the prejudices of those you govern by prejudices" (*E* 83).

Leopardi describes a similar condition, though his emphasis is more on the absence of happiness than the absence of freedom. Still, Leopardi does have his Academy of Sillographers remark, in its own pompous way, that it "has set itself diligently to consider the nature and character of our time and after long and mature examination has resolved that it may be called the Machine Age . . . because the men of today perhaps act and live more mechanically than anyone in the past."[17] Modern men are machine-like in their rote pursuit of happiness; and the conflicts between them that result from this pursuit are utterly unsurprising. Our actions are so predictable that machines could easily replicate them. Indeed, Leopardi has his Academy look forward to the day when machines can *feel* in our stead and we can then deploy their "parajealousy, [] paracalumny, [] paraperfidy or parafraud" to take the place of our own (*OM* 55). So long as we are enslaved to a vain chase after pleasure, we might as well be mechanisms. To act like human beings we would have to free ourselves from this

---

[17] *Sillographos* is an extremely rare Greek word for an author of lampoons.

behavior, which would mean, first of all, freeing ourselves from the belief that happiness and freedom are themselves coterminous.

Where Rousseau suggested that we have become a society of "artificial men," Leopardi gives this idea a literal embodiment. We are so close to such a situation, the Academy says, that we should take the next logical step. Thus the Sillographers, "determined to contribute with all the means in [their] power to this new order of things" (*OM* 55) propose a series of three prizes for those who construct robots that imitate, respectively, a friend, a man of virtue, and a loving woman (the latter, naturally, receives the largest prize). When these machines appear on the scene, our retreat from freedom in pursuit of a pain-free existence can be perfected. Leopardi's modern humans have been liberated only from a strong attachment to their lives; otherwise, they are as enslaved to the vain pursuit of happiness as Rousseau's Parisians.

Indeed, Leopardi holds that philosophers correspond to Rousseau's "greater slaves" in the sense of being the most deluded about their freedom. It is the philosophers who believe that unhappiness results from error and ignorance and can therefore be cured by knowledge and study. Philosophers thus believe themselves free from nature's dictates. But this is the greatest illusion of all. Filippo Ottonieri "often laughed at those philosophers who held that man can evade the tyranny of fortune, by . . . not entrusting his happiness or unhappiness to anything but what depends entirely upon himself" (*OM* 144). Here the philosophers rely on a supposed ability to "pay no more attention to one's own affairs than to those of others." But even if we implausibly suppose that this ability exists,

> Would fortune not hold sway over that very frame of mind, which these thinkers claim may enable us to evade her? Is not man's reason subject all the time to countless accidents, innumerable sicknesses that bring stupidity, delirium, frenzy, violence and one hundred other kinds of madness . . . ? It is great folly to admit that our bodies are subject to things beyond our control, and nonetheless deny that the mind, which depends on the body in almost everything, is inevitably subject to anything whatever outside ourselves. (*OM* 144–45)

So he concludes, in a manner reminiscent of Machiavelli, that "the whole man, always and incontrovertibly, is in the power of fortune" (*OM* 145). Here again we see the point, which Rousseau first made, that there is an optimism embedded in post-Socratic philosophy that misleads humans about the relation between reason and happiness.

This passage is also important because it marks one of pessimism's points of departure from Stoicism and other ancient philosophies of the self. While those philosophies also often depicted the material world as a place of unhappiness, they suggested escape through mental mastery of such circumstances. But to pessimists like Leopardi, this maneuver is just the last resort of a Socratic rationalism that, unable to change the world, still pretends to wield authority over it. The Stoic position, for example, requires a metaphysic of the soul that modern time-consciousness renders implausible. If the entire universe is subject to temporal change, Ottonieri suggests, the belief of ancient philosophers that they could permanently exempt their minds from such flux is an illusion. There is no immunity from the effects of time—and the delusion of such immunity is itself an element of our predicament, one to which philosophers are particularly prone, thus "even those who know the human condition best will persevere until death looking for happiness, and promising it to themselves" (P 42). If Stoicism is an art of living, from the pessimist's perspective it is a singularly impractical one in that it requires a constancy of purpose that its own analysis of worldly affairs would have (but for its metaphysical escape clause) revealed as impossible.

The modern condition, to the cultural pessimists, is one of self-delusion and unfreedom. The ironic narrative that begins with the appearance of time-consciousness culminates in a diagnosis of contemporary society mired in fantasies of self-authorship. But at this point Rousseau's and Leopardi's philosophies, to a certain extent anyway, part company. Their responses, though both pessimistic in their refusal to reverse their diagnoses, respond to it in different ways. Rousseau pursues special conditions that escape our temporal limitations while Leopardi, as I suggest below, demands a more direct embrace of them.

Pessimistic Solutions to Pessimistic Problems

Even as an old man, Rousseau retained the dream of escaping time's effects. Stretched out on a boat, bobbing gently on a Swiss mountain lake, he had the momentary feeling of being free of the world of reflection, desires, and comparisons, free to be simply Jean-Jacques, without interruption. Ashore, Rousseau's political theory retains this note of searching for a refuge from the awful power of temporality. Leopardi, on the other hand, seeks conditions in which one could find it bearable to live with the limitations that his pessimism requires. While one might be tempted here to call one of these responses more pessimistic than the other, I think this is a misguided approach. Rather, Rousseau and Leopardi should both be accounted pessimists on the grounds of their agreement on what has been set out to this point: the problem of time itself, the ironic narrative of human history, and the illusory character of modern freedom. Neither of their responses to this situation attempt to dislodge this fundamental problematic of the human condition caused by our emergence into time-consciousness. Rather, they have different strategies for coping with it.

In the 1750s, Rousseau saw little to be done about our situation. His suggestion in the *Second Discourse* (1755) that we will seek in a futile fashion after "the age at which you would wish your species had stopped" sets the tone for this period (*SD* 140). Both this discourse and the first (1749), apart from some stray thoughts about consulting our consciences, offer little in the way of concrete alternatives to the degenerate modern condition in which we find ourselves. In the *Letter to M. D'Alembert* (1758), however, one substitute, a fantastic one, is explored at some length. Rousseau recounts an alleged thirty-year-old memory of a nameless community of mountaineers "in the vicinity of Neufchâtel" that he claims to have encountered in his youth (*LD* 60ff.). Although he goes into considerable detail concerning their political and social circumstances, he acknowledges later that he in fact remembers nothing of their "moeurs, society, or characters." "I only remember that I continually admired in these singular men an amazing combination of delicacy and simplicity that would be believed to be almost incompatible and that I have never since observed elsewhere" (*LD* 62).

What Rousseau gives us here is a vision of the species "stopped" at a point where it garners some of the benefits of technological advance without the burdens of civilization. Although these farmers till the land and produce "countless artifacts," "each is everything for himself, no one is anything for another" (*LD* 60–61). Each builds his own house, makes his own furniture, and even (in an exceptionally ironic detail) produces his own clocks and watches. Conscious enough to be free, they are isolated enough to remain happy. Rousseau then proceeds to imagine his utopia disfigured by the introduction of a theater and finds that it will be destroyed in short order.[18] The fate of the mountaineers tells the story of civilization itself in miniature. But the very perfection of Rousseau's vision here is a clear signal that this is not a genuine memory but an idealization of what cannot be, a community frozen in time. The little mountain village is not just geographically isolated but set apart from the flow of history, until a little theater introduces the capacity for self-reflection into it and gives it, and its members, what Rousseau dreads, self-consciousness. Apart from such fantasies, Rousseau at this stage offers nothing that could counter the effects of time in a permanent fashion. Although he opposes the introduction of the theater to Geneva on the grounds that it will accelerate that city's corruption, he does *not* maintain

---

[18] Philonenko, in an excellent discussion, calls this passage Rousseau's "ideal genesis of vice" (1984, 2:237–41).

that the absence of a theater will preserve Geneva indefinitely. Nor could he, given the fundamentals of his theory.

It might be maintained that the proposals Rousseau makes in *The Social Contract* and *Émile* represent an alternative to this pessimism. As I said at the outset of this chapter, I will only insist on my thesis for Rousseau's early period. To explore these later works in all their complexity would require a much longer engagement than is possible here. However, I can at least offer some grounds for the view that Rousseau does not reverse himself in these later works. There is every indication that the structures of government he proposes, for example, in *The Social Contract* represent nothing more than temporary bulwarks against the flow of time, and that Rousseau acknowledges them as such.[19] While his advocacy on behalf of a republican form of government is certainly made in all earnestness, it is clear that *all* government, on his view, must fall prey to its own age. In chapters 10 and 11 of book III, Rousseau outlines the "the natural and inevitable inclination of the best constituted governments." "The body politic," he writes, "no less than the body of a man, begins to die as soon as it is born, and bears within itself the causes of its own destruction. Either kind of body may have a constitution of greater or less robustness, fitted to preserve it for a longer or shorter time" (*SC* 134–35).

The better constituted a state is, the longer it will last, but the best state does not last forever. To believe otherwise would amount to "flattering ourselves that we can give to the work of man a durability that does not belong to human things" (*SC* 134).[20] This point is not often made in as-

---

[19] Several commentators have emphasized how, for Rousseau, the General Will is something that exists only in the present tense, that is, it does not in any sense bind the future but only the current moment (Affeldt 1999, 308–15; Strong 1994, 90–94). I think this view is correct but emphasizes all the more that the egoism that opposes the General Will is not something that originates solely in selfishness but also, and more fundamentally, in temporality. That the General Will has to escape time in order to be effectual indicates not just its nature, but also its limits.

[20] Rousseau's view here is rooted, at least in part, in that of Machiavelli. The latter, in the *Discorsi*, also drew an image of a republic isolated and ultimately doomed by the flow of time, where its excellence was measured simply by how long it could hold out against such a force (Machiavelli 1970, 109, 123). The difference, however, lies in the sort of time to which political institutions are subject. Machiavelli, still in the grip of a premodern cosmology (see Basu 1990), speaks of circular patterns of history where the different forms of government, as in Aristotle or Plato, replace one another in a cyclical fashion. Rousseau's shift to a linear view is the root of the difference between his pessimism and what we might term Machiavelli's "fatalism." Hence, for Machiavelli, combining the three archetypical forms of government (monarchy, aristocracy, and democracy) in the "mixed constitution" is the best bulwark against time because it captures, as it were, the three principle "moments" in a single structure. Having abandoned the cyclical view, however, this strategy loses its value in Rousseau's theory.

sessments of Rousseau's political theory that compare his "ideal state" to that of Hobbes or Locke. But Rousseau's theory has a temporal and historical dimension that these others do not. Nor can any political structure provide more than a temporary refuge from the effects of time.

Both good and bad states are subject to the history of moral degeneration. A good constitution is a reprieve, but always a temporary one, from this history. This does not make it an idle pursuit by any means. But it puts such a pursuit in a pessimistic context. Just as human individuals, as the *Second Discourse* argues, are fundamentally changed by having their own death appear on the horizon of their world view, so the project of government must be changed when the dream of its immortality is abandoned. Whatever path we choose, its terminus has already been decided.

Similarly, the effects of the ideal structures of education that Rousseau develops in *Émile* are systematically dismantled in its sequel *Émile et Sophie* when this couple is introduced to the real world and its temporal effects. So long as Émile was under the watch of his tutor, he was isolated from the effects of time and could develop in an uncorrupted way. Like the picture of the mountaineers, however, this too is a fantasy on Rousseau's part and he is well aware that the project must end in failure. On the first page of *Émile et Sophie* (subtitled *Les Solitaires*), in recounting his misfortunes in a letter to his tutor, the disillusioned Émile reprises the theme of the *Reveries*, that our attachment to objects in time dooms us to unhappiness: "Everything has vanished like a dream; still young I have lost everything, wife, children, friends, in a word everything, including all traffic with my fellow-men. *My heart has been torn apart by all its attachments*" (*ES* 43; emphasis added). Again, the failure of the educative project does not mean it is not worthwhile; *but neither does the existence of the project refute Rousseau's pessimism*. As I have maintained from the outset, pessimism is not a paralyzing doctrine; it simply puts our projects in a particular light and reminds us of their necessary limitations.

Both *Émile* and *The Social Contract* indicate something else as well: while the individual pursuit of happiness is always vain for the self-conscious, the pursuit of freedom, though doomed, is not vain in the same way. Our second natures, in which we live outside ourselves, are incompatible with happiness at every moment. Freedom, on the other hand, is within the capacity of our second nature, even though that capacity will ultimately meet a superior foe in modern society and culture. Thus *Emile* and *The Social Contract* attempt to teach us what is within our power— not to *secure* freedom but to *experience* it, however temporarily. A well-educated conscience and a well-ordered polity cannot survive in this world. But they can exist for a little while. So long as they do, the individuals or citizens who inhabit them will have an experience that is worthwhile and genuine. While it is vain to seek freedom as a political *telos* (a

stable condition that is the guaranteed result of a certain structure of government), the experience of autonomy, though fugitive, is a possibility
precisely for those who have given up the search for such guarantees. It is
the result of a fortuitous alignment of social, political, and bodily circumstances over which we can only have partial and temporary control.[21]

All of Rousseau's various responses to his pessimistic diagnosis, whether
personal or political, involve isolating human beings, somehow, from the
effects of temporal consciousness. Leopardi's response is different in that
he does not think such an escape possible, even briefly or at the level of
theory. From his perspective, Rousseau's strategies remain a futile struggle for an unattainable happiness (*Reveries*) or freedom (*Social Contract*).
Instead, he argues, we should abandon the pursuit of happiness and pursue freedom at the individual level. His prescription takes the form of a
personal ethic rather than a larger social or political system. This ethic is
encapsulated in the advice that I quoted in chapter 1: "Live, and be great
and unhappy" (*OM* 65).

Where Rousseau seeks a polity fortified against the ravages of time,
Leopardi suggests instead that we fortify the individual. Having given up
the illusions that protected us in earlier eras, we are left, in one sense,
much weaker than before. In another sense, however, we are liberated and
strengthened when we lay down the burden of our previous pursuits.
Leopardi maintains that we will then be able to live more fully than before—if we live shorter lives, we may live better lives: "Life must be vital,
that is, truly life; otherwise death incomparably surpasses it in merit"
(*OM* 89–90; cf. *E* 42). Thus Leopardi's "Metaphysician" (*Metafisico*) re-
proves a "Physician" (*Fisico*) who proposes to lengthen life through modern medicine:[22]

> But if you wish, by prolonging life, to confer a real blessing on men, then find
> an art that multiplies the number and vigor of their feelings and actions. In
> this way you will truly increase human life, and by filling those interminable
> intervals of time in which our being is enduring rather than living, you will
> be able to boast of having prolonged it. And this without going in search of
> the impossible, or using violence against nature, but aiding her rather. Don't
> you think that the Ancients lived more fully than we do, partly because, on
> account of the grave continuous dangers they were accustomed to undergo-

[21] See Rousseau's remarks about the impossible necessity of aligning the three types of education in the opening pages of the *Émile* (*E* 38ff.).

[22] Translators have rendered these terms as "Philosopher" and "Intellectual," or "Metaphysician" and "Physicist." It is true that the normal Italian word for "physician" is *dot-
tore* or *medico*. However, these translations fail to capture the obvious play on words that
Leopardi makes here. The advice that the *Fisico* gives is clearly medical in nature, since its
goal is to prolong life. And the *Metafisico* is just as clearly a "higher physician" in that he
responds by pointing to a more important kind of "health" for human beings.

ing, they commonly died earlier than we do? And you will bestow the greatest blessing on men: whose life was always, I will not say happy, but less unhappy insofar as it was the more powerfully excited, and the more fully occupied. (*OM* 89–90)

Here we are returned to the figure of Columbus discussed in the previous chapter. Columbus, as described above, leads an active life that spares him from boredom. But there is more to it than that. Leopardi emphasizes how Columbus, in leaving dry land, has also left the guarantees of reason. The risks he takes are unjustified and, just because of that, they liberate him. So Gutierrez says to his captain that "you, when it comes down to it, have staked your life, . . . on no more than a mere speculative opinion" (*OM* 160). Columbus accepts this characterization, but in response emphasizes the benefits of his embrace of uncertainty. Reason may tell us how to preserve and extend our physical existence, but it does not tell us how to make life more bearable. Uncertainty, however, makes us value what we might have in a way that possessing it does not. "Every voyage", says Columbus, "is, in my opinion, like a leap from the cliff of Leucas" (*OM* 161). The reference is to an ancient fable about unhappy lovers who were freed from their passion by risking their lives. But Columbus generalizes the lesson: "It is commonly thought that men of the sea, and of war, being very often in danger of death, hold their lives in less esteem than others do. I for the same reason believe that life is by very few persons so loved and prized as it is by soldiers and sailors. . . . Who ever numbered among human blessings just having a little dry land under his feet? No one, except for sailors" (*OM* 161).

In making the leap, we accept that our fate will ultimately be determined by forces beyond our control rather than, as in Rousseau, trying to isolate ourselves from the effects of those forces. Yet in return, we receive a kind of freedom from fear and a vibrancy of existence that is otherwise unavailable. We are all unhappy lovers in pursuit of a happiness we cannot win; putting ourselves at risk liberates us both by distracting us from the unattainable and by removing us from the familiar so that it can be strange and valuable to us once again.

Unlike the cliff-jumpers, however, this sort of life does not reduce our suffering. In fact, Leopardi believes, it will only increase it. In the "Dialogue of Nature and the Soul," after being given the advice to be great and unhappy, the Soul inquires as to why the two are bound together. Nature replies that leading the vigorous sort of existence required for greatness will result in an intensification of all experiences, including the inevitable ones of suffering:

for the excellence of souls brings greater urgency to their lives; which in turn brings a greater feeling of their own unhappiness; which is as much as to say greater unhappiness. In the same way, the larger degree of life in these souls implies more active self-love, wherever this may lead or whatever form it may take: and this surplus of self-love induces a more intense longing for beatitude, and therefore more vexation and suffering at being deprived of it, and deeper sorrow at the adversities that come along. All this is contained in the primeval and perpetual order of created things, which I cannot alter. (*OM* 66; cf. 63–64)

Leopardi's response to his pessimistic diagnosis of life is not, as in Rousseau, an attempt to flee time in pursuit of happiness or to build bulwarks against time in pursuit of freedom. Rather, it is a decision to search for freedom in an embrace of unhappiness. Both acknowledge freedom and happiness to be opposite poles of human existence, kept apart by our time-bound condition. Leopardi does not conceive himself to be choosing freedom over happiness; on his account, we simply lack the ability to make ourselves happy. If we desire to achieve *something* rather than nothing, we ought to pursue that which the "primeval and perpetual order of created things" allows as possible, if not likely: a life that is robust and full of adventure. We should simply not confuse this vitality with happiness. As in Rousseau, we will have an *experience* of freedom, rather than the security of it. Unlike Rousseau, we will have that experience through an embrace of the universe, rather than by hiding from it.

It is true, however, that Leopardi believes this sort of life will also fortify us against the worst sort of unhappiness. This comes out in the "Dialogue of Plotinus and Porphyry," which discusses suicide. Here Leopardi confronts the conclusion to which many of his readers must be drawn, namely, that since life is full of unavoidable suffering, suicide is the logical "solution." Leopardi admits the logic, but to him, this is one last trick of reason, designed to assert its superiority at any price: "Allow it to be reasonable, to kill oneself; allow it to be against reason to resign one's mind to life: surely it is still a savage and inhuman act. And it ought not to gratify one more, nor should one choose, to be in accord with reason, and a monster, then in tune with nature, and a man" (*OM* 212). A decision against life as a whole, taken on account of its dearth of happiness, is just the final way in which we let ourselves be dominated by the pursuit of happiness. If we are actually able to liberate ourselves from this pursuit, our "reasons" for suicide will likewise be, if not eliminated, sharply reduced. One way in which this happens is that we come to value our own lives *less* than we did before. We inhabit, one could say, a bearable lightness of being and come to grasp the triviality even of our own suffering. Liberated from a cold rationality, we can allow ourselves to be seduced to life even when a strict calculation would cause us to reject it. Plotinus outlines a process to Porphyry by which suicidal logic can be defeated precisely by not "pondering the matter too deeply."

There is no disgust with life, no despair, no sense of the nothingness of things, of the worthlessness of remedies, of the loneliness of man; no hatred of the world and of oneself; that can last so long: although these attitudes of mind are completely reasonable, and their opposites unreasonable. But despite all this, after a little while; with a gentle change in the temper of the body; little by little; and often in a flash, for minuscule reasons scarcely possible to notice; the taste for life revives, and this or that fresh hope springs up, and human things take on their former visage, and show they are not unworthy of some care; not so much to the intellect, as indeed, so to speak, to the senses of the spirit. And that is enough to make a person, aware and convinced as he may be of the truth, as well as in spite of reason, both persevere in life, and go along with it as others do: for those very senses (one might say), and not the intellect, are what rules over us. . . . And life is a thing of such small consequence, that man, as regards himself, ought not to be very anxious either to keep it or to discard it. Therefore, without pondering the matter too deeply; with each trivial reason that presents itself, for grasping the former alternative rather than the latter, he ought not to refuse to do so. (*OM* 211–13)

The worst sort of unhappiness is produced by a lack of recognition of the limits to happiness. The yearning for suicide is the product of misplaced demands on life that life cannot respond to. "Ordinary" suffering, on the other hand, is bearable. Each of us may even find some elements of life, in Leopardi's hesitant formulation, "not unworthy of some care." We persevere in life "in spite of reason" and not for grand causes but for trivial ones, visible to the "senses of the spirit" rather than the "intellect." They are enough.

This sense of the preciousness of the quotidian (today we might say, the ordinary)[23] and the vitalization of life that comes through the embrace of uncertainty are further emphasized in the next-to-last *operetta*, "The Dialogue of an Almanac-Peddler and a Passer-by." A man selling guides to the new year is accosted by an inquisitive customer. In an exchange that anticipates Zarathustra's speeches about eternal recurrence, the customer asks the peddler whether he would like to have the last twenty years to live over again. The peddler readily replies that he would. But when the customer makes clear that "you had to relive the life that you have lived, no more and no less, with all the joys and griefs that you have had," the peddler replies, "That I wouldn't want" (*OM* 215). And when forced to consider the question, the peddler agrees that everyone else would probably feel the same way, that their own life would not be worth reliving.

---

[23] There is a real prefiguring here of the work of Stanley Cavell on the "ordinary" (Cavell 1988) and of those who have tried to follow Cavell's lead, for example, Strong 1994 and Dumm 1999.

What, then, did the almanac-seller want when he said he would like the last twenty years of his life over again?

> PEDDLER: A life just as it came, as God gave it, with no strings attached.
> PASSER-BY: A life accepted at random, knowing nothing of it beforehand, just as we know nothing about this new year?
> PEDDLER: That's it.
> PASSER-BY: I would want the same thing if I had to live over again, and so would everyone. But this shows that chance, until the end of this last year, has been treating everyone badly. And it's plain to see that everyone is of the opinion that the misfortune he has known is greater and more weighty than the good luck, if indeed on condition of repeating the same life, with all its good and bad, no one would choose to be born again. *That life which is a fine thing is not the life one knows, but the life one does not know; not a life of the past, but of the future.* (OM 215–16; emphasis added)

The passer-by does not suggest any escape from temporality. But he does suggest that the future becomes more bearable just to the degree that it is *detached* from a fixed historical narrative. That is the ordinary experience that is denigrated by an optimism that assigns our actions a value through a relationship to the progress of the self or the species.

We need not take on tasks as momentous as that of Columbus in order to have his sense of adventure. Every future is a voyage into the unknown and, for that reason, more enticing than anything that has happened to us, no matter how good. From the outside, it may appear to be quite ordinary, "a life just as it came." But to a pessimist, who has the perspective from which to appreciate it, the ordinary future is something worth living for, although it may be as full of pain as the past. We will see this emphasis on the openness of the future as the source of its attractiveness to the pessimistic spirit repeated in more detail in Nietzsche's writings. But it is already here in this late dialogue of Leopardi's and it sets his pessimism apart from that of Rousseau.

Leopardi's pessimist may not be happy, but he will have a perspective from which he can laugh at the triviality of human existence, in all its pleasures and pains. Laughter, in fact, is characteristic of the sort of pessimistic response to the burden of existence that Leopardi wants to recommend. Columbus's speeches are followed by *An Elegy to Birds*, in which birds are compared to human beings on the grounds that both partake in laughter. Birdsong, he says, is "so to speak, a laugh, brought forth by the bird when it feels well and comfortable" (*OM* 356). But laughter is even more characteristic of human beings, who could be described as "a risible animal" for "laughter is no less proper and peculiar to man than reason is" (*OM* 356). Laughter is all the more remarkable in human beings, however, because we do not only laugh out of pleasure but, just as often, out of pain. That is, we often laugh at ourselves: "It is certainly a wondrous thing, that in man, who of all creatures is the most troubled and wretched, we find the faculty of laughter. . . . Wondrous also is the use we make of this faculty: for we see many in some cruel mischance, others in great misery of mind, others who scarcely retain any love of life, utterly sure of the vanity of every human good, virtually incapable of any joy, and void of every hope; who nevertheless laugh" (*OM* 165–66).

Human beings are "risible" both in the sense that we have the capacity for laughter and in the sense that our lives are themselves laughable. Birds, with their capacity for flight, their constant energy, and their ability to see the whole world from on high, are never bored and laugh more directly out of joy. But humans "have no cause for laughter that is just and reasonable" (*OM* 166). Nonetheless, we laugh, and we laugh the most when we are at our most pessimistic, when we realize that we are the butt of the joke of the world, a joke created by time. So Leopardi, in the last of the *operette*, laughs at our fate and his own. This laughter does not alleviate our suffering, but it may give us courage for dealing with it.

> For my part, just as southern Europe laughs at husbands in love with their unfaithful wives, so I laugh at the human race in love with life; and I judge it very unmanly to let oneself be deceived and deluded like a fool, and in addition to the evils one suffers, to be as it were the laughingstock of nature and destiny. I'm still speaking of the deception that is not of the imagination, but of the intellect. . . . I trample upon the cowardice of mankind, reject every childish consolation and deception; and I have the courage to bear the privation of every hope, to gaze intrepidly on the desert of life, not to conceal from myself any part of human unhappiness, and to accept all the consequences of a philosophy that is grievous, but true. (*OM* 219)

Where Rousseau suggests that we attempt an escape from time-consciousness or build bulwarks against it, Leopardi counsels us to leap from the cliffs of Leucas, that is, to embrace our condition and learn to live with it by laughing at it. We will not, by this practice, be relieved of the sufferings of existence. But Leopardi believes that our souls can be fortified to a degree sufficient to confront our condition without lapsing into despair: "He who has the courage to laugh is master of the world, much like him who is prepared to die" (*P* 55). In addition, we will gain a kind of freedom. It is perhaps stretching Leopardi's meaning too far to call this freedom political in a direct sense. But I think it is fair to say that Leopardi describes an art of living that has freedom as one of its main goals, freedom from a vain striving for happiness and from social and cultural institutions that encourage such striving. The pessimist is never free from time-consciousness, but he is free from the illusions it encourages, free from a modern project in which he was enrolled without consent. The pessimist's activities partake of this freedom; they are unmoored from unattainable goals and pursued for their own sake, like the voyages of (Leopardi's) Columbus. While it might be wrong to call Columbus's voyages political acts, it would be equally wrong to claim that they were merely private adventures. Certainly, more than most political acts, they had very public consequences.

Conclusion: The Pessimist and the Misanthrope

The philosophies of both Rousseau and Leopardi are pessimistic in that they take their shape from the same problematic of time. Both operate principally at the level of culture. The difficulties of time-consciousness come to light in a social dynamic that results in extensive human suffering and yet is irreversible. In both, the course of human history is ironic and it issues in a condition that is full of illusions, above all the illusion of human freedom.

In neither case, however, do these pessimisms issue in despair, although Rousseau, in the moments when he prescribes withdrawal into the self, anticipates the philosophical resignation of Schopenhauer. In different ways, both seek to resist what they acknowledge to be irresistable, the effects of time-consciousness and time itself. Both, therefore, acknowledge that their prescriptions are no more than temporary remedies. Still, there is this difference between them: Rousseau, in seeking a semblance of animal unconsciousness, or political bulwarks against time, yearns to separate humans from that which is most distinctive to the human condition. In the *Letter to M. D'Alembert*, he rails against Molière's efforts in *The Misanthrope* to make the title character appear foolish. The misanthrope, Rousseau insists, is an honest and virtuous man—and Rousseau's philosophy is honestly and virtuously misanthropic in that it is deeply antipathetic to the human qua human. Rousseau's sympathies lie with the human animal, tormented by an alien self-consciousness that history and culture have foisted upon it. Our one natural feeling, Rousseau claims, is *pitié*, the fellow-feeling aroused in us by the sight of an animal in pain. In a sense, his philosophy is one long expression of such pity, extended from one human animal to another.

Leopardi, in contrast, while deploring our condition in terms that probably surpass those of Rousseau, does not turn his back on the modern human being in the same way. Although in moments he imagines how happy he would be to live as a bird, for the most part he recommends an embrace of our time-bound humanity. Our suffering may be unavoidable, but we can be distracted from it, learn to view it as trivial, and come to see it as a necessary part of achievement. All of these things can derive from a life of self-directed activity, where the activity is pursued for its own sake and not in the name of the progress of the species.

Versions of these contrasting approaches will recur in the next chapters. As I wrote above, pessimism is a problematic and not a doctrine. Its practitioners have conceived the dilemmas posed by time in different ways and elaborated a variety of responses to them. Nonetheless, the fundamental choice between humanism and misanthropy is one that every theorist must make. If the sympathies of this book lie finally with the humanists, it must be said of Rousseau that misanthropy has never been made more appealing than in his pages.

Chapter Three

"THE EVILS OF THE
WORLD HONESTLY ADMITTED"

METAPHYSICAL PESSIMISM IN

SCHOPENHAUER AND FREUD

> There is only one inborn error, and that is the notion that we
> exist in order to be happy. . . . So long as we persist in this
> inborn error, and indeed even become confirmed in
> it through optimistic dogmas, the world
> seems to us full of contradictions.
> —ARTHUR SCHOPENHAUER

PESSIMISM first achieved real recognition as a species of philosophy (a recognition that it quickly lost) through the popularity and influence of Arthur Schopenhauer. Although I have argued in the previous chapters that the true history of pessimism ought to be reckoned as beginning earlier, no account of the pessimistic spirit could deny pride of place to its most famous and relentless exponent. We should, however, resist the idea that Schopenhauer defines pessimism and vice versa. Schopenhauer himself certainly would not have claimed this.[1] He was well aware of his debts to earlier Western philosophers, from Heraclitus to Kant—indeed, his texts are riddled with citations that attempt to ground his views in an established Western tradition.[2] He also repeatedly declared his appreciation of Eastern religion and philosophy, especially the Buddhism whose first Sacred Truth is the well-known phrase, "Life is suffering."[3]

---

[1] Schopenhauer might well have claimed to have perfected pessimism, as he claimed to perfect every subject that he turned his attention to.

[2] In *The World as Will and Representation*, Schopenhauer makes an extended, fairly systematic attempt to catalogue his pessimistic predecessors (2:585ff.). Philonenko uses this fact to argue that pessimism is not in fact the distinctive element of Schopenhauer's philosophy (1980, 237ff.); but this argument is too clever by half. Schopenhauer is happy to report that others before him have remarked on, for example, the ubiquity of suffering. What he claims to have done is to give this pessimism a complete philosophical basis.

[3] Schopenhauer's interest in Buddhism only came after he had worked out the basic structure of his philosophy; it did not really have a role in the creation of that structure. While his appreciation for Buddhism was sincere, it should be noted that on his understanding its core insights could also be found in Christianity, albeit not as clearly. See Magee 1983, chap. 15.

Rather than building a definition of pessimism around Schopenhauer, then, I consider his to be a species of pessimism distinguished by its metaphysical character. In cultural pessimism, the effects of time on the species are filtered through the media of history and society. In metaphysical pessimism, the individual confronts his temporal condition directly. Schopenhauer thinks that there is nothing of importance to learn from history. He heaps scorn on Hegel and his followers for trying to reconcile history and philosophy: "The true philosophy of history . . . consists in the insight that, in spite of all the . . . endless changes [of historical circumstance] and their chaos and confusion, we yet always have before us only the same, identical, unchangeable essence, acting in the same way today as it did yesterday and always" (*WWR* 2:443–44).[4] Pessimism, to Schopenhauer, means not that our civilization or morality are declining, but rather that human beings are fated to endure a life freighted with problems that are fundamentally unmeliorable.[5] It is the unalterable conditions of our daily existence that are the source of Schopenhauer's pessimism, with our time-consciousness foremost among these.[6] Still, the arguments he presents follow a course that parallels, in a different key, those outlined in the last chapter—the burdens of time-consciousness are exfoliated such that most human action is rendered futile and ironic, freedom is fugitive, and redemption is found, as in Rousseau, largely by seeking an escape from the human condition.[7]

Sigmund Freud admitted once, in a backhanded way, that he had "unwittingly steered our course into the harbour of Schopenhauer's philoso-

[4] This point, and its importance for later pessimists like Nietzsche, is emphasized by Gottfried (1975).

[5] This is not the claim that pain will always outweigh pleasure. Although Schopenhauer makes the latter claim as well, it is, as I discuss below, a derivative point that is often mistaken for the central element of his philosophy. Bryan Magee, in his otherwise important analysis of Schopenhauer's metaphysics, tries to eradicate its association with pessimism entirely by arguing, in essence, that philosophy is always about facts and that pessimism and optimism are merely supplementary evaluations of those facts: "No general philosophy . . . can entail pessimistic conclusions. . . . it is true that his pessimism is compatible with his philosophy. . . . Non-pessimism is equally compatible with his philosophy. The traditional identification of him in terms of his pessimism is largely irrelevant to a serious consideration of him as a philosopher" (1997, 13). In addition to resting on a dubious premise (the "objectivity" of Schopenhauer's philosophy does not really support a human capacity for judgment that is in any sense value-free), this view seems to imply that all true ontological descriptions of the human condition can and should be met with equal equanimity no matter what their content, which seems absurd. Indeed, Magee himself cannot adhere to it—for example, "an essentially tragic course is programmed into us from the beginning" (219).

[6] This point, by itself, ought to be enough to dissolve the equation between pessimism and decline; for if the thought of decline is held to be a necessary element of pessimism, then Schopenhauer will have to be struck from the list of pessimists, which seems absurd.

[7] One of the better reconstructions of Schopenhauer's pessimism is to be found in Young 1987, chap. 10. It touches on many of the same points made in what follows; however it misses the centrality of the problem of time and, perhaps for this reason, fails to see the pessimistic tradition to which, by this thread, Schopenhauer is connected.

phy" (*BPP* 59). It will not be my concern here to determine just how witting or unwitting this navigation was.[8] Instead, Freud will provide a useful contrast to Schopenhauer and will allow us to fill out the category of metaphysical pessimist in a helpful way. As with Leopardi in the last chapter, Freud's theory follows many of the same paths as that of his interlocutor while nonetheless forming an alternative to it in rejecting the posture of resignation to which Schopenhauer was prone. While we are perhaps not used to thinking of Freud as a metaphysical philosopher, I will maintain that his understanding of the human mind as located in time profoundly shapes his psychology.[9] His so-called metapsychology in large measure translates Schopenhauer's metaphysics into phenomena of the mind—changing them less than one might imagine in the process. While much of Freud's work charts the subtleties of intrapsychic dynamics (with which we will not concern ourselves here), his pessimism—found in such texts as *Beyond the Pleasure Principle* and *Civilization and Its Discontents*—forms the philosophical framework within which these dynamics operate. As with the other pessimists, the dawning consciousness of time forms the horizon that separates the human from what preceded it and constitutes the context of all individual experience.[10]

Time and the Will

Schopenhauer, like the cultural pessimists before him, emphasized the distinction between human consciousness and the mental conditions of ani-

---

[8] That ground has been covered elsewhere. Freud mentions Schopenhauer at several other points, often to admit a consistency between their views while denying any influence. See Young and Brook 1994: although not focusing on pessimism, they catalogue many more parallels between the two than I consider here, concluding that Freud's denials that he was seriously influenced by Schopenhauer cannot be credible. Their bibliography also lists other useful discussions of the topic. Bilsker 1997 also notes many similarities, particularly those concerning the structure of the mind and the "death-drive."

[9] Ricoeur's magisterial account of Freud as a philosopher of language resists the view that his ideas rest on a metaphysic, though, on at least one occasion, he grants that Freud's view of time's relation to the unconscious is "quasi-metaphysical" (Ricoeur 1970, 444). Marcuse, strongly influenced by Heidegger, considers Freud's account "ontological" (Marcuse 1955, 107). Neither investigate Freud's relation to Schopenhauer at any length.

[10] Two previous discussions comparing Schopenhauer and Freud, both of which appear in the *Schopenhauer-Jahrbuch*, are Becker 1971 and Clegg 1980. The latter is an attempt to deny Freud's pessimism by contrasting his position with Schopenhauer's; but it draws so many connections between the two figures that the differences it then introduces seem paltry by comparison. Becker takes a psychological approach and attempts to document the common "character-structure" of the two men. While not drawing broad philosophical conclusions, this article contains a great deal of useful information about, for example, the Schopenhauerian inclinations of Freud's teachers as well as a complete catalogue of every place where Freud mentions Schopenhauer in print (there are seventeen).

mals. "The absence of reason," he wrote in *The World as Will and Representation*, "restricts the animals to representations of perception immediately present to them in time, in other words to real objects. We, on the other hand, by virtue of knowledge in the abstract, comprehend not only the narrow and actual present, but also the whole past and future together with the wide realm of possibility" (*WWR* 1:84). But while this may be to our intellectual advantage, from the perspective of happiness it is a burden. With a mental horizon that includes past and future, we are vulnerable to disappointment, worry, and regret. As with Rousseau, it is not just consciousness but *self*-consciousness that is the culprit: The animals "lack[] reflection, that condenser of pleasures and pains" (*PP* 2:294). Hence "animals are much more satisfied than we by mere existence; . . . due primarily to the fact that [they] remain[] free from *care* and *anxiety* together with their torment" (*PP* 2:296). Still writing before Darwin, Schopenhauer does not picture animal existence, as we might today, as a fearful struggle for existence, speaking instead of the "enviable tranquility and placidity of animals" (*PP* 2:294).

But where Rousseau's account was historical (giving an account of the transition from animal to human), Schopenhauer eschewed all questions of the origins of consciousness. He thought instead that, as the fount of all knowledge and experience, consciousness must itself be the starting point for all philosophical inquiry. This perspective on the proper ordering of philosophical questions Schopenhauer took over from Kant, along with the idea that proper answers to these questions must in some sense be metaphysical. Until the relationship between the knowing mind and the world that it knows is properly mapped (metaphysics), no particular conclusions about the world (physics) could be considered secure. Although today's Kantians might take exception to the claim, Schopenhauer never tired of repeating that he derived his principal ideas from Kant. From the perspective of this inquiry, in what respects he was or was not a genuine Kantian is unimportant, but understanding how Schopenhauer took himself to be building on his predecessor throws considerable light on his perspective.[11]

Schopenhauer was inspired, above all, by Kant's *Critique of Pure Reason*, which attempted to give a full account of the reasoning mind. Kant, though inspired by Locke and Hume, thought that their accounts of the mind were fundamentally incomplete. Where the empiricists declared that experience was the starting point for all human thought and the mind (in Locke's words) "blank paper," Kant argued that experience, by itself, could not account for our understanding of the world. Experience had to

---

[11] See, especially, Magee 1997, chaps. 3–4, and Young 1987. Guyer 1999 offers an excellent discussion of Schopenhauer's critiques of Kant that also lays out their similarities and differences in a systematic way.

be supplemented and, indeed, preceded by what he called the a priori structures of the mind. "Experience" to Kant would just be meaningless noise without conceptual categories to make sense of it. Of these, the concepts of *space*, *time*, and *causality* were the most basic. The existence of these was not a fact about the world that could be verified, but rather a structure of understanding that made it possible for us to organize our experiences into "facts."

Schopenhauer accepted these conclusions and emphasized one consequence—on this account, no conscious thought can be said to perfectly mirror the natural world. Instead thought is always conditioned by the a priori concepts that make it possible; subjective consciousness will always remain at some distance from the objective world. In Kant's terms, which Schopenhauer replicates, the *phenomena* we experience and know are always distinct from the *thing-in-itself*, which must always escape our understanding: "Space, time and causality belong not to the thing-in-itself, but only to the phenomenon, . . . they are only the forms of our knowledge, not qualities of the thing-in-itself" (*WWR* 1:134).

Of these primary forms of knowledge, Schopenhauer came to put the greatest emphasis on time. While perception of the external world requires all three, perception of the internal world—that is, self-consciousness—rests only on time: "Time is primarily the form of the inner sense. . . . Time is . . . the form by means of which self-knowledge becomes possible to the individual will, which originally and in itself is without knowledge" (*WWR* 2:35; see also 2:197). As with Rousseau, the idea is that the animal cannot see itself as a continuous being—cannot form the concept of an "I"—because it does not project itself either into the past or the future, while human beings can do both. But while knowledge of the external world also requires the a prioris of space and causality, "Our self-consciousness has not space as its form, but only *time*; therefore our thinking does not, like our perceiving, take place in *three* dimensions, but merely in *one*" (*WWR* 2:137).

In a perspective that foreshadows Heidegger's, Schopenhauer finds time to be "not merely a form *a priori* of our knowing, but . . . the foundation or ground-bass thereof; it is the primary woof for the fabric of the whole world that manifests itself to us . . . it is the archetype of everything" (*PP* 2:42–43). The fundamental horizon of our consciousness is constituted by temporality. Time is not in the world; rather it forms the boundary of our perceived world. Time here is linear time in the abstract, an infinity stretching both behind us and ahead of us (*WWR* 2:48–51). And from the perspective of our consciousness, there is nothing more fundamental. Even if Pythagoras was right, Schopenhauer says, in claiming that the whole world was reducible to numbers, yet "what are numbers? Relations of succession whose possibility rests on *time*" (*PP* 1:38; see also *WWR*

1:75). As the primary form of the sentient mind, time organizes all our experiences; and this, for Schopenhauer, is where our problems begin.

From the centrality of time in human consciousness, Schopenhauer draws a number of conclusions, the first of which is perhaps the most surprising, namely, the fundamental unreality of time. While Kant had acknowledged the impossibility of verifying the a prioris, he had nonetheless hoped that he could adduce evidence of their reasonableness and believed that their inescapability rested in some sense on the structure of the universe itself (Guyer 1999, 97ff.). Schopenhauer took the opposite tack. Just because of their status as fundamental structures of the mind, he took the a prioris to indicate what the universe was *not*. Real metaphysics, that is, knowledge of the thing-in-itself, was, to him, in some sense impossible. But we could gain an inkling about what lay outside the mind insofar as we could imagine (and it is the most difficult thing to imagine) a world without the a prioris, which meant, above all, a world without linear time.

In his "Fragments for the History of Philosophy," Schopenhauer claimed the proposition, "Time is the intuitive form of our intellect and is, therefore, foreign to the thing-in-itself," was "at bottom identical" with the idea that "the truly real is independent of time and hence is one and the same in every point of time" (*PP* 1:85). But imagining this "independence of time" was profoundly hard since it contradicts the very structures of our mind. We tend to think of eternity in terms of immortality—that is, we project our current existence infinitely forward along the straight line of time, rather than discarding time altogether. Thus, "of an indestructibility which is not a continued existence," Schopenhauer writes, "we can hardly construct even an abstract conception, because we lack every intuition for doing so" (*EA* 67–68). But whether or not we can form a clear conception of the "truly real," he argues, it must be there, bearing a co-responsibility, along with the a prioris, for our perceptions— unless we want to draw the conclusion that our experiences are simply one long dream. If the objects that we see "are not to be empty phantoms, but are to have a meaning, they must point to something . . . that is *not a representation*, but *a thing-in-itself*" (*WWR* 1:119).[12]

We should not think of the thing-in-itself as lifeless, intercelestial matter. We are prone to imagine it this way because we are used to thinking of the mind as the dynamic center of experience—but if time-consciousness is an illusion, we should look for the source of life in the substance, rather than the forms, of our experiences:

---

[12] One thinks here of the later Wittgenstein's description of language as "pointing toward" something, rather than mapping or picturing it. A large literature documents Schopenhauer's relation to Wittgenstein; see, e.g., Brockhaus 1991, Hallett 1977 passim.

Now how could nature throughout endless time endure the maintenance of forms and the renewal of individuals, the countless repetition of the life-process, without becoming weary, unless her own innermost kernel were something timeless and thus wholly indestructible, a thing-in-itself quite different from its phenomena, something metaphysical that is distinct from everything physical? This is the *will* in ourselves and in everything. (*PP* 2:95)

To understand why Schopenhauer refers to the thing-in-itself as the *will*, it is helpful to refer back to Rousseau. Indeed, I think it is a very plausible hypothesis that Schopenhauer derives his usage here from Rousseau's idea of the General Will.[13] For Schopenhauer's will is to the universe what Rousseau's is to a republic: that which animates everything but has no particular physical form. Everything that is truly a part of the republic, for Rousseau, is the product of such a will; everything that is not its product is illusory, unreal—even if a republic may be destroyed by such unrealities. In a parallel sense, for Schopenhauer, will is the intangible source of everything real in our world, although we can still lose ourselves in the illusions to which consciousness gives rise. Indeed, most people most of the time live within such illusions, just as, for Rousseau, few if any human beings have ever lived in a genuine republic. For both writers, as well, the first illusion of time-consciousness, what diverts us from the reality of the will, is a sense of our individuality—which both writers thus urge us to escape, but with little hope that we will succeed in doing so for more than a brief interval. Rousseau recommends the republican abnegation of self that submerges the individual in the general will of the polity; Schopenhauer suggests an ascetic abnegation of self that submerges the individual in the general will of the universe. Thus, Schopenhauer's idea of will also looks forward to Heidegger's "Being." Both indicate the fundamental substance of the universe, present in all things but fractured into individual objects (and thus rendered invisible to us) by our temporal consciousness—but that which we must understand our relationship to if we are to properly orient ourselves in the world.[14] What all

---

[13] There were, of course, many important predecessors to Schopenahauer's idea of will. But it should not be forgotten that it is Rousseau who provides the epigraph for *The World as Will and Representation* (*Sors de l'enfance, ami, réveille-toi!*). Schopenhauer cites Rousseau with enough frequency that one can safely assume a comfortable familiarity on Schopenhauer's part with Rousseau's main texts, which is in no way surprising given both Rousseau's intellectual standing at the time as well as his well-known influence on Kant.

[14] My terminology here is crude, but I hope my meaning is clear. In technical terms, neither Will nor Being would be considered "substances" by Schopenhauer or Heidegger; they are more primordial than that. But since these words are only markers for something that escapes the grammar of subjects and predicates, all other terms will be equally imprecise. There is a complicated relationship of all these ideas to those of Spinoza that I cannot adequately describe here.

of these perspectives share is the fear of a vital gulf that opens between the time-conscious mind and the timeless world that constantly eludes its grasp. It is this gulf that is the source of all the further burdens that Schopenhauer's pessimism elaborates.

Having traced his ideas to this point, we can begin to outline the parallels between Schopenhauer's pessimism and that of Freud. In *Beyond the Pleasure Principle*, Freud projects the timelessness of Schopenhauerian will to the deep interior of each human mind, as the *unconscious*, or *id*. The unconscious, which we can never access directly, is nevertheless that which gives the initial impetus to all our thoughts and urges. Like the will, Freud's unconscious, though it animates everything individual, is nonetheless apart from time, or rather "the idea of time cannot be applied" to its contents, which never change. Time and space are, instead, structures only of our conscious mind that give us our sense of self: "We have learnt that unconscious mental processes are in themselves 'timeless'. This means in the first place that they are not ordered temporally, that time does not change them in any way and that the idea of time cannot be applied to them. These are negative characteristics which can only be clearly understood if a comparison is made with *conscious* mental processes" (*BPP* 31–32. See also *CP* 4:119). By "negative characteristic," Freud means that "timelessness" is not even a real property of the unconscious, but an adjective applied to it by the conscious mind that can only view it across the gulf created by time-consciousness.

The unconscious is, in some sense, that part of us that is the most real ("truly real," Schopenhauer would have said). It is where the depth of our personality is stored. All of our emotions, wishes, and instincts, to Freud, originate there, "the core of our being, consisting of unconscious wishful impulses. . . . The unconscious is the true psychical reality" (*ID* 642, 651).[15] It thus occupies, in Freud's conceptual scheme, exactly the place of Schopehauer's metaphysical will. Like the will, it remains in a permanent state of disjunction from the conscious mind because of its different temporal condition. "To become conscious [for Freud]," as Drassinower puts it, "is to become involved in the universe of time" (2003, 30). Freud does not, as Schopenhauer does, insist that time is an illusion, but the idea that an unbridgeable separation exists between time-bound consciousness and a timeless source of all human motivation—between the will and its representation—and the further idea that this separation is the fundamental cause of human unhappiness, is common to both.

---

15 The individuality of the unconscious is an idea that distinguishes Freud from Schopenhauer, who maintained that individuality was, at bottom, illusory and that the will was both universal and singular. From this perspective, Jung's theory of a "collective unconscious" returns Freud more closely to his Schopenhauerian roots, which may well have been one of the reasons Freud rejected it.

The Reality of Unhappiness

Both Freud and Schopenhauer emphasize how, from a cosmic perspective, conscious life is a minor and temporary deviation from the normal state of things. Schopenhauer speaks of the infinite amount of time both before our birth and after our death, compared to which an individual life is but a moment. Freud describes consciousness as the detour an unconscious wish takes on the way to its satisfaction; and life as a detour from death to death. From this perspective, it is not really surprising that our experience is dominated by unhappiness. Our situation is out-of-joint with the universe to begin with. We cannot hope to set it right—we can only await the release from this predicament provided by death. In the meantime, we merely manage our condition—such management is, to Schopenhauer, the purpose of philosophy; for Freud, it is psychotherapy that serves this end. But the aim, in both cases, is not to create happiness or virtue but to minimize unhappiness by bringing us to greater knowledge of the gap between time-bound consciousness and the timeless reality consciousness defies.

The disjunction between the conscious and unconscious spheres is materialized for both authors in the idea that human beings teem with desires that cannot, in the ordinary course of things, have any hope of being satisfied. For Schopenhauer the idea that "human life must be some kind of mistake is sufficiently proved by the simple observation that man is a compound of needs which are hard to satisfy" (*EA* 53–54). Freud asks, "What do they [men] demand of life and wish to achieve in it? The answer to this can hardly be in doubt. They strive after happiness; they want to become happy and to remain so" (*CD* 24) But he observes that "life, as we find it, is too hard for us; it brings us too many pains, disappointments and impossible tasks" (*CD* 23).

Commentators on Schopenhauer and Freud often emphasize their common interest in sexuality and its inevitable frustrations. While this is correct, the point can obscure the more fundamental focus, in both writers, on the general frustrations of the will, of which sexuality is simply a prominent and tangible example. As I emphasized in the introduction, the primary source of this view for Schopenhauer is the idea that the flow of time constantly depletes our possessions of their value and makes them impossible to secure: "Time is that by virtue of which everything becomes nothingness in our hands and loses all real value" (*EA* 51). Freud does not task time directly but rather names, as Leopardi might say, the various daughters of Decay: the decline of the body, the loss of love from the death or departure of other people, and in general the "overwhelming and merciless forces of destruction" that the external world deploys against all our plans (*CD* 25, 31; see also *CP* 4:152ff.).[16]

But what exactly is the connection between our metaphysical status and the pessimistic conclusion of our permanent unhappiness? Note first of all that Freud follows Schopenhauer in assigning full reality only to unhappiness. As evil is, to Augustine, the absence of good, so, in a striking reversal of this Christian dogma, happiness is, to both thinkers, the absence of unhappiness. "All enjoyment," writes Schopenhauer, "is really only *negative*, only has the effect of removing a pain, while pain or evil, on the other hand, is the actual positive element and is felt directly" (*EA* 168).[17] While Schopenhauer is fond of illustrating this point with bodily metaphors ("we are conscious not of the healthiness of our whole body but only of the little place where the shoe pinches"), he clearly thinks of this as a characteristic feature of our mental life ("so we think not of the totality of our successful activities but of some insignificant trifle or other which continues to vex us") (*EA* 41).

Freud's "pleasure principle" is based on the same assumption. While it is often assumed that this phrase is simply shorthand for the idea that human beings are motivated by the pursuit of pleasure, what Freud actually says is somewhat different. In *Beyond the Pleasure Principle*, he argues that mental events are "invariably set in motion by an unpleasurable tension" and that as a result what we seek is "a lowering of that tension—that is, [] an avoidance of unpleasure or a production of pleasure" (*BPP* 3; see also *EI* 12). In other words, what we actually *experience* is something *unpleasant* and what we call "pleasure" is a reduction of that feeling, not anything with its own positive existence. That suffering is the essence of our mental life and pleasure only its reduction is, of course, an

---

[16] Drassinower calls attention to a brief, early paper of Freud's, "On Transience" (*CP* 5:79–82), in which he claims, against the view of an unnamed "pessimistic poet," that the transience of beauty is no bar to its enjoyment. But it seems clear that Freud abandoned this view, along with its associated idea of a brief, highly efficient mourning period for lost things ("mourning," he says here, "comes to a spontaneous end" [82]), in favor of something much more complicated, tragic, and dubious about our ability to take pleasure in the world.

[17] Rousseau had also written that "the happiest is he who suffers the least pain. . . . Man's felicity on earth is, hence, only a negative condition" (*E* 80). This view of pleasure is not wholly novel to pessimists; it has roots in Epicurean doctrine ("by pleasure we mean the state wherein the body is free from pain and the mind from anxiety" ["Letter to Menoeceus," Epicurus 1964, 57]). Schopenhauer follows Rousseau and Epicurus in describing humans as essentially equilibria-seekers who are moved to action by a disturbance in an existing equilibrium. "Only [when] power and desire [are] in equilibrium" is man "not unhappy" (*E* 80). Of course, nineteenth-century biology, of which Schopenhauer was an avid consumer, was also much concerned with equilibria, so the question of influence is complicated.

idea that greatly contributes to both thinkers' pessimism. But this idea too has a more fundamental root.

Consider Schopenhauer's elaboration of this point:

> All satisfaction, or what is commonly called happiness, is really and essentially always *negative* only, and never positive. It is not a gratification which comes to us originally and of itself, but it must always be the satisfaction of a wish. For desire, that is to say, want, is the precedent condition of every pleasure; but with the satisfaction, the desire and therefore the pleasure cease; and so the satisfaction or gratification can never be more than deliverance from a pain, from a want. (*WWR* 1:319)[18]

In other words, true pleasure is evanescent and constantly receding into the past. When our desires are satisfied, the pain they represented is ended. But as the desire disappears, the pleasure of its satisfaction disappears along with it. When we are thirsty, it is pleasurable to drink, but when the thirst is quenched, the pleasure is likewise ended. The gap between the timelessness of will and the time-boundedness of experience means that while desires are perpetual, satisfactions are constantly disappearing. Our thirst (and not just our thirst, of course) will recur perpetually and preoccupy us; the moments when it disappears, by contrast, are fleeting and leave no lasting pleasure.

Freud's view is much the same and, indeed, from this parallel we can draw a greater understanding of the relation of conscious unhappiness with the larger unconscious from which it arises. In *The Interpretation of Dreams*, he claims famously that "nothing but a wish can set our mental apparatus at work" (*ID* 606). That is, just as for Schopenhauer our consciousness is animated by a will that we cannot directly perceive, so for Freud our unconscious is a never-ending supply of desires that stimulate our mind to action. Freud adds, however, that *within* the unconscious, these desires *can* be instantaneously fulfilled—in dreams or hallucinations. Whatever we want we can instantly experience through the capacity of our mind to create images and sensations that answer to our requirements. And if we could remain forever unconscious we would remain perfectly satisfied. The unconscious "knows no other aim than the fulfillment of wishes and . . . has at its command no other forces than wishful impulses" (*ID* 607).[19]

For Freud, we could well have remained in a condition of perfect timeless unconsciousness—which he repeatedly likens to animality or child-

---

[18] This idea too has a Rousseauvian precedent: "Every desire supposes privation, and all sensed privations are painful" (*E* 80).

[19] The idea of dreams as episodes of wish-fulfillment can also be found in Schopenhauer; see 1974, 1:217.

hood—if only it worked; that is if, in addition to satisfying our desires, it also provided for our continued existence. But it does not. The "bitter experience of life" finally impresses on our mind that the hallucinatory "shortest path" from wish to fulfillment is ultimately inexpedient. Our consciousness emerges as an organ dedicated to helping our unconscious navigate the earth in a perpetual search to gratify its desires in reality rather than through delusion. That is, given ends that are defined by the unconscious, consciousness is that which searches for appropriate practical means: "Thought . . . is nothing but a substitute for a hallucinatory wish" (*ID* 606). It functions by recording the actual workings of the world and supplying the unconscious with the actual steps it must take to secure its ends. For the effects that we wish to produce, consciousness supplies the necessary causes.[20] But rather than the instantaneous gratification that hallucination produces, the *conscious* satisfaction of desires can only take place through a contingent time-bound succession of actual events.

For Freud, then, time first appears to the mind as that which *separates* the wish and its fulfillment. To be conscious is therefore to have emerged from a timeless happiness into a time-bound state that is defined by unhappiness. The "pleasure principle," where wishes were instantaneously fulfilled by hallucination, is replaced by the "reality principle," where wishes set in motion a series of actions that aim toward an unlikely, but more real, fulfillment (see *EI* 15).[21] Thus Freud chides us for thinking of the potential for happiness in terms that echo the Schopenhauer quotation that begins this chapter: "What decides the purpose of life is simply the program of the pleasure principle. . . . and yet its program is at loggerheads with the whole world, with the macrocosm as much as with the microcosm. There is no possibility at all of its being carried through; all the regulations of the universe run counter to it. One feels inclined to say that the intention that man should be 'happy' is not included in the plan of 'Creation'" (*CD* 24–25).

Unhappiness is not something that is created by a particular circum-

---

[20] In Freud too, then, we can hear the echo of Kant's definition of consciousness in terms of space, time, and causality (*BPP* 31). And this correlates with Schopenhauer's belief that "to know causality is the sole function of the understanding, its only power." Indeed, the understanding is just the "subjective correlative" of causality, the manifestation of causality in the mind (*WWR* 1:10–11).

[21] One of Freud's students, Marie Bonaparte, lays great emphasis on the "timelessness" of the unconscious and argues at length that time is the essence of the reality principle and that it is, for this reason, that generations of humans (and philosophers) have sought to escape from it into sleep, dreams, drunkenness, passion, and religious ecstasy (Bonaparte 1952, 24ff.). Her interpretation thus supports that offered here in making the conflict between a time-bound consciousness and a timeless substratum the central source of unhappiness in human affairs. Bonaparte's book also maintains that Freud endorsed her conclusions in conversation, but it is impossible to know what to make of this claim.

stance of our life, as we imagine, but rather by the conditions of conscious existence as such. What is for Schopenhauer the metaphysical conflict between will and representation is, for Freud, the conflict between unconscious and conscious mind. But in both cases the first term signifies a timeless reservoir of striving while the second is defined by a sense of temporality. Pain is more real than pleasure, then, because it is created by the will or unconscious (the core of human reality) in its initial encounter with the world. Pain is the primordial conscious sensation—the sensation of wish and goal being forcibly separated. Pleasure is just the lessening of that sensation, but pain can never be completely relieved so long as we remain conscious.

Even if we achieve an immediate goal, time attacks this achievement. As the desired end moves from the present into the past, it ceases to satisfy us. Schopenhauer likens this pattern to our desire for food, water, and sex. The longing for them is inevitably greater in duration than the experience of them. And the experience of them, however momentarily satisfying, cannot be retained. Hence, we are never (or only momentarily) released from desire, but we nevertheless pursue our objects as if they might satisfy us. The condition of unsatisfied desire is the true constant in our lives:

> We feel pain, but not painlessness; care, but not freedom from care; fear, but not safety and security. We feel the desire as we feel hunger and thirst; but as soon as it has been satisfied, it is like the mouthful of food which has been taken, and which ceases to exist for our feelings the moment it has been swallowed. We painfully feel the loss of pleasures and enjoyments, as soon as they fail to appear; but when pains cease even after being present for a long time, their absence is not directly felt, but at most they are thought of. (WWR 2:575)

But these material goods are just tangible examples of the more general case:

> absence of all aim, of all limits, belongs to the essential nature of the will in itself, which is an endless striving. . . . the same thing is also seen in human endeavors and desires that buoy us up with the vain hope that their fulfillment is always the final goal of willing. But as soon as they are attained, they no longer look the same, and so are soon forgotten, become antiquated, and are really, although not admittedly, always laid aside as vanished illusions. . . . the will always knows . . . what it wills here and now, but never what it wills in general. Every individual act has a purpose or end; willing as a whole has no end in view. (WWR 1:164–65)

The vast majority of our life is neither the moment of our wishes nor their fulfillment, but the time of unsatisfaction that stretches between these two points. And, if this were not enough, time constantly robs our goals and achievements of their reality while leaving untouched the desires that gave rise to them. From this Schopenhauer concludes that we "are" the one thing which remains constant in our lives—will. Beneath all particular desires lies that which ceaselessly generates them; just as for Freud psychic "reality" is the invisible, unconscious source of all our wishes.[22]

It is worth pointing out that here, as elsewhere, Schopenhauer takes a theme—our inability to experience pleasure—that had been articulated by earlier pessimists such as Leopardi, and attempts to give it a metaphysical basis. Though Leopardi had already linked this inability to time-consciousness, he treated this fact almost as a piece of bad luck or divine malevolence. Rousseau added an historical description of its emergence, but did not really seek to explain how the gap between the temporal and timeless was possible. Schopenhauer, however, makes this point the focus of his inquiry. He aims to have his analysis of consciousness yield an account of the structure of the universe such that the human time-bound condition fits neatly into it. Freud, repeating as metapsychology what to Schopenhauer was metaphysics, was not, of course, simply mimicking the pessimism that had preceded him. But even on Freud's own terms, his differences with Schopenhauer ought to be understood (as I argue below) as metaphysical in nature.[23] In both cases, though, if we hold at bay the presumptive superiority of metaphysical argument, their ties to the earlier generation of pessimists becomes more visible.

For Schopenhauer, such a metaphysical approach was by its nature superior to earlier pessimisms since it started from what was, to him, a more fundamental point of reference. But this stance we should view, I believe, more as a function of the passion for metaphysical finality that gripped nineteenth-century Continental thinking than as an inherent quality of Schopenhauer's philosophy. From our perspective, it seems more appro-

---

[22] In parallel fashion, both Freud and Schopenhauer maintain that the existence of the unconscious or will is something they have deduced (rather than seen or experienced) from facts that cannot be otherwise explained. For Freud, it is psychic phenomena such as dreams, which cannot be explained as products of the conscious mind, that point to the existence of the unconscious. For Schopenhauer, it is the repetition of behavior that has been repeatedly proved irrational (like trying to satisfy unquenchable desires) that points to a will beyond the reach of reason.

[23] I realize that a Freudian might object, at this point, that Freud's level of explanation is precisely the point at which he differs (and means to differ) from figures such as Schopenhauer. I maintain, however, that while many elements of Freud's vast argumentative structure may indeed be purely psychological, this psychology rests, in part, on an explicit metaphysics and, in part, on a secondary metaphysics lightly disguised as a metapsychology (e.g., the idea that the unconscious is "timeless"). But I do not say this to diminish Freud, but rather to make his position in the pessimistic tradition more visible.

priate to say that Schopenhauer took pessimistic topics from prior authors and elaborated them at a different level of explanation. Today, it is probably Schopenhauer's metaphysics that strikes us as the least plausible element of his overall philosophy. But the question of time-consciousness and its effects does not depend on this element; as we have seen (and will continue to see), it has arisen again and again in a variety of philosophical contexts. This is yet another reason why we should not wholly identify Schopenhauer and pessimism. The strength and significance of pessimism cannot be held to stand or fall along with the credibility of Schopenhauer's account of will and phenomena—any more than liberalism should stand or fall with Kant's account of the thing-in-itself.

Boredom and Vanity

To the picture of life outlined so far, Schopenhauer adds (as Freud does not) a final pessimistic irony: satisfaction of our desires, even when achieved imperfectly, inevitably leads not to bliss but to boredom. In terms that echo those of Leopardi, he depicts human existence as swinging "like a pendulum to and fro between pain and boredom, and these two are in fact its ultimate constituents" (*WWR* 1:312). Indeed, the very fact that boredom exists at all is proof for Schopenhauer that we are made for unhappiness: "For if life . . . possessed in itself a positive value and real content, there would be no such thing as boredom: mere existence would fulfill and satisfy us. As things are, we take no pleasure in existence except when we are striving after something" (*EA* 53–54). Like Leopardi, Schopenhauer takes boredom to be our reaction to bare conscious continuity as such, waking life uninterrupted by any activity. So long as we are engaged in pursuit of some goal, we are distracted from the empty, illusory nature of our lives. But in those brief periods when we are satisfied, we are thrown back on raw existence itself. And mere consciousness, founded on the illusions of space and time, has little to offer. It is then that we become most aware of what Schopenhauer refers to as the vanity, or nothingness, of existence (*der Nichtigkeit des Daseins*) (Schopenhauer 1972, 6:301).

As I argued in chapter 1, boredom is a special concern of the pessimists. While recognizing that boredom is an evil to be ranked below outright pain, Schopenhauer argues, as Leopardi did before him, that boredom is a form of suffering only possible in conscious beings. Indeed, for Schopenhauer boredom is the result of a kind of intuitive understanding of our metaphysical situation, the root of which is our location in time. When Schopenhauer speaks of the vanity of existence, he does not, as a Christian would, have in mind the emptiness of everything earthly as contrasted with the heavenly. Rather, he has in mind the illusion of the phenomenal, temporal, conscious world as opposed to the real but invisible world of the will: "The way in which this *vanity* [*Nichtigkeit*] of all objects of the will makes itself known and comprehensible to the intellect that is rooted in the individual, is primarily *time*. It is the form by whose means that vanity of things appears as their transitoriness, since by virtue of this all our pleasures and enjoyments come to nought in our hands" (*WWR* 2:574).

Just as there is a common element in all individual wishes that is the will, so it is proper to say that it is this *Nichtigkeit* that is "the only *objective* element of time, in other words, that which corresponds to it in the inner nature of things" (*WWR* 2:574).[24] *Boredom*, then, appears as a correlate of this essential emptiness of conscious experience, something we become aware of when we temporarily cease our striving for individual goals and are thrown back upon simple existence. Not a product of reason, it is nonetheless a cognizance of the evanescent quality of all worldly goods. This is yet another reason why the achievement of individual aims yields no satisfaction. Active suffering is our normal condition; but with pleasure having no positive existence, the relief of pain only delivers us to boredom, a lesser suffering. And to relieve boredom we seek out new goals. Schopenhauer's metaphor of swinging between pain and boredom "like a pendulum" is meant to be exact—each extreme impels us back toward the other.

Like the cultural pessimists, Schopenhauer's picture of human life is meant to yield an ironic conclusion. Here, however, the irony is not historical but, we might say, pedagogic. Our striving is, on the surface, futile; but at another level it achieves an end quite different (and to Schopenhauer more valuable) than what we intended. Although we may achieve our stated goals, they bring us little or no satisfaction. Through this process, however, we *do* achieve something real—namely, an *understanding* of the futility of our actions. We come to *grasp* the vanity of existence—the one thing we *can* hold onto—as our efforts to grasp at material objects are revealed as pointless. This decidedly unsentimental education is what Schopenhauer refers to in the opening quotation for this chapter: "Everything in life is certainly calculated to bring us back from that original error, and to convince us that the purpose of our existence is not to be happy" (*WWR* 2:635). It is in this fashion that our illusions about the purpose of life are replaced with the truth. And despite the abstract language that Schopenhauer uses to describe this truth, the

---

[24] Rather than puzzling over the apparent contradiction in the concept of an "objective nothingness," I think it is better to think of Schopenhauer's terminology here as the product of a very dry humor. While he is perfectly serious in maintaining that our conscious life is essentially an illusion, this means of expressing it is *also* meant to express, I think, the absurdity of the situation in which we find ourselves: where all that we can be sure of is that we cannot be sure of anything, or rather we can only be sure that nothing around us is real.

widespread experience of boredom confirms that its substance is easily grasped: "Hence the countenances of almost all elderly persons wear the expression of what is called *disappointment*" (*WWR* 2:635). The knowledge that Leopardi saw accumulating through history, Schopenhauer pictures as accruing in a single life:

> The fundamental characteristic of old age is disillusionment; the illusions which hitherto gave life its charm and spurred us to activity have vanished. We have recognized the vanity and emptiness of all the splendors of the world. . . . We have learnt that there is very little behind most of the things desired and most of the pleasures hoped for; and we have gradually gained an insight into the great poverty and hollowness of our whole existence. Only when we are seventy do we thoroughly understand the first verse of Ecclesiastes. (*PP* 1:494)[25]

As we have seen, Freud too mocks the notion that modern life is an especially happy existence. Unlike Schopenhauer, however, Freud says nothing about boredom—and this small difference affords us a window onto larger ones. From these larger differences, we will be able to see why Freud, though no less pessimistic than Schopenhauer, rejects the policy of resignation that the latter favors.

The great difference between Freud and Schopenhauer is at bottom metaphysical. Boredom, for Schopenhauer is the result of the unreality of our conscious life. But Freud, though he shares with Schopenhauer the sense of a deeper unconscious "reality," does not find conscious life wholly insubstantial. That this is obviously the case can be seen just in the name Freud gives to the lesson the mind receives in the necessity of navigating the world according to its causal structure—"the reality principle." In equating dreams and hallucinations and contrasting them with the everyday perceptions of waking life, Freud leaves little doubt that the world that the conscious mind makes out is real and that the temporality within which it operates is real as well, if unfortunate.[26] Like Rousseau,

---

[25] Actually, Schopenhauer has in mind the second verse. In the King James version: "Vanity of vanities, saith the Preacher, vanity of vanities; all is vanity" (Ecclesiastes 1:2).

[26] Freud never makes clear how the "reality" of the reality principle is related to the "true psychical reality" of the unconscious. Which, we might well ask, is more real? Or how can they both be real when their fundamental parameters (in time or out of it?) seem to differ so radically? Here, I think, we see Freud's desire to give his theory a conventional scientific basis struggling with the substance of the theory, which resists that frame. (He may also have thought that his "topographical" account of the mind somehow resolved this problem, though I cannot see how it would. There are also some scattered remarks on the "origin of the concept of time" that may also be attempts, unsuccessful in my view, to address the question. See *CP* 5:180; *BPP* 32) From a Schopenhauerian perspective, Freud's metaphysical stance may well be inconsistent. However, given the difficulties of Schopenhauer's own metaphysics, and given the way in which Freud's theory meets up more naturally with our intu-

he considers the human comprehension of time to be a true intellectual advance for our species, even if it affords us no pleasure and much misery. Rather than challenge the reality of our time-consciousness, as Schopenhauer does, he seeks only to cope with its effects. Our actions may be vain in the sense that they do not bring us the happiness at which they aim, but not in the larger sense—Freud never uses terms such as "nothingness" to describe them. So while Freud would certainly have acknowledged the existence of boredom, it simply did not have the far-reaching significance for him that it did for Schopenhauer.[27]

Our behavior, to Freud, is futile in a practical sense, not a metaphysical one. Indeed, in repeatedly identifying the pleasure principle with infancy and animality, Freud means to encourage our efforts to replace it more fully with the reality principle. To accept the limitations of our time-bound condition is for Freud the mark of emotional and intellectual maturity; to resist them is childish. Where Schopenhauer's philosophy, as we will see below, teaches us to leave this world behind to the greatest extent possible, Freud's psychotherapy attempts to give us the tools with which to engage it. Both approaches, to be sure, can be seen as responses to the dilemma of time. But the metaphysical differences between the two writers lead to very different prescriptions.

Vanity and Death

Death, as I argued in chapter 1, is a primary theme in all pessimistic theory. The close link between consciousness of time and consciousness of death that was evident in the cultural pessimists is equally evident in the metaphysical pessimists. For both Freud and Schopenhauer the centrality of death is a defining feature of their philosophies, and a refusal to acknowledge death is one of the chief weaknesses in the optimism to which they are opposed. Schopenhauer writes that "dying is certainly to be regarded as the real aim of life" and Freud repeats that "'the aim of all life is death'" (WWR 2:637; BPP 46). The condition of living is, to them, the exceptional condition, which thus always tends to return to the nonliving norm. Their differing metaphysics, however, also produce subtle differences here that are important to note.

---

itions (i.e., that both the inner and the outer world are in some sense real, even if we cannot explain their relationship), I do not think we should consider this objection a crippling one.

[27] In good pessimistic style, however, Freud does allow that pleasures, once achieved, lose their value: "When any situation that is desired by the pleasure principle is prolonged, it only produces a feeling of mild contentment. We are so made that we can derive intense enjoyment only from a contrast and very little from a state of things. Thus our possibilities of happiness are already restricted by our constitution" (CD 25).

Replicating Rousseau's argument, Schopenhauer emphasizes the element of dread that the presence of death adds to consciousness as such. Through "the addition of thought which the animal lacks," he writes, "the measure of pain increases in man much more than that of pleasure and is now in a special way very greatly enhanced by the fact that death is actually *known* to him" (*PP* 2:295). Man, in his ability to project his imagination into the future, can arrive at the hour of his own death. The animal, stuck in the present, never fears death and avoids it "merely instinctively" (*PP* 2:295; see also *WWR* 2:463). The animal never suffers death as such; rather, death puts an end to its sufferings. Humans, on the other hand, suffer from the anticipation of death; indeed, they suffer much more from the anticipation of it than from the event itself.

But ultimately, for Schopenhauer, this dread is needless. If we understand his philosophy, he claims, we will be free of it. To him, death is important not as a source of pain but as concrete evidence of the vanity of conscious existence and the pedagogic irony of our life-histories. Death is the ultimate expression of the meaning of our lives, or more precisely, of the absence of meaning of our lives—but even more precisely, of the meaning of our lives consisting in the gradual realization of the absence of such meaning. He continues the passage that begins by naming death as the aim of life with the following gloss: "Death is the result, the *résumé*, of life, or the total sum expressing at one stroke all the instruction given by life in detail and piecemeal, namely that the whole striving, the phenomenon of which is life, was a vain, fruitless, and self-contradictory effort, to have returned from which is a deliverance" (*WWR* 2:637).

Death, to Schopenhauer, is not the end of our existence but merely the end of our illusory *conscious* experience. The will, he believes, continues to exist—and its existence is more peaceful in death without the irritation produced by the illusions of consciousness. Death is thus the logical and desirable culmination of a life that teaches us not to want it: "As a mature consideration of the matter leads to the result that complete nonexistence would be preferable to an existence such as ours, the thought of a cessation of our existence, or of a time when we shall no longer exist, cannot reasonably disturb us any more than can the idea that we might never have come into existence" (*PP* 2:268). Thus we should be no more disturbed by the thought of our death, and our nonexistence thereafter, then we are disturbed by the idea that we did not exist for millions of years before our birth. And no one, he observes, ever complains about the latter.

This is perhaps the place to mention that Schopenhauer does not endorse suicide, as is sometimes assumed, though neither does he abhor it (see *PP* 2:306ff). His resistance to it guides us against a misinterpretation of the above. The "existence" he speaks of in the last quotation is conscious existence, existence of the individual self, which is all that suicide can put an end to. And since this existence is essentially illusory, suicide, as such, changes nothing, "it affords no escape" (*WWR* 1:366). It is just one more futile gesture in a lifetime of futile gestures. The genuine reality of our selves, our will, is unaffected by it, as it is not affected by any kind of death. So, for Schopenhauer, if we grasp his metaphysics, we will realize the evanescent quality of life and thus the insubstantiality of death, even a self-willed death. Naturally, we cannot entirely escape our dread of it, since this is built into the structure of our consciousness. But we can blunt the force of that feeling through an understanding of its origin.

It is yet another common misunderstanding of pessimism that it must lead to endorsement of suicide. While some of the pessimists, particularly Schopenhauer and Leopardi, have a great deal of sympathy for those who find the burdens of existence too much for them, none of the pessimists recommend suicide and indeed, for the most part, their aim is to find reasons to oppose it. What distinguishes pessimists from optimists here is their willingness to take the rationale for suicide *seriously* and to admit that it is sometimes difficult to make a case for remaining a part of this world. Schopenhauer does so, and he ridicules the Christian arguments against suicide as "feeble sophisms" (*PP* 2:309). But the *act* of suicide is, to him, a claim to a sort of knowledge that, as good Kantians, we should realize is beyond our grasp.

Schopenhauer brings together many of these views in a dialogue, reminiscent of those of Leopardi, between Thrasymachos and Philalethes that appears in the *Parerga and Paralipomena*. Thrasymachos expresses what Schopenhauer takes to be the ordinary human desire for earthly immortality, while his interlocutor attempts to condense the Schopenhauerian metaphysic and view on death into a few pithy sentences.[28]

> PHILALETHES: You as an individual end at your death; but the individual is not your true and ultimate essence, but rather a mere manifestation thereof. It is not the thing-in-itself, but only its phenomenon which man-

---

[28] The character names Schopenhauer uses here are very carefully chosen. Thrasymachos, of course, is Socrates' initial opponent in the *Republic*, where he tenaciously defends his self-interestedness "like a wild beast." Philalethes is normally translated as "lover of truth" (from the Greek *philos* and *alethia*; there was a seventeenth-century alchemist who wrote under this name). However, Schopenhauer may also have in mind Lethe, a river in the Greek underworld that erased the memories of those who crossed it and the root of the English words "lethal" and "lethargy." Philalethes would then mean "lover of death" or "lover of oblivion," which also fits well with the position Schopenhauer's character articulates.

"Philalethes" appears in another Schopenhauerian dialogue on religion with "Demophiles" (lover of the people) (*PP* 2:324–60). Philip Rieff discusses the way in which Freud's *Future of an Illusion* includes a dialogue that appears to closely parallel this one with, however, the difference that Freud tilts the argument much more strongly to his own Philalethian position than does Schopenhauer (Rieff 1961, 323ff.). My thanks to Verity Smith for calling my attention to this.

ifests itself in the form of time and accordingly has a beginning and an end. On the other hand, your true essence-in-itself does not know either time, beginning, end or the limits of a given individuality . . .

THRASYMACHOS: I, I, I want to exist! *That* is of importance to me and not an existence concerning which one must first convince me by arguments that it is mine.

PHILALETHES: Now look! That which exclaims "I, I, I want to exist" is not you alone but everything, absolutely everything, that has even only a trace of consciousness. Consequently, this desire in you is precisely that which is *not* individual, but is without distinction common to all. It springs not from individuality, but from existence generally, is essential to everything that *exists*, indeed is that *whereby* it exists, and accordingly is satisfied by existence *in general* to which alone it refers, and not exclusively through any definite individual existence. . . . [The latter] is a mere illusion to which indeed the individual's narrow-mindedness clings, but which reflection can destroy. . . . [I]ndividuality is no perfection but a limitation, and . . . to be rid of it is, therefore, no loss, but rather a gain. Therefore give up a fear that would seem to you to be childish and utterly ridiculous if you knew thoroughly and to its very foundation your own nature, namely as the universal will to life. (*PP* 2:279–82)

Thrasymachos is unconvinced by these speeches (just as he is not convinced, but merely subdued in the *Republic*), but of all Plato's characters, he is most famous for his stubbornness. The rest of us, Schopenhauer hopes, can be persuaded to at least combat our fear of death and, perhaps, to overcome it to some degree. Schopenhauer's pessimism, then, is not meant to accentuate our fear of death, but rather to place death in its proper context and to reduce its control over us. But that control is increased if we avoid the topic or deny how death ordinarily preoccupies us, as optimists do.

While Freud too views life as an unusual disturbance in a universal field of natural, nonliving matter, his metaphysical differences with Schopenhauer do not allow him to view death with quite the degree of equanimity that Schopenhauer does. Freud does not try to combat our instinct that, in dying, we lose something real and valuable. But he does offer an explanation of that instinct, which seeks to put it in a different light. As with Schopenhauer, death for Freud is the end of a struggle that we were born to lose. But Freud does not dismiss the struggle as illusory; to him, it is all too real. This means too that the individuality that we lose at the end of our lives is something real and that its loss is something to be regretted. Although Freud will admit that we may have been happier as animals, he cannot bring himself to prefer such a status of ignorance.

Just as, for Freud, a wish is an interruption of an equilibrium that our actions, in fulfilling the wish, seek to restore, so is all life a matter of a similar pattern of disturbance and return. Life, he tells us, was "at some time evoked in inanimate matter" by a process we can only make guesses about. But the result of that process, in the creation of instincts, can at least be outlined:

> The tension which then arose in what had hitherto been an inanimate substance endeavoured to cancel itself out. In this way the first instinct came into being: the instinct to return to the inanimate state. . . . For a long time, perhaps, living substance was thus being constantly created afresh and easily dying, till decisive external influences altered it in such a way as to oblige the still surviving substance to diverge ever more widely from its original course of life and to make ever more complicated *détours* before reaching its aim of death. (*BPP* 46)

Instincts (but, as we shall see, not all instincts) are in the service of a restoration of equilibrium. And many of the behaviors that we believe to be in the interest of self-preservation are actually meant to "assure that the organism shall follow its own path to death, and to ward off any . . . other. . . . [T]he organism wishes to die only in its own fashion" (*BPP* 47). This is Freud's instantiation of the idea that all life aims at death—death is the biological *telos* of life, rather than the meaning of it, as in Schopenhauer. Although it is a mistake to pretend that it can be avoided, Freud would never say that having death on our horizon teaches us not to want life.

When Freud refers to the "harbour of Schopenhauer's philosophy," he actually has something else in mind: the conflict *between* these instincts and the will to live, embodied in sexuality (*BPP* 59–60). Opposed to the original death-instincts, as Freud calls them, are the sexual instincts that seek to preserve life—to extend the detour taken by life in its inevitable course toward death. "One group of instincts rushes forward so as to reach the final aim of life as swiftly as possible; but when a particular stage in the advance has been reached, the other group jerks back to a certain point to make a fresh start and so prolong the journey" (*BPP* 49). The result is an unending conflict between life and death, played out as a battle of instincts within the psyche. Once again I think it is fairly clear that Freud has taken a metaphysical clash from Schopenhauer and rendered it into what he calls "metapsychological" terms. But with the difference that the two opponents now have equal status; life is not an illusion. Freud's pessimism thus focuses more on the tragic, perpetual conflict between these two sides of the human mind than on the emptiness of life. Schopenhauer too thought that we suffered from the struggle between life and death, but he thought that the struggle itself was pointless and, in some sense, avoidable. For Freud, the struggle defines our beings and can be

managed, but not avoided: "The sexual instincts . . . are the true life instincts. They operate against the purpose of the other instincts, which
leads, by reason of their function, to death. . . . It is as though the life of
the organism moved with a vacillating rhythm" (*BPP* 48–49). Where for
Schopenhauer we are tossed between pain and boredom, for Freud it is
Eros and Thanatos that take turns tormenting us. "This struggle is what
all life essentially consists of" (*CD* 77).[29] The irony of our situation consists not so much in the futility of our efforts, but rather in the fact that
the two sides to the struggle are part of the same being but do not acknowledge this.

The work of psychotherapy is thus the task of improving this condition
for us, of making the swings of the pendulum less violent. Freud famously
described it as the process of shaping "hysterical misery into common unhappiness" (Freud 1953, 2:305). And, in contrast to suicide, there are
some grounds for thinking this possible. We cannot escape the temporal
condition that creates this unhappiness. But we can, in understanding our
condition, come to a less painful accommodation with it. It is this, and
only this, limited project about which Freud can be said to be hopeful or
even, as he puts it in *The Future of an Illusion*, "optimistic" (Freud 1961c,
53).[30] Freud's therapy attempts to give individuals the tools they need to
fortify their position in this world. Schopenhauer, as we shall see, attempts
to give them the vehicle to escape it.

Pessimistic Resignation and the Fortified Self

The metaphysical pessimists, as we have seen, attribute much human unhappiness to our status in the universe, about which we can do nothing.
This can cause their work to appear apolitical as, for example, when
Schopenhauer writes that "people have always been very discontented
with governments, laws and public institutions; for the most part, however, this has been only because they have been ready to blame them for
the wretchedness which pertains to human existence as such" (*EA* 154).
But for Schopenhauer and Freud the point of such remarks is to turn our

[29] Like Schopenhauer, Freud exhibits little interest in describing or explaining how we
came to leave behind animal happiness. "Why do our relatives, the animals, not exhibit any
such cultural struggle? We do not know" (*CD* 78).

[30] Abraham Drassinower, who points to this text in an effort to rebut the idea of Freud
as a pessimist, nonetheless calls Freud's theory "less a call for resignation than an inter-
twining of a profound encounter with the necessity of unhappiness and an uncompromis-
ing indictment of the culture he describes" (2003, 13). My only disagreement with this is in
the equation of pessimism and resignation. Otherwise, Drassinower's analysis is very much
in agreement with the one presented here.

attention to the true sources of our difficulties and guide us in designing what limited remedies are possible. It is here, as I have indicated above, that their philosophies diverge. Schopenhauer advocates an ethic of resignation, descended from Rousseau's wish to absent himself from his individuality and float indistinguishably on the sea of time. Freud, while not perhaps the defender of heroic vigor that Leopardi was, nonetheless pursues an engagement with the world that is at odds with Schopenhauer's ethic. While only tangentially concerned with state structures (concerned enough, however, to denounce the false promises of socialism and fascism), it would be wrong to call Freud's project apolitical. Instead, Freud would claim, he is concerned with those social and cultural conditions that are vitally connected to human freedom and happiness.

Despite the tone of paternalistic certainty that both can employ, there is an inherent modesty of purpose in their attempts to aid human beings, born from the sense of limitations imposed by their theories. Schopenhauer writes that it would be "just as foolish to expect that our moral systems and ethics would create virtuous, noble, and holy men, as that our aesthetics would produce poets, painters, and musicians" (*WWR* 1:271). Nonetheless, he devotes an enormous section of the *Parerga and Paralipomena* to "Aphorisms on the Wisdom of Life," wherein he takes "the idea of wisdom of life entirely in the immanent sense, namely that of the art of getting through life as pleasantly and successfully as possible, the instructions to which might also be called eudemonology" (*PP* 1:313). He explains, however, that "Eudemonology must begin by informing us that its very name is a euphemism and that, when we say 'to live happily', we are to understand by this merely 'to live less unhappily' and hence to live a tolerable life" (*PP* 1:405). Freud's remark about "common unhappiness" echoes this theme. Whatever else their pessimism does, it does not make false promises.

For Schopenhauer, even if one were to set aside the metaphysical strictures, our happiness is largely dependent on the health of our body and the bodies of our friends and family—things that are also largely out of our control. While we do not have the power to make ourselves happy, we do have the power to limit our unhappiness through our capacity for self-denial or resignation. The resignation that Schopenhauer encourages is not exactly a suggestion of hopelessness or helplessness. Rather, resignation is a positive act, or set of acts, the one thing we can actually do to improve our situation, as when one resigns in protest.[31] To understand how Schopenhauer arrives at this position, we must recall his understanding of the problem. Our suffering is created by the striving of our will in a universe that can only punish such striving. Since we cannot

[31] See Dumm 1998.

change the nature of the universe, it follows that to improve our situation we must cease our striving.[32] But since this striving is the essence of our individuated existence, to put an end to it without suicide means to live in a state of pure self-denial or radical asceticism. We must attempt to abolish our own will, or rather, to use our will to subdue itself.[33] While Schopenhauer's atheism forbids him from endorsing Christianity, he nonetheless urges us to contemplate "the life and conduct of the saints" as our best example of this ethic—with one crucial difference. What the saint does from faith, the pessimist does from the *knowledge* that striving is pointless and his individuality an illusion. It is this knowledge, rather than obedience to a divine will, that motivates him.

> But we now turn our glance from our own needy and perplexed nature to those who have overcome the world, in whom the will, having reached complete self-knowledge, has found itself again in everything, and then freely denied itself, and who then merely wait to see the last trace of the will vanish with the body that is animated by that trace. Then, instead of the restless pressure and effort; instead of the constant transition from desire to apprehension and from joy to sorrow; instead of the never-satisfied and never-dying hope that constitutes the life-dream of the man who wills, we see that peace that is higher than all reason, that ocean-like calmness of the spirit, that deep tranquility, that unshakable confidence and serenity, whose mere reflection in the countenance, as depicted by Raphael and Correggio, is a complete and certain gospel. Only knowledge remains; the will has vanished. (*WWR* 1:411)

Perfect self-denial is an exceptional state that few can be expected to achieve. But there are, for Schopenhauer, a variety of experiences that enable us to simulate this condition and thus provide a kind of education for those seeking to draw closer to it. Foremost among these is aesthetic experience. Schopenhauer often speaks of the knowledge necessary to support self-denial as that which replaces subjectivity with objectivity— and objectivity is just what he takes great works of art to have achieved. (The portraits of Raphael and Correggio, referred to above, are thus doubly objective—the objective portrayal of a person who has achieved a state of objectivity). Old Master painting, especially, embodies Schopen-

---

[32] Another Rousseauvian echo: "The real world has its limits; the imaginary world is infinite. Unable to enlarge the one, let us restrict the other, for it is from the difference between the two alone that are born all the pains which make us truly unhappy" (*E* 81).

[33] Readers of Nietzsche will recognize the ethic Schopenhauer describes here as bearing a close resemblance to the general idea of modern "morality" that Nietzsche denounces in *On the Genealogy of Morals*. It is part of Nietzsche's debt to Schopenhauer that he takes his predecessor's account to have revealed things about morality as such that many of its exponents (especially the Christian ones) were unaware of. For more on this relationship, see chapter 5. For a useful study of the possibility of such a posture, see Clarke 1970.

hauer's meaning here and it is his most frequent example—these paintings abstract from time and capture the essence of their subject, whether in a still life or a portrait. They depict what is permanent and real about their subject, apart from the daily flux of existence.[34]

That we all have moments where we appreciate beauty is, to Schopenhauer, evidence that we are all capable of this experience of objectivity, which is equivalent to stepping out of time. The fact that there are naturally gifted artists, however, is equally evidence that some of us are more capable of it than others. "The artist," he writes, "lets us peer into the world through his eyes. . . . That he has these eyes, . . . is the gift of genius and is inborn" (*WWR* 1:195). But Schopenhauer's idea of genius is quite the opposite from how we think of it today. There is nothing, to him, individualized about the vision of an artistic genius. His personality does not enter in any way into his work; rather, it is his ability to shed his personality that distinguishes him. "Only through the pure contemplation described above, which becomes absorbed entirely in the object, are the Ideas comprehended; and the nature of *genius* consists precisely in the preeminent ability for such contemplation. . . . this demands a complete forgetting of our own person" (*WWR* 1:185). The artist's gift is not for displaying his individuality but precisely for surpressing it.[35]

Even for such geniuses, though, the escape that art affords is never permanent. Pure objectivity is not a stance we can perpetually occupy. We remain citizens of the natural world and sooner or later our wills and our bodies will reassert themselves. Then we experience once again the fall into time-consciousness that is the source of our ordinary unhappiness. "There always lies so near to us a realm in which we have escaped entirely from all our affliction; but who has the strength to remain in it for long? As soon as any relation to our will, to our person, even of those objects of pure contemplation, again enters consciousness, the magic is at an end" (*WWR* 1:197–98). The experience of the aesthetic is *like* losing yourself, it is *like* dissolving the boundary between the I and the not-I.[36] But ultimately it is not such a dissolving; the boundary always remains and always reasserts itself.

---

[34] This might be contrasted with Impressionist painting that, in an opposite fashion, seeks to capture a moment *of time*—that is, rather than escaping time, Impressionism seeks to depict the daily flux of existence by capturing the opposite of the permanent, namely, the moment that can never come again.

[35] Though he does not acknowledge this, Schopenhauer shares this theory of artistic genius with Hegel. See Hegel 1975, 280ff., and Dienstag 1997, chap. 5.

[36] Traditional aesthetic theory distinguishes between the experience of the beautiful and that of the sublime. Schopenhauer acknowledges the distinction but attempts to argue that, finally, they are the same experience of loss-of-self achieved by different routes (see *WWR* 1:195–207).

Likewise, aesthetic pleasure, just as with any other kind of pleasure, is essentially negative; it is nothing more than the relief of our ordinary sufferings by means of a temporary escape from our subjectivity. The metaphor of "losing yourself" in a work of art is, for Schopenhauer, exact: "On the occurrence of an aesthetic appreciation, the will thereby vanishes entirely from consciousness. . . . This is the origin of that satisfaction and pleasure which accompany the apprehension of the beautiful. . . . To become a pure subject of knowing means to be quit of oneself" (*PP* 2:415–16). Aesthetic experience is not limited to encounters with works of art. We may have it in the contemplation of nature as well. The important point is that people have the experience of "divesting themselves for a moment of their personality" (*WWR* 1:194).

In all of this we can see a desire, in Schopenhauer, for the same kind of happiness contemplated by Rousseau when he floated on a Swiss lake. As in the Stoic practice of asceticism, the self-denial that he recommends is not intended as a punishment but as a liberation. "Resignation," he maintains, "is like the inherited estate; it frees its owner from all care and anxiety for ever" (*WWR* 1:390). Optimism, in whatever form, demands that we see our life as a project, with achievement and happiness as goals at which everyone can justifiably aim and, indeed, is entitled to. "Optimism is not only a false but also a pernicious doctrine. . . . everyone then believes he has the most legitimate claim to happiness and enjoyment. If, as usually happens, these do not fall to his lot, he believes that he suffers an injustice" (*WWR* 2:584).[37] Pessimism liberates us from this narrative of individual progress as it denies the larger narrative of historical progress. It may not assure happiness, but it relieves us from the unhappiness that optimism, quite unwittingly, generates and guarantees. Although we cannot escape time any more than we can jump out of our skins (or think ourselves unconscious), we can free ourselves from a mindless, repetitive pattern of striving and suffering that an unthinking optimism condemns us to. We can fortify ourselves against the worst of time's effects: "It is really the greatest absurdity to try to turn this scene of woe and lamentation into a pleasure-resort. . . . Whoever takes a gloomy view regards this world as a kind of hell and is accordingly concerned only with procuring for himself a small fireproof room; such a man is much less mistaken" (*PP* 1:406).

Such a "fireproof room" is not something we can build once and then blissfully inhabit. Despite the remark above about an inherited estate, Schopenhauerian resignation is not a condition of listlessness or inactivity. Just because we remain bodily, time-bound creatures, we will forever

---

[37] We can see here the roots of Nietzsche's characterization of *ressentiment* as "the will's ill-will against time"; see chapter 5.

struggle to apply our knowledge to our lives. Once again, the lives of "saintly persons" are exemplary in this regard.

> We must not imagine that, after the denial of the will-to-live has once appeared through knowledge . . . such denial no longer wavers or falters, and that we can rest on it as on an inherited property. On the contrary, it must always be achieved afresh by constant struggle. . . . that whole will-to-live exists potentially so long as the body lives, and is always striving to reach actuality and to burn afresh with all its intensity. We therefore find in the lives of saintly persons that peace and bliss we have described, only as the blossom resulting from the constant overcoming of the will . . . for on earth no one can have lasting peace. (*WWR* 1:391)

The life Schopenhauer envisages, then, is one of constant self-fortification through efforts at self-denial. Each of us must struggle continuously to maintain his own defenses against the flow of time. In knowing what to do, the pessimist also knows that he will only be able to do it imperfectly. Correlatively, the freedom that is thereby achieved is never secure. It is always threatened by the same individuality that produces it.

That such a pessimistic ethic will *also* have the effect of motivating behavior that is conventionally moral is, for Schopenhauer, nothing more than a happy coincidence. His "eudemonology" aims at freedom and controlling unhappiness, to whatever extent these are possible. Like Stoicism, his is a philosophy of the self, a guide to practical existence on Earth, not a set of moral duties. It is only because peace of mind requires an end to selfish behavior that the pessimist ends up acting virtuously. Schopenhauer praises Stoicism precisely for this insight, which to him differentiates it from all other ethical systems: "the Stoic ethics is originally and essentially not a doctrine of virtue, but merely a guide to the rational life, whose end and aim is happiness through peace of mind. Virtuous conduct appears in it, so to speak, only by accident, as means, not as end" (*WWR* 1:86–87). If one wanted to complain that, on this account, neither he nor Stoicism offers a moral theory at all, but a eudemonology with moral consequences, Schopenhauer would no doubt reply "so much the better."

We might also say that Schopenhauer advises us to give up the search for positive happiness in the name of freedom—that to be truly free is to be free from the demands of one's desires. This too is a radicalization of Rousseau's idea that freedom is primarily a liberation from unnatural wants—a freedom obtained by a knowledge of the "vanity" of those desires. Of course, the idea of freedom as the ability to contradict one's own desires is an old one, appearing as far back as Augustine and the Stoics, reappearing in Calvin and Locke and also, between Rousseau and Schopenhauer, in Kant. But the likeness to Rousseau can also be seen in Schopenhauer's rejection of society, which can equal Jean-Jacques's in its extremity, for example, "Everyone can *be entirely himself* only so long as he is alone . . . only when a man is alone is he free" (*PP* 1:419).

Must we, then, give up happiness entirely on this account? Yes and no. What we must abandon is the idea that happiness is something we have a right to and something that we might obtain by some labor or technique. Instead, we must understand how subject we are to fate and chance, fortify our position, and expect little or nothing from life. We can build the strongest vessel possible and still have no control over where the currents take us. Happiness—the radical absence of unhappiness—is an occasion or a circumstance that we may stumble upon, or not, from time to time. We cannot reach it by any map or method. "Where [joy] actually makes its appearance," Schopenhauer writes, "it as a rule comes uninvited and unannounced, by itself and *sans façon* [unceremoniously]. Indeed, it quietly slips in often on the most unimportant and trivial occasions, in the most ordinary everyday circumstances. . . . It is scattered here and there, like the gold in Australia, by the whim of pure chance according to no rule or law, often only in tiny grains, and exceedingly rarely in large quantities" (*PP* 1:419; see also 1:468). Not expecting happiness, we may occasionally find it—Schopenhauer's pessimism does not rule out this possibility. To refrain from offering a guarantee of happiness is pessimism enough.

.   .   .   .   .

In contrast to all this, Freud's pessimism yields an ethic that is both more engaged with the world and more conventional. To use a phrase with a heavy history, Freud's is a more worldly asceticism. Since Freud does not share Schopenhauer's belief in the fundamental unreality of phenomena, the retreat from the world that Schopenhauer advises appears implausible to Freud and he never seriously contemplates it. Indeed, he repeatedly characterizes it as childish. The opening pages of *Civilization and Its Discontents*, for example, examine the persistence of an "oceanic feeling" of "oneness with the universe"—which seems like Schopenhauer's doctrine of the unity of the will lightly disguised—and concludes by tracing this feeling back to the "limitless narcissism" of infants (*CD* 20).[38] The reality of Freud's reality principle requires him to take a different approach.

Nevertheless, we can see in Freud's practice of pessimism many parallels with that of Schopenhauer. Despite Freud's efforts to establish psychoanalysis as a science, we might well understand its methods and purposes better if we treat it as a "eudemonology." Like Schopenhauer, Freud

---

[38] Freud puts his finger on something here—Rousseau's description of his moments of perfect happiness occurring when he is alone with his thoughts floating on a lake seems both reminiscent of Freud's description and deeply narcissistic.

too is concerned that our ordinary attempts to secure happiness, if un-aided by his insights, will regularly backfire and produce the opposite re-sult. He too suggests that the will must be turned against itself in order to alleviate this problem. And while he does not require that we live as the saints did, he agrees that our lives will be less unhappy as we moderate our demands for happiness. It is just that instead of setting escape from time and the world as our goal, Freud recommends that we accommodate ourselves to their inescapable presence in our lives. There are no fire-proof rooms in this world, so we are better off training ourselves to fight the in-evitable fires.

Since Freud grants equal status, so to speak, to the life- and death-in-stincts, the problem is how to lessen the conflict between them. The solu-tion is Schopenhauerian in its general structure—the instincts must be diverted from their natural aims and, especially in the case of the death-instincts, directed against themselves. But since, for Freud, these desires are not simply illusions of time-consciousness, they cannot cancel them-selves out in the perfectly mathematical fashion that Schopenhauer seems to envision. Their libidinal energy can be displaced, or redirected, but it will not disappear until it issues in something real. The sexual instincts are prevented from pursuing all but a few of their immediate aims (those that can be satisfied within marriage) and redirected toward creating so-cial structures that secure those few pleasures that are allowed. Putting it another way, we could say that energy that was used in unsuccessfully pur-suing pleasure is turned to the project of fortifying the individual (and the community) against the loss of those few pleasures that can be secured: "It is impossible to overlook the extent to which civilization is built up upon a renunciation of instinct, how much it presupposes precisely the non-satisfaction . . . of powerful instincts" (CD 49). We give up many of our natural aims but build protective structures around those aims that remain. Hence, unlike Schopenhauer, "The aim of satisfaction is not by any means relinquished; but a certain amount of protection against suf-fering is secured" (CD 28).

A parallel process takes place for the death-instincts. The difference is that the displacement of these instincts is purely internal and the result-ing structure—which also serves the purpose of securing our minimal pleasures—is a psychical one, our conscience. Just as the structures of cul-ture protect us against external threats, conscience protects us against in-ternal threats to our limited happiness. As with Schopenhauer, the moral behavior that results is only the side-effect of this technique, not its aim. "[A]ggressiveness is introjected, internalized . . . sent back to where it came from [and] in the form of 'conscience' is . . . put into action against the ego" (CD 78–79). Both sets of instincts, then, are set against them-selves to minimize the striving that either carries out.

In Schopenhauer, this process could be carried out, so to speak, without remainder. The instincts would cancel themselves out and leave the individual in, or near, Nirvana. For Freud, the procedure is far less tidy and we cannot avoid paying a price for its employ: "A threatened external unhappiness—loss of love and punishment on the part of the external authority—has been exchanged for a permanent internal unhappiness, for the tension of the sense of guilt. . . . the price we pay for our advance in civilization is a loss of happiness through the heightening of the sense of guilt" (*CD* 83, 91). But Freud does not object to this price. He considers it a fair bargain. Psychoanalysis only intervenes when the demands of the superego are out-of-kilter or excessively severe (*CD* 101). Indeed, the whole function of psychoanalysis is not to oppose these processes of repression or sublimation, but to enable them to function as smoothly as possible. The general bargain Freud summarizes in terms that constitute a kind of pessimistic social contract: "If civilization imposes such great sacrifices not only on man's sexuality but on his aggressivity, we can understand better why it is hard for him to be happy in that civilization. In fact, primitive man was better off in knowing no restrictions of instinct. To counterbalance this, his prospects of enjoying this happiness for any length of time were very slender. Civilized man has exchanged a portion of his possibilities of happiness for a portion of security" (*CD* 69).

But the general terms are not the whole story here. Freud's eudemonology has one further difference from Schopenhauer's that it is important not to miss. In recognizing the reality of time, Freud also recognizes the reality of individuality (the differences between individuals), which Schopenhauer considers an illusion. Although the conflict between life- and death-instincts is universal, the unconscious reservoir of desires in each person is unique. One result of this is that we each experience the necessary unhappiness of existence in different ways. Concomitantly, the practices that psychoanalysis means to encourage must be tailored to each individual. While Schopenhauer maintained that anyone who read his books with an open mind could learn everything he needed to know for the least unhappy life possible, Freud never made such a claim—the problems of individuals required individual treatment. Freud's books drew general conclusions from these treatments, but the actual practice of psychoanalysis does not take place in them; it only takes place between the analyst and patient. Where Schopenhauer can recommend the lives of the saints to all of us without differentiation (either of them or of us), Freud uses a countervailing theological metaphor: "Happiness, in the reduced sense in which we recognize it as possible, is a problem of the economics of the individual's libido. There is no golden rule which applies to everyone: every man must find out for himself in what particular fashion he can be saved" (*CD* 33). Indeed, Freud lists a variety of "arts of living" or "techniques of living," as he calls them, and insists that the individual character of each person will determine which is the most appropriate in his or her case (*CD* 31, 34).[39]

Self-fortification, to Schopenhauer, was the project of a lifetime. From Freud's perspective, it is importantly an *individuated* project, but one that, just for that reason, has a social and political dimension that Schopenhauer's does not. It is in this sense that Freud stands as a counterpoint to Schopenhauer in much the same way that Leopardi did to Rousseau. Pessimism is not an inherently anti-individual ethic. Although all the pessimists agree that we suffer for, and from, our individuality, they are divided on whether it is possible, or desirable, to abandon it. Though perhaps with less enthusiasm than Leopardi, Freud also suggests that we embrace the individuality we have been given and secure it as best we can against the force of time with appropriate arrangements, both personal and social. If we can speak of a Freudian freedom, then (and it is not a term that he often used), it can only partly be understood by reference to Schopenhauer's idea of liberation from desires. The elimination of individuality was not what Freud sought—rather, his goal was the freedom of the individual to pursue that art of living most appropriate to his or her character (free, on the one hand, from social oppression that limits our choices and, on the other hand, from psychic disorders that have the same effect). Or, in more pessimistic terms, we might say, each being should be free to choose its poison and "follow its own path to death." In recognizing that our freedom to follow this path has something to do with our relations with others, Freud at least begins to indicate the way toward pessimistic politics (to be discussed further in the next chapter), even if his main concern is to point out the limitations that optimistic political theories fail to acknowledge.

Conclusion

It is perhaps a sign of the close relation of these two metaphysical pessimisms that each author at times entertains the other's conclusions. Toward the end of *Civilization and Its Discontents*, Freud writes that "I can at least listen without indignation to the critic who is of the opinion that when one surveys the aims of cultural endeavour and the means it em-

---

[39] Freud does mention both the "killing off [of] the instincts . . . practiced by Yoga" and "break[ing] off [of] all relations" with reality practiced by the religious hermit as possible life-techniques, but he seems to classify these Schopenhauerian arts, along with intoxication, as suicidal or madness-inducing measures that are best to be avoided (*CD* 27–31).

ploys, one is bound to come to the conclusion that the whole effort is not worth the trouble" (*CD* 103), which echoes Schopenhauer's famous conclusion that "life is a business that does not cover the costs" (*WWR* 2:574). Schopenhauer, for his part, once offered an alternative to pure resignation as follows: "A *happy life* is impossible; the best that man can attain is a *heroic life*, such as is lived by one who struggles against overwhelming odds in some way and at some affair that will benefit the whole of mankind, and who in the end triumphs, although he obtains a poor reward or none at all" (*PP* 2:322). Indeed, in this passage, he sounds very much like Leopardi, and with good reason.

Metaphysical pessimism shares with cultural pessimism the problematic of time and time-consciousness. Approaching the problem in more cosmological terms than the cultural pessimists, Schopenhauer and Freud still manage to translate many of the themes of their predecessors into a distinct new language. In this chapter, I have stressed this continuity at the expense of highlighting the many differences that could, of course, be noted (both between Schopenhauer and Freud and between both of them and the earlier writers). I have done so, and do so again in the next chapter, for the purpose of making as clear as possible the existence of a pessimistic tradition of political philosophy. As important a figure as Schopenhauer may be, his arguments and conclusions have been easier to dismiss so long as he is seen as an isolated, cranky figure with no significant antecedents or successors. It is better, I believe, to view him as a vital link in an historical chain that stretches both forward and backward from the time of his writing. This chain connects writers with a philosophical disposition to foreground the burdens of temporal existence; but it has nothing to do with feelings of depression or despair. Even Schopenhauer's "resignation," as we have seen, is not an emotion or even a stance of passivity, but instead an art of living or technique of the self that prescribes a set of activities for human beings to pursue.

I have argued that this art of living, for both Schopenhauer and Freud, centers on a kind of fortification of the self against the burdens of temporality. The techniques are not identical for these two figures because of their underlying metaphysical differences—but the structures built on top of these differences, because of their shared pessimism, bear a great likeness to one another. Each finds that conscious human existence, insofar as it aims at satisfying unconscious desires, must issue in frustration and suffering. Each suggests that, the structure of the universe being unalterable, such desires must be curbed in some way by the individual. And each describes a technique of self-inhibition whereby the necessary defenses can be constructed and maintained. From this perspective, the main difference between the two is that Schopenhauer, believing as he does that the phenomenal, conscious world is fundamentally illusory, holds out a greater prospect for the success of this project than does Freud. In the terms used at the end of the last chapter, Schopenhauer's is finally a "misanthropic" ethic and Freud's "humanistic." Freud is a more tepid humanist than Leopardi, perhaps, but he does not glorify isolation and loneliness as Rousseau and Schopenhauer do. Indeed, the very idea of "civilization" in Freud (even as *Kultur*) contains the sense that our techniques of fortification can at least be carried out in tandem with others, if not exactly in harmony with them.

The metaphysical pessimists also share with the other pessimists the sense of the irony or absurdity of ordinary human existence. Though they do not stress the historical irony that was a prominent feature of cultural pessimism, the idea that human actions regularly issue in results that are the opposite of those intended is a prominent feature of their theories. Well-known for their atheism, they both still have repeated recourse to the idea of a "cosmic joke" as the only way to make 'sense' of our position in this world. One passage of Schopenhauer that captures this mood runs as follows: "The life of every individual, viewed as a whole and in general . . . is really a tragedy; but gone through in detail it has the character of a comedy" (*WWR* 1:322). As I discuss in chapter 6, this perspective (and this passage in particular) resonates well with the themes of *Don Quixote* and provide some justification for the view advanced there that we should understand Quixote as the embodiment of the pessimistic ethic.

In the next chapter, the thread of pessimism will be run forward through the middle of the twentieth century with those writers I label the "existential" pessimists. The problematic of time remains but—in the wake of Nietzsche's critique of metaphysics—the level of argument shifts once again. Camus, Cioran, and Unamuno pitch their philosophy at what we would today term, I think, an "existential" or "ontological" level, somewhere between the metaphysical and the psychological. One consequence of this, as we shall see, is a pessimism that, while still individualist, can advance further on to the plane of the political.

Chapter Four

"CONSCIOUSNESS IS A DISEASE"

EXISTENTIAL PESSIMISM IN CAMUS,

UNAMUNO, AND CIORAN

If there are happy people on this earth,
why don't they come out and shout with joy,
proclaim their happiness in the streets?
Why so much discretion and restraint?
—E. M. CIORAN

IN the twentieth century, pessimism has been the philosophy that dares not speak its name. Although the writers I will discuss here—Albert Camus, Miguel de Unamuno, and E. M. Cioran—often went out of their way to defend the idea of pessimism,[1] they did not always adopt this label for themselves, or not with any consistency. My concern, however, is not with their practices of self-identification. Each of these writers, in fact, tried to disassociate themselves from *all* affiliations and often presented themselves as writers "without party." Thus Camus frequently rejected the tag of "existentialist" with which he was (and is) often associated. Cioran, a Romanian who lived in France from the late 1930s onward, remarked that his situation of exile was "the best possible status for an intellectual" (*FT* 185).[2] Unamuno was forcibly exiled from Spain by a mil-

---

[1] See, e.g., Cioran *DAQ* 133; Camus *RRD* 57; Unamuno *TSL* 144.

[2] It has now been well-established that, in the 1930s, Cioran was a sort of fellow traveler with the protofascist political movement in Romania that became the Iron Guard. His 1937 work *The Transfiguration of Romania* (written in Romanian and still untranslated) is full of nationalist sentiment and antisemitic cliches (based, in some sense, on a self-disgust at the backwardness of Romanian society). Alexandra Laignel-Lavastine, in her book documenting this (2002, chap. 4) and to which I am indebted for this information, compares his political writings in this period, not unfairly, to those of such "revolutionary conservatives" as Ernst Jünger—both had no use for the "old" politics of the church or the aristocracy, but nonetheless sought a "modernized" society that would be highly unified in purpose and devoted to national ends. Laignel-Lavastine also demonstrates that, in his later French career, Cioran obscured, rather than acknowledged, his earlier political associations (chaps. 9, 10). He rarely mentioned the Humboldt fellowship that took him to Germany in the early 1930s, and *Transfiguration*, unlike some of his other early works, was never translated into French or any other language.

While this research must cause us to tread carefully with Cioran's texts, it also seems clear

itary government and later removed from his university position by *both* the republicans and the fascists. Yet it is right to name these authors pessimists because they are, among others, the inheritors and perpetuators of the tradition of thought that I have outlined in the previous chapters. Their philosophy issues from, and focuses on, the problematic of linear time that has preoccupied pessimists since Rousseau.

Unlike the metaphysical pessimists, however, Camus, Unamuno, and Cioran all avoided the grand structural approach that characterizes the philosophies of Schopenhauer and Freud. This reflects, in large part, the common influence of Nietzsche, who discredited that style of thinking for many in the last decades of the nineteenth century.[3] Instead, the "existential pessimists," as I am calling them, reconstitute the issues that preoccupied earlier pessimists (the burden of temporality, the dearth of happiness, the futility of striving, boredom, and many others) by focusing on the life-conditions of the modern individual. One way to put this difference might be to say that while, for the earliest pessimists, time was inflected as history, and later as metaphysic, for the pessimists of this generation it is inflected as narrative. By "narrative," I here mean to indicate an ontological fabric of political and social life that is more than a psychological state and less than an historical destiny. It is in this sense that I think the adjective "existential" is appropriate—not to indicate an affiliation with Sartre or Heidegger—but to mark the level of explanation at which they aim.

Like Leopardi, Unamuno and Cioran are less familiar to English-speaking audiences today, but important figures in their own national litera-

---

that his philosophy, like that of many in his generation, underwent some kind of transformation (e.g., from 1956, "A fatherland . . . is a moment-by-moment soporific. One cannot sufficiently envy—or pity—the Jews for not having one"), which left him embarrassed by his earlier position (*TE* 106). If anything, the result of Cioran's political involvement seems to have been to push him to the other extreme such that he embraced a radical individualism typified by the condition of exile. "A whole period of my life seems scarcely imaginable to me today, so alien to me has it become. How could I have been the man I was? My old enthusiasms seem ridiculous to me" (*DAQ* 156–57). As with Heidegger, then, one cannot ignore the potential political implications (or the occasional elements of self-pity) of the work (less frequent than Heidegger's but still present); however, looking at Cioran's texts from the 1940s forward, even with a skeptical eye, it would seem very difficult to me to derive a fascist politics from them. Laignel-Lavastine, focusing on Cioran's career rather than the substance of his work, seems disinclined to acknowledge this, but offers no real argument or evidence against this conclusion. For a more balanced approach, see Parfait 2001.

[3] I realize there is some awkwardness here in that I am postponing a detailed discussion of Nietzsche's philosophy to a later chapter. As I have said repeatedly, however, it is not the goal of this book to trace a history of the influence of some pessimistic writers on others, although such a work could surely be done. In any case, my point here does not rely on the details of Nietzsche's pessimism, which I discuss in chapter 5, but on his effect as an antimetaphysical philosopher, which is widely acknowledged.

tures and in European discussions more generally. Unamuno, at least, was
well-known for a period as a leading member of the Spanish "Generation
of '98"—those stimulated to develop a new political model for Spain in
the wake of the disastrous defeat in the Spanish-American War. His work
of 1913, *The Tragic Sense of Life in Men and Nations*, was quickly translated into many languages and made him an international figure. Cioran,
in fact, was under Unamuno's inspiration in originally planning to study
in Spain before the Civil War in 1936 prevented it. While I will not be
tracing out the influence of these three writers on one another, it should
at least be noted, then, that Unamuno, a generation older than the other
two, was well-known to both. While Cioran (b. 1911) and Camus (b.
1913) were near-contemporaries, Cioran only published his first work in
French (*Précis de Décomposition*, translated as *A Short History of Decay*)
in 1949, when Camus was already an international figure.[4] In recent
decades, however, Cioran's many books, including those written in Romania in the 1930s, have been translated into English and many European languages and a substantial secondary literature has grown up
around him, one that often puts him in Camus' company.[5]

Yet, again like Leopardi, Unamuno and Cioran are figures whose importance to political theory has been unseen or forgotten, largely, I would
claim, on account of their pessimism. This is in part a problem of intellectual reference: when the pessimistic tradition itself is invisible, it is difficult to characterize their arguments or understand what questions they
are asking and answering. The preceding chapters, I hope, will have given
the background necessary to see both the seriousness and the originality
of their work. The problem of reference, however, also extends to matters
of style: Cioran's writing is largely composed of aphorisms. Even his essays (like Unamuno's), are aphoristic—they sometimes seem to consist of

---

[4] Camus' last major theoretical work, *The Rebel*, was published in 1951, so it is hard to
imagine Cioran's book having much impact. The two men knew each other but did not have
a good relationship: according to Cioran's biographer, the Romanian felt snubbed by
Camus' initial rejection of his work in his capacity as an editor at Gallimard (which went
on to publish all of Cioran's books). What notice Camus took of Cioran's work as the latter's reputation grew in the 1950s is hard to say (Camus died in 1960). Cioran makes almost no direct reference whatsoever to any living writers in his own work, so it is equally
difficult to gauge Camus' effect on him. (I thank Prof. Ilinca Zarifopol-Johnston for private
communication regarding the Camus-Cioran relationship.) One should also note their connection through the Romanian-French playwright Eugène Ionesco, who was Cioran's old
friend and Camus' fellow contributor to the "theatre of the absurd."

[5] E.g., Cahn 1998, Jarrety 1999. Jarrety's book, *La morale dans l'écriture*, usefully aligns
Camus and Cioran, comparing both to the French *moralistes* of the eighteenth century. He
also describes their common efforts to fashion an art of living, however different in practice
those arts may be. Like many writers, however, Jarrety mistakenly equates pessimism with
nihilism and, thus, is quick to insist that the authors he examines are neither (16ff.).

a series of emphatic declarations rather than the various stages of an argument. As a result, both writers are sometimes praised as vivid stylists or "moralists," without considering that their style or morals are deeply related to a unified philosophy. In chapter 7, I will consider in more depth the link between pessimism and the aphorism, a relationship that begins, perhaps, with Leopardi and continues through Schopenhauer and Nietzsche. At this stage, all I would suggest is that ideas about the proper form of philosophy are more linked to the substantive content of it than we sometimes care to admit. It is therefore one of my contentions that learning to appreciate the pessimistic perspective and learning to appreciate the aphoristic style, while not identical endeavors, are closely allied—just as understanding Plato cannot by fully separated from feeling the effects of the dialogic form. The dismissal of pessimism has, in some sense, been the product of a vicious cycle where misunderstanding of the content leads to incomprehension of the form and vice versa. Placing Unamuno and Cioran within the pessimistic context can thus also lead to a revaluation of the form of writing that they chose to employ.

It is therefore worthwhile to note (without getting into the details of influence-tracing) that each of these writers, often depicted as iconoclasts, were very conscious of being members of a tradition. Indeed, at times this tradition seems so substantial to them that they curtail or telescope discussions of certain points because they fear being repetitive. Camus refers to it as the tradition of "humiliated thought" and he begins his survey of it in the *Myth of Sisyphus* with the observation that the critique of rationalist optimism that he is about to make "has been made so often that it seems unnecessary to begin again" (*MS* 22). Likewise Unamuno, who begins *The Tragic Sense of Life* by describing how personality is intimately connected to "continuity in time" cuts short his discussion with the observation that "I know very well that all this is sheer platitude" (*TSL* 12). Cioran, who is most candid about his influences in his early work, writes, "The more I read the pessimists, the more I love life. After reading Schopenhauer, I always feel like a bridegroom on his wedding night" (*OHD* 101).[6] In each case, the tradition that we have called "pessimism" appears to them as a living one to which they are indebted and to which they react.

If they hesitate to embrace the label for themselves, it seems to be largely because the psychological or dispositional use of the term "pessimism" has already begun to overwhelm the older meaning in everyday language; they fear how they will be perceived if they adopt the term. Thus Cioran, who in his first book refers to his own "somber pessimism," argues explicitly that "it is wrong to surmise that a pessimist has an organic deficiency or weak vital instincts" (*OHD* 110, 122). Unamuno complains

[6] Not, one must admit, the most common reaction.

that the terms "optimism" and "pessimism" "often come to mean the opposite of what their user intends," while tacitly allowing that his fundamental views are pessimistic (*TSL* 144). Camus' remark that it was "puerile" to believe that "a pessimistic philosophy is necessarily one of discouragement" comes in an article where he complains that the idea of pessimism is being used as a simplistic *reductio* that equates non-optimistic perspectives with submissiveness and Naziism (*RRD* 57–60). His heart, it appears, is with the pessimists even if, as I mentioned earlier, he disdained to be grouped with anyone. In all of these authors' rhetorical declarations we see no rejection of pessimistic ideas, but rather a simple (and well-founded) concern that allowing themselves to be labeled "pessimistic" will result in misunderstanding.

Furthermore, each writer is vehement in rejecting the historical optimism that they see as prevalent in their times. This is particularly Camus' theme in *The Rebel*, concerned as he is there with refuting the historical Hegelianism and Marxism that he takes as the dominant intellectual force in postwar France.[7] Unamuno and Cioran are, as we shall see, more concerned with the general modern theme of progress, as much in its liberal as in its Marxist variety. Not only do they doubt the claims of progress made to this point in time, however—their main concern is that the *telos* of progress has become an idol, and is used to justify violence and a loss of freedom in the present. When we become captive to historical thinking, they argue, we forget how to live in the here and now.

If each of these writers is well-ensconced within the pessimistic tradition, they nonetheless, as with the figures examined in the previous chapters, embody different responses to it. Cioran is the most misanthropic. While not seeking to eradicate the spirit to quite the same degree as, say, Schopenhauer, he does suggest a detachment from life in all but its most minimal respects. Like Rousseau and Schopenhauer, he repeatedly contrasts animal happiness with human misery and if he, in the last judgment, tepidly embraces the latter, it is only because he feels he has little choice in the matter, since he refuses as unreal all the metaphysical, mystical, or transcendent alternatives he can conceive of. Unamuno and Camus, on the other hand, while agreeing with Cioran on the prevalence of unhappiness, both embrace more heartily the life offered to us under the pessimistic diagnosis. Decades before the current interest in agonal politics, they both spoke of "contradiction," "conflict," and even "agony" as fundamental conditions of political life (and life in general) that could nonetheless be affirmed and, even, occasionally, enjoyed. "Battle," Unamuno wrote, "is a form of association" (*TSL* 124).

What is more, while pessimism remained for them primarily a personal

---

[7] This point is especially well-made in Isaac 1992, chap. 3.

ethic, both Unamuno and Camus clearly saw it as authorizing and encouraging political participation. Indeed, both men were in their lives directly and extensively occupied with public debates and politics. This behavior runs counter to the common conception of pessimism as issuing in political detachment. I do not, by this statement, mean to say that their philosophy is somehow validated by their personal behavior. (I do not examine their political lives here in any detail.) I only mean to indicate that their philosophical interpretation of pessimism pointed toward an engagement with, rather than a retreat from, politics. That they then acted on that conclusion speaks only to their personal integrity, which was, of course, enormous. Nonetheless, it certainly *ought* to disturb the ordinary interpretation of pessimism to realize that two of the most active, politically engaged intellectuals of the twentieth century fall within its ranks.

On this point, there is one fascinating parallel between Cioran and Camus that I will give some attention to in what follows. In describing Cioran's philosophy as one of detachment and Camus' as one of engagement, as I did in the previous paragraph, I am speaking of their mature, post–World War II positions, the one expressed in Cioran's French-language books and in Camus' *The Rebel*. Yet for both men these works represented something of a change from their prewar stances. Though each had a pessimistic outlook before the war, Cioran's Romanian books suggest an "ecstatic" interpretation of it that he later went to pains to disparage. And Camus' *Myth of Sisyphus*, written in 1940, before the invasion of France, is almost entirely focused on the individual with little attention given to political questions. While both men then endured World War II as noncombatants in France, and primarily Paris,[8] this common experience seems nonetheless to have driven them in entirely opposite directions. Camus emerged as a critic of solipsism and an advocate of participation (though, as we shall see, of a special kind) while Cioran abandoned the political sphere entirely.[9] While this was not, in either case,

---

[8] Camus, of course, was a participant in events as a member of the Resistance and editor of the underground newspaper *Combat*. Cioran was briefly attached to the Romanian diplomatic legation in Paris, but was quickly dismissed and never again in his life held a regular job, surviving as a free-lance writer and translator.

[9] Camus explains this shift with the claim that his first book was written in "the age of negation" while his second is written in "the age of ideologies" (*R* 4), but, of course, the two books were written only ten years apart, separated by the war. Camus makes no real attempt to defend these historical characterizations, which, in any case, seem arbitrary—one could just as easily argue for reversing them. Cioran had less to explain to his French-language audience since they, initially, had no access to his Romanian books. Because, as I have noted, he was, at a minimum, embarrassed by some of this work, he made almost no reference to it apart from the occasional "follies-of-youth" remark. It was only late in his career that several of the Romanian books were translated into French and English and he began to address his past in interviews.

an absolute reversal of their previous positions, it was a significant swerve and it emphasizes for us the political stakes involved in questions of pessimism.

Time, Consciousness, and the Absurd

The term "absurd" is by now indelibly associated with Camus and, to a lesser extent, with the other French philosophers and dramatists of the mid-twentieth century commonly referred to as "existentialists." Camus made the absurd character of existence the lynchpin of his analysis of the human condition in *The Myth of Sisyphus*, and it continues to play a central role in the more fully developed theory that appears in *The Rebel*. But his pithy formulations of the concept can sometimes create the impression that it is largely a matter of juvenile angst or personal alienation: "The absurd is born of this confrontation between the human need and the unreasonable silence of the world" (*MS* 28). While Camus was clearly intrigued by Heidegger and Kierkegaard (writers whose relationship to pessimism needs further exploration), however, the concept of the absurd can be best understood as Camus' interpretation of the problem posed by earlier generations of pessimists.

This connection will perhaps be clearer if we consider first the intervening and important figure of Unamuno. Like the earlier pessimists, Unamuno focuses on the price that man has paid for becoming a conscious animal. He emphasizes, as did Rousseau, both how consciousness distorts animal health and happiness and how it catapults man into a state of self-reflectiveness:

> There is something which, for want of a better name, we shall the call the tragic sense of life, and it carries along with it an entire conception of the Universe and of life itself . . . man, because he is man, because he possesses consciousness, is already in comparison to the jackass or the crab, a sick animal. Consciousness is a disease. (*TSL* 21–22)

> A real disease, and a tragic one, is the one that arouses in us the appetite to know for the sole pleasure of knowing, the delight of tasting the fruit of the Tree of Knowledge of Good and Evil. . . . [Animals have knowledge but] what distinguishes us from them is reflective knowing, the knowledge of knowing itself. (*TSL* 25–26)

Consciousness is thus identified as the central feature of human (as opposed to animal) being and identified as the ability to mirror ourselves. But this same fruit, which teaches us to reflect, because it also allows us access to the temporal realm is laced with the poisonous knowledge of the vanity of existence. That is why Unamuno calls consciousness, powerful though it is, a disease: "Everything passes! That is the refrain . . . of all who have savored the fruit of the Tree of Knowledge of Good and Evil" (*TSL* 45).

If, for Unamuno, the problem is more directly existential than for the previous pessimists, this is because for him time is the source, both of human desire, and of that which thwarts it. For Rousseau and Schopenhauer, it was the constant dissolution of the objects of our desire (material, social, sexual, et cetera) that produced frustration. For Unamuno, our ultimate goal is immortality, which we can only come to grasp within the sphere of temporality; our ultimate enemy, which enters our imagination simultaneously, is death. Unamuno's analysis is parallel to that of Schopenhauer in making temporality, as it were, a condition of knowledge. But while for Schopenhauer, temporality is a cognitive structure, for Unamuno it is the existential condition that temporality engenders that is key: "The longing not to die, the hunger for personal immortality, the striving to persevere indefinitely in our own being, . . . constitutes the affective basis of all knowledge" (*TSL* 42). In addition Unamuno understands this "condition" in an individual way—time is not just the basis of cognition, but also, as Rousseau argued, of memory, personality, and whatever constitutes our distinct existence: "And that which determines a man, that which makes him a certain man, one man and not another, . . . is a principle of unity and a principle of continuity. . . . Memory is the basis of individual personality" (*TSL* 11–12). The human individuality that temporality makes possible is, for Unamuno, haunted from the start by this tragic conflict between immortality and death.

It is at this point in the analysis that Unamuno announces that this position is "sheer platitude." The centrality of temporal questions is not just something he takes for granted, but he also expects his audience to be satisfied with a relatively cursory account of them. And, in a certain sense of course, it is not very controversial to claim that human consciousness has a temporal element that that of animals lacks. But, like the other pessimists, both before and after him, Unamuno believes that we do not focus sufficient attention on the implications of this fact.

Human beings are caught, then, between the desire for permanence and the knowledge of decay and death, both equally the product of temporal consciousness. Unamuno tends to refer to this as the conflict between "reason" and "life." "Reason," to him, is shorthand for the reflective consciousness of the human mind: "Reason, what we call reason, reflex and reflective knowledge, [is] the distinguishing mark of man" (*TSL* 29). But reason, once activated, cannot be forced to serve the impulse toward life that is born its twin. Indeed, reason is ultimately compelled to oppose the hunger for immortality, just because the latter is irrational. Whatever else we learn, through the employ of reason, we learn first of all of our own mortality. Here Unamuno follows the other pessimists: through reason, humans have foreknowledge of death, rather than the animal's instinctive aversion to it. This knowledge poisons our every attempt to give our lives immortal meanings by "rationalizing life and forcing it to submit to the inevitable, to mortality" (*TSL* 127–28).

But the image of death is, for Unamuno, as much a symbolic problem as a direct one. Death threatens our individuality, but only at the end of our life. Reason, however, in its capacity to generalize, also threatens our personal distinctiveness, not just at a later time, but at every moment:

> Reason confronts our longing for personal immortality and contradicts us. And the truth is that reason is the enemy of life. Intelligence is a dreadful matter. It tends toward death in the way that memory tends toward stability. That which lives, that which is absolutely unstable, absolutely individual, is, strictly speaking, unintelligible. *Logic tends to reduce everything to identities and genera, . . . But nothing is the same for two successive moments of its being. . . .* Identity, which is death, is precisely what the intellect seeks. The mind seeks what is dead, for the living escapes it. . . . Everything vital is irrational, and everything rational is anti-vital. (*TSL* 100–101; emphasis added; cf. 39)

Unamuno's point here is more subtle then, perhaps, the last line makes it appear. Reason, as reflection in time, allows us to form a continuous sense of ourselves by comparing one state of ourselves to others, both future and past. Being embedded in time means that we, like all creatures, are in a process of continuous flux and change—but reason can only perceive this change, as it were, in a negative fashion. In order to constitute a continuous identity within an ever-changing being, reason must identify that which remains the same within the flow of becoming. But to do so means to discount as inessential that which changes. If reason did not focus on the "genera," then consciousness would erase itself—there would be no self with "continuity in time"; this is the animal condition. The ability to perceive the genera as genera (that is, to hold identity constant over time) is just what consciousness is. But to Unamuno, this means that what is genuinely individual and alive is "strictly speaking, unintelligible." The only being that ceases to change is one that is dead. The "death" that truly concerns Unamuno, then, is not the one at the end of our lives but the death-in-life that consciousness creates at every moment. So reason and life, rationality and vitality, are housed together unhappily in one body, perpetual antagonists, both owing their existence to time-consciousness.

The human being as a house divided: this is for Unamuno the primary condition in which we find ourselves. We are trapped between reason and life, between heaven and earth. *And we must remain so.* To escape entirely to either side would make life unbearable. If we could truly give up the hunger for immortality, we would lose the will to live. Reason alone cannot provide one. Hence, "The vital consequence of rationalism would be suicide" (*TSL* 128) If, on the other hand, we gave ourselves over entirely to faith in immortality, we would lose our humanity: "faith—life—can sustain itself only by depending upon reason, which will make it transmissible—transmissible, especially, from me to myself; that is, reflective and conscious" (*TSL* 125).[10] Pure faith would be too akin to an animal's instincts: unwavering, unquestioned—and thus unreflective, inhuman, and pathetic. What separates the will to life from the instinct for self-preservation is precisely the former's reflective character. Animals do not commit suicide, but neither do they keep their dead. To return to this condition would be to give up our human distinctiveness. Though some people, of extraordinary shallowness, may follow this route, it cannot be seriously recommended.[11]

Fortunately, humans rarely achieve either form of certainty. For both the most committed rationalist and the most committed believer, "A muffled voice, the voice of uncertainty, murmurs in his spirit's ear: 'Who knows?' . . . How, without this uncertainty, could we ever live?" (*TSL* 131). The tragedy lies, then, not particularly in the conflict between reason and life, but in the irremediability and violence of that conflict, which Unamuno calls "warfare" (*TSL* 118):

> Some reader may see a basic contradiction in everything I am saying, as I long on the one hand for unending life, and on the other hand claim that this life is devoid of the value assigned it. A contradiction? I should say so! The contradiction between my heart which says *Yes*, and my head which says *No*! Naturally there is a contradiction. . . . Since we live solely from and by contradictions, since life is tragedy and the tragedy is in the perpetual struggle without hope or victory, then it is all a contradiction. (*TSL* 17)

---

[10] It should be said here that Unamuno thought the desire for immortality was also the source for all religious feeling and that his own philosophy had a complicated relationship to Catholicism. I will not discuss his religious views here (he was raised Catholic but is said to have had a crisis of faith in the 1890s), but one can only describe them as extremely eclectic and complicated. He believed himself to be a kind of Catholic but it would be difficult, I imagine, to find any church authority that would agree. His writing, though, did have an influence on such tragic Catholics as Graham Greene, whose novel, *Monsignor Quijote*, could almost be seen as a tribute to Unamuno.

[11] "And as regards today, all these wretches are quite satisfied merely because they exist today, and for them it is enough to exist. Existence, pure and naked existence, fills up their entire soul. . . . But, do they exist? Do they really exist? I think not. For if they existed, if they really existed, they would suffer from existing and they would not be content with it. If they truly existed in time and space, they would suffer from not existing in eternity and infinity." (*OLDQ* 11)

No truce between the two forces may be called. We can ignore neither our presentiment of death, nor our desire for immortality, nor the conflict between them. But, as the passage above implies—"we live solely from and by contradictions"—this condition is not only a source of pain. In the next section we will trace the way in which Unamuno, along with other existential pessimists, makes this contradiction into a basis for activity.

It deserves emphasis, however, that, as with the earlier pessimists, this conflict must be understood as a product of time and, more specifically, as something that appears with particular force within modern, linear time. Mortality, in the sense Unamuno means it—the final and complete end to one's existence—is not the same issue in the context of circular time, in which everything recurs in one form or another. Not that a circular notion frees us from the fear of death, of course; but to fear death *as* that which puts a permanent end to one's existence in every sense requires a simultaneous belief that nothing recurs, that there are no cycles of existence, only a straight, unbroken path. Whatever truth there is in Unamuno's contention that the fear of death is universal, it should be clear that this fear is intensified by the emergence of linear time.

A parallel point can be made about the desire for immortality. Though Unamuno deems it something inalterably human, this drive makes little sense without modern ideas of temporality. A certain kind of permanence, after all, is already promised to those whose notion of time is circular; to have immortality as a *goal* of human life (as something we might or might not achieve) only becomes possible when life is subjected to linear time. To say that humans strive for immortality is to say they fear they do not naturally possess it. The fear and the desire are only intelligible within linear time.

The idea of a contradiction, deeply felt within the individual and framed by time, is the kernel of existential pessimism that Cioran and Camus share with Unamuno. What to Unamuno is the *tragic sense of life* is, to Cioran and Camus, each using the term independently of the other, the *absurd*. Both are preoccupied with the problem of suicide, each judging it to be a central issue and a special danger. The degree of interest in suicide (which far exceeds the relatively brief discussions of the earlier pessimists) is another marker of the existential character of their pessimism. The problem of time is not, to them, something one must reflect upon philosophically in order to feel. In their earlier works, both Camus and Cioran respond to the challenge of suicide with a philosophy that embraces life, but at the price of a certain degree of self-involvement and, perhaps, solipsism. Later, in rejecting that position, Cioran reverts to a kind of asceticism (akin to Schopenhauer's, but in some respects unique) while Camus and Unamuno search for an alternative that is more personally active and politically engaged while avoiding the dogma of modern optimisms.

Like Unamuno, Camus equates consciousness with reason and considers both to be that which separates human beings from nature and from a simpler animal existence: "If I were a tree among trees, a cat among animals, this life would have a meaning, or rather this problem would not arise, for I should belong to the world. I should *be* this world to which I am now opposed by my whole consciousness. . . . This ridiculous reason is what sets me in opposition to all creation" (*MS* 51). This immediately produces, for Camus as for the other pessimists, a crisis centering around the questions of death and the potential meaninglessness of human activity: "If nothing lasts, then nothing is justified; everything that dies is deprived of meaning" (*R* 100–101). Also, as in Unamuno and Rousseau, there is the element of backward-glancing regret, the "nostalgia for unity," as he calls it (*MS* 50). The irreversibility of time means that our animal past is a homeland to which we can never return. Thus, Camus thinks, we could easily consider ourselves to be faced with a stark choice in which we either accept the empty, fruitless nature of our life or put an end to it by our own hand.

Camus' presentation of the problem is condensed—it only occupies a few pages of *The Myth of Sisyphus*. But this is in part because he believes that, in stating it, he is merely repeating a problem posed by others. It is his response that he thinks of as original.

Despite the seeming universality of the problem, both pessimists and suicides, Camus acknowledges, are rare creatures and this, he feels, needs to be explained. His explanation lies in the nearly universal human act of *eluding (l'esquive)*.[12] Eluding is that mental maneuver that allows human beings to exist in linear time without being deflated by it, but without fully facing its challenge either, thus "the typical act of eluding . . . is hope. Hope of another life one must 'deserve' or trickery of those who live not for life itself but for some great idea that will transcend it, refine it, give it a meaning, and betray it" (*MS* 8). In this criticism, Camus means to sweep together both the transcendent hope of Christianity and the hope of historical optimists that, to him, is typified by Marxism. Both ultimately "betray" human life because they do not accept it in the time-bound, absurd state that is, in fact, its single unalterable condition. Even the contemporary philosophers whom he most respects (like Kierkegaard,

---

[12] Camus' noun has more strength than the English gerund so, unable to improve on O'Brien's translation, I use the French below. *L'esquive* covers a range of meanings from "dodging" or "ducking," as in sports, to "evading" or "escaping" or "the slip," as in "giving the slip" to someone.

Chestov, and Jaspers) do not get beyond a clear statement of the problem. "Without exception," Camus writes, they all "suggest escape. . . . That forced hope is religious in all of them" (*MS* 32).

In *The Myth of Sisyphus*, Camus sets himself the task of defining a philosophy for the individual that copes with our temporal condition without recourse to *l'esquive*. He repeatedly refers to our situation as one of "divorce": "It lies in neither of the elements compared; it is born of their confrontation" (*MS* 30). We are all children of this divorce "between the mind that desires and the world that disappoints, my nostalgia for unity, this fragmented universe and the contradiction that binds them together. . . . It is essential to know whether one can live with it or whether, on the other hand, logic commands one to die of it" (*MS* 50). As this passage makes visible, Camus' theme reintroduces the problem of the earlier generations of pessimists. The "unity" between the desiring subject and the object of its desire, they all agree, simply cannot exist; we can only recollect it dimly as part of our animal past, hence our "nostalgia" for it (a term Cioran will also use).

But we cannot cope with this divorce simply by choosing which parent we prefer. "If I attempt to solve a problem," Camus writes, "at least I must not by that very solution conjure away one of the terms of the problem" (*MS* 31). This is especially the case here because all of our thinking, as Unamuno argued, has its roots in this confrontation between the two opposed forces of desire and logic. To "solve" the problem by erasing one element is to undermine the possibilities of reasoning itself. Camus is fundamentally committed to this point—it is his version of the Kantian a priori—the condition of thinking that thinking has no choice but to affirm. In *The Rebel*, when much about his political thought has changed, he repeats this point practically word-for-word in his conclusion: "[Rebellion's] movement, in order to remain authentic, must never abandon any of the terms of the contradiction that sustains it" (*R* 285).

Just as Unamuno argues that "we live solely in and by contradictions," so Camus believes that "it is a constant confrontation between man and his own obscurity" that is our initial spur to thinking (*MS* 54). This is the basis for Camus' argument against suicide. While we cannot clearly say why life is worth living, suicide, for him, is not so much a judgment against life as an abdication of judgment. If we are honest about the source of the problem, then, we cannot condone a solution that pretends, in essence, that the problem does not exist. Suicide does this by eliminating the value of the mind, that is, of the thinking being, man. Suicide is the ultimate performative contradiction. If we understand the confrontation that is the a priori of our thinking, we will see that suicide attempts to ignore it, and thus cannot be the conclusion of any clear reasoning. Rather than solve a problem or make a judgment, it declines to wrestle with or endure the actual difficulty that confronts us in favor a simple exit from mental distress. It is not the *wrong* answer to the crisis of meaninglessness; rather, it is no answer at all. Like the leap of faith, it is a form of *l'esquive*, "acceptance at its extreme" (*MS* 54).

To abjure from *l'esquive* is to admit that "the absurd cannot be settled"—though we live in a state of divorce, the ex-spouses remain preoccupied with one another. And we, their progeny, cannot pretend to be other than the product of their meeting. Summarizing and endorsing, in *The Rebel*, the conclusions of his earlier essay, he writes, "Suicide would mean the end of this encounter, and absurdist reasoning considers that it could not consent to this without negating its own premises" (*R* 6).

In *The Rebel*, Camus is more concerned with what Unamuno would call the "antivitalism of reason." In a long discussion of the French revolutionaries, and especially Saint-Just, Camus describes how their passion for reason became the implacable basis for the Terror: "To abandon oneself to principles is really to die—and to die for an impossible love which is the contrary of love" (*R* 129–30). By this last phrase, Camus means that the revolutionaries' "love" was of a perfect justice and a perfect future that could not exist in this world. This love deprived them of any sympathy for human frailty or complication. They thus lost the ability to empathize or love their fellow citizens (hence their love became "the contrary of love") and sent them to the guillotine without remorse. Nor could they appreciate individual distinctiveness, since that too is something that occurs within life rather than outside of it. When "rebellion" (Camus' word for our protest against the absurd) is converted into revolution (an abandonment of the absurd for the safe harbor of rationalism), the nostalgia for a time outside of time becomes unhealthy: "All revolutionaries finally aspire to world unity and act as though they believed that history was concluded" (*R* 107).

Despite Camus' efforts to depict his arguments against suicide and murder as being in accord with the existential reality of our situation, he is conscious at the same time that there is an element of choice involved, and that his choice is rooted in a value of humanism that he cannot really defend but only describes: "The creature [man] is my native land. This is why I have chosen this absurd and ineffectual effort" (*MS* 87). Indeed, part of the value of keeping the absurd alive is that it creates, in part through its destruction of historical hopes, an expanded arena of choice for the individual. It restores to us our independence and unpredictability, which are our truly special capacities as human beings. While the various "hopes" of the past, both religious and historical, gave us (specious) reasons to live, they did so at an enormous cost. By presuming to tell us our future, they also told us what our role in history was to be. This prescripting of our lives relieved us of the burden of making our own decisions, but also, thereby, of the freedom to make them. Confronting the absurd anew, Camus believes, "restores and magnifies . . . my freedom of action. That privation of hope and future mean an increase in man's availability" (*MS* 56–57).

In returning to our original dilemma, then, we confront the true burdens of temporality and admit that our response must always be, at some level, a personal one: "I understand then why the doctrines that explain everything to me also debilitate me at the same time. They relieve me of the weight of my own life, and yet I must carry it alone" (*MS* 54–55). Hope and optimism are condemned not because it is wrong to want something better in life for oneself or others, but because in pre-scripting history, they allow humans to elude their responsibility for making their own choices—just like suicide. All these forms of *l'esquive* hide from view the enormous range of potential lives, good and bad, with which we are actually confronted. We cannot rely on the flow of history or transcendental faith to give us our identity; to be truly human (to "really exist," as Unamuno might say) we must make that identity ourselves.

Cioran's Pessimism

Cioran's pessimism, as we shall see, gives us much the same diagnosis as that of Unamuno and Camus; it is their reactions to it, discussed in more detail in the next section, that differ. Cioran's writings display in more depth the many strands of the pessimistic tradition on which he draws. His aphoristic style allows him to take up different elements of this tradition and put them side-by-side and, indeed, sometimes he seems to rely largely on their thematic similarities to give coherence to his texts. I will have more to say about this in chapter 7, where I take up the question of aphoristic writing directly. But the exposition of the pessimistic tradition to this point should also allow the reader to perceive the consistency, which might otherwise be hard to see, between the historical, metaphysical, and existential elements in Cioran's philosophy, for all three are present.[13]

In his first book, *On the Heights of Despair* (published in 1934, when

---

[13] In discussing Cioran, then, the limits of the typology of pessimism that this book proposes will become more visible and I am happy to admit this. That typology is intended as a heuristic for understanding the evolution of pessimism and, I think, it serves that purpose well. But it is not intended to draw impenetrable barriers between the many authors discussed here. To do so would be to invite an Unamunoesque critique of devitalizing logical genera. Especially for the later writers, the availability of the pessimistic tradition means that there are bound to be vectors of influence that make their works resonate with earlier ones.

Cioran was only twenty-three), Cioran took "the demonic character of time" to be the pivotal problem for human beings (*OHD* 28). In terms more dramatic even than those of Camus and Unamuno, Cioran deplores our emergence into time from our animal condition and the irreversibility of that step: "*Knowledge is the plague of life, and consciousness, an open wound in its heart*. Is it not tragic to be man, that perpetually dissatisfied animal? . . . If I could, I would renounce my condition on the spot, but what would I become then, an animal? I cannot retrace my steps" (*OHD* 43).

This nostalgia for an animal condition (and sometimes, with Cioran, for a *plant-like* condition) is coupled, as one would expect, with the presence of death on the horizon of consciousness: "When consciousness becomes independent of life, the revelation of death becomes so strong that its presence destroys all naiveté, all joyful enthusiasm" (*OHD* 24; cf. 68). As in Camus' and Unamuno's analysis, the self becomes divided and doomed to unhappiness since "the secret of happiness lies in this original nondivision of an impenetrable unity" (*OHD* 78). Although his later books will no longer refer to time as "demonic," the theme of a self divided on the frame of time-consciousness remains central. One of his French books bears the title *Ecartèlement*, which refers to the form of execution known as drawing and quartering. But all his books emphasize the agony of ordinary human existence and the inescapability of it.

More clearly than Camus and Unamuno, Cioran also repeats elements of the metaphysical pessimism of Schopenhauer and Freud. Especially in his earlier works, human beings are sometimes depicted as confronting time directly. He reproduces Schopenhauer's concern with nothingness: "The presence of death in life introduces into one's existence an element of nothingness. . . . the nothingness inherent in the temporal" (*OHD* 26). All events and moral judgments, to Cioran, seem meaningless in a time that is infinite and linear: "Eternity does not lead to the triumph of either good or evil; it ravages all. . . . Nothing created by man will endure" (*OHD* 63). And he even repeats Freud's judgment that life is a diversion from the natural condition of inorganic being: "It is not *normal* to be alive. . . . Death . . . is no more than the cessation of an anomaly" (*DAQ* 171). This is a minor theme for Cioran—his main focus, as with Camus and Unamuno, is at the existential level of analysis, the conflict produced in the thinking mind by its consciousness of time. But these passages show, at the very least, how there can be a general pessimistic horizon of understanding that includes the various levels of argument in a larger perspective.

Cioran refers to the general calamity that subsumes all these problems as the "fall into time"—one of his books even bears this as a title—but he does not actually interpret this event in a religious fashion.[14] Rather, like Leopardi, he uses Christian (and pagan) imagery as a kind of mythological language to explore and explain a phenomenon that is almost beyond our imagination.

> Already Adam showed signs of that inaptitude for happiness, that incapacity to endure it which we have all inherited. Happiness was within his grasp, he could have appropriated it forever, and he cast it from him. Ever since, we have pursued it in vain; yet suppose our pursuit were *not* in vain—we should accommodate ourselves to success no better. What else is to be expected of a career that began by an infringement of wisdom, by an infidelity to the *gift of ignorance* our Creator had bestowed on us? Cast by knowledge into time, we were thereby endowed with a destiny. For destiny exists only outside Paradise. (*FT* 35–36)

This last phrase—"destiny exists only outside Paradise"—indicates the extent to which Cioran, like the other existential pessimists, is concerned with historical narrative as both a product of our temporal condition and a crutch to help us endure such a condition. To make sense of our situation, we adopt a destiny, a *telos* located in the future that enables us to explain our suffering by reference to a supposed historical trajectory. But such hopefulness, he argues, amounts to no more than eluding the consequences of time and evading the reality of the present: "Hope is the *normal* form of delirium" (*DAQ* 167). This delirium is not far removed from Camus' *l'esquive*: to hope means simply "to lie and to lie to *oneself*" (*SHD* 83–84). Cioran also decries "modern optimism" as the false hopefulness that has been substituted for the traditional religious hopefulness. Such optimism blinds us to the perpetual cycle of destruction that an honest perusal of history would reveal: "Hegel is chiefly responsible for modern optimism. How could he have failed to see that consciousness changes only its forms and modalities, but never progresses? Becoming excludes an absolute fulfillment, a goal: the temporal adventure unfolds without an aim external to itself, . . . each period is perfect in itself—and perishable" (*SHD* 146).

Cioran's *Short History of Decay* was published just two years before Camus' *The Rebel* and there are many parallels to be drawn between the two books.[15] While Camus' book is now mainly recalled for its defense of the politically engaged artist and its exhortation to participation under

---

[14] Cioran's father was an Orthodox minister but he seems to have given up his faith early. *On the Heights of Despair* is already irreligious and his second book, *Tears and Saints*, was actually pulled from the presses in mid-run by his publisher who, from Cioran's account, feared the consequences of publishing something so sacrilegious.

[15] Cioran's *Précis* is the book that Camus initially turned down for publication at Gallimard.

the sign of decency, the better part of the book is a long exploration of the history of "rebellious" thought—a history that proves to be deeply ironic. Over and over, Camus attempts to demonstrate, ideas that began as beneficial ended up being used to defend murder and oppression. This is especially true, he thinks, of historical ideals, which allow one to defend violence as a "sacrifice" to be redeemed by a better future to come. Rejection of some aspect of current conditions is transformed into a wholesale denigration of the present in the name of an ideal but non-existent future. This is one of the reasons that historical "hope" is not just wrong, but dangerous. Though Cioran does not consider the history of modern ideology in the same sort of detail, he likewise views history as having an ironic character. "History", he writes, "is irony *on the move*" (*SHD* 147–48). "*Every step forward is followed by a step back*: this is the unfruitful oscillation of history—a stationary . . . becoming" (*SHD* 178). Faith in the future, for Cioran, is in fact itself evidence that our mental powers do not produce the results we expect: "That man should have let himself be duped by the mirage of Progress is what renders his claims to subtlety absurd. Progress? Perhaps we can find it in hygiene. . . . But anywhere else?" (*SHD* 178).

Just as Camus believes that abandoning hope is, perhaps surprisingly, a liberating step, so Cioran thinks that it is precisely the lack of order to history that is what gives possibility to an individual human life, and which should therefore be embraced: "That History has no meaning is what should delight our hearts. . . . The universe begins and ends with each individual, whether he be Shakespeare or Hodge; for each individual experiences his merit or his nullity *in the absolute*" (*SHD* 149). By this last phrase, I believe, Cioran means that the value of an individual life cannot be a function of its place in history. We cannot understand each other, and should certainly never understand ourselves, as a precursor of X or a culmination of Y; that is the effect of thinking in terms of history or destiny. Nor can we ever really direct our actions beyond ourselves. This does not mean, however, that we cannot think past the end of our life-span. The idea is that we ought not to do so (and ought not to let others suggest that we do so) if it means debasing our own life in favor of a future that we somehow allow to count for more than the present. For, in the end, the unpredictability and destructiveness of history mean that actions carry their meaning, Shakespearean or Hodgist, only in the present. We can, of course, *care* about the world that our children will inherit. But if we begin to evaluate ourselves *only* in terms of that future, we have fallen into an "idolatry of tomorrow" (*FT* 47). For our lives to have merit, they must have it in the here and now, and not by reference to an unactualized future.

Since, unlike the present, tomorrow is always imaginary, such idolatry can be manipulated in many ways. On the one hand, of course, the Stalins of the world can demand the death of millions in the name of a future paradise. This is an especial concern of Camus, who complains of those who "glorify a future state of happiness, about which no one knows anything, so that the future authorizes every kind of humbug" (*RRD* 263). Cioran is concerned about this, but like Camus he is just as concerned with the way in which even a humane future, even one individually chosen, can act as a straitjacket for the chooser and close down possibilities in the present. The entire effort to make our choices *via* a complicated process of attempting to divine what the future holds distracts us from simply confronting the world that is all about us and asking ourselves what, if anything, we actually care about in that world. Avoiding the idolatry of tomorrow is therefore liberating in that one has options apart from simply reacting to perceived historical processes. We can ask not what is important to history but what is important to us.

Given the ironic character of history, we should, at the very least, make sure that our actions have some value in the present. The future that we imagine is unlikely to come about, if it does come about it will not last, and when it does come about we will probably despise it. *That*, at any rate, is what history suggests, if it suggests anything; and that is the only way in which it can guide us. Here too Cioran's conclusions parallel those of Camus: "The historical revolution is always obliged to act in the hope, which is invariably disappointed, of one day really existing" (*R* 251). And both are preceded in this thought by Unamuno. The latter, in explaining the ethic of Don Quixote, who simply leaves his house and confronts whatever evils come his way on the road, writes: "What is known as the future is one of the greatest lies. The true future is today. . . . What is happening to us today, right now? That is the only question." (*OLDQ* 11) For all of the existential pessimists, then, optimism has functioned to displace attention from the real world of today onto an imaginary future. Not only does this future denigrate the present, it causes us to lose touch with the present. When the present, which should be the richest and most vivid thing in our minds, is flattened out in our imagination, it makes our options seem fewer than they are. In fact, the present is the island on which we are stranded. But if, instead of looking offshore, we explore that territory, it may be richer than we initially imagine.

This focus on the present does not abjure all concern for the future. Unamuno's claim that "the true future is today" indicates not that we are forbidden to think about what is to come, but only that we should not make the future into an idol. *If we care about the freedom of later generations, we must respect it—and we respect it best by refusing to script their lives for them*. Respecting the radical openness of the future is hard to do because it can seem like choosing not to care. But, the pessimists insist, we express our care better if we focus on the present and stop considering the openness of the future a problem. The unpredictability of the future represents our freedom and that of future generations. Like the absurd, it is not a problem to be solved but a difficult condition that must be not just endured, but actively preserved.

It is from this perspective on history that Cioran's response to suicide originates. Looking on the meaninglessness of history as liberating, rather than depressing, is the means by which Cioran, like Camus, finds the tenuous grounds to avoid self-imposed death: "Everything that breathes feeds on the unverifiable; . . . Give life a specific goal and it immediately loses its attraction. The inexactitude of its ends makes life superior to death" (*SHD* 10–11). When we know (or think we know), the *telos* of history, even if it is a wonderful one, it renders our life one-dimensional. We exist as a means of transit from point A to point B. We can only appreciate our potential for multidirectional behavior if we abandon the conceit of a transhistorical aim for humanity. While this is no proof, of course, that life is worth living, this perspective at least removes one of the common reasons for suspecting it is not: the fear that we lack, or will not reach, such a destiny. The fruitlessness of human aims is less of a burden if we do not think of it as a failure but as an opportunity.

Like the other pessimists, then, Cioran does not so much build an argument against suicide as attempt to describe how the act itself would make no sense. Putting it laconically in *The Trouble with Being Born*, he writes: "It's not worth the bother of killing yourself, since you always kill yourself *too late*" (*TBB* 32). The act can never really catch up with the suffering that instigates it. While not presenting it as a rational deduction in the manner of Camus, Cioran does insist that the suicidal *thought* is the product of life-conditions that would, in a sense, be contradicted by the *act*:

> Since all that has been conceived and undertaken since Adam is either suspect or dangerous or futile, what is to be done? Resign from the race? *That would be to forget that one is never so much man as when one regrets being so.* And such regret, once it seizes one, offers no means of escape: . . . man still has his road to travel. . . . And since he advances by virtue of an acquired illusion, he cannot stop until the illusion disintegrates, disappears; but it is indestructible as long as man remains an accomplice of time. (*FT* 52–53; emphasis added)

The idea that the condition of regret is endemic to humans also explains why, though Cioran does not endorse the act of suicide, he understands why the habit of thinking about it is something that we can never entirely escape. Just as it cannot be logically carried out, so it cannot be logically refuted: it stems from a fundamental condition of consciousness. At the

same time that it is our burden, it is also, in a strange way, our honor to
have this possibility before us at all times:

> No church, no civil institution has as yet invented a single argument valid
> against suicide. What answer is there to the man who can no longer endure
> life? . . . Suicide is one of man's distinctive characteristics, one of his discov-
> eries; no animal is capable of it, and the angels have scarcely guessed at its
> existence; without it, human reality would be less curious, less picturesque:
> we should lack a strange climate and a series of deadly possibilities which
> have their aesthetic value, if only to introduce into tragedy certain new so-
> lutions and a variety of denouements. (*SHD* 38)

The fact that humans are permanently haunted by suicidal thoughts
means that we feel the seriousness of our situation in a way that animals
and angels do not. This too may not prove that life is worth living, but it
does add to a sense of our existence as a precious opportunity that is not
to be lightly dismissed. Systematic moralities that attempt to forbid suicide can only do so, ironically, at the cost of diminishing their appreciation for the variety of human life.

This incapacity to free ourselves from the thought of suicide is balanced, in a way, by an equal inability to eliminate our tendency to hope.
As in Camus and Unamuno, our tendency to look to the future is not simply a mistake on our part; it is also a product of the embedding of our
consciousness in time: "All men have the same defect: they *wait* to live,
for they have not the courage of each instant. . . . we do not live in the living present but in a vague and distant future." We can perhaps free ourselves from some of its illusions but we cannot return to the animal condition of living entirely in the present. Our hoping is part and parcel of
our no-longer-animal status. "There's no salvation without the immediate. But man is a being who no longer knows the immediate" (*OHD* 111).
Hence, there is no longer any salvation; hoping is the after-effect of this
loss.

And so Cioran, like Unamuno and Camus but perhaps more hellishly,
depicts an immutable conflict as the ordinary human condition. "Agony
means a battle between life and death. Since death is immanent in life, almost all of life is an agony" (*OHD* 16). The result of his approach is no
reason to live, but simply what he calls a "state of non-suicide". Trapped
between two conflicting impulses, we can only negotiate the unpleasant
space between them:

> To do away with oneself seems such a clear and simple action! Why is it so
> rare, why does everyone avoid it? Because, if reason disavows the appetite
> for life, the *nothing* which extends our acts is nonetheless of a power supe-
> rior to all absolutes; it explains the tacit coalition of mortals against death;

it is not only the symbol of existence, but existence itself; it is everything. And this nothing, this everything, cannot give life a meaning, but it nonetheless makes life persevere in what it is: *a state of non-suicide*. (*SHD* 19; cf. *NG* 53, 58)

Cioran thus shares with the other pessimists discussed in this chapter what I have called *the problematic of linear time* manifested at a level of existential narrative. The most important implication, to them, of a consciousness predicated on linear temporality is the personal agony it creates in a human being perpetually poised between hope and suicide.

So far I have largely described the problem that the existential pessimists depict while only hinting at their proposals for an ethic that copes with this situation. As I mentioned before, there are, at least for Camus and Cioran, both an earlier and a later position. The later response represents, for both, but in very different ways, their attempt to make pessimism politically responsible, if not respectable (they are always suspicious of respectability!). Since Unamuno's position is more unswerving and since it dovetails, to a considerable degree, with that of the mature Camus, I postpone discussion of it to the second section below.

First Responses: Boredom and Living the Moment

Of the three authors we are considering here, Cioran is the one who takes up the pessimistic theme of boredom in a serious way. Unamuno, certain that we are all as preoccupied with our own immortality as he is with his own, cannot really conceive of it. Camus' discussion of a possible withdrawal from life comes closer, but he tends to think of that withdrawal only in terms of suicide, with boredom as a subsidiary problem. But from first to last boredom is a topic of which Cioran never tires.

Following Leopardi and Schopenhauer, Cioran considers boredom a model of bare human existence—one embedded in time but without the comforting illusions that we normally use to shield ourselves from the effects of that condition. "Life is more and less than boredom," he writes, but "it is in boredom and by boredom that we discern what life is worth" (*DAQ* 139). When we are not in pain and not distracted by some purpose we have given ourselves, we are left alone with unadorned life. And this existence does not, by itself, prove very stimulating: "Boredom will reveal two things to us: our body and the nothingness of the world" (*TS* 88). It is in part to relieve this feeling of nothingness that we engage in any activity whatsoever. Like Leopardi, Cioran views boredom as one extreme in a pendulum-flow—when we reach it, we are impelled in the opposite direction: "Life is our solution to boredom. Melancholy, sadness, despair, terror, and ecstasy grow out of boredom's thick trunk" (*TS* 89). Inevitably, though, the search for activity will result in feelings of futility and meaninglessness that return us to boredom: "What should I do? Work for a social and political system, make a girl miserable? Hunt for weaknesses in philosophical systems, fight for moral and esthetic ideals? It's all too little" (*OHD* 43).

The bass-note that boredom sounds throughout our lives can be amplified: for example, by insomnia. Cioran suffered from insomnia for many years and he made this condition into a minor theme of his writing. Though insomnia is not quite the same thing as boredom, both of them give Cioran the sense of experiencing the naked flow of time. The very first aphorism of *The Trouble with Being Born* refers to it: "Three in the morning. I realize this second, then this one, then the next: I draw up a balance sheet for each minute. And why all this? *Because I was born.*" (*TBB* 3). Cioran puts this at the beginning of the book so that we will understand that everything that follows is framed by this fundamental experience. Time is what we are born into—we may only realize it when we step back from our daily activities but it is the baseline of all experience. In this sense, insomnia is a blessing since it allows us to tap directly into the pure feeling of happening, as Cioran documents here. But this feeling turns out not to be a pleasant one: everyone with insomnia seeks to escape it, which should not be the case if pure conscious existence were something good in itself. Schopenhauer and Leopardi thought that the fact of boredom proved the inherent misery of existence; Cioran copies that argument and extends it to insomnia. If being conscious were delightful, then we would think of insomniacs as the blessed.

The problem of boredom is especially important for understanding the response to the pessimistic diagnosis that Cioran pronounces in his early Romanian works. Conceiving of the problem as a personal, if universal, agony, he sought a solution that was also, in some sense personal, even private. *Tears and Saints* is a meditation on the agony of the saints—but especially the female mystical saints like Teresa of Avila—and an attempt to convert their experience into an ethic of ecstasy, divested of its religious content. Already in *On the Heights of Despair* he speaks of evading the burden of time and the boredom it delivers us to by, as it were, living entirely within the moment: "Eternity can be obtained only, . . . if one lives the instant totally and absolutely. Every experience of eternity presupposes a leap and a transfiguration" (*OHD* 64). "Eternity," here, while not divine in nature, is meant to signify some realm of existence outside the normal flow of time. Access to eternity is the essence of the mysticism that he credits to the saints, but which need not be limited to them: "The failed mystic is the one who cannot cast off all temporal ties. . . . As with music and eroticism, the secret of successful mysticism is the defeat of time and individuation" (*TS* 67). The ecstasy of the saints was real enough, Cioran maintains; their error was to ascribe it to divine intervention. But as the examples of music and passion show, there are other paths to this kind of experience, which many can share. The success of the saints lies, not in their touching the divine, but in achieving ecstatic moments that relieved their temporal suffering.

Cioran is vague about what it would mean to "live the instant" in such a fashion, but it is reasonably clear that he means to associate himself with a kind of radical romanticism that tells us to abandon all thought of the past and future to experience as deeply and intensely as we can whatever is in front of us: "Suffer, then, drink pleasure to its last dregs, cry or laugh, scream in despair or with joy, sing about death or love, for nothing will endure" (*OHD* 63). Every moment, in this view, is equally valuable, or valueless—that is the view from eternity. But, since we are not gods, we can only experience this view by withdrawing entirely from a historical perspective and narrowing our vision to the immediate, the instant. Living the moment is the attempt to reverse, or cancel, the fall into time.

To be sure, there is something irredeemably juvenile in this kind of stance and Cioran, indeed, gave it up in his later writing. As we have seen, Cioran is clear in his French works that there is no exit or withdrawal from temporality. But he does not come to endorse history as meaningful or to admit the benefits of incremental efforts. Rather, in dismissing the option of ecstasy, he simply cuts off his last avenue of escape and leaves himself stranded. "Only ecstasy cures us of pessimism," he writes in *Tears and Saints*, "Life would be unbearable if it were real" (*TS* 101–2). His later books start from that unbearable reality of life—*leaving him with a pessimism that must remain uncured*. Without the escape-hatch of ecstasy, the burdens of temporal existence become all the heavier to him.[16]

As implausible as this ethic of ecstasy sounds to us now, there *is* a more developed version of the idea of valuing the present moment that can give us some sense of its seriousness—Camus provides it in *The Myth of Sisyphus*. In the middle section of that work, there is a sequence of sketches, as he calls them, that are meant to give substance to the idea of a vocation that does not presuppose an historical destiny. Like Cioran, Camus endeavors to devise an art of living that does not rely on, or attempts to combat, linear temporality. He too displays this art of living by outlining an exemplary existence (as Cioran, in his way, does with the saints). And while Camus also came to view his early essay as, in some sense, imma-

---

[16] The ethic of ecstasy is also the (narrow) point of contact between *Tears and Saints* and *Romania's Transfiguration*: the "transfiguration" in the latter title presumably refers to a kind of miraculous transformation by which backward Romania, through an ecstatic leap, will become a leading, modern European nation. The abandonment of this ecstatic ethic by the postwar Cioran leads him to abandon this kind of nationalism as well.

ture, the "ethic of quantity" it defends is, if not persuasive, far more plausible and instructive than Cioran's early efforts (*MS* 72).

The most famous of these sketches—Camus' imaginative, ambivalent rendering of Don Juan—is apt to be misunderstood (the term "ethic of quantity" is especially unhelpful here). Camus' Don Juan is not a sexual predator, but someone who seeks to repeat genuinely the experience of passionate love. He is not an insincere seducer; rather he loves "each time with his whole self" (*MS* 69). Nor does he collect victories or memories, "collecting amounts to being capable of living off one's past," and Don Juan does not do this (*MS* 72). Equally, he does not plan for future conquests; he "does not hope" (*MS* 70). Rather, he acknowledges the tragedy of our condition by accepting that the intensity of feeling we call "love" is not actually extended over time, as we pretend it is by insisting that love only finds its meaning in long-term, linear narratives. "There is no noble love but that which recognizes itself to be both short-lived and exceptional" (*MS* 74). Camus does not exactly endorse Don Juan's behavior, but he believes that it conforms to the conditions of life that the absurd perspective lays out. It accepts the inherent contradictions of temporal life and lives in moments by multiplying them rather than by trying to assemble them into a false narrative: "The absurd man multiplies here again what he cannot unify. Thus he discovers a new way of being which liberates him. . . . It is his way of giving and of vivifying. I let it be decided [*Je laisse à juger*] whether or not one can speak of egoism" (*MS* 74).

Even if one judges that Don Juan is not an egotist, what Camus describes is only an improved version of Cioran's mystic—his is a sober pursuit of ecstasy. With less ambivalence, however, Camus also describes the theatrical life as embodying an art of living that embraces the moment equally but more productively. Indeed, one can see here the origin of Camus' lifelong allegiance to theater as *the* essential form of art. He does not think at all of the texts of classic plays that endure and are repeated over time. His perspective is that of the actor and his performance: "The actor's realm is that of the fleeting" (*MS* 77). Theater, to Camus, is an art form that, in its nature, is impermanent. Each presentation leaves no trace of itself behind and therefore makes no claims upon the future. To record a theatrical performance would be to violate the terms on which it is offered. The actor succeeds or fails in the moment—but, as with Don Juan, this pursuit of the moment can be a life-long vocation, even if the moments do not accumulate or cohere into a narrative of their own. "Entering into all these lives, experiencing them in their diversity" is an end in itself (*MS* 77). The actor's performance has no goal beyond the performance itself; nor (qua actor) does his career have any goal beyond the repetition of such performances. Yet the actor gains something from experiencing so many different aspects of the human condition. He gains greater understanding of the depth and complexity of the human condition, even if his actions cannot meliorate it. Such a life preserves, in rebellion, the conditions of the absurd.

Camus here embraces exactly those qualities of the theater that repelled Rousseau, but his fundamental reasoning about them is largely the same. For Rousseau the illusions of the theater were contrasted with a natural identity, in comparison with which they seemed shallow. But the theater, for Rousseau, exemplified our modern time-bound existence. And this is exactly the case for Camus as well, only, without the contrast of a natural identity, the theater's exemplary ephemerality becomes something to be embraced.

> [The actor] demonstrates to what a degree appearing creates being. For that is his art—to simulate absolutely, to project himself as deeply as possible into lives that are not his own. At the end of his effort his vocation becomes clear: to apply himself wholeheartedly to being nothing or to being several. . . . He will die in three hours under the mask he has assumed today. Within three hours he must experience and express a whole exceptional life. That is called losing oneself to find oneself. (*MS* 79–80)

Rather than pursue a long-term project of creation or pine for a primordial natural existence—both projects that must end in failure or frustration—the actor's vocation is one of a sequence of transfigurative moments, each independent of the others. The theater, to Camus, is a place where temporality can be acknowledged but where, in the repetition and reenactment of that temporality, a certain kind of freedom is created. Where Don Juan's experiences are, one supposes, more or less the same from night to night, the actor, playing a series of different roles, experiences a life that is more varied and, for that reason, more full of insight into different realms of life. The actor's life explores a wider territory than the libertine's—harkening back to Leopardi's invocation of a Columbian life as the one that best embodied the pessimistic spirit. It offers, at least, an individual solution to the problems that the pessimistic perspective identifies without denying the limits that perspective imposes or pretending to escape them.

Camus thus gives a deeper and more persuasive account of what it would mean to respond to the pessimistic diagnosis by attempting to live in the moment. But even here, it must be said, an air of solipsism hangs over the text. It is not just that Don Juan or the actor are selfish; rather, their vocation is described in such a way that their actions seem to have no effect whatsoever on others. One imagines a great deal of spontaneous monologue. For the earlier generations of pessimists, the problems they described were meant to be understood, at least, as general, social conditions. If the solutions they offered often amounted to individual ethics, that did not mean that the situation of others simply disappeared from view, as it seems to here. While not as juvenile as Cioran's ethic of ecstasy, then, Camus' ethic of quantity still seems a rather narrow response to the sort of problem that his own pessimism put before him.

To his credit, it was not his last response. And while Cioran, as we shall see, still seeks a kind of withdrawal from life in his later work, the absolutism and love of excess of his early books is largely muted.

Second Responses: Into Life or out of It

In their post–World War II works, both Cioran and Camus altered, significantly if not radically, their responses to the pessimistic diagnosis. Cioran, as I have said, gave up his ecstatic solution and concentrated on finding a mode of existence that accommodates itself to the conditions of life in this world.[17] His new position, as we shall see, is a retreat into and valorization of solitude, akin to that proposed by the other misanthropic pessimists, Rousseau and Schopenhauer. Camus, as is well-known, was galvanized by the experience of war in the opposite direction. He strove to connect the situation of absurdity to a defense of vigorous political participation, albeit of a certain kind, one linked to the activities of the artist. His particular form of devotion to politics echoes that of Unamuno, who found, in the figure of Don Quixote, an exemplar of a pessimistic form of life that is nonetheless activist. This transformation is of particular importance because, if it is indeed the case that Camus' activism is consis-

---

[17] While it seems clear that Cioran was chastened by the disastrous consequences of wartime radicalism, as well as by the behavior of those with whom he had been associated in prewar Romania (as well as his own behavior), he referred to the transformation of his views only obliquely, as in this passage where he describes the effects of learning to write in French:

> After having frequented certain idioms whose plasticity gave him the illusion of an unlimited power, the unbridled foreigner, loving improvisation and disorder, tending toward excess or equivocation by an inaptitude for clarity, if he approaches French with timidity, sees it nonetheless as an instrument of salvation, an *askesis* and a therapeutics. By practicing it, *he cures himself of his past*, learns to sacrifice a whole background of obscurity to which he was attached, simplifies himself, becomes *other*, desists from his extravagances, surmounts his old confusions, increasingly accommodates himself to common sense, to reason; . . . How can one be mad—or a poet—in such a language? (*TE* 128–29; second emphasis added)

Of his enthusiasm for the mystics he writes: "I lived for years in the shadows of these women, these saints, believing that no poet, sage, or madman would ever equal them. I expended, in my fervor for them, all my powers of worship, my vitality in desire, my ardor in dreams. And then . . . I stopped loving them" (*SHD* 131).

tent with his pessimism, it answers one of the most persistent criticisms of pessimism, namely, that it cannot be effectively political. While it is part of my claim in this book as a whole that this charge should be taken with a grain of salt and that the term "political" should be understood in an expansive sense that includes the antisystematic views of the pessimists, it must nonetheless also expand our view of pessimism if we can see its fruit in Camus' political engagement. While Leopardi and Freud both resisted the temptations of misanthropy and resignation, it is still the case that what they offer is more or less a philosophy of personal conduct adapted to an unresponsive world. Camus' ethic at least allows us to see how such a philosophy can orient us toward the political arena.

Cioran, in modifying his original conclusions, did not change the fundamental perspective of his philosophy. He still felt that our separation from the animals was a regrettable event, from the standpoint of happiness or any other: "We would be better off, verminous and serene, if we had kept company with the animals, wallowing beside them for millennia to come, . . . dying of our diseases and not of our remedies" (*FT* 62). But such statements of regret can only be illustrative of our position; they hold no option for us. Indeed, we are, as Rousseau feared, no longer *lately* removed from our animal condition, but very far away from it indeed: "Nothing is better proof of how far humanity has regressed than the impossibility of finding a single nation, a single tribe, among whom birth still provokes mourning and lamentations" (*TBB* 4). At best we can say that humanity has adjusted itself to its temporal condition and learned to survive it without suicide, but that is not much to show for millennia of conscious existence: "After having botched the true eternity, man has fallen into time, where he has managed if not to flourish at least to live; in any case he has adjusted himself to it. The process of this fall and this adjustment is called History" (*FT* 180).

In this circumstance, what Cioran can suggest amounts to no more than an adjustment to that "adjustment." Like Schopenhauer's instructions for the construction of a fire-proof room, he attempts to adapt to a situation that is fundamentally hellish. And like Schopenhauer, his suggestions have a *tone* that is ascetic and, to a point, stoic. But whereas Schopenhauer predicated the idea of withdrawal or resignation from life on the claim that time-consciousness was something fundamentally unreal and that, in approaching nirvana, we actually approach true knowledge, Cioran does not comfort himself with the idea of an alternate reality or a compensatory knowledge. Our withdrawal from life is a purely practical matter: "As for happiness, if this word has a meaning, it consists in the aspiration to the minimum and the ineffectual, in the notion of *limitation* hypostatized. Our sole recourse: to renounce not only the fruit of action, but action itself" (*FT* 65). Cioran's technique, then, is to radicalize the isolation that our time-consciousness creates, almost to the point of hermitage. Rather than strive after an impossible reunification, we should rest (not rest content, just rest) within our boundaries. In this way we will minimize our unhappiness, be free from illusion, and do the least harm to others. These are the only goals we can hope to obtain.

Like the earlier pessimists, Cioran associates ends-oriented activity with frustration and suffering. On the daily level, this suggests that we ought to cease our pursuit of objects outside of ourselves, whatever their nature: "Civilization instructs us how to take hold of things, whereas it is the art of letting them go that it should teach us. . . . Every new acquisition signifies a new chain" (*FT* 69). But this behavior, if generalized, amounts to an "art of living", albeit a monastic one—a withdrawal, insofar as humanly possible, from the effects of time. While we cannot leap out of time, in an ecstatic fashion, we can hunker down, as it were, mark our doors with blood, and let the worst of it pass over us. This, to Cioran, is the condition that we ought to call freedom: "If we were to wrest ourselves from our desires we should thereby wrest ourselves from destiny; . . . by the sacrifice of our identity we would accede to freedom, inseparable from a training in anonymity and abdication. 'I am *no one*, I have conquered my name!' exclaims the man who, rejecting the degradation of leaving tracks, tries to conform to Epicurus's command: 'Hide your life'" (*FT* 66). While this passage makes the freedom Cioran desires sound entirely negative, elsewhere, as we have seen, he describes the release from destiny as something that should "delight our hearts" on the grounds that it liberates the individual in the most radical way possible (*SHD* 149).

Epicurus is a figure to whom Cioran recurs on several occasions, always as an example of the sort of philosopher he would like to emulate, one who has "stopped thinking and . . . begun to search for happiness" (*TS* 50). While showing no interest in Epicurean metaphysics, Cioran directly identifies with the idea of a search for an "art of living" and with a practical approach to pleasure and pain. But where Epicurus recommended friendship as a core element of personal happiness, Cioran's stringent search for nothingness ends in isolation: "I suppressed word after word from my vocabulary. When the massacre was over, only one had escaped: *Solitude.* I awakened euphoric" (*TBB* 92). To escape our destiny, we must escape from all the trappings of social existence, which constantly threaten, as Rousseau argued, to generate new desires and aims for which we will futilely strive. Even more than hiding our lives, Cioran's advice, in effect, is to hide your soul. He replaces the ecstasy of transfiguration with the satisfactions of solitude. The atheistic mystic has become an atheistic monk. It goes too far to say that Cioran, in his later work, is recon-

ciled to this kind of existence. One might say he accepts it as the best freedom there is, having given up all alternatives.[18]

None of this changes for Cioran the fundamentally pessimistic diagnosis. Always bleak, his tone becomes, if anything, even more laconic in his
later works. "To live," he writes, "is to lose ground" (*TBB* 96). Having
prescribed solitude and inactivity as the preferred form of existence, his
ethics now amounts to a universal pact of noninterference, similar to
Freud's injunction to let each person find his own path to death: "The
originality of a being is identified with his particular way of losing his footing. Primacy of noninterference: let each live and die as he wants, as if he
had the luck to resemble no one, as if he were a blessed monster" (*DAQ*
161). Anything more, to him, even the attempt to help another find their
footing, would be inhumane.

Though Cioran's ethic resembles Schopenhauer's perhaps more than
anyone else's, he did not, in his later writings, romanticize or aestheticize
the inactivity he recommended. If anything, he satirized it, and his writings are full of self-mockery: "And who was ever bold enough to do nothing because every action is senseless in infinity? . . . Who has become a
hero of total sloth?" (*SHD* 43–44). More clearly than Schopenhauer too,
Cioran insists that we cannot make much headway in our efforts to minimize the unpleasantness of life. It is not just a matter of reducing our desires; time's destructiveness cannot, by such a maneuver, by avoided.
"Resignation to becoming, to surprises that are no such thing, to calami-
ties that pretend to be uncommon" (*AA* 189). Except for rare moments,
Cioran sees the randomness of events in a world that is linear but not pro-

---

[18] Cioran is also motivated to affirm conscious life by his capacity to imagine another
form of being—one that is worse than our own. Though this world is a hell, yet, he thinks,
there are circles of it even beneath our own. Having been ejected from eternity into history,
Cioran conceives a possible further ejection into what he calls "posthistory." Posthistory
will occur when we lose touch with the temporal consciousness that now sustains us. If this
happens, he seems to think, we might look back with nostalgia even on our current world
of suffering.

> Now it will no longer be a matter of falling out of eternity, but out of time; and, to fall
> out of time is to fall out of history; once Becoming is suspended, we sink into the inert,
> into the absolute of stagnation where the Word itself bogs down, unable to rise to blas-
> phemy or prayer. . . . And then, having lost even the memory of the true eternity, of
> his first happiness, he will turn his eyes elsewhere, toward the temporal universe, to-
> ward that second paradise from which he has been expelled. (*FT* 180–81)

The condition Cioran pictures here is not a return to unconsciousness or he would welcome
it. He appears to be imagining the sort of nightmare where one is pinned or trapped but unable to even call out for help or lament one's condition. In posthistory, we would be neither
human nor animal. And regrettable as our condition is, it is, to Cioran, apparently preferable to a posthistorical quagmire—as he prefers the state of nonsuicide to suicide.

gressive as uncompensated for—surprises are always bad surprises. And even in the exceptional moments ("That History has no meaning is what should delight our hearts"), the compensation is insufficient. What it amounts to is mostly the pessimistic knowledge that we are not enslaved to history. We can at least say then, in a Leopardian fashion, that in acknowledging this, we achieve the freedom of the person who has torn the last shreds of illusion from his vision of the world and sees it as it is. "Lucidity," he writes, "is the only vice which makes us free—free *in a desert*" (*TBB* 12).

The Pessimistic Rebel

Camus in his later writing also changed the direction, if not the foundations, of his pessimism. But from an initial position that was similar to Cioran's, Camus moved in the opposite direction. In *The Rebel*, Camus returned to the problem of absurdity that he explored in *The Myth of Sisyphus*, but it is clear from the start that he views it differently. Whereas in his earlier essay he had stressed the isolation of the individual within a meaningless universe, *The Rebel* takes pains to emphasize that this condition is one that is the common lot of humanity: "In absurdist experience, suffering is individual," he writes, "But from the moment when a movement of rebellion begins, suffering is seen as a collective experience. Therefore the first progressive step for a mind overwhelmed by the strangeness of things is to realize that this feeling of strangeness is shared with all men. . . . The malady experienced by a single man becomes a collective plague" (*R* 22).

This last phrase, of course, is a reference to Camus' highly successful novel *The Plague*, published immediately after the war. In that book, the "plague" (*la peste*) is an allegory for the pernicious spread of fascism, which the characters in the book respond to in a variety of ways, from servile acceptance to heroic resistance. By linking the problem of the absurd to the plague of fascism, Camus signals that his question is no longer simply the personal one of whether an individual can find a reason to avoid suicide. The dangers of absurdity he now considers to be importantly social and political—*l'esquive* is not just a personal failing, but, he now maintains, one that can lead to compliance with monstrous evil: "The longing for rest and peace must itself be thrust aside; it coincides with the acceptance of iniquity" (*R* 248). While Camus' novel was criticized for seeming to depoliticize fascism by using the metaphor of an anonymous, biological force, Camus' intention was, in a sense, precisely the opposite. His desire (successful or not) was to represent political danger as a species of the absurd condition, which perpetually confronts us not just as individuals but as a population and a community. For the eminently personal question of suicide in *The Myth of Sisyphus*, *The Rebel* now substitutes the very political question of murder.

As we have seen, however, there is also a great deal of philosophical continuity between the early and late Camus. In both periods, he continues to reject historical optimism and to deny the existence of natural or permanent moral structures to guide our behavior. Indeed, as I described above, a large portion of *The Rebel* is given over to repeating and deepening these claims: "Thought that is derived from history alone, like thought that rejects history completely, deprives man of the means and the reason for living" (R 249). How, then, will Camus reformulate his pessimism so that it can address the political questions he now considers pressing? The answer, I believe, is by returning to the figure of the actor and by demonstrating that there is a kind of antiteleological political activity that is like the actor's in finding its purpose in the enacted moment.[19] He now emphasizes something he did not before, but which nonetheless grows naturally out of the idea of the theater: activity that preserves the absurd can be undertaken not only in the presence of, but in active concert with, others, as an actor does with his troupe. In *The Myth of Sisyphus*, the actors had appeared only to soliloquize. But "art," he now writes, "cannot be a monologue" (RRD 257). The purpose of the endeavor, he now maintains, though contained in the present, may be something more than the personal transfiguration of the participants.

Although still indebted to theatrical metaphors, at this point Camus no longer speaks exclusively of the theater but of art as such. Art is that which can represent both sides of the absurd divorce—the unresponsive universe and the human who demands a response. "If," he writes, "rebellion could found a philosophy it would be a philosophy of limits. . . . Injustice, the transience of time, death—all are manifest in history. . . . But confronted with [history], he [the rebel] feels like the artist confronted with reality; he spurns it without escaping from it" (R 289–90). What Camus means here is that art, when it is serious, does not reject the human condition but, *by the process of representing it*, manages to escape enslavement to it. Just as the actor, in representing a life, finds a freedom of expression that is the opposite of rote imitation, so the work of art in general, in representing life in general, amounts to a form of freedom that is not found in the world itself. Here is the element of liberation in the theater that Rousseau, who compared the actor to a prostitute, missed. The artist

---

[19] This point has been emphasized by Isaac who links Camus' theories here, rightly in my opinion, to those of Hannah Arendt. Both took as their model the activities of the French Resistance, which were, in this view, not undertaken in the belief that they would necessarily be efficacious or successful, but simply with the thought that they were the necessary human response to tyranny. See Isaac 1992, chaps. 4–5.

"spurns [reality] without escaping from it." The limits of the actor's performance are still set in advance by the boundaries of the character she inhabits. But within that horizon, the actor can, in a reenactment, find a moment of freedom that was not present in the original.

Important to Camus here is the example of Proust's *In Search of Lost Time*, which, in perfectly capturing our experience of life in the flow of time, is anything but a carbon copy of life: "Proust's work . . . appears to be one of the most ambitious and most significant of man's enterprises against his mortal condition. He has demonstrated that the art of the novel can reconstruct creation itself, in the form that it is imposed on us and in the form in which we reject it" (*R* 267). Proust does not escape reality; he rebuffs it by lovingly reproducing it in a beautiful form. Indeed, it is just Proust's radical dedication to reproducing the experience of the flow of time that is the center of his artistry and, therefore, of his individuality and his freedom. Though a novel, obviously, lacks the spontaneity and fleetingness of an acted performance, *Proust's* novel finds a way to reproduce that sensation and make it available to us outside of the theater. It is the element of creative reenactment, which Camus first associated with the actor, that he generalizes here into a broader theory of art. Proust's work "is allied to the beauty of the world or of its inhabitants against the powers of death and oblivion. It is in this way that his rebellion is creative" (*R* 268). Like an Impressionist painting, Proust's novel respects the fleetingness of the moment but also, in preserving it, rebels against its sinking into oblivion. The rebellion that Camus describes here is, to him, not mere artistry or simply a personal art of living but also, finally, a model for politics. Art of this kind can produce moments of beauty and freedom off the stage as well as on it.

For the later Camus, rebellion of this sort is the only kind of aim that it is reasonable to possess in an absurd world. The rebel must not just admit to limits but his actions, like the artist's, must "express fidelity to the human condition" (*R* 290). In politics, this means not directing one's efforts to a far-off future, but rather enacting the present in a way that does not merely replicate it. "Every great reformer tries to create in history what Shakespeare, Cervantes, Molière, and Tolstoy knew how to create: a world always ready to satisfy the hunger for freedom and dignity which every man carries in his heart. . . . The procedure of beauty, which is to contest reality while endowing it with unity, is also the procedure of rebellion" (*R* 276). Of course, the world is not remade simply by being reimagined and Camus readily concedes that "beauty . . . does not make revolutions" (*R* 276). Nonetheless, these great humanistic artists, by depicting an ugly world in which people suffered intensely, in their very act of doing so as human beings succeeded in establishing a human place in the world and in humanizing that world. In creating characters of universal appeal, they make the commonality of the absurd apparent and thus contribute to human solidarity. At the very least, then, such artists might help us to feel at home in our homelessness (in Heidegger's phrase) and, perhaps, they thereby contribute to an atmosphere conducive to "freedom and dignity." This, to Camus, is a model for political behavior.

In a later essay, Camus went somewhat further in describing what such behavior would look like: "Beauty . . . cannot serve any party; it cannot serve . . . anything but men's suffering or their liberty. The only really committed artist is he who, without refusing to take part in the combat, at least refuses to join the regular armies and remains a free-lance" (*RRD* 267). Here it is clear that Camus' ethic, though it may be more political than that of other pessimists, remains individualistic. In *The Rebel*, the moment of danger for any idea comes when it is converted into an ideology. When the thought of an individual becomes a template for group behavior, the element of freedom is removed. Performances become rote, they lack the spontaneous creativity of the initial instance, whether in the theater or outside of it. Thus, although Camus is committed to "taking part in the combat" (recall that *Combat* was the name of the resistance newspaper he edited), he insists that the sort of activism he recommends cannot include becoming a member of a party. This does not mean, of course, that his ideas cannot coincide with those of others or that he cannot work with others in the short term—but such coincidence will be just that and will not imply a long-term binding of destinies. Such destinies his pessimism, like Cioran's, continues to reject. An actor might join with others, with great unity of purpose, to mount a particular production, without thereby committing to the group for anything further. What sort of political activity, then, remains to a person without party?

The references to the artist as a "free-lance" and to Cervantes as a rebellious artist here point us back to Unamuno and to his hero, Don Quixote. While I will discuss Cervantes's actual text in chapter 7, it will be helpful here to consider briefly in what way Unamuno regarded the quixotic ethic as the upshot of his pessimism. As we have discussed, Unamuno also believed that human existence only takes place within an absurd contradiction. Like Camus, he believed we must banish any concrete image of the future from our decision making. Yet, like Camus, he rejected the withdrawal and misanthropy of someone like Schopenhauer or Cioran and used the exemplar of Don Quixote to explain his alternative.

In Unamuno's rendering, Don Quixote has no plan of justice, not even a system of beliefs. To be a free-lance is to wander the world as it is, lending a hand to whomever you meet who is in need of assistance: "Redress whatever wrong comes your way. Do now what must be done now and do here what must be done here" (*OLDQ* 16). In doing so, however, Quixote does more, Unamuno maintains, than merely behave commendably. He performs an art of living that enhances the world by its appearance without fundamentally altering its temporal horizon. There is a fine line to walk here since Unamuno wants to say simultaneously that Quixote's actions do not improve the world in any permanent way even though we are all better off for having his example. Like Camus' actor, Quixote was all along *enacting* a piece of the world, yet transforming both the part and the whole in the process. Although Quixote's efforts never reach their stated goals and do not appear to directly make the world any safer, happier, or freer, his *performance* of freedom leaves a kind of afterglow that can inspire us to seek a similar relationship to our absurd condition:

> The Knight allowed himself to be led at random along the pathways of life by his horse. . . . He sallied out into the world to right the wrongs that would come forth to meet him, but with no previous plan, no program of reform. *He did not set out to apply prearranged decrees, bur rather to live as knights-errant had lived; his model he had found in the lives created and narrated by art*, not in systems constructed and explained by any sort of science. (*OLDQ* 33; emphasis added)

Unamuno's Quixote is thus the instantiation of Camus' artistic rebel. *His success lies not in the later consequences of his actions but in the freedom that their occurrence represents.* While the vigorous execution of these actions does not negate their ultimate futility, it does manage to express simultaneously the essence of their author along with the inevitability of his demise. It is this unpredictable expression that marks the occurrence of something new, individual, and free. As Camus puts it: "The loftiest work will always be . . . the work that maintains an equilibrium between reality and man's rejection of that reality, each forcing the other upward in a ceaseless overflowing, characteristic of life itself at its most joyous and heart-rending extremes. Then, every once in a while, a new world appears" (*RRD* 265). The "new world" Camus refers to here, however, is not a different place or a better place than our own. Rather, it is the world of freedom that can exist within a human being, even while bound to a pessimistic universe: "There is not a single true work of art that has not in the end added to the inner freedom of each person who has known and loved it. Yes, that is the freedom I am extolling, and it is what helps me through life" (*RRD* 241). This sort of freedom is not a social or political *condition*—it cannot be locked into place by constitutional means and, strictly speaking, it cannot be shared with others. Less strictly, however, just as Camus now considers the problem of the absurd, though individual in structure, to point toward a political commonality, so the freedom he speaks of here is not *just* a private experience, but can at least be related to political and social interaction. An actor's performance is always her own but, if she shares the stage with anyone, there is a sense in which the various performances can mutually enhance one another. Moreover, it is always the actors' goal to share these performances with the audience. It is a goal that, like all others, can never really be achieved—but the repetition of such failures, the continuous reaching out and falling short, is, one might say, the real activity of the theater itself. Failing from the perspective of its goal, it is just this representational activity that, to Unamuno and Camus, generates a genuine experience of freedom, an experience compatible with the burdens of temporality.

If there is a difference between Unamuno's and Camus' ideal of a freedom, it lies in Camus' continuing emphasis on the "collective experience" of the absurd. "Rebellious art," he writes, "also ends by revealing the 'We are'" (R 275). When it is truly successful, as in Cervantes or Proust, the plight and triumph of the delineated individual makes visible to us our common situation. "The common dignity of man" is what is illuminated, what we see, during the experience of freedom we have in rebellion (R 277). This is why a rebel in politics seems, to Camus, so much like an artist who appears to work in solitude. In describing our condition, even in the most pessimistic terms, both figures call us together and call us to action. This call to action may have a specific content, but the only content that all such calls will share is to recognize the equality of our circumstances and, on this basis, to communicate. The common dignity of man is not a moral status but an existential condition—that is why it does not generate permanent rules of behavior:

> Far from obeying abstract principles, [rebellion] discovers them only in the heat of battle and in the incessant movement of contradiction. . . . If injustice is bad for the rebel, it is not because it contradicts an eternal idea of justice, but because it perpetuates the silent hostility that separates the oppressor from the oppressed. It kills the small part of existence that can be realized on this earth through the mutual understanding of men. . . . The mutual understanding and communication discovered by rebellion can survive only in the free exchange of conversation. (R 283)

Where Freud offered a pessimistic social contract, Camus rejects the idea of fixed terms of social engagement—but he does provide a model of pessimistic citizenship. The pessimist's engagement can be predicated on an equality of condition thrust upon us by our common situation of absurdity. While this equality generates no permanent principles, it is at least a distinct standpoint from which to view politics and to make one's own decisions about how best to intervene. And in establishing the grounds for communication with others, it offers a structure for politics that allows the radical individuality of the pessimistic spirit to come into contact with others on a regular basis. Camus rejects the conclusions of Cioran and the other pessimists who insist on insulating the individual while still remaining within the larger pessimistic perspective.

As Camus' readers, it can seem frustrating that little about these political actions or conversations can be specified in advance. A quixotic ethic, the wanderings of a free-lance, can seem vague to the point of emptiness. But the vagueness is largely a product of the demand for a politics based on a specific future. Over and over, Camus insists that dedication to the present is in fact the more concrete political commitment in a world where the future cannot be known.

> Origin of form, source of real life, [rebellion] keeps us always erect in the savage, formless movement of history. . . . He who dedicates himself to . . . history dedicates himself to nothing and, in his turn, is nothing. But he who dedicates himself to the duration of his life, to the house he builds, to the dignity of mankind, dedicates himself to the earth and reaps from it the harvest that sows its seed and sustains the world again and again. (R 301–2)

If we devote ourselves to the problems that appear on our doorstep, we will not want for concrete steps to take. It is when we try to orient ourselves by means of a specific but imaginary future that our ethic descends into vagueness. Although we may seem to narrow our political engagements when we disdain to join any party, from Camus' perspective it is the parties that narrow the realm of the political by linking all behavior to the various destinies they pursue. The free-lance is the only political actor who can strike out in any direction at any time—the only one, therefore, who truly keeps the entire vast terrain of the political within the horizon of possibility.

Camus' activist philosophy thus continues to honor his pessimistic assessment of the world. Indeed, it echoes the concern first voiced by Rousseau that our consciousness of time distracts us from the reality in front of our faces: "What madness for a fleeting being like man always to look far into a future which comes so rarely and to neglect the present of which he is sure" (E 82). Camus has specific political desires, of course; no human being could fully divest himself of those. But he does not plan for the future or aim at it. That would be to invite frustration. Precisely because the future always remains for him open and unspecified, he leaves room for the surprises and spontaneous events that separate human freedom from historical destiny. That is why he also insists that "the 'We are' paradoxically defines a new form of individualism. . . . This individualism is in no sense pleasure; it is perpetual struggle, and, sometimes, unparalleled joy" (R 297). It is only when we attempt to release ourselves from historical narratives that we are able to appreciate the multiple potentialities of our being and thereby more fully respect the freedom of our peers and those who will come after us. If we care for others, we can best express that care by exploring those potentialities as Quixote explores himself in the process of exploring the world: "Real generosity toward the future lies in giving all to the present" (R 304).

While he speaks of "giving all to the present," it should be noted that it is no longer Don Juan who exemplifies this attitude. Camus has left behind his absolute focus on the moment. Rather than seeking to escape from linear time into the moment, the rebel is someone who no longer relies on teleological narratives but still acts under the aegis of her time-consciousness. The "present" (as opposed to the "moment") is admitted to connect to past and future; we are simply not the masters of this connection. This is the "real generosity toward the future": neither hiding from it nor attempting to imprison it in advance. *Expecting nothing* from the future is not in any way a hostility toward the future—just the opposite, Camus claims.

Here too it should be clear that Camus as well as Unamuno (like Leopardi and Freud) are in possession of a humanistic impulse that separates them from the misanthropy of Cioran (and Rousseau and Schopenhauer). Cioran's self-disgust is only partly personal; it also extends to his status as a member of the species. Where Cioran offers the option of dying of our diseases or of our cures (and prefers the former), Camus counters with the advice of Abbé Galiani to Mme. d'Epinay: "The important thing," Camus repeats, "is not to be cured, but to live with one's ailments" (MS 38). Living with one's ailments is precisely what Camus' activist pessimism aims to do. It neither denies the limitations on our condition nor seeks to escape them. But it also is not paralyzed by them. Though it offers no ideological orientation in the ordinary sense, the quixotic ethic that Camus arrives at is without question intolerant of complacency. If the simultaneous injunction to explore oneself and to confront whatever injustices appear before one seems schizophrenic, one can only reply that this is in no way obvious and did not appear so to Camus. "There shines forth fleetingly the ever threatened truth that each and every man, on the foundation of his own sufferings and joys, builds for all" (RRD 272).

Indeed, the conjunction of the two seems to have occurred to him at the height of his political participation. In a famous editorial in *Combat* that was published on the night Paris was liberated, he wrote as follows: "Nothing is given to men, and the little they can conquer is paid for by unjust deaths. But man's greatness lies elsewhere. It lies in his decision to be stronger than his condition. *And if his condition is unjust, he has only one way of overcoming it, which is just to be himself*" (RRD 39–40; emphasis added). It is only, it seems, on the basis of a pessimistic acknowledgment that Camus could find simultaneous grounds for *both* individualism and human solidarity. The actions of the Resistance, he argues, were not justified by their eventual success. They were justified because they simultaneously gave dignity to individual life under occupation while allowing those who respected such dignity to create a common political space where they could have the experience of freedom. While the actions generated may have played a part in the demise of fascism, their failure to do so could never have invalidated the enterprise. Resistance, rebellion, if they are genuine, validate themselves in the moment of their occurrence, not by reference to some desired outcome, no matter how noble. While this, for Camus, is all the justification we should require for political acts, it is probably worth noting here that over the years such actions have proved more productive of freedom in politics than is often recognized.[20]

. . . . .

The typology I have set out in this chapter and the preceding two is, of course, a schematic one. The history of pessimism that it begins to describe could be expanded and deepened in a variety of directions. In the twentieth century alone, for example, detailed study of Weber, Adorno, Heidegger, Foucault, and Arendt from this perspective would be useful. But my intent has not been to offer an exhaustive history, but rather, as I said at the outset, to recreate the pessimistic perspective in order to trouble and interest the reader and to disturb the standard histories of political thought that exclude pessimism or treat it as a psychological condition. What I hope to have established to this point is simply the existence and seriousness of a pessimistic tradition in political philosophy, structured around the problematic of a time-bound human life and offering a variety of perspectives on that problem. In the second half of the book, I will focus more directly on that pessimism I am most concerned to defend.

One of the themes of this chapter has been the struggle of the twentieth-century pessimists, especially Camus, to define a philosophy that is not based on truths that somehow escape the destructiveness of time and yet that is equal, in some sense, to the murderous destructiveness of modern politics. Camus' critique of "dandyism," for example, betrays an impatience with an ethic that is purely personal or *in a narrow sense* aesthetic. Though Camus has in mind largely figures from the nineteenth century (as well, I believe, as his own earlier self), there is no question that this is a shoe that at times fits Cioran disturbingly well: "To make for the end of time with a flower in one's buttonhole—the sole comportment

---

[20] It seems to me that a very strong case exists that it was on the basis of just such a pessimistic solidarity that, for example, the rebellious dissident movements of Eastern Europe in the 1970s and 1980s coalesced. The writings of Václav Havel—and the veneration of iconoclasts like Frank Zappa by the Czech underground—echo Camus' injunction to combat oppression with individuality.

worthy of us in time's passage" (*SHD* 117–18; cf *R* 47ff.).[21] But Camus rightly believes that the evils of totalitarianism (whether or not they constitute something called Evil) simply cannot be ignored this way.

Yet, surprisingly perhaps, Camus returns at just this point to the subject of art and defends a kind of activity that is rooted in aesthetic values even when it is political. One might say, of this turn in his thought, that by means of a long detour through ideology, he comes back to Nietzsche, who was clearly one of his starting points. Though Camus faulted Nietzsche for writing words that lent comfort to fascism (while acknowledging that such was never his intent), his efforts to use aesthetic practices and techniques to craft a political ethic were perhaps more Nietzschean than he himself realized. It is in this spirit that I suggest we approach Nietzsche's own efforts to define his philosophy as a kind of pessimism. The pessimism that he suggests we practice, like that of Camus, has aesthetic models, but it is not meant to be limited to an artistic realm. Rather its aim is to break the hold that optimistic discourse has had on the political realm for many centuries—and it perhaps does so with more consistency and depth than Camus was able to register.

Unamuno, who endured the precursors of modern fascism in Spain, also felt that it was a human duty to right wrongs—but rather than search for a theory of justice to ground such a duty, he turned instead to the narrative of *Don Quixote*. This too is unexpected and, seems, at first, an aesthetic detour away from political engagement. But, as I hope the next chapters will show, the figure of Don Quixote is in fact one that is perfectly apt in the effort to make pessimism an ethic that is practicable and political. "Quixotic," like "pessimistic," is not an adjective we should blithely use as a form of denigration. I also hope that these chapters will flesh out in more detail the pessimistic sense of freedom and individuality that this chapter only began to develop.

Cutting against the typology that ordered the last three chapters, I have also relied on a distinction between those pessimisms that are misanthropic versus those that are humanistic. This distinction is also schematic: humanism and its opposite are not clear-cut categories. The figures I have discussed—as I think the substance of what I have written demonstrates—offer a range of opinions on our species that I would not want to see simply reduced to pro- and anti-. I have used this distinction, as I have used the typology, to give the reader a handle on the issues involved and to provide a preliminary sorting that might encourage further study.

---

[21] Parfait, whose study of Cioran is one of the best, reaches a similar conclusion, though she does not view it as necessarily a criticism (2001, 168–71). Cioran, one might say, also acknowledges the horrors of the twentieth century—by the energetic attempt to hide his life from politics altogether. *Je laisse à juger si l'on peut parler d'égoisme.*

Nonetheless, I do, of course, believe that the distinction gets at something real, even if in a crude way, and that there is within the pessimistic problematic a fundamental issue about whether the human condition is something to be embraced or, insofar as this is possible, rejected. In part III, I will attempt to give a better accounting for my preference for the humanist pessimists.

PART III

Chapter Five

NIETZSCHE'S DIONYSIAN PESSIMISM

That there still *could* be an altogether different
kind of pessimism, . . . this premonition and
vision belongs to me as inseparable from me,
as my *proprium* and *ipsissimum.* . . . I call this
pessimism of the future—for it comes! I see
it coming!—*Dionysian* pessimism.
— FRIEDRICH NIETZSCHE

THE PRIOR chapters have attempted to give the reader a sense of the
breadth and complexity of the pessimistic spirit. It is a long and diverse tradition, sympathetic to the plight of the human condition but, on
the whole, not pitying of it. The pessimists, more than any other group of
theorists, have attempted to come to grips with the burden placed on
human beings by virtue of our residency in linear time. If we cannot return to a cyclical view of history and if narratives of progress now seem
suspect, it is pessimism, I submit, that holds the richest set of resources
with which to confront the human condition as we know it today. Nonetheless, while I hope that the pessimistic tradition in its entirety will, in
the future, receive the broad attention it deserves, it remains the case that
any individual, after surveying this vast terrain of possibility, must choose
his or her own path through it.

Having presented a variety of overlapping pessimisms in the preceding,
this section of the book attempts to crystallize something more particular. The preference I have shown for the pessimists who reject resignation
and withdrawal in favor of more activist life-practices cannot have escaped the reader's attention. The next four chapters attempt, in various
ways, to specify what I take to be the best sort of pessimism—that is, the
pessimism that best accomplishes the task this tradition sets itself, namely,
to define a life-practice compatible with linear temporality. Just as any liberal can appreciate the diversity of the liberal tradition while nonetheless
believing that a certain rendering of its principles best captures its core
identity, so will I attempt to identify a pessimism that is maximally valuable and persuasive.

In this project, Friedrich Nietzsche is a crucial figure. I have limited discussion of his texts in the previous chapters in order to give his pessimism
sustained and direct attention here. In the vast literature that Nietzsche

has generated, there is very little direct attention paid to his self-definition as a pessimist. But this self-definition is crucial, not just for understanding Nietzsche, but for helping us to see the possibilities of pessimism; indeed, it is probably more important for the latter. Since World War II, many excellent studies of Nietzsche have been published and most corners of his thinking have been adequately rendered in some portion or another of this literature.[1] Because the reputation of pessimism has been in such eclipse in this period, however, it has been impossible to see Nietzsche as connected to this tradition or as an exemplar of it.[2] I mean to show here that he is both. But while it may be interesting enough to learn that Nietzsche was a pessimist, I believe it is vital to understand that a pessimist can be a Nietzschean.

Nietzsche's relationship to the pessimists who preceded him was hardly one of uniform celebration. While his allusions to Leopardi are only positive, he called Rousseau a "moral tarantula." And although initially inspired by Schopenhauer's philosophy (and while always respecting its critical spirit), he eventually dissociated himself from its systematic conclusions. Nietzsche was also unkind toward the pessimists popular in the Germany of his day, especially the prominent Berlin philosopher Eduard von Hartmann; Nietzsche called him "completely abysmal" (*BGE* 204).[3]

---

[1] Among the commentaries I have found most useful are Kaufmann [1955] 1974, Deleuze [1962] 1983, Klossowski [1969] 1997, Strong [1975] 1988, Derrida 1978, Kofman 1983, Nehamas 1985, Salomé 1988, Theile 1990, Blondel 1991, Kateb 1992, as well as Borges 1962, which can be usefully read as a series of Nietzschean thought-experiments. A more extensive discussion of the Nietzsche literature can be found in Dienstag 1997.

[2] Thus, the one exception to my earlier statement that commentators have ignored Nietzsche's self-identification as a pessimist dates from 1911. Emily Hamblen's *Friedrich Nietzsche and His New Gospel* is not read much today—no doubt the title gives the impression of a too-worshipful approach that did often appear in this period. But the title is misleading; there is actually much to admire in this little book. In addition to foregrounding Nietzsche's pessimism, it makes a serious and in many ways successful attempt to understand Nietzsche's ironic and multifaceted language, his attack on metaphysics, his interest in dreams—indeed, a whole series of topics are usefully discussed. Although the book is hobbled by the distortions of Nietzsche's sister and by an insistence on Nietzsche's biologism, it does not deserve its present obscurity. (It appears in the International Nietzsche Bibliography of 1960/8, but in no other bibliography that I have consulted.) Heidegger would have profited from reading it, for example, "It is a facile judgment which decides that Nietzsche, while scorning a metaphysical interpretation of the world, has himself been caught in the metaphysical snare" (83). Hamblen (again despite the title) rightly emphasizes the antisystematic nature of Nietzsche's thought.

The title of Roger Hollinrake's book (*Nietzsche, Wagner and the Philosophy of Pessimism*, 1982) suggests more of a focus on pessimism than is the case. It is largely concerned with the Nietzsche-Wagner relationship and the possible connection between *Thus Spake Zarathustra* and Wagner's *Ring* operas.

[3] Little-remembered today, Hartmann would, in the 1870s and 1880s, have been second only to Schopenhauer in the minds of many of Nietzsche's German readers as an exemplar

Nietzsche believed (and I will discuss this in more detail below) that the pessimism of both Hartmann and Schopenhauer led directly to nihilism. Indeed, the very popularity of this form of pessimism in the late nineteenth century was one of the factors that convinced Nietzsche that nihilism would soon enjoy a temporary dominance of European society.

Intermixed with his critique, however, is an account of another kind of pessimism. Nietzsche viewed it as distinct from the popular one and called it "that courageous pessimism that is . . . the way to 'myself,' to *my* task" (*AOM*, "Preface" 4). In this chapter's epigraph, he singles out pessimism as "my *proprium* and *ipsissimum*," that is, "my very own and quintessence." While Nietzsche distinguished between what he frequently called "my pessimism" and those that preceded it, his adoption of the term "pessimism" is also meant to indicate the tradition from which his philosophy sprang. His debts to both the pre-Socratic Greeks and Schopenhauer are widely acknowledged, but his many references to Leopardi (and his pessimism) indicate clearly that he does not construe the origins of this tradition narrowly.[4] Ultimately, he gave his alternative the name "Dionysian pessimism" (*GS* 370).[5] What exactly Nietzsche meant by this term and what appeal it may still have, it is the aim of this chapter to discover. In part, this is a project of disentanglement since Nietzsche made many references to "pessimism" without always indicating which variety he was talking about. When these references are viewed as a whole, however, clear patterns begin to emerge. Nietzsche speaks of many types of pessimism, "the unclear word," only one of which he can embrace (*KGW* 8:1:129; see *WP* 38).[6]

"Pessimism," by itself, is not a very specific term to Nietzsche, and this is not surprising. The late nineteenth century in which he wrote was the one period in which pessimism enjoyed wide respectability, if not alle-

---

of pessimism. A self-proclaimed pessimist, he published extensively and inspired a large secondary literature while remaining a private scholar. His best-remembered work today is probably *The Philosophy of the Unconscious* (1869), an attempt to integrate the systems of Hegel and Schopenhauer, which went through at least nine editions in his lifetime, but in 1880 he also published *On the History and Foundation of Pessimism*. Many nineteenth-century commentaries (e.g., Saltus 1885 and Sully 1891) consider Schopenhauer and Hartmann as pessimism's two principal exponents, though the superiority of Schopenhauer is generally recognized.

[4] In those parts of the Nietzsche corpus that are available for electronic search (all the published work and most of the *Nachlass* for the 1870s and 1880s), Leopardi's name appears more than two dozen times, about the same frequency as that of Emerson and more frequently than those of Dostoevsky and Tolstoy combined.

[5] Nietzsche also occasionally spoke of "the pessimism of strength" (*KGW* 8:2:133), which, as we shall see, has a parallel but not quite identical meaning.

[6] All translations from *KGW*, the authoritative German edition of Nietzsche's writings, are my own responsibility, though I have often drawn on those in *WP* and other published versions when these exist.

giance, in popular and intellectual discussions.[7] The word was used by and applied to a wide spectrum of authors in an indiscriminate way. Nietzsche's notes in the 1880s contain several lists of the various types of pessimism. Whether he composed these lists simply to distinguish among the possible varieties or because he planned to write about them in sequence is unclear. One list reads, in part: "Russian pessimism. Tolstoi, Dostoevsky / aesthetic pessimism *l'art pour l'art* 'description' / romantic and antiromantic pessimism / epistemological pessimism. / Schopenhauer. "Phenomenalism". / anarchistic pessimism," and so on, down to an entry for "moralistic pessimism," which Nietzsche identifies with himself (*KGW* 8:2:73–74).[8] Nietzsche did not address all these varieties of pessimism in depth, but when he did so, it is clear that he did not consider them interchangeable. From his perspective, what these pessimisms had in common was their practice of rejection and denigration or, in his vocabulary, "no-saying." But the *object* and *means* of no-saying were far more important to Nietzsche than the negativity itself. After another such list of pessimisms ("of sensibility, . . . of 'unfree will', . . . of doubt"), he sets out a clarification: "What must not be confused with all this: pleasure in saying No and doing No out of a tremendous strength and tension derived from saying Yes . . . the *Dionysian* in will, spirit, taste" (*WP* 1020). Dionysian pessimism, then, although it too is a no-saying and related to the others, is something explicitly set off from them. For Nietzsche, as for the other pessimists we have examined, it is a philosophy of personal conduct, a suggestion of how to manage the human condition and cope with the basic problems of existence. Far from being a psychological disposition, it is a set of practices intended to guide an individual through the chaotic and disenchanted world in which he finds himself.

The phrase "art of living," having been repopularized by Pierre Hadot with reference to an ancient conception of philosophy ("an exercise practiced at each instant"), has been pressed into service by a variety of commentators as a description of what Nietzsche prescribes as a substitute for ethics.[9] This literature, while pointing us in the right direction, has missed

---

[7] One interesting account of this, with many useful citations to the contemporary literature, appears in Dale 1989, chaps. 9–10.

[8] A version of this jotting appears in *The Will to Power* as "aphorism" 82. However, the editors inserted a variety of punctuation marks in order to clarify and associate various lines with one another; all this punctuation is suppositional and some of it appears mistaken (apart from the obvious awkwardness involved in pretending that a list is an aphorism). In Nietzsche's notebook, but not in *WP*, the note goes on to list other topics that apparently are to be considered related, such as "nationalism / industrial competition / science." To the best of my knowledge, Nietzsche does not refer to his own pessimism as "moralistic" elsewhere.

[9] Hadot 1995, 272. See Nehamas (1985, 1998) who applies the phrase to Nietzsche, as well as Theile 1992, Strong 1988, Rorty 1989, Orlie 1997 and Connolly 1991. Foucault

something crucial in ignoring Nietzsche's self-characterization as a kind of pessimist. The implications of that label will be explored below, but they can at least be prefaced as follows: pessimism has a particular understanding of the burdens of the human condition that these interpreters have not fully acknowledged. For Nietzsche, the time-bound character of our existence forms the basic problematic (and sets limits to the possibilities) of any life-practice that he can recommend. While the phrase "art of living" has been taken by some to indicate an infinitely protean perspective on life, its Nietzschean sense must include the idea that an "artist of living" works with the materials that life provides. Nietzsche's pessimism is what sets the terms of those materials or, more simply, what describes the "life" we have to work with.

Nietzsche's use of the term "Dionysian pessimism"—and his insistence in the 1880s on its centrality to his work—indicates a crystallization of ideas that takes place relatively late in his philosophical growth, but of which there are many precursors in earlier periods. Understanding this term is therefore best accomplished by tracing the development of Nietzsche's thoughts on pessimism and, relatedly, the process by which he disentangled his own thinking from that of Schopenhauer.[10] Nietzsche began by quoting Schopenhauer uncritically, but he ended by proclaiming his views to be the opposite of Schopenhauer's—while still calling Dionysian pessimism his "quintessence."[11]

Of course to his critics, Nietzsche is more often a nihilist than a pessimist. As is the case with many attacks on pessimism, this view mistakes what Nietzsche predicts for what he desires. But the related charge of in-

---

(1986) credits Hadot for inspiring his Nietzschean search for "techniques of the self" in ancient texts; Hadot, in response, politely declined to equate his interpretations with Foucault's (Hadot 1995, 206–13). This whole strand of interpretation has received strong criticism from those who believe Nietzsche meant to offer philosophical truths (though very novel ones) in the traditional meaning of that term. See, e.g., Clark 1990, Leiter 1994, Berkowitz 1995, Appel 1999. While I cannot address this controversy directly in any detail, it will be clear that my position demonstrates an affinity with (and perhaps presents further evidence for) the view of the first group.

[10] I cannot accept the view that Nietzsche's writings, from first to last, are all of a piece, as some commentators have contended. In exploring the earlier writings, I attempt to identify themes that, although they have rivals at the time, later become dominant. I accept, in broad outline at least, the division of Nietzsche's work into an early, middle, and late period as proposed by Warren (1988).

[11] I cannot therefore agree with Cauchi's contention that "the seemingly antipodal route taken by Nietzsche out of Schopenhauerian pessimism was in fact circular" (1991, 260). Cauchi's insistence that Nietzsche merely repeats Schopenhauer's metaphysics (258) is insupportable and her treatment of pessimism as a disposition, while understandable, distorts her interpretation of Nietzsche's terms. While Nussbaum oversimplifies in calling Nietzsche "profoundly hostile" to Schopenhauer's pessimism (1991, 78), her account of the relation between the two is thorough and illuminating.

citing resignation or apathy is one that is often lodged, with some justification as we have seen, against other pessimists as well as Nietzsche. Consequently, if this charge turns out to be false in Nietzsche's case, then it must change our opinion both of his political theory and of pessimism more generally, including all those pessimisms that followed in his wake—"the pessimism of the future" that he predicted. That pessimism need not lead to resignation, that it *properly* leads to spirited activity, is Nietzsche's main contention in his long campaign to rid pessimism of the deformations with which it was saddled by earlier exponents.

Greek Pessimism

Nietzsche first wrote of pessimism and its connection to the Dionysian in *The Birth of Tragedy* of 1872. Although it was certainly anachronistic to apply the term "pessimism" to the ancient Greeks,[12] Nietzsche's use of it here explains a great deal about its meaning in his later work. The focus on pessimism in *The Birth of Tragedy* has often been attributed to the influence of Schopenhauer, but the Greek pessimism Nietzsche claimed to identify is in many ways distinct from Schopenhauer's.[13] In retrospect (though not at the time), Nietzsche himself recognized this. In the "Attempt at a Self-Criticism," which he added to the book upon its republication in 1886, he lamented that he had "obscured and spoiled Dionysian premonitions with Schopenhauerian formulations" (*BT*, "Self-Criticism" 6). But this retrospective judgment did not, as might be expected, lead him to withdraw the characterization of the pre-Socratic Greeks as pessimists. That was not the "Schopenhauerian formulation" he had in mind. Indeed, in the 1886 edition he *added* the subtitle "Hellenism and Pessimism" to the work and emphasized in his new introduction that what he still approved of in the book was its examination of "the good, severe will of the older Greeks to pessimism" and its contrast with the "optimism" initiated around the time of Socrates (*BT*, "Self-Criticism" 4).

The mistake that the new introduction identifies is the *confusion* of Greek pessimism with that of Schopenhauer. The Dionysian pessimism of

---

[12] See chapter 1. Nietzsche's characterization, however, was taken up with enthusiasm by a generation of classicists. See Opstelten 1952.

[13] That Schopenhauer strongly influenced Nietzsche is generally uncontested by scholars; but the degree and timing of that influence are matters of considerable debate. For example, Kaufmann (*BT* 60n) believes Nietzsche had already "broken loose from Schopenhauer" in *The Birth of Tragedy*, whereas Nehamas believes it is precisely on the issue of tragedy that "the influence of Schopenhauer became dominant" (Nehamas 1985, 42). Janaway, in a judicious formulation, maintains that, in *The Birth*, "the Schopenhauerian system hovers eerily in the background, unasserted but indispensable" (1998, 22).

which Nietzsche had had a premonition through his exploration of the Greeks was obscured (he now thought) by his equation of it with Schopenhauer's philosophy. Even to the post-Schopenhauerian Nietzsche of the 1880s, then, the ancient Greeks were indeed pessimists—but were simply another kind, as was Nietzsche himself. In *The Birth of Tragedy*, in fact, we have an early version of Nietzsche's own pessimism. Greek pessimism is not the same as that of Schopenhauer or Nietzsche, but it is an instructive model, both to Nietzsche (who called it "the only parable and parallel in history for my own innermost experience" [*EH*, "*BT*" 2]) and to us in our attempt to understand his later attachment to this term.

The task that *The Birth of Tragedy* set itself was to explain not only the appearance of Greek tragedy, but also its disappearance, at least in its traditional form, after Euripides. As is well-known, Nietzsche hypothesizes that Socrates' introduction (and Plato's furtherance) of a rationalistic philosophy destroyed the preexisting cultural grounds for Greek tragedy (*BT* 12–15). But what exactly did Socrates destroy and how was this possible? Why, in any case, should a philosopher have had the power to affect the theater? The answer lies in the pessimism that Nietzsche associates with the pre-Socratic philosophers and his belief that their ideas reflected the original character of early Greek culture. "Tragedy," he as he put it in a note from this period, "is the outlet of mystic-pessimistic knowledge" (*KGW* 3:3:73). Pessimism was the philosophical basis for the plays of Aeschylus and Sophocles. This was the wisdom that the pre-Socratics possessed and that later generations first denied, and then forgot. Socrates is the agent of this change because his philosophy is essentially *optimistic* (*BT* 14).[14]

In the period in which he wrote *The Birth of Tragedy*, Nietzsche did not think of optimism and pessimism as two equal, if opposite, ways of looking at the world, as we might today; rather "pessimism . . . is older and more original than optimism" (*KGW* 4:1:208). Pessimism is the domain of the Ionian philosophers who preceded Socrates and whose teachings we possess only in fragments. Instead of trying to construct a systematic, ordering philosophy, as Socrates and Plato were to do, the pre-Socratics, Nietzsche believed, grasped the chaotic and disordered nature of the world and only attempted to cope with it insofar as that was possible: "Pessimism is the consequence of knowledge of the absolute illogic of the world-order" (*KGW* 3:3:74).

In some notes from this period, Nietzsche first attributes to Democritus the doctrine that "the world [is] without moral and aesthetic meaning" and calls this idea "the pessimism of accidents" (*KGW* 3:4:151). In

---

[14] A parallel analysis, but without the emphasis on pessimism, is offered by Strong (1988, 152ff.).

Philosophy in the Tragic Age of the Greeks (written at about the same time as *The Birth of Tragedy* but only published posthumously), he likens Anaximander to Schopenhauer and calls him "the first philosophical author of the ancients." He goes on to describe Anaximander as a "true pessimist" and quotes his only extant fragment to justify the label: "Where the source of things is, to that place they must also pass away, according to necessity, for they must pay penance and be judged for their injustices, in accordance with the ordinance of Time" (*PTG* 4; see *KGW* 3:2:312).[15] The comparison with Schopenhauer follows directly in Nietzsche's text and emphasizes the moral quality in both of their philosophies; both view "all coming-to-be as though it were an illegitimate emancipation from eternal being, a wrong for which destruction is the only penance" (*PTG* 4; see Cartwright 1998, 122). Later, as I discuss below, Nietzsche would distinguish between Schopenhauer's moralizing pessimism and that of the Greeks, which is only ontological.

But setting aside the association with Schopenhauer, Nietzsche's consistent point is that the pre-Socratics, as he interpreted them, grasped the animating principle of pessimism as I have described it in the preceding chapters: that time is an unshakable burden for human beings because it leads to the ultimate destruction of all things—and that this fate belies any principle of order that may, on the surface, appear to guide the course of events. Of course, whether any of the pre-Socratics would have put things this way is debatable (although Heraclitus, in particular, is certainly often understood in this fashion). What is important here is that Nietzsche took them to be doing so, that he understood the root of pessimism to be, as he later wrote, "time-sickness [*Zeit-Krankheit*]" (*KGW* 7:2:51). It is the destructive power of time that stands behind any particular cause of suffering in the world.[16]

---

[15] This is a translation of Nietzsche's German translation of the Greek original, which he slightly adapted to suit his own understanding. A standard English translation renders Anaximander's fragment thus: "And the source of coming-to-be for existing things is that into which destruction, too, happens 'according to necessity; for they pay penalty and retribution to each other for their injustice according to the assessment of Time.'" (Kirk, Raven, and Schofield 1983, 118).

[16] In fact, it seems to me, Nietzsche is mistaken here in not recognizing what I argued for in chapter 1, namely, a considerable distance between the time-consciousness of the ancients and the moderns. Anaximander's fragment, for example, can easily be understood to be describing a cyclical view of existence, in which case its implications, though dire, are less sinister than Nietzsche makes them sound. It is for this reason that I think Nietzsche's characterization of the Greeks as pessimists is ultimately a substantive (rather than merely nominal) anachronism, and that it would be more correct to say that the Greek-tragic view, rooted in the destructiveness of cyclical time and (relatedly) a strong concept of fate, is a precursor to modern pessimism, including Nietzsche's. Nietzsche tends to take account of the differences between ancient and modern temporality by speaking of the increasing "historical consciousness" of the moderns. While it is certainly correct to do so, it seems to me that this cannot quite cover the incongruity of calling the Greeks "pessimists."

Nietzsche considered tragedy to be the outgrowth of this view of the world as something constantly in flux, constantly in the process of becoming, and thus constantly in the process of destroying. The ravages of time could not be cured or compensated through tragedy, only understood: "Tragedy . . . is in its essence pessimistic. Existence is in itself something very terrible, man something very foolish" (*KGW* 3:2:38). Nietzsche rejects the conclusion, popular since Aristotle, that tragedy offers some kind of purification of the emotions generated by the terrible truths of the human condition (*TI*, "What I Owe" 5; *WP* 851). He also rejects the idea that tragedies contain some sort of moral lesson meant to instruct us in ethical behavior. Instead, he argues, tragedy simply serves to lay bare for us the horrible situation of human existence that the pre-Socratic philosophers describe, a situation from which our minds would otherwise flee: "The hero of tragedy does not prove himself . . . in a struggle against fate, just as little does he suffer what he deserves. Rather, blind and with covered head, he falls to his ruin: and his desolate but noble burden with which he remains standing in the presence of this well-known world of terrors presses itself like a thorn in our soul" (*KGW* 3:2:38). The tragic outlook is thus generated from a base of pessimistic knowledge. It recommends no cure for the pains of existence, only a public recognition of their depth and power.[17]

From the beginning too this view is associated with the Dionysian, "the mother of the mysteries, tragedy, pessimism" (*KGW* 3:3:309). The Athenian public theatrical festivals were known as the Dionysia and Nietzsche goes so far as to claim the existence of a tradition "that Greek tragedy in its earliest form had for its sole theme the sufferings of Dionysus" (*BT* 10).[18] Just as time stands behind any immediate cause of suffering, even in mature tragedy it is always the god, he claims, who stands behind any particular character and wears his face as a mask. Dionysus, in Nietzsche's account (which here certainly parallels Schopenhauer's depiction of the human condition) suffers the prototypical agonies of existence inflicted by time. He is severed from the eternal flux and individuated, then torn to

---

[17] In the vast literature on tragedy, George Steiner's *The Death of Tragedy* is still notable for its emphasis on this point: "The wounds are not healed and the broken spirit is not mended" (Steiner 1961, 129).

[18] Nietzsche calls this tradition "undisputed," which seems doubtful, if only because very little is undisputed in classical philology. Again, however, the accuracy of Nietzsche's construal of philological literature and traditions is less important here than how these were related to his own views. For a useful discussion of the relationship of Nietzsche's conception of Dionysus to the preexisting philological literature, see Murray 1999. For a more complete account of the complex history of the cult of Dionysus, see Kerényi 1976. Kerényi's narrative is written, one might say, under the aegis of Nietzsche's interpretation and is doubtless contentious on many points, large and small—but it is not written in slavish obedience to Nietzsche and disputes many points of his account, often in favor of Nietzsche's friend, the more traditional philologist Erwin Rohde.

pieces and reunited with the whole: "This view of things already provides us with all the elements of a profound and pessimistic view of the world, together with the *mystery doctrine of tragedy*: the fundamental knowledge of the oneness of everything existent, the conception of individuation as the primal cause of evil, and of art as the joyous hope that the spell of individuation may be broken in augury of a restored oneness" (*BT* 10).

Dionysian suffering is essentially human suffering. In tragedy, this is indicated by a connection between the various elements involved in the public performance of the drama. The tragic hero, to Nietzsche, simply personifies the "Dionysian state" of the chorus as a whole (*BT* 10). The chorus is likewise "the mirror-image in which the Dionysian man contemplates himself" and also "a vision of the Dionysian mass of spectators" (*BT* 8). Thus, actor, chorus, and public are all connected in tragedy through their Dionysian character (see Strong 1988, 165); each is a fragment torn from the whole. Nietzsche is here critiquing, but also reconstituting, the traditional philological stance that the chorus represents the Greek public itself. Although, he sharply attacks the original proponents of this view, he in fact proposes not to reject it but to modify it. What he truly dislikes about the association in its original form is the implication that the connection between Athenian performers and spectators is somehow reflected in contemporary (i.e., nineteenth-century) relationships between artists and their public. He will only accept the connection of citizens and chorus on the condition that the Greek public is understood as a unique phenomenon, a "Dionysian throng," that is, as a public already infected with the pessimistic wisdom of the pre-Socratics.[19] Because modern audiences no longer share this outlook, comparisons of the moderns to the Greeks are, to Nietzsche, specious.

Against this account of pessimism and tragedy as a kind of Dionysian wisdom, Nietzsche counterposes Socratic philosophy, whose characteristic feature now appears to be its optimism.[20] Even while proclaiming its ignorance, Socratic inquiry rejects the pessimistic idea that inquiry, like every human activity, is ultimately doomed: "For who could mistake the *optimistic* element in the nature of dialectic, which celebrates a triumph

[19] Nietzsche identifies A.W. Schlegel as the originator of the other view; but while he proclaims that he gives Schlegel's formulation "a deeper sense," he certainly also exaggerates his own distance from contemporary German thought about the Greeks.

[20] My brief account of tragedy has underplayed the role of the Apollonian as a contrast to the Dionysian. I do not mean to suggest that the Apollonian is unimportant in *The Birth*. In the context of this discussion, however, it is less salient since it is the Dionysian element of tragedy that is particularly linked to pessimism and that Socrates is particularly supposed to object to. Though the Apollonian/Dionysian contrast is what the book is famous for, it largely disappears from view after the first forty pages and is replaced by "the new opposition: the Dionysian and the Socratic" (*BT* 12). I offer a fuller discussion of tragedy in Dienstag 2004.

with every conclusion . . . the optimistic element which, having once penetrated tragedy, must gradually overgrow its Dionysian regions and impel it necessarily to self-destruction" (*BT* 14). Socrates does not promise eternal happiness, but he does affirm both that virtue results in happiness and that virtue can be taught—thus happiness is theoretically within the grasp of all (*BT* 15).[21] He denies that there is anything ultimately mysterious about life or inevitable about suffering: "By contrast with this [tragic Greek] practical pessimism, Socrates is the prototype of the theoretical optimist who, with his faith that the nature of things can be fathomed, ascribes to knowledge and insight the power of a panacea" (*BT* 15).

Notwithstanding Socrates' fate at the hands of his fellow citizens, Nietzsche has no doubt that this approach, developed by Plato, was ultimately victorious in its struggle with tragedy: "Optimistic dialectic drives *music* out of tragedy with the scourge of its syllogisms" (*BT* 14). Just as the pessimism of an older generation of Greeks explains the origin of tragedy, so the Socratic turn in Greek philosophy explains its demise. When the population adopted the optimistic perspective, the cultural context for tragedy evaporated (see Strong 1988, 161). From Nietzsche's perspective, this was anything but a theoretical advance. Greek pessimism may have been somewhat soporific in its consequences (see below), but it had a fundamental honesty that Socratic-Platonic philosophy lacks. This point, in particular, he reemphasized in the 1886 introduction to *The Birth of Tragedy*. While pessimism today, as it was in Nietzsche's time, is commonly associated with ideas of cultural decay, he takes the Greek experience to indicate precisely the opposite:

> Is pessimism *necessarily* a sign of decline . . . as it once was in India and now is, to all appearances, among us, "modern" men and Europeans? Is there a pessimism of *strength*? . . . And again: that of which tragedy died, the Socratism of morality, the dialectics, frugality, and cheerfulness of the theoretical man—how now? might not this very Socratism be a sign of decline. . . . Is the resolve to be so scientific about everything perhaps a kind of fear of, an escape from, pessimism? A subtle last resort against—*truth*? (*BT*, "Self-Criticism" 1)

The Greeks of Socrates' generation could no longer *bear* to live with the brutal truths of the human condition and sought refuge in an optimistic philosophy. To Nietzsche this was "morally speaking, a sort of

---

[21] Throughout *The Birth*, Nietzsche's characterizations of Socrates are given without reference to their source; here it seems clear that he has in mind the conclusions of the Platonic Socrates of *Gorgias, Protagoras,* and *Republic* that true happiness can only come from virtue and that virtue is equivalent to knowledge. This picture is common enough, but it ought at least to be pointed out that it is far from the only possible characterization of Socrates; an opposite one could perhaps be constructed from the Socrates of the *Meno*.

cowardice . . . amorally speaking, a ruse" (*BT*, "Self-Criticism" 1). Either way, it was an active self-deception that made life more tolerable but less genuine. It was a retreat from a real look at the abyss to a pleasing fantasy of progress and happiness. Thus, Nietzsche concludes, it is the *optimists* who are the true harbingers of cultural decline. What else can we call their weakening of resolve in comparison with the stance of the earlier Greeks? Nietzsche's attack on Socrates and Plato is sometimes taken to be a defense of irrationalism, but from his perspective it is they who have retreated from an honest assessment of the world. The pessimistic vision of the world as fundamentally disordered, untamable, unfair, and destructive is the "truth" against which they close their eyes and withdraw to a cave.

If this, then, was Greek pessimism, and if it was in some sense Dionysian, then what separates it from Nietzsche's own later pessimism? We are dealing here only with matters of degree, but the differences are real enough (a fuller answer will be given below). Ultimately, the "Dionysian man" of ancient Greece is likened by Nietzsche to Hamlet—both are paralyzed by the knowledge of "the eternal nature of things." Both, that is, have gained an understanding of the primordial chaos of the world, next to which their own efforts will always amount to nothing. Both, therefore, draw the conclusion that acting is pointless:

> the Dionysian man resembles Hamlet: both once looked truly into the essence of things, they have *gained knowledge*, and nausea inhibits action; for their action could not change anything in the eternal nature of things; they feel it to be ridiculous or humiliating that they should be asked to set right a world that is out of joint. Knowledge kills action; . . . true knowledge, an insight into the horrible truth, outweighs any motive for action, both in Hamlet and in the Dionysian man. (*BT* 7)

The pessimism of the Greeks resulted in a quiescence that tragedy, rather than purging, encouraged and strengthened.[22] This Schopenhauerian conclusion that pessimism must issue in resignation is reversed in Nietzsche's later thought. Ultimately, for Nietzsche, the combination of the Dionysian and the pessimistic served to stimulate activity rather than passivity. In some notes for *Ecce Homo*, he wrote of *The Birth* that it contained, in embryonic form, "the conception of pessimism, a pessimism of strength, a classical pessimism. . . . The antithesis of classical pessimism

---

[22] Again it could be objected here that this account ignores the Apollonian element of tragedy that allowed the Greeks to put a mask of "cheerfulness" over these conclusions (*BT* 8). But this point should not be overstated. The Apollonian elements do not, in Nietzsche's account, cause the Greeks to *forget* Dionysian insights; they are simply a means for avoiding suicide. They do not fundamentally alter the posture of resignation, but rather redirect its effects.

is romantic pessimism . . . e.g., the pessimism of Schopenhauer" (*KGW* 8:3:21). But while it is true that *The Birth* held many of the elements of Nietzsche's later account of pessimism, this statement probably exaggerates its distance from Schopenhauer.[23] After all, in the first edition Nietzsche still maintained that the Greeks derived some sort of "metaphysical comfort" from tragedy; later, in rejecting that conclusion, he suggested that "you ought to learn the art of *this-worldly* comfort first; you ought to learn to laugh, my young friends, if you are hell-bent on remaining pessimists" (*BT*, "Self-Criticism" 7).[24] Ultimately, then, Nietzsche's Dionysian pessimism was to stimulate action—but how could the elements of Greek pessimism be recombined to draw the conclusion nearly opposite to that of *The Birth*?

Pessimism-to-Nihilism

It will be helpful at this point to identify Nietzsche's objections to the pessimism of his day, especially that of Schopenhauer and Hartmann. Although he considered the latter to be a comically simplistic version of the former, his mockery of it is still instructive, for it reveals a great deal about how he understood the pessimism of his contemporaries.

Nietzsche judged Hartmann's pessimism to be a kind of reverse utilitarianism. That is, he took Hartmann to be posing the question of life as if it were a simple cost-benefit analysis: "Whether it be hedonism or pessimism or utilitarianism or eudaemonism: all these modes of thought which assess the value of things according to *pleasure* and *pain* . . . [are] naïveties" (*BGE* 225). These approaches are all naive both because they take reports of pleasure and pain at face value—and because they never imagine that something other than simple pleasures could be a justification of life. Finding the pains of life to outweigh the pleasures, Hartmann draws the "logical" conclusion that life itself is best rejected. To Nietzsche, this entire way of thinking is absurd, hardly meriting the title of "philosophy"; Hartmann's "pessimism" is really no more than a mathematical summation of peoples' feelings.

[23] Maudemarie Clark characterizes *The Birth* as "an attempt to save Schopenhauer's metaphysics by showing how to avoid Schopenhauer's own inconsistency" (1998, 45). See also Janaway 1998, 24.

[24] This phrasing may also be a jab at Hartmann who, in 1869, published an essay titled "*Ist der Pessimismus trostlos?*" which suggested combining Schopenhauerian pessimism with a faith in Providence (Hartmann 1876). (It appeared in an English translation with the apt title "The Comforts of Pessimism" [Hartmann 1895].) This sort of work—and its popularity—was no doubt among the reasons for Nietzsche's belief that Schopenhauer's philosophy, though apparently anti-Christian, ended up sliding back into traditional Christian habits of thought.

"The sum of displeasure outweighs the sum of pleasure; consequently it
would be better if the world did not exist"—"The world is something that
rationally should not exist because it causes the feeling subject more displeasure than pleasure"—chatter of this sort calls itself pessimism today! . . .
I despise this *pessimism of sensibility*: it is itself a sign of deeply impoverished
life. I shall never permit such a meager [one] as Hartmann to speak of his
"philosophical pessimism." (*WP* 701; see *WP* 789)[25]

Nietzsche's objection was not that Hartmann performed his calculation
incorrectly. Nietzsche certainly did not maintain that life was or would be
justified when pleasures outweighed pains (see *KGW* 4:2:414). Aside
from its sheer simple-mindedness, what condemns this approach is the
impossibility of making such a calculation. We lack the necessary mea-
suring-stick. Hartmann assumes that it is possible to stand outside life as
a whole and, as it were, tote up its pluses and minuses. This is inconceiv-
able, in Nietzsche's view, both because there is no perspective *sub specie
aeternitatis* from which to make such an assessment *and* because the
world itself, as the pre-Socratics recognized, is in a constant state of transformation, or becoming, which render any such calculations transient and
useless.

> Becoming is of equivalent value every moment; the sum of its values always
> remains the same; in other words, it has no value at all, for anything against
> which to measure it, and in relation to which the word "value" would have
> meaning, is lacking. *The total value of the world cannot be evaluated*; con-
> sequently philosophical pessimism belongs among comical things. (*WP* 708)

The world as a whole cannot be said to have any particular value and
it cannot be said to have a higher (or lower) value at one time rather than
at another. We can never say that things are getting better or worse over-

---

[25] Nietzsche's characterization of Hartmann is only mildly unfair. Hartmann really does
suggest that an "algebraic sum" is the ideal, if only hypothetical way, to judge the merits of
existence: "There remains, then, in fact, nothing for it but to judge every phenomenal stage
of the Unconscious by its own standard, and then to draw from all these special judgments
the algebraic sum, which then at the same time represents a real unconscious unity, namely,
the totality of all the subjective determinations of feeling posited in the All-one Being."
(1931, 3:6). His 1880 book argues for a scientific measure of the "pleasure-balance" (*Lust-
bilance*) of the world (1880, 65ff.), which proves the "objective truth" of pessimism. And
he does at points seem to suggest that the end of man is some sort of mass suicide or "world-
redemption" (1931, 3:120ff.) However, Nietzsche's vitriol is no doubt animated in part by
the concern that readers will confuse his views with those of the better-known Hartmann—
they *can* sound similar from time to time—and Hartmann even asks his readers in the *Philosophy of the Unconscious* to consider a dilemma that resembles the famous episode in
Thus Spoke Zarathustra where a demon asks if we are willing to live life over again (1931
3:4–5). All this suggests, then, not so much that Nietzsche took Hartmann seriously, but
that he was keenly aware that his readers might have done so.

all, or that the world as a whole is of high or low value. At best, we might say that, taken as a whole, things get neither better nor worse since whatever exists is always in a process of transformation.

Nietzsche found Hartmann's pessimism comical—rather like an infant who rejects the world the moment its milk goes missing—and did not worry that, in the long run, many would be convinced by it. Or, if they came to espouse such a view, it would not be because the arguments were persuasive but because, as decadents, they were already inclined to this position—like the later Greeks (see *TI*, "Problem of Socrates" 2).

Even as he grew less enamored of Schopenhauer, however, Nietzsche's response to him was quite different in tone. Although Schopenhauer too had famously likened life to a business whose receipts did not match its expenses (Schopenhauer 1966, 2:574), this was only one element of his argument and, to Nietzsche, a minor one, even if it had been emphasized by successors like Hartmann.[26] More importantly, in Nietzsche's view, Schopenhauer had made a *moral* judgment against life and not merely an economic calculation in its disfavor. Schopenhauer, unlike Hartmann, recognized the fundamental disorder of the world first identified, in a different way, by the Greeks.[27] This, to Nietzsche, was Schopenhauer's great advance on all philosophy since Plato. It should have led him back to something like the tragic view of the pre-Socratics. But he drew a judgment *against* such a world, based on a moral standard.[28] That is, he at-

[26] This point has been overlooked by several commentators on the relationship between Schopenhauer and Nietzsche. Soll, for instance, seems to assume that it is the surplus-of-pain argument that defines Schopenhauer and links him to Nietzsche (Soll 1998, 83ff.; 1988, 113). Cartwright calls Schopenhauer a "quasi-hedonist" but admits that Nietzsche is not (1998, 136). Simmel's condemnation of Schopenhauer also seems to rest on this point (1986, chap. 4), which he finds illogical and which he attributes to Schopenhauer's personality. The oddity of Simmel's interpretation, written in 1907, can only be further confirmed by reading his characterization of Nietzsche as a Darwinian optimist and by his confident declaration of Schopenhauer's superiority both as a philosopher *and* as a prose stylist (13). Simmel's book seems to be organized by the desire to have Schopenhauer and Nietzsche form a perfect antithesis toward one another so that, in comparing them, Simmel was in effect comparing two equal and opposite perspectives on life. While this creates an elegant (too elegant) structure to his book, it does violence to the substance of both men's philosophies as well as to the relationship between them.

In an important and useful article, Mark Migotti (1995) recognizes that the surplus-of-pain argument is not Schopenhauer's main point and emphasizes instead the absence of "the Unconditioned Good" as the source of pessimism. He also acknowledges in a footnote (651) that Schopenhauer relies on an argument about temporal existence but, strangely, declines to incorporate this into his discussion.

[27] Despite his belief that life was dominated by suffering, Hartmann's Hegelianism (and his attempts to root pessimism in the "facts" of biology) caused him to modify Schopenhauer's metaphysics so that it (somehow) accorded with the Hegelian Idea and its ordered sense of nature and history (see Hartmann, 1869, vol. 2).

[28] There is strong evidence for this interpretation. Schopenhauer wrote, for example, that

tempted to account such a chaos generically "evil," but could only do so based on an imagined "good" stability, a timeless world of Being, against which our transient, everyday world could be measured. "Given these two insights, that becoming has no goal and that underneath all becoming there is no grand unity in which the individual could immerse himself completely as in an element of supreme value, an escape remains: to pass sentence on this whole world of becoming as a deception and to invent a world beyond it, a *true* world" (*WP* 12; see *WP* 6, 9, 11).

This is the pessimism that leads to nihilism. It is pessimistic in the sense that it rejects the optimism inherent in the idea of an ordered universe. On this point, Schopenhauer remains, to Nietzsche, a great critic of the nine-teenth-century social philosophies of progress, whether of the liberal-En-glish or Hegelian-German varieties—and certainly a stimulant to Nietz-sche's own rapprochement to the pre-Socratics. But rather than embrace the natural chaos, as Greek tragedy did, Schopenhauer devised one final strategy to keep it at bay, namely, to sit in judgment over it and deem it bad. This, to Nietzsche, is something worthy of being called nihilism, and it is much more serious than Hartmann's calculation that for most indi-viduals, or even the species as a whole, the quanta of pain exceed the quanta of pleasure. It is instead a judgment against the world *as a whole*, a wish that it would not exist. Schopenhauer's pessimism is more severe because it cannot be cured, even in theory, by increasing the amount of pleasure in the world. Rather life, in its very nature, is something worthy of rejection. Schopenhauer's pessimism endorses the "wisdom of Silenus": "Not to be born is best," and for man "the next best thing by far is to go back / back where he came from, quickly as he can."[29]

Ultimately, this position too can be met with the objection Nietzsche made to Hartmann: no observation-point exists from which to make such a judgment. Furthermore, there is no evidence for such a "true" world, only our "psychological need" for it to exist. Nietzsche makes these ob-jections, but they are not really his main concern. Schopenhauer, he ar-gues, though known as the father of modern pessimism, did not, finally, follow his pessimism all the way through. He allowed it to be diverted from its natural conclusion by a conventional morality he was unwilling to abandon. Schopenhauer did not, in the end, have the courage of his own convictions: "A pessimist, a world-denier and God-denier, who *comes to a halt* before morality—who affirms morality and plays the flute [a pastime of Schopenhauer's], affirms *laede neminem* [harm no one]

"nothing is more certain than that, generally speaking, it is the grievous *sin of the world* which gives rise to the manifold and great *suffering of the world*; whereby is meant not any physical-empirical connexion but a metaphysical one." (*EA* 49).

[29] Sophocles, *Oedipus at Colonus*, lines 1388–91 (1982, 358). Nietzsche discusses "the terrible wisdom of Silenus" in *BT* 3 and 4.

morality: what? is that actually—a pessimist?" (*BGE* 186). In other words, Schopenhauer betrayed the logical outcome of his own pessimism at the last possible moment, by denying the results of his ontology *solely on a moral basis*, and an unverifiable moral basis at that (See Higgins 1998, 167ff.). The true implications of pessimism, then, remained to be fully explored. Schopenhauer had shown the way but had not taken it. But the consequences of Schopenhauer's failure were far more dangerous then pessimism itself.

At least for Socrates, optimism was based on the idea that the world had an order; when this idea was abandoned, the Socratic morality should have disappeared as well. But Schopenhauer denied the results of his own ontology. That he sought to preserve morality with a transcendental projection was transparently a failure of nerve. When morality no longer claimed to have a basis *of any kind* in the real world of events, it was free to condemn that world in toto (as Socrates never would), to develop into genuine philosophical suicidalism. Although Nietzsche found the roots of this sort of thinking stretching back to Socrates' final request that his debt to Asclepius be paid (that is, Socrates' personal death-wish), it was not until Schopenhauer completely uncoupled morality from ontology that this tendency could fully develop (*TI*, "The Problem of Socrates"). Nihilism, at least of this variety, is pessimism mixed with morality in a kind of devil's cocktail.[30]

At this point, we are in a position to understand Nietzsche's repeated (and otherwise very perplexing) claims that, rather than rejecting Schopenhauer's pessimism, he "deepened" it and "first really experienced it" (*WP* 463). Whereas Schopenhauer mixed up and adulterated his pessimism with morality, Nietzsche takes himself to be purifying pessimism of the imperfections that Schopenhauer, its modern inventor, introduced to it (see *BGE* 56). In the introduction to the second volume of *Human, All-too-Human*, also written in 1886, Nietzsche looks back on his *Schopenhauer as Educator* and explicitly traces this development: "I then went on to give expression to my reverence for my first and only educator, the *great* Arthur Schopenhauer. . . . I was . . . already deep in the midst of moral skepticism and destructive analysis, *that is to say in the critique and likewise the intensifying of pessimism as understood hitherto*" (*AOM*, Preface 1; see also *WP* 463). The critique of Schopenhauer is rooted in a moral skepticism: Schopenhauer relies on moral categories in passing a final judgment on the world, and Nietzsche rejects these categories. But

---

[30] Perhaps this was one of the examples Nietzsche had in mind when he wrote of "the hidden history of philosophy, the psychology of its great names" that "error is *cowardice*— every achievement of knowledge is a consequence of courage, of severity towards oneself" (*WP* 1041). See also *WP* 382.

the critique is likewise an *intensification* because it liberates Schopen-hauer's pessimism (which is, after all, his original contribution) from the commonplace morality within which it has been encased.[31] The at-tack on Schopenhauer is thus, in spirit, an act of loyalty. And it leaves Nietzsche free to "experience" pessimism in a way that was not available to Schopenhauer—not available, in fact, to any philosopher in the West since Socrates poisoned Greek pessimism by his introduction of an opti-mistic ontology.

Stripped of its moral overcoat, pessimism thus means confronting the terror that Schopenhauer, and (to Nietzsche) the pre-Socratic Greeks, found in the prospect of a world of flux and becoming. But Nietzsche's perspective at least offers the advantage of not succumbing to a nihilism that rejects life as a whole (See Soll 1998, 101ff.). Pessimism recognizes that "becoming aims at *nothing* and achieves *nothing*," and pessimism *does not sit in judgment of this condition* (WP 12). What is the result? "The *innocence* [*unschuld*] of becoming restored" (TI, "Four Great Er-rors" 8).[32] This idea Nietzsche considers "a tremendous restorative" just because we are released from the burden that morality imposes on us (WP 765). Morality causes us to judge the world as a whole (an impossibility) and to judge it negatively (a mistake predicated on an impossibility): "In-sofar as we believe in morality we pass sentence on existence" (WP 6), we "find existence a misfortune" (KGW 7:1:192). Along with the terror, then, there is also "a great liberation" involved in pessimism (TI, "Four Great Errors" 8). We no longer give credence to the world-hatred and self-hatred bound up with morality; the burden of its judgment is removed.

Pessimism, then, is a terror that liberates. (I will say more about this below.) But how is it that this pessimism does not return us to the Hamlet-like impotence of the pre-Socratics that was the result of the "Dionysian" in *The Birth*? This always remains, to Nietzsche, a possibil-ity; indeed, it is the most likely response. What changes after *The Birth* is just that Nietzsche now spies another possibility. To the innocence of be-coming, he now believes there will be two broad categories of response, which he characterizes as arising out of "strength" and "weakness," where these terms indicate a capacity (or lack of capacity) to tolerate the meaninglessness of life. Those who cannot bear this sort of existence, who

---

[31] On Schopenhauer's self-consciously unoriginal morality, see BGE 186.

[32] This translation makes it appear as though Nietzsche is replacing one moral judgment about the world (i.e., that it is "guilty") with another (that it is "innocent"). But "*unschuld*," the opposite in everyday speech of "*schuld*," or "guilty," while it can only be felicitously translated as "innocent," is more literally "not guilty" or "lacking guilt." Thus Nietzsche's use of it here does not reverse the moral judgment but, insofar as possible, removes it en-tirely. To say that becoming is *unschuld* is to adopt an agnostic position as to its moral worth and, moreover, to suggest that such a valuation is, in itself, inappropriate.

require an ultimate meaning to life (the Hamlets), end up once again as nihilists, though now in a psychological rather than a moralistic sense: "One grants the reality of becoming as the *only* reality, forbids oneself every kind of clandestine access to afterworlds and false divinities—but *cannot endure this world though one does not want to deny it*" (WP 12). This sort of pessimism *does* result in despair and resignation and "the weak perish of it" (WP 37). This is what Schopenhauer's position, stripped of its illusions of a thing-in-itself, would amount to.

Yet, in his writing after *The Birth*, Nietzsche argues that it is a mistake to believe that human beings need such premanufactured meanings. The "strength" of a pessimism of strength is just this ability to forgo them. "It is a measure of the degree of strength of will to what extent one can do without meaning in things, to what extent one can endure to live in a meaningless world *because one organizes a small portion of it oneself*" (WP 585). He now considers Schopenhauer's final inferences to be a product of weakness: It is one thing to know that there is no natural or God-given meaning to the world as a whole or to life as a whole. But from that point to make "the inference that there is no meaning at all" is a "tremendous generalization," one that Nietzsche considers "pathological" (WP 13). Such a generalization represents an absolute disfaith in humanity—a presumption that humans can create no meaning other than that which they are given—that in itself is as without foundation as the earlier belief in a natural moral order to the world. The alternative to this is based on the human capacity to create meanings of a temporary nature in our own corner of the cosmos. The lack of an overall meaning in the universe is no argument that adequate meaning cannot be generated by individuals. Nietzsche may have made this same faulty generalization at the time of *The Birth*, but he abandons it in his later work and reproaches himself for having made it.[33]

Aphorism 370 of *The Gay Science* encapsulates this transformation. In it, Nietzsche describes his initial attraction to "philosophical pessimism" (Schopenhauer) and "German music" (Wagner) as based on a misunderstanding. What appeared to him at first to be a cultural "earthquake" emerging from a Dionysian "over-fullness of life" was in fact the product of "the impoverishment of life" that Nietzsche now labels "romanticism."

---

[33] Soll (1988, 116) and Higgins (1998, 174), among many others, tend to view the difference between the two alternatives as a matter of temperament, so that the choice for strength or weakness is either something inborn and unalterable or, alternately, a radical choice with no philosophical basis. I think the passages quoted above make clear that this is not the case. Though every philosophical choice, for Nietzsche, is in some respect a matter of character, it is clear that the two positions here are separated by ideas, and not just moods. The pessimism of strength rests on the idea that human beings have a creative potential that survives the demise of natural foundations of meaning.

Romanticism only *simulates* something revolutionary; its radicalism is feigned. It seeks "above all mildness, peacefulness, and goodness in thought and deed . . . also logic, the conceptual understandability of existence . . . in short, a certain warm narrowness that keeps away fear and encloses one in optimistic horizons." Just as Wagner began his career as a partisan of the 1848 revolutions but ended as an unctuous courtier to German princes, so Schopenhauer began with a seeming rejection of Socratic optimism, only, in the final analysis, to retreat to it. This "romantic pessimism" is thus "an altogether different kind" from Nietzsche's own, which he names here for the first time as "Dionysian pessimism." "That there still *could* be an altogether different kind of pessimism, . . . this premonition and vision belongs to me as inseparable from me, as my *proprium* and *ipsissimum*. . . . I call this pessimism of the future—for it comes! I see it coming!—*Dionysian* pessimism" (GS 370).

Romanticism, although it was Nietzsche's own starting point, turns out to be a kind of sham pessimism and Nietzsche here declares his independence from it. Unadulterated pessimism is only now coming into existence; only when it does can we fully appreciate its promise and dangers. Nietzsche (grateful for the education he provided) nonetheless rejects Schopenhauer, not because the latter is too pessimistic, *but because he is not pessimistic enough*.

The Pessimism of Strength

Having, by a process of elimination, come some distance closer to understanding the pessimism of which Nietzsche could and does approve, it remains to give a more detailed account of it. Certainly his pessimism remains a kind of "no-saying," a rejection of traditional morality. But he emphasizes the *activity* involved in such a no-saying and considers it, by itself, to be something valuable. The alternative title Nietzsche gave one of his final books is perhaps a good starting point. *How to Philosophize with a Hammer* is the second name provided for *Twilight of the Idols*. Throughout the book, however, there is little reference to this "hammer" and readers are often left wondering just what it is.[34] In the foreword,

[34] The distance between the text and title is partly explained by the fact that Nietzsche only hit upon the latter after the book was written. The working title "Idleness of a Psychologist" Nietzsche discarded after his friend Peter Gast objected. Certainly the word "idleness" (*Müssiggang*) seems particularly inapposite for such vibrant and violent prose as the book contains—but perhaps it was Nietzsche's original intention that the title be understood ironically (i.e., "*our* idleness seems vigorous to you? Imagine what it would be like if we psychologists ever exerted ourselves!"). All the other book-titles of 1888 (*Ecce Homo, The Anti-Christ, The Case of Wagner*) are ironic to the point of sarcasm. Nietzsche concluded, we

Nietzsche likens the hammer to "a tuning-fork" with which he sounds out the hollowness of idols. But this does not square well with his characterization of the work as "a declaration of war" and does not, in any case, help us to understand the *nature* of the hammer. The final section of the book is entitled "The Hammer Speaks" but is simply a short quotation from *Thus Spoke Zarathustra*. Perhaps the hammer is Zarathustra himself then? But this is only to further beg the question.[35]

In his notes, however, Nietzsche repeatedly refers to pessimism as a kind of "hammer," one used to break down and break apart traditional ways of thinking (e.g., *WP* 132, 1055). This destruction is healthy and recuperative on its own, even apart from some rebuilding that may come: "The hammer: a teaching which through setting loose the death-seeking pessimism brings about an extraction of the most vital" (*KGW* 8:1:108). What does it mean to wield pessimism as a tool? In the first place, of course, it means to attack existing moralities, "to teach destructive ways of thinking" (*KGW* 7:3:210). In this task, pessimism is an all-purpose instrument because it attacks the basis of all moralities, not just some of them. By denying the existence of any natural order to the universe and emphasizing the continuous flow of becoming and time, pessimism is as critical of utilitarian morality as it is of the Christian or Kantian variety. But its effect is not *simply* a critical one. Even if destruction is a necessary prelude, that is not the end in itself. Hammers can also be used to put something together—or, as a smith does, to reconfigure some existing object or material into a new shape. Likewise pessimism, "In the hand of the strongest becomes simply a hammer and instrument with which one can make oneself a new pair of wings" (*KGW* 8:1:109). This metaphor would seem to indicate, again, that the liberation of pessimism is not just a negative one (liberation *from* morality) but also a positive liberation, a new arena of possibility or technique of life is to be opened. To remove chains is one thing—to build wings another.

But again, one wants to ask: Wings of what sort? At this point, we can begin to perceive the difference between Nietzsche's pessimism and pre-

---

might suppose, that if his friend and admirer failed to get the joke in the original title neither would any of his other readers, and so he produced the more obvious pun, *Götzen-Dämmerung*.

[35] This question is directly addressed by Thomas Brobjer in a short article that contains much useful information and suggests that the question has an easy solution, namely, that we read "hammer" simply as short-hand for "eternal recurrence." While there are some notes to suggest this reading, Brobjer ignores others that connect hammers with pessimism. And while there is merit in the idea of connecting the two terms, simply equating them creates as many problems as it solves—it hardly seems plausible, for example, that we are meant to grasp hold of eternal recurrence and use it as a tool in the way that the metaphor suggests. If anything, eternal recurrence is something that takes hold of us, not vice versa. See Brobjer 2000.

vious ones. Even the past pessimisms Nietzsche admired, like the Greeks', came to an end with the destruction of illusions. In his account, the pre-Socratics evoked an ethos of virtual paralysis. They taught one (as Buddhism does) to be at peace with the world's chaos but not to seek to alter it. In a long note entitled "Critique of previous pessimism," Nietzsche outlines his alternative:

> *Our* pessimism: the world does not have the value we thought it had. . . . Initial result: it seems worth less; . . . simply in this sense are we pessimists; namely with the will to admit this revaluation to ourselves unreservedly and not to tell ourselves the same old story, not to lie to ourselves.
>
> That is precisely how we find the pathos that impels us to seek *new values*. In sum: the world might be far more valuable than we used to believe; . . . while we thought we accorded it the highest interpretation, we may not even have given our human existence a moderately fair value. (*KGW* 8:1:248)

Nietzsche is treading a delicate line since, as we have seen, he has also said that it is a mistake to try to give the world *any* overarching value. But, as is indicated here, this does not mean we should cease to value anything at all. Rather, the withdrawal of an overarching account of the world's value impels one to seek (importantly plural) "new values." No single one of these can replace the old value-system. But separately and collectively, they might give us more reasons to continue living than can any overarching Meaning of Life. Christian morality and its offshoots sought to overcome thoughts of suicide with one ultimate duty, or ultimate happiness. Nietzsche's pessimism advises each of us individually to cobble together a meaning for life out of lesser goals, to organize small portions of the world ourselves—but with the ultimate result that, when these are gathered together, "the world might be far more valuable than we used to believe." Finding the will to live is not a problem that admits of a universal solution—but the individual solutions we each can arrive at may, in any case, be more credible for us than a set of prefabricated values we are instructed to reenact.

Nietzsche's inspiration here, as in so many other matters, is the example of a certain kind of art.[36] Of course, his is not the romantic idea that art puts us in touch with greater truths or the Schopenhauerian belief in the artist's "objectivity." Rather art represents that organization of a small portion of an otherwise meaningless world that gives purpose to an indi-

---

[36] His praise of art is not indiscriminate. He goes to great lengths to distinguish the sort of art he has in mind from that produced by the "artists of decadence" and "romanticism in art" (Wagner is always his chief example), which proceeds from "an impoverishment of life" and ends in "hatred of the ill-constituted, disinherited, and underprivileged . . . one who, as it were, revenges himself on all things by forcing his own image, the image of his torture, on them, branding them with it" (*WP* 852, *GS* 370).

vidual existence (*WP* 585). Art is the attempt to impose a temporary form on the inevitable transformation of the world; since the world must acquire *some* particular forms in its metamorphoses, art is "repeating in miniature, as it were, the tendency of the whole" (*WP* 617)—only now by an effort of will. Thus art for Nietzsche, as it would be as well for Camus, is not really an attempt to fight the pattern of existence, but rather to shape that pattern into something recognizable, "*to realize in oneself the eternal joy of becoming*—that joy which also encompasses *joy in destruction*" (*TI*, "What I Owe" 5). The creativity of artists is thus an enactment of their "gratitude for their existence" (*WP* 852), even when that existence is constant turmoil. Pessimism impels us to this artistic "pathos," which then itself impels us to seek new values. And pessimism impels us to this pathos because it shows us that the sense of order and timeless meanings that we have taken for granted are themselves the product of an artistic pathos—doomed in time but also replicable as achievements of the human spirit. Pessimism shows us our continuity with the universal chaos—and equally with universal creativity, for they are one and the same. Pessimism is thus a "set of wings" that helps us to traverse and navigate the fluid medium we inhabit.

When art assumes this shape, it becomes "the great seduction to life, the great stimulant to life" (*WP* 853). This is *not* to say, however, that such art must be "uplifting" in the conventional sense. Since joy in destruction may be a stimulant to life, even depictions of the most miserable things may be included: "The things they display are ugly: but *that* they display them comes from their *pleasure in the ugly*. . . . How liberating is Dostoevsky!" (*WP* 821). Nietzsche does not mean, of course, that we should all be artists but that we should approach our lives as artists do their work. If we can understand *why* an artist like Dostoevsky, who knows that art is devoid of metaphysical value and that the universe is as apt to produce ugliness and depravity as beauty and virtue, would still want to write, then we can understand why Nietzsche thinks pessimism can result in a creative pathos. Similarly, if we can see how tragedy, the "repetition in miniature" of worldly chaos can represent the liberating "joy of becoming," then we can get a sense for the political productivity of a pessimistic ethic.

Now "liberating" is not the adjective most frequently applied to Dostoevsky, but it is instructive here to consider the art that Nietzsche praised after he came to view Wagnerian opera as romantic pseudo-tragedy. In *The Case of Wagner*, Nietzsche tells us that he returned to hear Bizet's *Carmen* no less than twenty times. And every time, he claims, "I seemed to myself more of a philosopher, a better philosopher," and even "a better human being" (*CW* 1). What creates this effect? "This music is evil," Nietzsche writes, by way of praise. "Have more painful tragic accents ever been heard on the stage? How are they achieved? . . . Without counter-feit." The language and metaphors that Nietzsche uses for pessimism are here transferred directly to Bizet's aesthetic vision. His music "liberates the spirit" and "gives wings to thought" (*CW* 1). On the one hand, a (very modern) tragedy is depicted, one in which the characters suffer and die without redemption. Nor is this an isolated case but, we are meant to un-derstand, a repetition in miniature of the general path of love. And yet viewing it is depressing only to the most literal-minded. The liberation consists in the opera's acknowledgment of love as a fatality, equal parts passion and terror, which the protagonists do not control. The "tragic joke" of existence is revealed and the viewer, if not the characters, un-derstands simultaneously his (or her) freedom and powerlessness (*CW* 2). Indeed, it is precisely the recognition of our powerlessness that is liberat-ing. So long as we cleave to the illusion that we are perfect masters of our fate, we are burdened with a bad conscience, an unredeemable debt for our own flawed character. We can never be finished with justifying what we *are*. The witnesses of *Carmen* are better, freer philosophers and human beings for setting down that burden and replacing it with a future for which they can take their genuine share of responsibility, rather than a past that they can never alter. As in the Greek tragedies, it is the ac-knowledgment of fate (understood here not as a particular destiny for a particular individual but simply as a general term for the forces that ex-ceed that of the individual will), rather than the resistance to it, that lib-erates the spirit. It is that much easier to begin projects that are genuinely our own when they do not have to bear the responsibility of justifying their creator.

Likewise, the characters of Dostoevsky's fiction, horrible though they may be, and populating a landscape utterly devoid of morality, reveal to us the dizzying freedom that a pessimistic horizon creates, along with ter-rible possibilities that go along with that freedom. Though we may find the story of Raskolnikov repulsive, we grow by the exercise of measuring our distance from it, and finding that distance to be small. Equally, though, we grow from understanding that the subject of art can be the terrible and the ugly as well as the perfect and the beautiful—it helps us again to unburden ourselves of the self-despising that a retrospective morality enforces.[37] Not that we should liberate our worst impulses; rather, we should own up to them and understand those parts of ourselves as a fact rather than a sin. Modern tragedy, no less than ancient, for Nietz-sche, is thus a source of solace and liberation. While I will not exaggerate

[37] Nietzsche never mentions the work of his near-contemporary Auguste Rodin and there is no evidence that he knew of it—but I think Rodin's sculptures give some sense of what is meant here.

its directly political effects, it should at least be clear why Nietzsche saw pessimism as, at root, a productive and creative ethic, rather than a soporific one. It invites us to explore along every dimension, and not just the one that the "path of history" marks out. It expands, for better or worse, the horizon of human possibility. From his perspective, it is optimistic rationality that is stifling, for it insists that there is only one path and one means with which to walk that path. Pessimism, by contrast, demonstrates the remarkable openness of the future and the remarkable diversity of trajectories open to the human species, even if they all end in death. That is the "liberation" (a word Nietzsche uses repeatedly) that is available here.

A helpful image for this situation, one that demonstrates its potential for effects beyond the individual, can be found in the practice of architecture: any sane architect must know that no building lasts forever. Built in opposition to nature (as to some extent every human structure must be), it will be attacked by nature (by wind, by water, et cetera) the moment it is completed. Whatever the purpose for which it is initially designed, that purpose will someday be superceded. However beautiful it may seem when erected, it will someday, to another set of eyes, appear ugly. Yet knowing all this, architects pursue their craft. Knowing that the universe will ultimately not tolerate their work, they continue to organize a small portion of that same universe for local purposes. The lack of an objective or metaphysical meaning for the work is no obstacle; indeed, architects often think of the generation of locally meaningful environments out of meaningless nature to be a particular goal. Equally, the lack of a preordained path to such production is the origin of an incredible variety of styles rather than of despair at the absence of a natural best form.

Of course, knowing all this does not make one into an architect, anymore than listening to Bizet makes one into a musician. But Nietzsche's claim that Bizet's music had made him a better human being is both less and more than that. One can enjoy music and admire architecture all one's life without being liberated by either. This is what Nietzsche has in mind when he complains that, although moderns claim to revere Greek tragedy, we do not experience it as a Greek audience did—and not just because of the gap in time that separates us. Pessimism is not just an ethos of artistic productivity but also, as I discuss further below, of human receptivity. It is the latter that makes the former possible. It is not just that Greek artists and viewers happened to share a perspective. Nietzsche's point is rather that the substance of pessimism, its teaching of the fundamental impermanence of the boundaries of self, rendered Greek audiences open to the suffering they witnessed on stage. This same openness is what Nietzsche claims to have rediscovered when he says that he, alone among modern philosophers (alone, perhaps, among all modern humans), "first really experienced" pessimism. While Nietzsche is no democrat, the openness that pessimism fosters is a far cry from the elitism that he is often accused of promoting and it should be no surprise that Nietzsche once remarked, in a lecture on Sophocles, "Tragedy has always contained a pure democratic character, as it springs from the people" (*KGW* 2:3:17).[38]

·   ·   ·   ·   ·

The lack of order in the universe can also fuel nihilism, as Nietzsche (like Dostoevsky) is well aware. Unlike the nihilist, the pessimist does not just reveal the tragic character of existence but achieves a degree of equanimity about it. This aspect of pessimism often comes across as indifference to the suffering of others, something Nietzsche is regularly, but mistakenly, accused of. What he does insist on, however, is that we not sanctify our concern for others by giving it an otherworldly origin. He advises that we not look to nature or God to express a horror of suffering on our behalf (and therefore to think of ourselves merely as concurring in their judgments). Nor should we imagine that such suffering is any less natural than happiness:

> The benefit consists in the contemplation of nature's magnificent *indifference* to good and evil. No justice in history, no goodness in nature: that is why the pessimist, if he is an artist, goes *in historicis* to those places where the absence of justice is revealed with splendid naïveté . . . and also in nature, to those places where her evil and indifferent character is not disguised. (*WP* 850)

If we choose to rebel against the suffering to be found everywhere in existence, we must take responsibility for that rebellion as our own and recognize the degree to which it is, so to speak, unnatural. Of course, the fact that nature is indifferent to good and evil is no reason for us to be so—indeed, if we succeed in creating values for ourselves to live by, such a stance would be impossible. What the pessimist is particularly opposed to is the optimistic view that suffering is to be eliminated by "history," "nature," or "reason." (Pessimism is also opposed to the idea that suffering is always unproductive—I discuss this in the next section).

Note here too Nietzsche's desire to dispel the view that pessimism leads to a disinterest in the workings of the world. Instead, he sees it as an invitation to a new critical investigation of nature and history—and even to those elements of life that we consider ugly and evil. One effect of this situation is that when we look at the world once again—without the grey-

---

[38] Cited in an unpublished paper by Tracy Strong, "The Tragic Ethos and the Spirit of Music," p. 15. I thank Tracy Strong for sharing this paper with me.

colored glasses of morality—we may see things differently. We may now find ourselves curious about that which, for millennia, we have been taught to shun. Curiosity about what has been considered evil is, to Nietzsche, one of pessimism's greatest benefits. This does not mean that we will simply celebrate what we once abhorred, but rather that we will seek it out on its own terms and come to our own fresh evaluation of it—and this goes for what was once called "good" as well:

> Let us dwell a moment on this symptom of highest culture—I call it the pessimism of strength. Man no longer needs a "justification of ills"; "justification" is precisely what he abhors: he enjoys ills *pur, cru*; he finds senseless ills the most interesting. If he formerly had need of a god, he now takes delight in a world disorder without God, a world of chance, to whose essence belong the terrible, the ambiguous, the seductive. In such a state it is precisely the *good* that needs "justifying." (*WP* 1019)

Nietzsche is quite clear that what we previously called "good" may well *find* a justification, only it will not be "justification" in its previous sense: "If he *in praxi* advocates preservation of virtue, he does it for reasons that recognize in virtue a subtlety, a cunning, a form of lust for gain and power" (*WP* 1019). In other words, pessimism promotes an unblinkered reexamination of the world, and of the self, without built-in moral assumptions. From this perspective, it is actually optimism, relying on such assumptions, that inhibits truly free inquiry.

Pessimism as a hammer—as a philosophical technology—both destroys and builds. Pessimism is both a critique of existing moralities and an instrument in the construction of an alternative apart from morality. Far from ending in despair and resignation, Nietzsche considers the moment when "my type of pessimism" appears "the *great noon*, . . . [the] great point of departure" (*WP* 134). Pessimism may not be the end of the journey, but all roads to the future lead through it—and it may be necessary to remain pessimistic for "a few millennia" (*KGW* 7:3:210). Can we say more about this alternative? Again, what is *Dionysian* pessimism?

Pessimism as a Quest

Nietzsche was less interested in assigning content to the hypothetical new values he encouraged than in demonstrating that they should exist. One note on "the pessimism of the energetic" emphasizes that "the 'to what end?' after a terrible struggle [is] . . . itself a victory" (*KGW* 8:2:62). Just the desire to formulate new goals after overcoming earlier moralities (the end of the repression of desire those moralities enacted) is something to be celebrated. Although Nietzsche speaks often of a "revaluation of values," he never provides a new set of values to replace the old. Indeed, given his well-known sentiment that "a will to a system is a lack of integrity" (*TI*, "Maxims" 26) and his radically individualistic belief that the formulation of new values is something each of us should undertake on our own (*Z* 1:22), it would be unfair to expect this from him.[39] Still, we are not left simply with the imperiously vague injunction to "create new values." Dionysian pessimism is not itself a value-system, but it is an ethos that sheds some light on what it might be like to live a good life in the era following the death of God—it is, in short, an art of living. It is a life-practice that Nietzsche recommends, although not for everyone.

Some sense of what is meant by "Dionysian" is given in *The Birth*, but Nietzsche's use of this word continued to evolve (though he would often write as if all the later meanings were implicit in the earlier ones). If Dionysian pessimism is the one "no" that evolves out of "yes," then it is important to know what one is approving with a Dionysian "yes." From the various texts and notes that bear on this question, the answer seems to be something on the order of "life as a whole" or "the world as it is and will always be." But since, as Nietzsche was fond of pointing out with regard to Hartmann, there is really no perspective from which to view life as a whole (either to praise or condemn it), such an assent can only be a kind of gamble or risk-taking. It is an affirmation in the dark, an approval given in ignorance. Above all, it is a decision to welcome the unknown future, to wager on futurity, and accept the unseen past rather than clinging to a familiar present (*Z* 2:20). While all pessimisms conclude that the universe has no order and human history no progress, Dionysian pessimism is the one that can find something to like about this situation: "My new way to 'yes.' My new version of pessimism as a voluntary quest for fearful and questionable aspects of beings. . . . A pessimist such as that could in that way lead to a Dionysian yes-saying to the world as it is: as a wish for its absolute return and eternity: with which a new ideal of philosophy and sensibility would be given" (*KGW* 8:2:121).

The phrase "fearful and questionable" (*furchtbaren und fragwürdigen*), which recurs frequently in Nietzsche's texts, is carefully chosen to indicate what is at issue here.[40] The aspects of existence that we will have the greatest difficulty grasping and affirming are not the cruel and disgusting; they are those whose existence is so threatening to our sense of order that we have heretofore denied their very being, so that initially we

---

[39] Gooding-Williams, in an important discussion, also concludes that, having taken on the task of proving that the creation of new values is possible, Nietzsche leaves the act of creation itself to others (2001, chap. 5).

[40] These words could also be translated as, say, "terrible and doubtful." For other uses of this term, see, e.g., *WP* 852, *GS* 370. The phrase always refers to those things that the pessimist can bear the sight of which others cannot.

find their very existence "questionable" or "dubious." Which are these? In *Twilight of the Idols*, Nietzsche ridicules "the almost laughable poverty of instinct displayed by German philologists whenever they approach the Dionysian." Why laughable? Because these philologists cannot recognize what is, so to speak, right under their noses. The "Dionysian mysteries" are simply "the mysteries of sexuality . . . the *sexual* symbol was to the Greeks the symbol venerable as such, the intrinsic profound meaning of all antique piety" (*TI*, "What I Owe" 4; see Higgins 1998, 170ff.). The absurdity of post-Socratic philosophy is ultimately demonstrated in its attitudes toward sex and the body. What ought to be the most obvious and immediate source of knowledge and pleasure is not merely obscured but almost entirely obliterated. Cruelty may be *condemned* by morality but at least it is acknowledged; sexuality is *eliminated* from view through a process of "moral castrationism" (*WP* 204, 383).

Sexuality, not cruelty, represents that part of life with which it is most difficult to come to terms. It is the most difficult *not* because it is inherently shameful ("It was only Christianity . . . which made of sexuality something impure" [*TI*, "What I Owe" 4]). The difficulty lies in affirming the necessity for pain and suffering that accompanies any pleasure and growth. That is, it involves admitting that we ourselves *and not just the world* are essentially time-bound, that we too are flux and change. With its constant dissolution of boundaries, sexuality is more threatening to the optimist than is the human tendency to cruelty. The violation of self at the core of human sexual exchange (of whatever variety)—simultaneously painful and pleasurable—is the simplest and best evidence that our own nature is as unstable and tumultuous as that of the rest of the universe and, therefore, that no calculation of our best interest can ever be permanent.[41] The openness that pessimism recommends has, as its cost, the invasion of self that has always been symbolized and exemplified by sexuality. To truly make contact with another human being means to be open to their touch and alteration of us, to unfreeze our self-understanding and ego-boundaries long enough to acknowledge and model the distinctive qualities of the other, a transformative experience the outcome of which cannot be known in advance. Sex (like any true encounter with the world but more obviously) changes us in ways we cannot predict or master. It should thus be obvious why Nietzsche found Socratic rationalism and asceticism to be tightly linked. Maintenance of an optimistic perspective relies, in some sense, on denying the fluidity of self that the experience of

[41] Obviously I do not refer here to the brute fact of intercourse, which is no different in humans and animals, but to a sexual relationship between thinking beings. The boundaries of this category may be vague, but we are rarely uncertain about whether we are or are not within or without it.

sexuality manifests and repeatedly reminds us of. Shunning sex (and, to the degree that it is unavoidable, demonizing and mechanizing it) is therefore the practice of the self most necessary to the denial of pessimism.

Nietzsche calls the Dionysian "the triumphant Yes to life beyond death and change; *true* life as collective continuation of life through procreation." But this can only come at the cost of suffering, the rending of self that is the price to be paid for continuous rebirth: "In the teaching of the mysteries, *pain* is sanctified: the 'pains of childbirth' sanctify pain in general—all becoming and growing, all that guarantees the future, *postulates* pain. . . . All this is contained in the word Dionysus" (*TI*, "What I Owe" 4). Childbirth, that is, the emergence into the world of a new individual, stands in here for the enlargement and transfiguration of the self ("all becoming and growing") that pessimism enables in people over the course of their lives. In Christian morality, the pains of childbirth are the Curse of Eve, and sexuality the sin that enables and stands for sin in general; it is this symbolism (and this generalization) that Nietzsche urges us to reverse. The Dionysian is not *simply* sexuality (Nietzsche is not Freud); rather, the repression of sexuality represents the repression of the "fearful and questionable" as such. Accepting the necessity of these things, accepting the pain and loss that comes with any experience that transforms us, thus *setting aside the goal of happiness as the ultimate aim of a human life*, is what the Dionysian "yes" requires.

This does not mean that happiness must disappear from human life. Setting it aside as the final goal does not mean banishing it altogether. But if happiness is to be found, it can only be on these new terms. We can only take our pleasures in an acceptance of a chaotic and, we now know, painful condition. Pleasure and pain simply cannot be separated as the utilitarian or simplistic pessimists contend with their efforts simply to seek one and avoid the other. In *The Gay Science*, Nietzsche suggests that the Stoics were far closer to the truth when they contended that "pleasure and displeasure were so tied together that whoever *wanted* to have as much as possible of one *must* also have as much as possible of the other" (*GS* 12). But where the Stoics, on this basis, drew the inference that both are to be avoided, Nietzsche rejects this as wholesale life-denial and concludes the opposite. Destruction must be known and acknowledged as part of anything creative or good. To truly embrace becoming at the expense of being means *to take pleasure in the suffering that accompanies the demise of whatever is*: "The joy of becoming is only possible in the destruction of the actuality of 'Beings,' the beautiful visions, in the pessimistic annihilation of illusions. [I]n the destruction also of beautiful illusions, Dionysian joy appears as its climax" (*KGW* 8:1:114; see also *EH*, "Destiny" 4).

This is something we have great difficulty doing. Nietzsche knew such an idea would sound dreadful to most. It is not enough simply to withdraw our condemnation of suffering. It is not enough to retreat to an agnostic shrug and agree to coexist with "necessary" suffering; that would be equivalent to being agnostic about life itself. Instead, we must approve of it.[42] That is why Nietzsche depicts the idea of eternal recurrence as something proposed by a "demon" and the "greatest weight" upon one's conscience (GS 341). To will the eternal recurrence is to will endless suffering. Why should we sanction suffering, even our own, much less that of others?[43]

If Nietzsche's reply is simply "because it is an unalterable part of life," then we are tempted to return to the position of Schopenhauer. Indeed, perhaps now we can see the attractions of that position most clearly. Why *not* reject this life we are offered, as Schopenhauer suggested, if to endorse it means to endorse endless and unalterable suffering? Nothing, after all, requires us to participate in the suffering of others. Our every moral instinct rebels at the thought. If we are truly powerless against suffering, as Schopenhauer argues (and here the parallels between Schopenhauer and Stoicism become more visible), why not just withdraw? To this question, Nietzsche cannot give the sort of answer that provides any comfort. He cannot offer any irrefutable reason for preferring affirmation to denial. In a world of flux, no such "reason" could permanently exist. This is why Nietzsche calls it a "question of strength"—*not* because the strong survive and the weak die, but because those who affirm have the "strength" to control their disgust long enough to give themselves a local reason to live.

The Dionysian "yes" is not a matter of taking a sadistic pleasure in the suffering of others. But it is a decision to be glad that ours is a world of becoming rather than being, to be glad that things are always changing and that the future is always being born and the present always passing away. It means detachment from whatever exists at present—something that will inevitably appear as callousness toward others: "*Dionysian wisdom.* Joy in the destruction of the most noble and at the sight of its progressive ruin: *in reality joy in what is coming and lies in the future, which triumphs over existing things, however good*" (WP 417, second emphasis added). This is what Nietzsche had in mind by such phrases as "*amor*

---

[42] Gillespie overstates the point when he writes that "doing Yes" amounts to "putting one's hand to the throats of all the innocent children and squeezing their lives away," but he is not wrong to demonstrate to us our own likely revulsion at the implications of Nietzsche's philosophy and his reference to Dostoevsky is also apt (2000, 146). His ultimate conclusions about Nietzsche's historical anthropology, however, strike me as condescending and dismissive. A more sympathetic discussion of this point can be found in Murray 1999, though it is marred by the author's insistence that Nietzsche's aim is to "overcome pessimism."

[43] Neiman (2002, 219ff.) shows a keen appreciation of this dilemma.

fati" or eternal recurrence. *Not* the idea that we must relive the past again and again, but rather that this pattern of destruction and creation is unalterable and must be borne (*WP* 1041). *And it cannot be withstood by means of faith in progress.* We must learn to hope in the absence of an expectation of progress. If this sounds almost nonsensical to the modern ear, perhaps it is because we have been told for so long that progress is the rational thing to hope for.

The difference between the incomplete pessimism of Schopenhauer and Nietzsche's version is explicitly outlined in *Thus Spoke Zarathustra* as a difference in their respective attitudes toward our fate of temporality. In the twentieth section of the second book, titled "On Redemption," Nietzsche traces two approaches to our time-bound condition. First he describes the preaching of "madness." Madness speaks as Nietzsche once did himself, by citing the aphorism of Anaximander—in a slightly altered form so as to bring out what Nietzsche now considers its vengefulness "'Everything passes away; therefore everything deserves to pass away. And this too is justice, this law of time that it must devour its children.' Thus preached madness" (*Z* 2:20). Madness then continues to speak more directly in the voice of Schopenhauer, whose solution to the problem of time is to withdraw from the life of the will insofar as is humanly possible. "Can there be redemption if there is eternal justice? Alas, the stone *It was* cannot be moved: all punishments must be eternal too. . . . No deed can be annihilated: . . . This, this is what is eternal in the punishment called existence, that existence must eternally become deed and guilt again. Unless the will should at last redeem itself, and willing should become not willing" (*Z* 2:20). To Nietzsche, this attitude of resignation toward our place in time can only be called madness, the product of "the spirit of revenge" or "the will's ill will against time."[44] It moves too quickly from the inescapability of time to the idea that it enslaves us.

Next, Nietzsche contrasts this false redemption with a better one, one in which our temporality conditions us, but does not imprison us: "I led you away from all these fables when I taught you, 'The will is a creator.' All 'it was' is a fragment, a riddle, a dreadful accident—until the creative will says to it, 'But thus I willed it.'" Rather than hate backwards, as it were, Nietzsche suggests that we aim forward, that is, be open to the future to result from this past. If the present is the result of an unalterable

---

[44] Hartmann also speaks with the voice of madness: "Pain, once endured, can never be compensated for. The past can never be made good" (Hartmann 1895, 89). Wendy Brown has written eloquently on the way in which *ressentiment* is generated by a kind of narcissistic dwelling on prior injury to the point that it can infiltrate and infect much supposedly affirmative identity politics. Release from this form of political subjectivity is a singular attraction of Nietzsche's pessimism, as Brown (without using that term) points out (1995, 66–76).

past, it is also the source of a very alterable future: "I walk among men as among the fragments of the future—that future which I envisage." Instead of a false redemption that is essentially an abandonment of society, the true pessimist (pessimistic still because he accepts our time-bound condition and all it entails) sees an opportunity where the false pessimist sees only a conclusion: "To redeem those who lived in the past and to recreate all 'it was' into a 'thus I willed it'—that alone should I call redemption." Schopenhauer's romantic pessimism acknowledges the power of the past but not the open horizon of the future. It is madness because it seems to be based on a hostility to existence that Nietzsche ultimately finds inexplicable except as self-hatred. Temporality is not just a limitation but also a source of potential.[45] The redemption of the past to which Nietzsche looks forward may be unlikely, but at least it is not an impossibility. His characterization of pessimism as a "voluntary quest" (*freiwilliges Aufsuchen*) thus captures many of its essential qualities. It must be voluntary in the strongest sense, because the option of resignation cannot be rationally foreclosed. Nor can the quest be fully motivated by its object since to choose a quest for the questionable is to choose a path to the future that is unknown, but known to be something different from where one sets out. It is an exploration that is bound to be frightening, but holds the potential to be liberating. It is, as I argued in the first chapter, to value human life primarily for its natality and its futurity, its ca-

---

[45] I cannot agree, therefore, with Gianni Vattimo's contention, in his interpretation of this section, that Nietzsche seeks "redemption from time" as such. Vattimo's interpretation recognizes the burdens of linear temporality as Nietzsche describes them but posits an imagined escape from this condition that Nietzsche would have considered quite impossible (Vattimo 2001, 116–20). Much more interesting are Joan Stambaugh's attempts (1972, 1987) to understand Nietzsche's remarks on time as a contravening of Schopenhauer's views that are revolutionary in their originality. I cannot give Stambaugh's analysis here the attention it deserves—I will only say that, however sympathetic I am to some of her formulations, I find the analysis in the end too separated from the "historical" element of Nietzsche. That is, in Stambaugh, the whole topic of time, under Heidegger's influence, becomes hypostatized in a way that, I believe, is alien to Nietzsche's thinking. Likewise Gooding-Williams, also acknowledging Heidegger's influence and despite extraordinary and enlightening attention to Nietzsche's imagery in *Thus Spoke Zarathustra*, ends by suggesting that Nietzsche's solution to the problem of time is to "spatialize" it—that is, to subordinate linear time to a spatial eternity where all moments are simultaneous (2001, 214ff.). But this interpretation rescues Nietzsche from the "contradiction" of willing backward only at the price of making him into a metaphysician who posits a plane of reality outside of time where all our problems can be solved. But Nietzsche, I think, is perfectly clear in his text that we are not to imagine solutions that contravene our experience, but rather embrace our experience of time, with all its costs, so that we can see its possibilities. Gooding-Williams also includes an excellent discussion of Nietzsche's relationship to Schopenhauer but, like so many others, assumes that Nietzsche's opposition to Schopenhauer must entail opposition to pessimism as well.

pacity to produce something new and different, without knowing what that something will be.

Here at least Nietzsche is at some distance from the Greek tragic view, which, however liberating, remains finally within the ambit of a nonlinear temporality and thus is unable to generate this kind of openness to the future. Nietzsche's rhetoric tends to suppress this distance, but in his later self-criticism of his romantic identification with the Greeks in *The Birth* ("in sum, a first book, . . . in every bad sense of that label" [*BT*, "Self-Criticism" 2]) and in his injunctions that we must "go beyond the Greeks" we can see some acknowledgment of it. Ultimately, the Greek tragic view cannot generate an interest in an open future for, from that perspective, what is to come is already foretold. When Nietzsche speaks of "*amor fati*" he has in mind accepting the history that constituted us as we find ourselves not, as a Greek would, accepting a future that is already scripted. If Nietzsche continues to call his view "tragic," as he sometimes does, he at least does not mean to replicate that element of the outlook of the original tragedians. That would leave us unalterably in the position of Hamlet.

As I argue in the next chapter, we can see in Cervantes's *Don Quixote* a better example of the quest-for-no-object Nietzsche has in mind. The lack of object throws into relief the idea of pessimism issuing not in a fixed judgment, but in a *quest*, that is, not in an idol of the future but in a *task* that can only be described in narrative. If Nietzsche is reluctant to specify the *content* of the new values he calls for, he is clear enough that these new values must have a new *form*. In the form of narrative, values cannot fall victim to the sort of metaphysical hypostatization that has been the result of the Socratic turn of philosophy outlined in *The Birth*. And the quest-narrative puts particular emphasis on the openness of the future as well as the encounter with the unexpected along the way.

Dionysian pessimism may be "fearful and questionable," but the alternative is worse. In a famous note, Nietzsche embodies the two choices as "Dionysus and the Crucified": "It is *not* a difference in regard to their martyrdom," i.e., in whether the two personifications of different life-practices suffer and die, "it is a difference in the meaning of it" (*WP* 1052).[46] In other words, it is not a question of how death and suffering can be minimized—all human lives include suffering and end in death. "The problem is that of the meaning of suffering: whether a Christian meaning or a tragic meaning." We are only given the choice of accepting

---

[46] As Murray points out, this dichotomy is also what Nietzsche has in mind when terming his alternative source of redemption "eternal recurrence" (*ewige Wiederkunft*); it contrasts with the *Wiederkunft Christi* (the Second Coming of Christ) (1999, 234).

this life as a whole or rejecting it as a whole. There are more than two possible meanings for suffering and we can surely struggle to alter those elements of life within our purview, but we will still be faced with the larger question where we cannot pick and choose. One alternative is to reject life as a whole: "The god on the cross is a curse on life, a signpost to seek redemption from life." The other is to embrace life, with all the suffering entailed, both for ourselves and for others: "Dionysus cut to pieces is a *promise* of life: it will be eternally reborn and return again from destruction" (*WP* 1052). Here is the "this-worldly redemption" that Nietzsche spoke of in *Thus Spoke Zarathustra*. It is nothing permanent. Every local solution to the burden of time-consciousness will, ultimately, itself be destroyed by time. But it can serve its local purpose of creating reasons to embrace life and leave a legacy that itself may be fodder for further incarnations.

If one accepts the pessimistic assessment of the time-bound world as a place of chaos and dissonance, one faces the choice of retreating from it or embracing it and trying to "let a harmony sound forth from every conflict" (*WP* 852). Dionysian pessimism, understood as a quest, is a life-practice designed to meet this challenge. It does not deny the structure of time or the difficulties this creates for human life, but it converts those difficulties into the stimulus for a project of worldly exploration and self-renovation. Pessimism fortifies us, not against the effects of time itself (death, change, suffering), but against the possible dispiriting that can come from facing time and its effects in pessimism's absence. It looks toward the future, not with the expectation that better things are fore-ordained, but with a hope founded only on taking joy in the constant processes of transformation and destruction that mark out the human condition.

The Future of Dionysian Pessimism

Nietzsche wrote about pessimism throughout his career, but there is a remarkable degree of concentration on the subject in the series of prefaces prepared in 1886 for all his pre–*Thus Spoke Zarathustra* writings, which were then in the process of being republished. Looking back over the development of his thought, he identifies a principle that has guided it, unseen hitherto in its entirety, even by himself—and he desires now to reemphasize it, and by doing so, to draw together his various poses into a unified attitude. Read together, these introductions (to *The Birth, Untimely Meditations, Human, All-too-Human, Assorted Opinions and Maxims,* and *Daybreak*) describe a pessimism that "has no fear of the fearful and questionable that characterizes all existence":

This has been *my* pessimistic perspective from the beginning—a novel perspective, is it not? a perspective that even today is still novel and strange? To
this very moment I continue to adhere to it and, if you will believe me, just
as much *for* myself as, occasionally at least, *against* myself. . . . Do you want
me to prove this to you? But what else does this long preface—prove? (*AOM*,
"Preface" 7)

Here Nietzsche is playing on the meaning of *beweisen* (prove). The root
weisen means "show," so that *beweisen* can mean "show" in an intransi-
tive sense, that is, to "show oneself." In other words, the last sentences
can be read to ask, in effect, whether the reader desires that Nietzsche ex-
pose himself to his audience—and then to respond that he has already
done so by displaying his pessimistic perspective.[47] And yet the preceding
sentences suggest that Nietzsche's pessimism has struggled with other elements of his psyche and that this struggle is not over. Taken together with
the quotation with which this chapter began, where Nietzsche declares
pessimism to be his "quintessence," we can see that the self is not meant
to be excluded from the small portion of the universe that the pessimist is
to organize. Indeed, if anything, the self is the starting point (though certainly not the ending point) from which pessimistic quests must begin.
Tracy Strong describes Nietzsche's as a "politics of transfiguration" and
it is this theme of self-shaping and self-transformation against a fundamentally chaotic background that is the key link between Nietzsche and
such later figures as Camus, Arendt, Foucault, and William Connolly.
Critics of postmodernism have considered Nietzsche a dubious foundation for politics because of his clearly antidemocratic tendencies.[48] But
what each of these later, more democratic writers has found in Nietzsche
is a portrait of energetic individuality that can be supportive of political
action while remaining distinct from the liberal assumptions that are often
held to be a necessary complement to democratic participation.

Nietzsche's pessimism authorizes a process of identity-renovation based
not on an assumption of the self's natural integrity but, to the contrary,
on an acknowledgment of its fundamental instability and perishability.
The lack of perfect boundaries to the self means that these projects need
not (indeed, cannot) be solipsistic or limited to self-perfection (as some
critics imply). The pessimistic spirit, I wrote above, is a restless one, unlikely to be enamored of the status quo either in the self or in the world.

---

[47] Note again here the association of pessimism with sexuality and the suggestion that in
affirming pessimism, Nietzsche also affirms himself as a (vulnerable, exposed) sexual being.

[48] See Leiter 1994, Berkowitz 1995, and Appel 1999, among many others. Of course,
these works, and those they attack are only the latest iteration in an old debate. See Brinton
1965 [1941] for an earlier example that itself surveys this debate in the first half of the twentieth century.

As I argue in the next chapter, the story of Don Quixote gives us a good example of what such a project would look like. Quixote begins by changing his own identity from a man who sits at home to one who engages the world as a knight-errant. This project begins with Quixote liberating himself from a social role into which he has been cast without his consent and arming himself against the forces of the chaotic world, but the project is not completed when this is accomplished or when some aesthetic criteria of the self have been met, but only when he has succeeded (against all sound advice) in launching himself into the world and, indeed, altering it. Don Quixote is free and active in the world. He is never happy, but he accepts this condition as necessary to his quest. Doubtless he is not an ordinary democratic citizen; but he would not be a bad citizen in such an order even if it is not his goal to sustain it. And, importantly, his qualities are not dependent on the variety of regimes in which he finds himself. Like Camus' rebel, he acts in a way that exemplifies freedom regardless of circumstance, illuminating a human dignity that we all share. If Nietzsche's politics are not always democratic, then, they are quixotic—and that should be taken as no more of an insult than calling them pessimistic.

Nietzsche's connections to the pessimists who preceded him have heretofore been difficult to see, in large part because of the invisibility of the pessimistic tradition itself. If it can now be acknowledged that such a tradition has existed, then we can recognize Nietzsche as one of its principal exemplars. What is more, however, we can also see later Nietzscheans as extensions of the pessimistic tradition, even if they have not always used that name for themselves. Concerns about the burdens of temporal existence have continued to animate political theorists in the twentieth century and they have often attempted to use a Nietzschean language to address those concerns. While it is beyond the scope of my efforts here to rewrite the history of twentieth-century thought from a pessimistic perspective, it seems to me an eminently possible task.

. . . . .

To believe that pessimism must lead to resignation is to make one of two errors: It is either to mistake Schopenhauer's pessimism (or Wagner's or Buddha's) for the whole of pessimism, or it is to believe that no other response is possible to the realization that we live in a tragic, disordered, immoral world. Why is it commonly thought that human beings must be disappointed at the prospect of a world of constant flux and chaos, where no moral order can be sustained? Because, I believe, it is assumed that human beings are creatures of order, that we will somehow be discomposed if forced to exist in this chaotic world. But to Nietzsche we ourselves are no different from the world to which we are condemned; we are not islands of being in a sea of becoming. We too are nothing else but a constant transformation and development. So he famously calls it a "*Dionysian* world of the eternally self-creating, the eternally self-destroying . . . without goal. . . . [D]o you want a *name* for this world? . . . *This world is the will to power—and nothing besides*! And you yourselves are also this will to power—and nothing besides!" (*WP* 1067).[49] To restore "the innocence of becoming" to the world means likewise to restore it to *ourselves* and to face this chaotic world not as a creature alien to it or fallen from it, but as part and parcel of that which we find most threatening. Those who believe pessimism leads to resignation see humans as "weak," creatures that must have transcendental meanings in order to survive. It is *not* the pessimists, then, at least not all of them, who believe that the demise of traditional beliefs must lead to aimlessness and suicide. *It is rather those who fear pessimism*, or fear the repeal of traditional moralities, that maintain this.

What does it mean to go through life with no expectations, or more precisely, with an expectation of nothing? To be sure, one is deflected from a certain kind of global ambition. The desire *wholly* to remake the world in one's image, in whatever manner, must be set aside once it is realized that the world will hold no image at all for very long.[50] Yet nothing deters us from entering on local projects or organizing "a small portion" of the world (How small? One person? One city? One state? One culture?). As I have argued, this does not mean cultivating one's own garden so much as knowing the limits to one's actions, however ambitious.

Furthermore, there is a freedom to be gained when one's existence is detached from the narrative of progress. If human history is pregiven as a story of progress, then one's fate (however worthy) is already scripted, in a sense, by what has come before, and one becomes nothing more than

---

[49] To be sure, there is something paradoxical about this formulation. To imagine ourselves as will would normally imply that our will had some object. Yet if there are no permanent objects, but only an eternal flux, including ourselves, how is this possible? The paradox is not eliminated, I think, but it is mitigated in light of Nietzsche's critique of our subject-object grammar and his related critique of our ideas of causality as such. In *GS* 370, Nietzsche explicitly links these to the emergence of Dionysian pessimism. To him, the strangeness of what he proposes emerges as much from our ordinary grammar of "will" as it does from the propositions themselves. In this passage, in any case, it seems clear that Nietzsche gives us what he knows to be an inaccurate shorthand "name" for what he describes only because we, his readers, demand it. Nietzsche's critique of causality is especially vivid in his discussion of dreams (see *GS* 22, 112; *TI*, "Four Great Errors" 4; *WP* 479; and Dienstag 1997, 96–100).

[50] Or rather, the desire to wholly remake the world is permitted so long as one does not regret the fleeting character of such a remaking. The art of Christo, geographically grandiose but always temporary, is perhaps an example of this.

"an angry spectator of all that is past" (*Z* 2:20). Pessimism, by freeing us from this script, simultaneously frees us from enslavement to the past. This is not to say we are immune from the effects of history, merely that they do not bind us.

The destruction of all things by time is not a judgment of their worth, as Anaximander maintained, but simply a condition of life and an opportunity for each person to chart their own course free of "the stone *It was*." "Thus," Nietzsche concluded, "the belief in time is good for one's health (pessimists after all)" (*KGW* 7:1:390). The constant transformation reminds us that our fate is not set. We have at least a role in determining it. The burden of the past is thus lessened and the prospect of the future brightens. "The trust in life is gone: life itself has become a *problem*. Yet one should not jump to the conclusion that this necessarily makes one gloomy. Even love of life is still possible, only one loves differently" (*GS*, "Preface" 3). Instead of being a creature of the past, one can be "a bridge to the future" (*Z* 2:20). Instead of valuing oneself for being part of a long chain of progress, one can value the fresh start that one makes of oneself. Instead of searching for transcendental meanings, one can "give the earth a meaning, a human meaning" (*Z* 1:22:2). Dionysian pessimism encourages us to act while seeking to avoid the hubris so common to more systemic philosophies.

The reference to pessimism as "good for one's health" is not, I think, a casual phrase. Nietzsche often refers to pessimism as a life-technique with medicinal qualities "a remedy and an aid in the service of growing and struggling life" (*GS* 370). This language reflects his continuous struggle to set the proper level for his philosophy's charge: somewhere beneath the imperious universal demands of categorical rationalism, but above the mere prudential advice of Galenic medicine. I have used the phrases "art of living" and "life-technique" interchangeably to indicate my understanding of what Nietzsche takes that level to be. Such a technique will not be to everyone's taste or, he thinks, within the ability of all. While it is not clear to me that this last judgment is entailed by Nietzsche's view of the substance of pessimism, he clearly does not expect it to be a universal ethic. But even Nietzsche's antidemocratic moments are not all that they are often cracked up to be. His philosophy, he wrote in 1887, will be best suited to those he calls "the most moderate": "Those who do not require any extreme articles of faith; those who not only concede but love a fair amount of accidents and nonsense; those who can think of man with a considerable reduction of his value without becoming small and weak on that account" (*WP* 55). These are the humans he considers "the strongest"—not those who can destroy the most, or the towering egotists of Ayn Rand's imagination, but those pessimists who can withstand the most destruction without giving way to pity and resignation. "*I assess the power of a will by how much resistance, pain, torture it endures and knows how to turn to its advantage*" (WP 382). Like Don Quixote, the best pessimists have a strength of character and a sense of humor—for this world, both are needed.

Chapter Six

CERVANTES AS EDUCATOR

DON QUIXOTE AND THE PRACTICE
OF PESSIMISM

Don Quixote . . . is an allegory of the life of every man who,
unlike others, will not be careful merely for his own personal
welfare, but pursues an objective, ideal end that has taken
possession of his thinking and willing; and then, of course,
in this world he looks queer and odd.
—ARTHUR SCHOPENHAUER

Today we read *Don Quixote* with a bitter taste in our
mouths, almost with a feeling of torment, and would thus
seem very strange and incomprehensible to its author
and his contemporaries: they read it with the clearest
conscience in the world as the most cheerful of books,
they laughed themselves almost to death over it.
—FRIEDRICH NIETZSCHE

IN THE last chapter, I depicted Nietzsche's Dionysian pessimism as an
ethic of radical possibility linked to radical insecurity. The lack of natural boundaries both between and within humans permits, simultaneously, our capacity for novelty and distinctiveness as well as our capacity
for enormous cruelty. We cannot, on this account, have one without the
other. But if Dostoevsky provides a horrible image of what such a world
would look like, he does not offer the only one. As the quotations above
indicate, Nietzsche, and Schopenhauer before him, felt a profound affinity between the worlds they describe in philosophy and the one Cervantes
created in *Don Quixote*. Nor are they the only pessimists to have done
so. Both Miguel de Unamuno and José Ortega y Gasset devoted entire
books to this text.[1] Leopardi praised Cervantes and spoke of his desire to

---

[1] Miguel de Unamuno, *Our Lord Don Quixote* (orig. 1905); José Ortega y Gasset, *Meditations on Quixote* (orig. 1914); Unamuno's is a page-by-page commentary, Ortega y Gasset's, as his title suggests, is a more thematic reflection. As the remainder of the chapter will
make clear, my interpretation of Quixote owes a great deal to their efforts. Since I have discussed Unamuno at some length in chapter 4, more attention is given here to Ortega y Gasset's interpretation as a way to expand the reader's understanding of the pessimistic tradi-

imitate him (*P* 17). Cioran called the Knight of the Mournful Countenance "the most truthful image ever created of man" (*SHD* 83). And given
his other references to Cervantes, Camus may well have had the book in
mind when he wrote: "The novel is born at the same time as the spirit of
rebellion and expresses, on the aesthetic plane, the same ambition" (*R* 259;
cf. 276). That *Don Quixote* has attracted and continues to inspire pessimistic readers and readings would be enough reason to probe it further
in this context. But the main benefit of such an investigation will be the
ability of this fiction to aid in generating a picture of what it might mean
to lead a pessimistic life, as well as to understand the relation between
such a life and pessimistic writing.

Of course, as the quotations above indicate, different pessimists have
read *Don Quixote* in different ways and it will not be my concern here to
reconcile these various readings. But the uniform praise of this novel by
the pessimists should cause us to wonder at the source of the commonplace understanding of its protagonist as an enemy of pessimism. Though
the reader may reflexively think of Don Quixote as an inveterate optimist,
charging at windmills and the like, I would suggest that this has more to
do with the popularity of the musical *Man of La Mancha* than with Cervantes's actual text. Whatever merits this lachrymose bit of theater may
possess, fidelity to the spirit of *Don Quixote* is not actually one of them.
If anything, *Man of La Mancha* resembles the heavy-handed, Wagnerian
operatic romanticism that Nietzsche so feared being associated with.
Though I am not concerned here with cultural analysis, the reworking
that *Don Quixote* receives in *Man of La Mancha* is an interesting example of the kind of imperialism of optimism that has succeeded in making
pessimism invisible today. As Nietzsche reminds us, however, Cervantes's
book was received by its first readers as a bright comedy and was, indeed,
internationally successful on that basis.[2] While we cannot read too much
into this success, I want to at least suggest that the popularity and influence of *Don Quixote* are at least an interesting piece of evidence against
the oft-repeated canard that pessimism must somehow be an elite or mi-
nority perspective. Though it is never really stated why this should be so,
one suspects that, in an American public culture that is both optimistic
and democratic, there is a tendency to assume that these two traits have
some kind of elective affinity. But *Don Quixote* in its time was far more

---

tion. I regret that I cannot, otherwise, give Ortega y Gasset's writing the attention it deserves
in this volume.

[2] Published in 1605, *Don Quixote* was an immediate bestseller. The first edition sold out
almost instantaneously and it was then reprinted several times and very quickly translated
into other European languages; Cervantes became a kind of literary celebrity. So successful
was the book that it inspired several very modern phenomena, namely, pirated editions and
at least one unauthorized sequel (which Cervantes lampoons and derides in his own sequel).

successful than *Man of La Mancha* has been in ours, so we should at least consider the possibility that this assumption is wrong.

The purpose of this chapter, however, is to use Cervantes to further illuminate the Dionysian pessimism described in the previous chapter and, in the process, to give some substance to the idea of a "pessimistic ethic"—a term that I have used but that might, on its face, strike some as an oxymoron. An "ethic," after all, suggests a way of living and pessimism has often been taken to suggest a withdrawal from life as such. It is the latter characterization, of course, that this book means to question. While pessimism does indeed suggest to us that we must lower, indeed abandon, many of our expectations about what is possible, it need not, I have claimed, prescribe an attitude of resignation. As I argued in the last chapter, Nietzsche's pessimism issues in a "quest for the fearful and questionable." Quixote's journey, I maintain here, can serve as a useful exemplification of that idea. His is a quest motivated neither by an anthropological curiosity to explore the alien nor by an imperial desire to conquer it, but rather by something else. Quixote, to give a preliminary formulation, having transformed himself into something new, can be understood as seeking to bring the example of himself into an encounter with those who have not heard of him and, in doing so, to make it possible for others to transform themselves in a similar fashion. And in this he is, in a strictly limited way, successful—even if by every conventional standard his quest is a failure. One of the most remarkable things about the text, as I discuss below, is the way in which many characters, having initially described Don Quixote as "mad," eventually choose to adopt his way of looking at the world or, at least, desist from attempting to dissuade him of it. Even when they do not adopt his goals, they come to admire his example, as does the reader. His presence has (often literally) a liberating effect on those with whom he comes into contact, even if after being liberated they do not follow him.

"Become who you are," a phrase adopted from Pindar, was Nietzsche's strange counsel to his readers in the fourth book of *The Gay Science*. He describes those who follow this path as "human beings who are new, unique, incomparable, who give themselves laws, who create themselves" (*GS* 335). This depiction of the sort of human Nietzsche's philosophy aims at is also, I would contend, perfectly apt for Don Quixote, for Quixote can be said to deserve each one of these adjectives and phrases. That he is unique and incomparable is something the novel remarks upon hundreds of times: there is simply no one else like him, no one crazy enough to act as he acts and speak as he speaks. That he gives himself laws cannot be questioned either: it is the defining act of Quixote's character that he adopts a code of chivalry that is currently in force nowhere—and in so doing, renames and transforms himself. "Quixote" (literally, the piece of armor that protects the thigh) is a name that Cervantes's character gives himself in the first pages of the book, abandoning his given name of Quijada (or Quesada or Quejana—Cervantes is purposely vague on this point, presumably to thwart us from referring to it as his character's "real" name).

Though Quixote himself does not believe his code to be "new" (he claims to have adopted it from the past), this is the one area in which he is gravely mistaken. The narratives that he takes to be the records of past heroism are in fact poetic fabulations. Although there were actual knights-errant in Spain, and records of their deeds, these were not the "books of chivalry" that Quixote is said to have read. Quixote's books were popular fictions with as much resemblance to history (and with a parallel place in the literary culture of the time) as modern romance novels. If Quixote followed a code of knight-errantry, he was the first to do so in this fashion. At first glance then, Nietzsche's formulation finds a rough instantiation in Don Quixote.[3] As to what it *means* to say that Quixote has "created himself," that is obviously the crucial question to which we shall return.

We can say immediately, however, that at all times Cervantes keeps us focused on the costs of such a self-transformation. He does not depict it as a joyous or undifficult process—most of the time, Quixote is neither happy nor "gay," though he often expresses a kind of pacific satisfaction with his quest and its results. Not only does Quixote suffer the physical costs of his many unsuccessful adventures, he also suffers from the separation from the rest of humanity that his new practice of self inevitably brings. That Quixote does not always consciously register these costs (sometimes he does, other times not) does not mean that the reader is meant to ignore them. The "real Quixotism," as Ortega y Gasset put it, "is that of Cervantes, not that of Don Quixote" (1961, 52).[4] But neither

---

[3] There are further parallels one could pursue. As many commentators have noted, Nietzsche's "Gay Science" derives from the literary culture of the Provençal troubadors (on his title page, in the second edition, the German *Die fröhliche Wissenschaft* is followed by the Latinate "*la gaya scienza*") and refers, loosely, to their art of poetry (*la gai saber*). It was this same culture, of course, that produced the books of chivalry that are Quixote's initial inspiration. One could press the point still further (if more speculatively): *The Gay Science* is the only one of Nietzsche's books to be both preceded and followed by verses, which is also the case with *Don Quixote*—and this is *also* the case with the books of chivalry that both Cervantes and Nietzsche mean to mock and imitate, in varying degrees.

[4] This puts Ortega y Gasset at odds with Unamuno, who proclaimed his desire to "free Don Quixote from Cervantes" (*OLDQ* xxix). Unamuno's ecstatic interpretation thus reflects, and is intended to reflect, more Unamuno then Cervantes.

It should be noted that this "Quixotism of Cervantes" is not at all the same thing as Cervantes's politics, which, as far as can be determined, seem to have been quite conventional for his time—royalist, Catholic, and, to some extent, militaristic (Cervantes had been a soldier at Lepanto) and aristocratic (though perhaps it could be said that he favored an aris-

does Cervantes suggest that his protagonist is simply a fool. Even more so than Nietzsche, Cervantes has no particular hope of reforming the dismal and corrupt world into which he was born; he seeks only to resist and survive it, and to do so with a modicum of dignity and self-respect. In Quixote, he offers an example of how to do so and, what is more, to have an experience of freedom in the process. Quixote's quest is an art of living, not in the sense that it produces anything beautiful, but in the sense that it is a means of coping with a world that is chaotic, unpredictable, "fearful and questionable," and, therefore, incapable of preserving anything good.

If Quixote hopes, at first, to right wrongs with a wave of his noble sword, the sad truth about the world eventually destroys that expectation, both in him and in the reader. But if the narratives of chivalry that Cervantes mocks have been a dubious education for Quixote, *that is not at all the case for Quixote's own narrative of chivalry*, which is an education for Sancho Panza and, through him, for the rest of us. And, as certain episodes in the novel suggest (particularly those in which Sancho is called upon to govern), it is even a useful *political* education. For Sancho, the unlettered peasant, to the surprise of everyone, governs wisely when given the opportunity. The justice that the insane Quixote is unable to effect with the sword, Sancho brings about through a sane and brave administration inspired by Quixote's example. Sancho's success is limited (indeed, ultimately it is destroyed), but it is (temporarily) genuine. For a time, Sancho organizes a small portion of the universe under something like a decent political regime. And all the characters in the novel, except Quixote, find this astounding.

Though Cervantes, of course, was not a Nietzschean, it is fair, I believe, to characterize the universe he created as a pessimistic vision and to say that his book aims at a goal that pessimists would recognize (and have recognized)—a mode of action that acknowledges the insuperable barriers that time-bound existence throws up against justice and happiness, but which does not respond to this situation with resignation. *Don Quixote* represents what I am terming a "practice of pessimism," a mode of conduct and action founded on an absence of expectation and hope. Cervantes is not a Nietzschean; can we understand Nietzsche as a *cervantista*?

．　．　．　．　．

Political theorists concerned to articulate a radical alternative to the status quo have often embarked on historical expeditions, most frequently

---

tocracy of the spirit rather than one of blood or custom). Nonetheless, in this work, he created an outlook that was much greater than the sum of these parts.

to ancient Greece, but also to such places as the republican city-states of early modern Italy. Though wisely hedged round with caveats, there can be little doubt that the aim of such writers is, in some sense, to reintroduce premodern values into the modern world. This attempt is exactly what Cervantes lampoons in the figure of Don Quixote. Quixote has a headful of faux-medieval "values" that he has learned only from the study of old books, which themselves turn out to be full of lies. When he attempts to act on these values in the modern world, which knows nothing about them and cares little when informed, the effects are regularly comic. This is Cervantes's initial point: he believes the "detestable books of chivalry" then popular in Spain (such as the *Amadis of Gaul*) to be a pernicious influence on the public. Yet, miraculously, by the end of the book, Don Quixote, for all his craziness, has come to seem one of the saner people in the jaded, unsentimental, early modern Spain that the novel depicts. What, then, is admirable or worthy of imitation in Don Quixote, if not his attempt to import premodern values into the modern world? If Cervantes means, through the figure of Don Quixote, to educate us, what is it he means for us to learn?

Don Quixote is thoroughly modern in its acknowledgment of and reliance on linear time. It is for this reason that some literary critics have referred to it as the first true novel.[5] As with the texts discussed in the earlier chapters, however, it is unusual in rejecting both progressive and eschatological versions of such time. If pessimism consists in accepting the burdens of linear time, without being broken by them or seeking to escape them, then *Don Quixote* is a book that seeks to exemplify what a pessimistic ethic might look like. In what follows, I will lay out several ways in which Quixote embodies the attitude toward life that emerges from this perspective, a practice of pessimism that is active rather than resigned, one that contains "joy in what is coming and lies in the future, which triumphs over existing things, however good" (*WP* 417).

Don Quixote, of course, is an immense book, dense in allusions, references, and meanings, most of which I will not even touch on in this short chapter. My intention is not to offer a complete interpretation of this

---

[5] This characterization was perhaps more common a generation ago than today. Debates about what would constitute the "first" novel have become more complicated and admit of no clear answer, especially since there is no agreed-upon list of characteristics for a "novel." However, *Don Quixote* is still accurately characterized as the first extended prose narrative in a European language shorn of mythical or supernatural elements and roughly respecting modern novelistic conventions, especially those of linear time. Carlos Fuentes has recently reaffirmed the "first-novel" characterization with the argument that the book "really inaugurates what we understand modern fiction to be—a reflection of our presence in the world as problematic beings in an unending history" (2003, 15b).

work, but rather to demonstrate how it can be usefully and not incorrectly understood as an illuminating instance of the sort of pessimistic perspective I described in the previous chapter. It will thus help us to fill out a description of what pessimism can mean as a lived philosophy.

Don Quixote's Struggle with Time

By several devices, Cervantes indicates to us that Don Quixote's true enemy is not anyone he meets up with on the road, or the dragons or giants that he imagines confront him, or even the modern world as a whole, but rather, as with Nietzsche, time itself. "Human affairs are not eternal," he writes, "but all tend ever downwards from their beginning to end, above all man's life" (*DQ* 2:74).[6] Don Quixote's adventures take place, not in the timeless arena of myth like that of the premodern books of chivalry he has read, but in a very real world where the passage of time takes its toll on the characters. Beyond the accumulating injuries and ultimate death that beset Don Quixote, this threat manifests itself most frequently as a disruption of narrative. In addition to the main plot, *Don Quixote* is a book full of other, subsidiary stories (which often go on for several chapters), some related by characters in the main plot, others presented as whole texts that have been found by chance and read out. One of the most remarkable things about these various stories is that they are regularly threatened with noncontinuance. That is, circumstances conspire to break off the tales and end them prematurely, before they can be properly concluded. Most are then resumed later, but not without some effort or sheer luck. Thus, for example, in part I the story of Cardenio is broken off in chapter 24 when its speaker is rudely interrupted by Don Quixote, even though the latter has been explicitly warned that such an interruption may lead to a fit of madness on the part of the teller and thus halt the story. The reader is thus left hanging for several chapters until

---

[6] *Don Quixote* is notorious for the different levels of narration that exist side-by-side in the text, making it very difficult to say when, if ever, Cervantes is speaking directly. I cannot, at each instance of citation, discuss my reasons for believing the quotation in question to reflect an authentic concern of the author—that, in any case, is not my main concern. I can only say that, as in any circumstance with this sort of hermeneutic barrier, it is my understanding of the meaning of the whole that has, in turn, shaped my choice and, analysis, of the various portions of the text I discuss directly. I would thus ask the reader to suspend the question of the status of any particular passage until they can assess the larger understanding that is laid out in this entire chapter. Note that throughout this chapter I use the italicized title *Don Quixote* to refer to the text as a whole and the unitalicized name Don Quixote to refer to its protagonist.

Cardenio (who runs off) can be tracked down and persuaded to continue in chapter 27. Similarly, in chapter 35, the reading of a manuscript is interrupted by "the heroic and prodigious battle Don Quixote had with certain skins of red wine" while sleepwalking. Only when the hero is awakened, calmed down, and some claims against him settled is the reading concluded. With each of these embedded narratives, then, the reader has the experience of wondering, not merely *what* the dénouement will be, but *whether* she will even see the end of the tale.

From these examples, it might be thought that Cervantes is merely pointing to the fragility of narratives and using this device to heighten suspense and, indeed, both are doubtless part of his concern. But the point is deepened when we consider that Don Quixote's *own story*, the main plot of the book, is similarly threatened with disruption. Book 1 of the novel ends at a particularly dramatic moment.[7] Don Quixote and another man are charging at one another, swords raised. On the first pages of book 2, however, the unnamed narrator does not complete the episode but instead tells us of his problems in continuing. He admits that he has been working from a manuscript, but the manuscript has broken off and he has been unable to locate the succeeding chapters. He does not for a moment doubt that the story exists somewhere, but perhaps it has fallen a victim to time: "I could not bring myself to believe that such a gallant tale had been left maimed and mutilated. I laid the blame on Time, devourer and destroyer of all things, which had either concealed or consumed it" (*DQ* 1:9). Eventually, he runs across the rest of the manuscript, by chance, in the bazaar in Toledo, buys it, and then the story can continue. But a crucial point has been made: what can really bring Don Quixote to a halt (even in the midst of a battle where he is apparently threatened with death by another character) is no corporeal enemy but time itself. Don Quixote's struggle is to have his story continue; his success is that he lives from day to day (or page to page) until his natural death arrives.[8]

As if to underline the point, Cervantes gives us an example of a story that does *not* get finished—and this story is one told early on by Sancho Panza, one who is in need of Don Quixote's instruction. Sancho begins to tell a story in which a goatherd is ferrying a pack of goats across a river,

---

[7] Part 1 of the novel is composed of four books, perhaps in imitation of *Amadis of Gaul*; Part 2 is undivided.

[8] The resumption of the story is even more complicated than my summary can convey. The found manuscript is said to be in Arabic, which the narrator must pay to have translated. Between the unknown Arabic author, the translator, and the narrator (all of whom, at various points, speak directly and none of whom are in the least objective), the reader is at least triply removed from the "events" of Don Quixote's life, a distance Cervantes seems very concerned to emphasize.

one at a time. For some reason it is necessary to mention the passage of each goat individually, "he came back and carried another one; he came back again, and again brought over another—let your worship keep count of the goats the fisherman is taking across, for if one escapes my memory there will be an end of the story" (*DQ* 1:20). Sure enough, when Don Quixote loses count of these goats, Sancho *forgets* the rest of story. "So then," asks Don Quixote, "the story has come to an end?" Sancho's plain answer is: "As much as my mother has." It does not take too much imagination to postulate that these goats, ferried across a river, represent the days of our lives, where one passes each day from the bank of the future to the bank of the past over the flowing water that is the present— with the whole held together only by memory. And Sancho directly likens the abrupt ending of the story to death. In contrast to Don Quixote, Sancho is unable to finish his story, and this disruption is compared to the real end of our lives brought on by time.

Time is the true enemy of the knight and the end of narrative symbolizes its power. The problem is not just that narratives end—all narratives end as all lives must end. The threat is that they will do so abruptly or prematurely; the destruction and turmoil caused by time are not just problems that we face at the end of our life but on a daily basis, even when we are busy with other things. Don Quixote succeeds where Sancho fails in staving off the demise of his narrative and in giving his narrative a coherence that the abruptly terminated story lacks. From this perspective, Don Quixote's charge at the windmills, the first of his adventures, and the one that has become emblematic for the entirety of his endeavor, takes on another meaning. Though the phrase "charging at windmills" is now synonymous with an act of futility, that is not the only way to view what happens. The windmills themselves are an apt metaphor for time—turning slowly in the wind at a steady pace, they grind nature into powder between two enormous stones, and from this powder we make the staff of life. When Quixote tilts at this "giant," it picks him up by his lance and flings him to the ground, severely injuring him in the process. But Quixote survives and he is not discouraged; he goes on to his next encounter. This, in itself, is a victory of sorts. In struggling with time, any day you continue to live is a battle won. The lesson need not be the futility of Quixote's efforts (only from an optimistic perspective is he a failure), but his success in avoiding being ground to bits and his further success in having his story survive "the devourer and destroyer of all things" to reach us. Quixote fails in his efforts to bring peace and justice to the world, but he succeeds in remaking himself and in living by his own lights for the natural span of his existence. The novel ends with Quixote's death, but only after he has chosen to bring his travels to a conclusion.

Fixed Values, Narrative Exemplars, and Techniques of the Self

In the opening chapter of part 2,[9] Don Quixote and his friends (who are hoping that he has "recovered" from his earlier behavior) have, we are told, a long philosophical conversation in which everyone agrees he speaks sanely and wisely about politics and in which he and his interlocutors "remodel the state" (we are not told how). Cervantes then has Quixote return to the subject of knight-errantry, which his friends have avoided, and deride the contemporary valuation of "theory over practice" in political matters (*DQ* 2:1). His complaint is not particularly elaborated, but from what follows it appears that he is not concerned with degrees of particularity and abstraction, but rather with something more fundamental, namely, the way in which we come to identify and act on our central values. Instead of looking to works that purport to give timeless rules of political behavior, we would be better off, he maintains, attending to the records of actual participants in politics, like those of the knights-errant that Quixote steadfastly believes to be genuine.

If Don Quixote's death is threatened in the demise of his narrative, the meaning of his life is likewise contained in narrative form. His "values," such as they are, are neither arrived at deductively nor systematically expounded, but rather come to light largely through stories. Despite Quixote's constant repetition of his fidelity to the norms of chivalry, an extended discussion, or even description of those norms, is strangely absent throughout the entire book. Indeed, it would be better to say that Don Quixote does not really have a "theory" or "code" of chivalry at all; what he has are narrative exemplars. When, for example, he is asked directly to describe his system of beliefs, he responds, remarkably, by recounting the history of King Arthur in considerable detail, concluding, "That, sirs, is what it means to be a knight-errant, and that is the order of chivalry I have spoken of. . . . What the aforesaid knights professed that same do I profess" (*DQ* 1:13). But in fact he has said practically *nothing* about what those knights "profess"; he has instead recounted who they were and what they did. For him, that seems to be enough.

If our temporal existence is to be not just a burden to us, but also a structure to which we can both express our fidelity while simultaneously experiencing freedom, as I have been maintaining, then the narrative-based identity that Quixote performs here is helpful in describing how we might go about this. Cervantes's pessimistic ethic is contained in the quest that forms the substance of the novel and this relationship is metonymi-

---

[9] That is, at the beginning of the sequel to the original novel, published ten years after the first part and now routinely reprinted alongside it.

cally related to Quixote's finding his own orientation in relation to the quests which have inspired his. These relationships help us to understand the Nietzschean idea that values have a different form, and not just content, in light of the time-bound character of existence. Insofar as Quixote has created himself and created new values, he has done so out of narratives that preceded him. Even if the books he settled upon were, unfortunately, wildly untrue, his act of self-definition sets him apart from his contemporaries (who never question the values they inherit) and marks him out as a "unique, incomparable" individual. He is unique, no doubt, because his values are not the common ones—but he is "incomparable" because his values and character do not even have the *form* that those of others do. This is perhaps one of the reasons why his adherence to the books of chivalry is so disturbing to his friends, who are otherwise happy to speculate wildly about remodeling the state (Cervantes seems to go out of his way to emphasize this). While Ortega y Gasset attributes the focus on narrative to the book's conformity to the rules of the epic genre (1961, 130), this reading needs, at the least, to be supplemented by reference to the temporal, or protopessimistic, stance toward character and values in which Cervantes's approach is rooted. If time is the fundamental obstacle, then addressing it in narrative form has a power that no systematic philosophy, however moral, can obtain. The book as a whole, of course, is just such a narrative, but, at a further level, Don Quixote is a character whose identity has been shaped by the narratives he encounters, rather than by the laws or rules that he obeyed as Quijada.

Narrative is the form of speech that starts from linear time, and is bound by it; but narrative is also that which preserves what time destroys (that is, the past) and, in that sense, frustrates the destructiveness of time.[10] Certainly, this is the sense of narrative that Camus had in mind when he claimed that a novel like that of Proust can both "reconstruct creation itself, in the form that it is imposed on us" and yet at that same time reject that form and work "against the powers of death and oblivion" (R 267–68). It is thus particularly apt that a pessimistic perspective takes its inspiration from narrative exemplars and decries synchronic "theory." Cervantes's approach here anticipates that of Nietzsche in proceeding as if the narrative unity of the self, rather than the consistency of one's beliefs, is the proper goal of human life. Thus Zarathustra can say, "The time is gone when mere accidents could still happen to me" and "I

---

[10] The sense in which I use "narrative" here is, obviously, a restrictive one. A cycle of events can, of course, be narrated—but in that case, I think it makes more sense to speak of "mythic" discourse rather than narrative per se. I rely here on Hayden White's account of the three levels of narrative utilized by historians, of which the most mature—narrative proper—is strictly bound by modern linear time-conventions. See White 1987, chap. 1.

taught them . . . to create and carry together into one what in human be-
ings is fragment, riddle and dreadful accident" (Z 3:1:12).[11] But even be-
yond Zarathustra's particular declarations, the very idea of Nietzsche de-
picting his philosophy through a narrative representation, the story of
Zarathustra's quest, indicates the broad affinity in approach at work here.
When Don Quixote is asked what he believes, he replies with the name of
King Arthur; when Nietzsche asks himself the question, he answers with
Zarathustra.[12]

In a discussion concerning the best sort of painters, Don Quixote is
more explicit about the way in which one should go about learning from
the past. Again, it is not a theory or a doctrine that one attempts to glean
from history; one simply seeks to imitate what is worthy of imitation: "I
say, too, that when a painter desires to become famous in his art, he endeavors to copy the originals of the finest painters that he knows. The
same rule holds good for all the most important crafts and callings that
serve to adorn a state" (DQ 1:25).[13] Foremost among the latter, of course,
is the calling of chivalry itself. Little wonder, then, that, when asked to explain himself, Don Quixote will simply invoke some episode or character
from *Amadis of Gaul* or *Orlando Furioso*. These two epic narratives are,
for him, the equivalent of a visual masterpiece worthy of a student's imitation. Since they are *narratives*, however, and not static images, the imitation of them is not something that can be carried out standing in one
place, as it were. Rather, Quixote's art of living simply consists in imitating, that is *living out*, the narrative art that describes previous lives he finds
admirable. And what is admirable about such lives are not the fixed values of their subjects but their *activity*, their attempts to change the world.

The greatest change that comes over Don Quixote when he decides to
take up knight-errantry is *not* that he becomes more virtuous. Indeed, we
are told that in his original persona, he was already known as "Alonso
the Good" (DQ 2:74). The transformation is from a man who quietly sat
at home and read books to one who felt it necessary to travel the world,
seeking out injustice and correcting it: "Churchmen in peace and quiet
pray heaven for the world's welfare, but we soldiers and knights put into
effect what they pray for" (DQ 1:13). If these efforts largely come to nothing, it is as much because "our depraved age does not deserve to enjoy
such a blessing" (DQ 2:1). What Don Quixote learned from these narra-

---

[11] See Nehamas 1985, chap. 5, esp. 160–69.

[12] The better parallel, perhaps, is with Cervantes himself. In the penultimate paragraph
of the novel in the voice of the narrator we read, "For me alone was Don Quixote born, and
I for him; it was his to act, mine to write; we two together make but one" (DQ 2; 74).

[13] I take the second sentence to indicate that Cervantes means for this idea to have application in the political sphere as well. In fact, the examples Quixote goes on to offer are
Homer's depiction of Odysseus and Virgil's of Aeneas.

tives was *not* what to believe, but how to act and, more importantly, *that* he must act. As Alonso, we might say, his ideas were correct and just but his narrative was empty. In becoming Quixote, he transforms himself, not just by leaving his home, but by coming into contact with others and acting both with and against them. His constant encounters with the unfamiliar make his transformation a continuous one, in the fashion, as Ortega y Gasset rightly observes, of epic narrative: "The good is, like nature, an immense landscape in which man advances through centuries of exploration" (1961, 37). But before he became Quixote, Alonso did not explore this landscape at all, something Cervantes emphasizes by recording next to nothing of his life in this earlier condition. It was only when he became Quixote that his life reached the level of narrativisability (exploring not just the "good," as Ortega y Gasset has it, but the "fearful and questionable" as well). Before this, he was just another *hidalgo*, literally, a "son of somebody," which is to say, a nobody. In parallel fashion, when, at the end of the book, he renounces his status as Quixote, now against the wishes of his friends (and the narrator, who will only refer to him as Quixote), he promptly dies.

Quixote as Political Educator

As we would expect from the above discussion, Quixote himself serves as an inspiration to others not as a purveyor of ideas, but as the author of his own actions. Almost all the other characters in the novel determine to "play along" with Don Quixote for one reason or another—that is, to join his plot. At first this strikes the reader as comic happenstance as when, in his first excursion, two prostitutes he meets at an inn take up the role of court maidens, which Quixote has assigned them (*DQ* 1:2). As the novel progresses, however, it becomes clear that this is, in fact, his principal effect on the world. Some play along with Don Quixote because it is in their interest to do so, as with the criminals that he frees on questionable grounds (*DQ* 1:22). Others do so strictly for comic effect, like the Duke who arranges for Don Quixote to encounter the wizard Merlin who will tell him how to disenchant Dulcinea (Sancho must beat himself senseless) (*DQ* 2:35). Still others do so out of concern for Quixote, thinking that, by means of such deceptions they will be able to bring him home.

While this play-acting is the source of much of the novel's comedy, its repetition also suggests another purpose. Ultimately, Don Quixote is an exemplar to the other characters, and if they do not take on the profession of knight-errant, they set about imitating Don Quixote in other ways. Don Fernando, for example, becomes courtly and generous, for once, in Don Quixote's enchanted inn (*DQ* 1:36). Indeed, so enamored does Fer-

nando become with Quixote's perspective that, when others doubt it, he
stages a vote among those present in which a clear majority endorse it
(*DQ* 1:45). When Cervantes has characters vote and take up arms to defend Don Quixote's view of the world, we have clearly passed beyond the
limits of simple satire. The others, it seems, gradually begin to understand
how Don Quixote's story is truly a better one than their own, such that,
when he renounces knight-errantry on his death-bed, they beg him to
recant.

Another way of putting this is to say that Quixote does not persuade
anyone of the validity of his ideas, but rather inspires their imitation of
his example. The clearest example of this phenomenon is Sancho Panza.
Sancho agrees to travel with Quixote because he believes that the journey
will make him rich and powerful, but he remains with Quixote long after
he has come to realize that he will never attain these goals and indeed,
when he no longer has these goals at all. When it is suggested to Sancho
that he has been seduced by Don Quixote's ravings, he responds quite
sharply: "I have not been seduced by anyone, nor am I a man to let myself be seduced, if it was by the king himself. . . . Each of us is the son of
his own works" (*DQ* 1:47). Sancho has *chosen* to follow Quixote, initially perhaps, out of greed, but finally out of admiration and loyalty. Indeed, this very capacity of Sancho's (loyalty) is something new, something
he has learned from Quixote himself. And, as we shall see, the kind of
protoexistentialism that Sancho now espouses ("each of us is the son of
his own works") is also part of Quixote's "code" of knight-errantry that
has rubbed off on him.

Sancho's entire journey with Quixote is, of course, a form of education,
but there are a few particular episodes that call attention to the nature of
this education. Only rarely does Quixote explicitly attempt to "instruct"
Sancho (usually he lets his own behavior stand for instruction) but one of
these attempts occurs before Sancho takes up the "governorship" to
which he has been appointed by the obliging Duke as a joke. The first
counsel is, predictably, to fear God, but the next one is more surprising:
"Secondly, you must keep in view that you are striving to know yourself,
the most difficult thing to know that the mind can imagine" (*DQ* 2:42).
Why this Delphic counsel when the challenges that face Sancho are explicitly material and political? Though Quixote goes on to counsel fair-
ness, mercy, modesty, and the like, for him these all follow from self-
knowledge. Why? Because for Quixote, knowledge of self is knowledge
of one's own limitations—and knowing one's own limitations, one is apt
to be more tolerant of the limitations of others. But self-knowledge is not
merely knowledge of one's limitations. If it were, it would be easy, rather
than difficult, to acquire.

Given the narrative conception of identity that we have discussed above, the command that Quixote issues to Sancho is to acquire knowledge that is, at least in part, narrative in character: "Glory in your humble birth, Sancho; and be not ashamed of saying you are peasant-born" (*DQ* 2:42). Although Sancho does not (yet) have much about his person that is worth narrating, we can get some sense of what is involved from Quixote's own self-description. When Quixote proudly proclaims "I know who I am," he follows this statement with the words, "and I know that I may be not only those [several knights] I have named but all the twelve Peers of France and even all the Nine Worthies" (*DQ* 1:5). While it is easy to see how such statements create the impression that Quixote is mad, his identification with the heroes of earlier legends is not senseless if identity itself is something that takes a fundamentally narrative form. Quixote is not delusional; he is not claiming to be a reincarnation of these figures.[14] Rather, he is claiming that his identity is in some sense continuous with theirs. What does this mean? When, in *Ecce Homo*, Nietzsche claimed to continue the figure of Zarathustra in himself, he did so not because his views were the same as Zarathustra's or because he was a second coming of Zarathustra, but because Zarathustra represented "the self-overcoming of morality, into his opposite—into me," (*EH*, "Destiny" 3). Nietzsche did not seek to impersonate the old Zarathustra. Rather, he contended that he could *redeem* that narrative (that is, in a sense, liberate it) by making it a necessary past to a desirable future, that is, to himself. Similarly, Quixote takes up these old figures, not to lose himself in them, but rather to find himself in them by adding to them, as one adds to a narrative one has inherited.

If Quixote has come to know who he is through his contact with chivalric romances of dubious quality, Sancho, in turn, comes to know who he is through his contact with Quixote, his narrative, and the various other narratives embedded in the text. And, as I mentioned above, the episode of Sancho's governorship suggests that this has been a surprisingly useful political education. When he takes up his post and is confronted with liars and tricksters, Sancho sees through them. When legal cases are brought before him, he is a shrewd judge of the motives and wiles of others. Several of these cases involve, essentially, two lowlifes who accuse one another of having cheated them. Sancho always finds a way to punish both while doing justice to both (*DQ* 2:45, 47, 49). The townspeople, who both present and observe these cases, have not been let in on the Duke's joke and come to have great admiration for Sancho: "In a word, he made so many good rules that to this day they are preserved there, and are called

---

[14] That would mean that he had previously been Joshua, David, Judas Maccabee, Hector, Alexander, Caesar, Arthur, Charlemagne, and Geoffrey of Bouillon—the traditional "Nine Worthies" (Geoffrey led the First Crusade).

The ordinances of the great governor Sancho Panza" (*DQ* 2:51). Since, up to this point, the reader has been told repeatedly of Sancho's intellectual shortcomings, this is a remarkable transformation.

On Sancho's part, while he first sought a governorship in order to get rich, he later has cause to boast that "without a cent I came into this government, and without a cent I go out of it" (*DQ* 2:53). Once his common sense has been unburdened of greed and ambitions, it is more than adequate to the task at hand. The justice that Quixote is repeatedly unable to effect by force, Sancho brings about through a sensible administration inspired by Quixote's ideals and Sancho's embrace of his own humble background. One of Sancho's "advisers" (planted by the Duke to observe and report on what are expected to be hilarious blunders), is amazed at what he has seen and reports, "Every day we see something new in this world; jokes become realities, and the jokers find the tables turned on them" (*DQ* 2:49). But the lesson is not just that the Duke's mildly sadistic plan has backfired. Quixote's quest for justice, which everyone considers mad and impossible, has shown itself to bear fruit indirectly and in the most unlikely of places. In Don Quixote, quixotism is a joke; in Sancho, it becomes real.

Why is Sancho more successful than Quixote? Perhaps because he knows himself better than Quixote. Quixote claims to continue the personality of the Nine Worthies, but Sancho knows himself only as Sancho, Quixote's squire. Without Quixote's example, he would, perhaps, never have been able to see the value of this. While at the start, Sancho wanted nothing else than to be a governor, by the time he actually takes on the role, he has changed. The Duke suggests that he pick out a new wardrobe when assuming office, but he replies, "Let them dress me as they like. However I'm dressed I'll be Sancho Panza" (*DQ* 2:42). Sancho reassures Quixote that the position will not distort him by saying, "I'd rather go to heaven as Sancho than to hell as a governor." And this draws a rare compliment out of Quixote: "For those last words you uttered alone, I consider you deserve to be governor of a thousand islands" (*DQ* 2:43). In learning from Quixote, Sancho has not become another Quixote, but the first and only Sancho Panza. Following a knight with delusions of grandeur, Sancho has lost his own delusions and become who he is. What success he has in politics stems from this. Sancho's policies are not, perhaps, what we might expect from a pessimist, but the entire episode may perhaps be taken to indicate that the best governor is one with a pessimistic education. Having dismantled his extravagant plans for the future, Sancho is better at seeing each case that comes before him for what it is. In knowing himself, he also knows what justice is.

But the success that Sancho meets with is limited, in more ways than one. First of all, there is the inability of Sancho's state to withstand a violent attack staged by the Duke who put him in power. More importantly, despite Sancho's fitness to govern, he finds the process itself agonizing. An "advisor" concerned with his health refuses to let him eat anything and this symbolizes the lack of reward involved in governing: "I am dying of discouragement, because when I thought I was coming to this government to get hot food and cold drinks, and take my ease between holland sheets on feather beds, I find I have come to do penance as if I was a hermit" (*DQ* 2:51). Sancho has forsworn the acceptance of bribes or any such similar material rewards, so his post is no more rewarding financially than nutritionally. It might be expected, though, that his successful government might give him some feeling of satisfaction. It does not. Sancho, in coming to know himself, learns that the task of government is more than he can bear, nor does Cervantes suggest that another would find it any easier. Sancho leaves his governorship even more hastily than he accepted it.

Finally, Cervantes warns us, in his usual comic fashion, not to become too enamored of Sancho's new-found "wisdom." When Quixote remarks on his improvement, Sancho replies, "It must be that some of your worship's discretion sticks to me. Land that, of itself, is barren and dry, will yield good fruit if you fertilize it and till it. What I mean is that your worship's conversation is the fertilizer [!] that has fallen on the barren soil of my dry wit, and the time I have spent in your service and company has been the tillage" (*DQ* 2:12). This way of putting things sets them in proper perspective. Though Sancho has improved, he has not improved much. At best, he repeats garbled versions of old maxims whose meaning he only half-understands. In imitating Quixote, he has unlearned a few of his worst habits and acquired some better ones. If Sancho is successful at governing, it is as much because an honest half-wit is already a great improvement on the greedy, corrupt, and conniving men who ordinarily hold such posts. Quixote had suggested to Sancho that knowing who he is would be enough for him to govern, and, as Cervantes lets the events unfold, this turns out to be the case. At some level, the joke, which appeared to become real, remains a joke—what more, Cervantes seems to say, could one expect from a chaotic world such as this one? But this attitude too is perfectly consonant with a pessimistic perspective. What we learn from Sancho's government is not how to bring order and justice to the world in any permanent way, but that the attempt to do so is worthwhile.

Quixote's Madness, Narrative, Dionysus

Those who want to help Don Quixote attempt to convince him to return to a common, contemporary narrative, to a world he could more readily share with others. He simultaneously tempts them to join his plot. The difference is that they, largely, make rational appeals, while he provides an exemplar for them to follow. The actions of each side must appear to the other as madness. What is surprising is not so much the failure of those who attempt to reclaim Quixote, but rather his success in claiming them for his own story.

The one character that attempts to persuade Quixote on his own terms is Sanson Carrasco, who dresses up as a knight in order to best Quixote in a contest of arms and thereby force him to return home. The result, however, is that Carrasco is one of the few who actually loses a physical contest to the aged, weak Quixote. Afterwards, Carrasco's squire remarks, "Don Quixote a madman, and we sane; yet he goes off laughing, safe and sound, and you are left sore and sorry. I'd like to know now which is the madder, the man who is mad because he cannot help it, or the man mad of his own free will?" (*DQ* 2:16). Carrasco, whom we are told is a learned university graduate, is no match for Quixote on the latter's own terms. And the squire pinpoints the reason: the true madness is to pretend to beliefs insincerely. Quixote's outlook is at least his own genuine way of looking at the world, and it is just as (in)effective, in its own way, as Carrasco's. Although Carrasco does ultimately succeed in forcing Quixote home (and is denounced for it: "May God forgive you the wrong you have done the whole world" [*DQ* 2:65]), he too, in the end, becomes an admirer and, on the last pages of the book, gives one of the most fervent pleas for Quixote to take up his role again when the latter renounces it.

Quixote is well aware that he projects an appearance of madness, but he has a simple explanation of how what appears to be madness is largely a matter of perspective. After he has captured the "legendary helmet of Mambrino" from a passing barber, Sancho attempts to convince him that it is, after all, only a barber's basin. Don Quixote denies this, but he is ready to explain Sancho's confusion:

> Is it possible that all this time you have been going about with me you have never found out that all things concerning knights-errant seem to be illusions and nonsense and ravings, and to be done topsy-turvy? And not because it really is so, but because there is always a swarm of enchanters around us who change and alter everything with us and turn things as they please. . . . Thus what seems to you a barber's basin seems to me Mambrino's helmet, and to another it will seem something else. (*DQ* 1:25)

Quixote does not expect the world to appear to others as it appears to him, and not because he is crazy but because such conflict of perspectives is the normal course of things. Thus Quixote does not bridle at the charge of being "mad"; it is only when it is suggested that he has a genuine mental illness that he gets annoyed (*DQ* 2:1). While it would perhaps be going too far to say that Quixote is a "perspectivist" in the Nietzschean sense of this term, it is easy to see how Nietzsche could have perceived in Quixote a kindred spirit. The "swarm of enchanters" that Quixote says surround him produce an effect not unlike the Dionysian world view: things are unpredictable, magical, always changing, "topsy-turvy" (*hechas al revés*, lit. "made into their reverse or opposite"). If Cervantes does not, at this point in the text, attribute these things to the effects of time as Nietzsche might, the picture of a turbulent, chaotic world produced by the first Western fiction to adopt the conventions of modern linear time is still a striking one.

Cervantes emphasizes, as does Nietzsche, that to model one's life on a quest is to isolate oneself. Even when Quixote is in physical contact with other people, as he often is, the fact that they do not share his perspective leads them to consider him mad. This is the ordinary course of things. Yet there is also the possibility that the others, in agreeing to join Quixote's plot, will join him in his madness. Most of the characters that do so only do so temporarily. In a topsy-turvy, Dionysian world, it cannot be otherwise. But in joining forces with Quixote this way, each of them has the opportunity to learn something from him as he does from them. Though isolated in one sense, in another Don Quixote spends his time in contact with the panoply of human possibility through his wide travels in the varied landscape of La Mancha, just as Nietzsche suggests his Dionysian pessimist will be both lonely and constantly changed by being viscerally exposed to the most "fearful and questionable" elements of the species.

The Practice of Pessimism

There is another way, however, in which Quixote can more properly be called "mad." The quest that he exemplifies has no prospect of success in the corrupt, declining world in which he finds himself. Cervantes's outlook is pessimistic in the sense that there is no chance for Quixote (or, so far as we can tell, anyone else) to defeat injustice and corruption. Indeed, he is bound to suffer in the attempt to do so. If it is madness to persevere in such an effort, then Quixote may justly be labeled mad. But that is not, I think, the conclusion we are meant to draw. As if to highlight the special quality of Quixote's perseverance, Cervantes gives us a contrasting figure, a truly discouraged fatalist, in the character of an unnamed canon who has "sanely" abandoned his own plans to write theatrical works of moral instruction in the face of an unappreciative world:

If the plays that are now in vogue . . . are, all or most of them, downright
nonsense, having neither head nor tail, and yet the public listens to them with
delight, and regards and approves them as perfection when they are far from
it, and if the authors who write them and the players who act them say that
this is the way they must be, because the public wants them that way and
will have nothing else, . . . and that for themselves it is better to earn a living from the many than praise from the few; then my book will fare the same
way, after I have burned the midnight oil trying to observe the principles I
have spoken of, and I would end up like "the tailor on the corner" [that is,
practicing a useless, unrewarded trade]. (*DQ* 1:48)

The canon's position is of course the sensible one, well-reasoned and
well-justified—it is very nearly that of Rousseau in the *Letter to M.
D'Alembert*. But Quixote takes the opposite view, knowing full well the
consequences of it. Though he often tells Sancho that a kingdom to rule
is right around the corner, when he is more candid, he knows that he will
not meet with any success: "This adventure and those like it are not adventures for winning but are merely crossroads encounters. Nothing is to
be won except a broken head or an ear the less" (*DQ* 1:10). But Quixote
is not discouraged. He does not measure his efforts by the metrics of happiness or worldly success. It is only in terms of his consistency in produc-
ing the person he aims to be that Quixote takes stock of the quest he has
enacted. And unlike the canon, he does not require an audience to appreciate him.

When at last Don Quixote heads home for the final time, he does not
claim victory but he admits to self-respect: "In a word, I took a chance, I
did my best, I was knocked off, but though I lost my honor, I did not lose
nor can I lose the virtue of keeping my word" (*DQ* 2:66). Far from mock-
ing Quixote's cheerfulness, Cervantes depicts it as a superior response
consistent with a pessimistic outlook. The only thing that truly depresses
Quixote is not losing battles or being knocked off of his horse, but being
constrained to go back to his village and end his quest. Only the end of
his narrative, that is, rather than its low moments, threatens his posture.
As Michael Oakeshott put it: "Cervantes created a character in whom the
disaster of each encounter with the world was powerless to impugn it
as a self-enactment." (Oakeshott 1975, 241). The quixotic life is not
thwarted by a lack of results; its value lies in the experience of freedom
that it enacts. That is why it is possible for the pessimistic ethic to persevere in the most adverse circumstances, when optimism has nothing to
offer except an unfounded hope that is little more than wishful thinking.

All narratives, as all lives, must end ("human affairs are not eternal but
all tend ever downwards")—this is the pessimistic knowledge that
grounds Cervantes's perspective. But if we all face destruction at the hands

of time, this need not convince us to resign ourselves prematurely. Although in one sense, nothing about the world has been changed for the better by Quixote's actions, his success consists in having led a life consistent with who he is. Like Sisyphus with his stone, he has achieved dignity by accomplishing nothing. Or rather, what he has accomplished is to have enacted the value of pessimism in the form of a quest. He has made his life unpredictable, memorable, and narrativisable by bringing his life-practice into contact with the world. And a small portion of the world responds by allowing itself to be inspired by this practice.

Camus went wrong, perhaps, in concluding his early essay with the sentence, "We must imagine Sisyphus happy." Certainly we must *not* imagine Quixote "happy." He is simply in too much pain for that word to be the apt one. If we are to speak of a success in Quixote's story, it cannot be in terms of his effects in the world or in terms of his personal happiness. While it is true, as I have argued, that Quixote has converted others to his outlook, they are not likely to be any more successful than he in changing human prospects, except perhaps in the limited, temporary way that Sancho Panza succeeds. We can, however, imagine Quixote, like Sisyphus, taking a certain amount of satisfaction in having created and enacted a "new, unique, incomparable," law-bound identity.

What *Don Quixote* offers is not any moral program, then, but no more (and no less) than a certain kind of pessimistic wisdom. Quixote may believe, at first, that he can make the world safe for Dulcinea; but Cervantes certainly does not, nor, in the end, do Quixote or the reader. And beyond Quixote's human enemies, there is time itself, monstrous and implacable, grinding one slowly to bits, like the windmills that are his first foe. In his wanderings, however, and his encounters with multifarious humanity, there is a kind of facing up to reality in Quixote that most humans never experience. Most remain in blissful (or willed) ignorance of this world's terrors as well as its possibilities. Yet as Quixote comes to grips with the forces that thwart his will and ultimately defeat him, he never doubts his task. And in continuing his quest in the face of overwhelming odds, he creates a narrative that inspires those around him—even if the narratives *he* follows are themselves deceptive fictions.

We can also think of his quest for the "fearful and questionable," as Ortega y Gasset does, as simultaneously an intellectual exploration. Knights-errant, Quixote tells Sancho, "ought to know everything" (*DQ* 1:19). And in another conversation that precedes Sancho's government, Cervantes suggests that what Quixote possesses is a knowledge akin to philosophy. He has Quixote argue that knight-errantry is, after all, a science, even the master science: "It is a science that comprehends in itself all or most of the sciences in the world" (*DQ* 2:18). He then goes on to list the roles that are comprised in that of a knight: jurist, theologian, physician,

astronomer, mathematician, and a host of others. To truly carry out a
knight's task, one would have to master all these different sorts of knowledge and doing so would constitute a full education in knight-errantry.
This account simultaneously emphasizes the heroism and futility of those
like Quixote whose purpose is good but whose task is hopeless. To take
up this role in a sane fashion would be to admit, from the start, that one's
goal was unreachable. But this is really no argument against doing the best
we can. Cervantes depicts his ideal knight-errantry as Nietzsche depicts
his ideal philosophy: as an open-ended quest for understanding whose
destination is unknown and must always appear unreachable. Here we
return to the *"la gai saber"* as a point of contact between Cervantes and
Nietzsche. The gay science is a questing logic at once mental and existential. Where Socrates took the Delphic command, "Know thyself" to propose a life of internal reflection, Cervantes takes it to suggest instead a
perpetual examination of oneself through one's encounters with the
world. Cervantes maintains that an education of the kind Quixote offers
to his squire is the best sort of education one could have, both as a human,
and as a potential governor of others. Likewise, Nietzsche claims that his
pessimistic quest is the (gay) science of living best suited to our universe
and our age.

.   .   .   .   .

"To become what one is," Nietzsche wrote, "one must not have the
faintest notion *what* one is" (*EH*, "Clever" 9). As with the list of adjectives from *The Gay Science*, one does not need to stretch the text very far
to find in Quixote the sort of character, and personal transformation, that
Nietzsche has in mind. In one sense, of course, Quixote "knows" who he
is very well—he "is" the knights of the Round Table, the Nine Worthies,
and so on. At another level, of course, he does not seem to know himself
at all—at least he seems to be constantly astonished at how he appears to
others. While in one sense, then, Quixote radically overestimates himself,
and what he has accomplished, in another sense, as Nietzsche suggests,
he radically "underestimated his own courage because his head was filled
with the miraculous deeds of the heroes of chivalric romances" (*HH* 133).
Believing that what he does is little different from what has been done before, he does not realize how "new, unique, [and] incomparable" he is.
Believing in fictions, he becomes a fact that is stranger than fiction.

The sum of this is that Quixote can truly be said to have created himself—not out of whole cloth, to be sure. Before he was Quixote, he was
Alonso Quisano the Good. And without the chivalric romances, Quisano
would never have become Quixote. But this neither lessens Quixote's
achievement nor does it contradict the idea that in becoming Quixote,

Quisano has become who he is—that is, in making himself over anew, he has become more himself, *become more that which is uniquely him* and less that which is common and contemporary. He claims that knowing yourself is the key to sound government, and yet he does not engage in prolonged introspection but in a quest that defines him as a character. Quixote says to Sancho that "one man is no more than another unless he does more than another" (*DQ* 1:19). Quixote's transformation, though symbolized by his adoption of a new name, is certainly not *contained* in the renaming. That only marks the beginning of the quest. It is Quixote's *doings* that make him who he is and not another. It is his acts that set him apart from other people. All humans act; but not all "give themselves laws." Ortega y Gasset put it thus: "A hero, I have said, is one who wants to be himself. . . . Don Quixote . . . is a hero" (1961, 152).

What kind of hero is it, though, who loses nearly every battle? I think the best reply is: a pessimistic exemplar. If we too are tempted to join Quixote's plot, we will not do so by putting on armor and mounting an old horse, or by reading books of chivalry. But we might do as Quixote did in taking his quest for himself to the most fearful and questionable aspects of existence, however we define them, and seeing what happens.

Cervantes, as I have said, describes the suffering, as well as the satisfaction, that accompanies this self-transformation. Though Quixote is, very occasionally, joyful as he wanders the plains of La Mancha, he is not immune to the pain of his many injuries or the embarrassment that comes with his many rebuffs and humiliations. To be unique is to be different from all the rest, and to follow one's own law is necessarily to run afoul of the laws of the community. One episode in *Don Quixote* encapsulates this problem in the most efficient possible way. In the nineteenth chapter of part 1, Quixote (famously) adopts the epithet "Knight of the Mournful Countenance" (*Caballero de la Triste Figura*) at the suggestion of Sancho. The moment he resolves to do so—*the moment he puts on a pessimistic face*—a priest appears and, without ceremony, pronounces him excommunicated (*DQ* 1:19). This episode, at the very least, ought to underscore just how far Cervantes understood his hero to have traveled from his comfortable life in his ancestral home.

· · · · ·

If we consider *Don Quixote* an educative parody of a literature of moral education (the books of chivalry), then we might regard *Thus Spoke Zarathustra* as its successor in this genre, with its relation to the Bible paralleling *Don Quixote*'s relation to the books of chivalry. Though there are doubtless limits to this comparison, one is naturally tempted to look for echoes of Quixote in Nietzsche's narrative exemplar Zarathustra: Both leave their homes at a middling age and roam about in the countryside, dispensing wisdom. Both are ignored, perceived as comic, or, occasionally, listened to in such a way that they would rather be ignored. Both suffer from and complain of the loneliness of being misunderstood. Both find an enemy in contemporary values, especially contemporary religious values.[15] And both respond, in effect, by exemplifying a set of values that, while couched in terms that appear old, is in fact radically new, in form as well as content. Both books, in effect, offer to replace a fixed set of judgments with a narrated quest of a fortified self—an art of living, but more specifically, a practice of pessimism.

Zarathustra, of course, has been compared to many other figures, both of literature and of real life, and I do not want to privilege this connection above all others. However, it seems clear enough that Nietzsche, like Cervantes before him, wrote a book that very nearly escaped the categories of genre that preceded their work. In doing so, each sought to create a character adequate to the modern conception of time that structured each of their narratives and created the fundamental problematic for their characters' lives. Nietzsche, of course, is more explicit about this. But, at the very least, Cervantes's attention to temporal disorder and chaos in the "first" Western novel gives some indication that the problem Nietzsche identifies is not idiosyncratic to him.

In the practices of both Quixote and Zarathustra, there is no suggestion of resignation or suicide. Rather, each takes up the burden of time by furthering the narratives they have inherited, by redeeming what has been handed down to them as well as they can. Each attempts to give their lives meaning through a self-renovation and self-fortification, a living out of a unique set of values, with no expectation that their acts will leave any permanent mark on the world. Their lives must be their only reward, along with a greater-than-ordinary portion of human suffering. To us, they hand down, not any doctrine, but techniques and narratives that can be reexampled, but not copied—continued, but not repeated.

· · · · ·

[15] The second book of *Don Quixote* did receive the approval of the royal censors with the statement that "it contains nothing against our holy Catholic faith or good morals" (no approval was required at the time the first book was published)—but though the censors were very far from credulous, this does not mean that they were not, in some sense, fooled. Quixote's excommunication (and death-bed return to the faith) may well have been the means by which Cervantes legitimized his characters' exploration of a world view that was far from orthodox. Though the censors accepted the novel (not entirely without reason) as an example of "moral reproof," it is hard to imagine that it was on this basis that the book became an international bestseller.

In *Schopenhauer as Educator*, Nietzsche, while reporting all he had learned from that philosopher, did not say that he wanted to become another Schopenhauer, or that he wanted others to do so. He instead suggested that his encounter with Schopenhauer had enabled him to become who he was. Similarly, being educated by Cervantes does not mean that the result is a desire to become another Don Quixote. Ortega y Gasset, in his best formulation, described the effect of *Don Quixote* as the liberation that comes with news of a world ruled by certain gods "under which the impossible is possible:"

> The normal does not exist where they reign: all-embracing disorder emanates from their thrones. The constitution they have sworn to obey has one single article: adventure is permitted. . . . Adventure shatters the oppressive, insistent reality as if it were a piece of glass. It is the unforeseen, the unthought-of, the new. Each adventure is a new birth of the world, a unique process. How can it fail to be interesting? (1961, 129, 132)

Here Ortega y Gasset finds a thought in Quixote that we can properly call Dionysian: the disorder of the world can be viewed as a horizon of opportunity so long as we do not cling insistently to what exists at any one time. *Quixotic disorder is the antidote to the ruling power of normality.* The fundamental chaos of the universe is the ultimate source of freedom, even if it also guarantees us a dangerous existence. An impossible desire to preserve the present can be put aside more easily when life is viewed as a quest where the encounter with the new is the ordinary course of things. Quixote's adventures, properly understood, should not trigger a desire that they be *repeated*, but could prod us to *continue* them in the sense Quixote continues, by radically transforming, the narratives that have shaped him. Static norms demand to be affirmed; narrative values ask only to be extended.

This freedom toward the future, or better, *constant tending to the rebirth of novelty in human affairs*, is something that Nietzsche too is concerned with (and which he handed down to his pessimistic inheritors like Camus, Hannah Arendt, and Michel Foucault). From Schopenhauer, he learned that the world was a place of constant change, flux, and transformation. For Schopenhauer, as we have seen, this was a reason to reject existence and find it meaningless. Nietzsche, perhaps because he encountered books like that of Cervantes (or, as the epigraphs to this chapter indicate, encountered such books in a way that Schopenhauer was not capable of), suggested instead that we view the chaos as a landscape of constant adventure, often painful, but never boring, worth traversing and continuing.

Apart from varying degrees of suicide, to the pessimist, this is our only real choice.

Chapter Seven

APHORISMS AND PESSIMISMS

1

THE APHORISTIC FORM

To collect one's thoughts, to polish up certain denuded
truths—anyone can manage that, more or less; but the *edge*,
without which a pithy shortcut is only a statement, a mere
maxim, requires a touch of virtuosity, even of charlatanism.
—CIORAN, *DAQ* 169

THE APHORISM is not dead—but it *is* in danger of being misplaced.
Is it not remarkable that aphorisms are not in use more widely? They
seem so appropriate for our age, where the average attention span is
rapidly diminishing. And yet, in a perverse way, this is probably the reason for their rarity in contemporary Anglophone philosophy. Thinking to
fight against the banalization and abbreviation of our culture, philosophers write ever-longer, more serious, more studious tomes—while publishers beg them to write shorter, sexier ones. But while our culture may
become truly simple, an aphorism merely appears so. Its gnomic quality
has a purpose: it stimulates one to investigate, to *look into* it. To pause.
Even to stop dead and look round for a moment. To stop dead: to take
oneself out of the stream of life. To look up to the farthest reaches of one's
circumstances: to the horizon. As noted previously, "aphorism" is from
the Greek *ap-horeizen*, to set a horizon, a boundary, hence to define. A
good aphorism sets a new horizon, which forces one to reconsider old
ones.

The poet Frank O'Hara once claimed that a poem ought to be the
chronicle of the creative act that produced it. While this may or may not
hold true of poetry, something parallel to this could be claimed for the
best aphorisms. Aphorisms are not epigrams or maxims. These two,
which make a virtue of extreme brevity, are an attempt to encapsulate
some piece of wisdom in one, two, or at most three sentences. They do
not necessarily derive from a single experience and, indeed, are meant to
have a broad, if not general, application. An aphorism, on the other hand,
is an attempt to communicate to the reader not just the content, but the
experience of the glance to the horizon, of stepping out of the stream of
life, if only for a moment. Though it may be short, it may also be extended,

even to the length of a few pages, but no further. If it has not achieved its purpose by this point, it is a failure and there is no point in going on. The vista will remain the private experience of the writer, unavailable for others to call on.

To my mind, the maximum length of an aphorism is whatever can be written in one sitting. *Written*, not read—for many aphorisms may be taken in at once. An aphorism can be revised, of course, before it is released into the world. It may be improved, simplified, polished; but if it is complicated, if another train of thought is added, even one fully consequential to the first . . . then it is an essay, no matter how short. The reason is, so to speak, phenomenological. Deriving from one glance to the horizon, an aphorism can only contain as much as the eye can take in in a moment. This is more for some than for others, but not very much more. If its essence is not set down in one sitting, usually immediately, then it is lost.

The reader's capacity to take these in, then, depends on many things. Ordinarily, the moment that was so vivid to one is not necessarily so in its reproduction to another. The horizon of the reader and that of the writer do not initially coincide. And aphorisms, self-contained and hermetic in their moment of vision, appear to make little attempt to explain themselves. Hans-Georg Gadamer has suggested that every act of understanding is a result of the "fusing of horizons." That is, two worldviews truly come into contact only when their horizons can be made to connect, when their fundamental terms and categories of meaning can be related to one another. The efforts of both parties (here: writer and reader) are equally important to the success of this task. But even with such efforts, the necessary connection will be rare.

Think of the situation like this: we often wander through a museum—or a collection of aphorisms—taking in, in a few minutes, works that took considerably longer to create until by chance we arrive at the one work that strikes *us* dead, roots us to the spot, lifts us out of our ordinary relationship to the world. Some works do this to no one or almost no one; others only to certain people in certain moods; a few to nearly everyone (everyone at least who is willing to pick up a book or set foot in a museum). Aphorisms are like that.

2

PESSIMISM AND APHORISM

Aphorisms and pessimism are fitted to one another. There can be little doubt that different philosophical orientations are particularly well-suited for certain formats of writing. When Theodor Adorno, in his own aphoristic work, wrote that "the presentation of philosophy is not an external matter of indifference to it but immanent to its idea" (1973, 18), he did not express an original idea but a very old one. The seemingly fragmentary form of the collection of aphorisms communicates, ahead of the content, the condition of disorder that pessimism as a whole describes in the world. While each aphorism of course has its own subject, the genre itself contains the perspective that all who use it partake of to some degree— just as Plato's use of the dialogue form communicates something about his outlook, even though Socrates and his companions express a bewildering variety of opinions within that form. Of course, not all aphorists are pessimists nor are all pessimists aphorists—but the constant recourse that pessimists have had to aphoristic writing is a clear indication that philosophical form and content have here a natural comfort with each other.

Plato's early dialogues are often characterized as "aporetic" in that they often fail to come to conclusions about the questions with which the conversation is initiated. But, on another level, the dialogues are often highly successful—Socrates usually succeeds in convincing his interlocutors to abandon their original positions and to join him in his condition of enlightened ignorance. In this sense, the dialogue form communicates the success of communication itself, even as it often documents the failure of inquiry. Plato's characters and readers are (with some exceptions) strengthened by the process of dialogue itself, as they grow to trust and appreciate one another and to gain mutual respect for systematic discussion.

But the aporia that early Platonic dialogues display only at the end is in evidence throughout a collection of aphorisms. This is in part an effect of the discontinuity that occurs between one aphorism and the next. But this also occurs within the individual aphorism when it reproduces the problem of temporality that I have claimed as the core of pessimism. In attempting to set a momentary experience into words, aphorisms attempt to render the transitory permanent. Inevitably they fail, and often comment on this failure. Thus F. H. Bradley, in his own book of aphorisms: "Our life experiences, fixed in aphorisms, stiffen into cold epigram."[1] That the aphorism has failed, in a sense, before it has begun is one of the elements of its pessimistic cast. When Derrida writes that "all writing is aphoristic," it is this quality of an attempt that documents its own failure that he has in mind (1967, 107).[2] From the beginning, the scholarly literature on aphorisms has emphasized their "discontinuous," "contradic-

---

[1] 1930, 25. Cited in Neumann 1976a, 3.

[2] In what appears to be a lapse by the translator, this sentence is missing in the English edition (Derrida 1978, 71). My attention was first called to this sentence by Lafond 1984, 117. Derrida appears here to be extending the thought of Bergson, quoted below.

tory" nature (e.g., Fink 1934, 91). But it is also this experience of contradiction that the pessimistic writers, as we have seen in earlier chapters, have stressed as the constant effect of time-bound existence. The effects of temporality constantly undermine the value of any particular moment. So the attempt to hold on to any instant, even in written form, is futile. And yet if, as Bergson maintained, "discontinuity is thought itself, it is the thinkable in itself," then the documentation of failure that the aphorism produces is simultaneously the most direct and undistorted reflection possible of the time-bound mind (1907, 155).

The discontinuous form of writing is, from this perspective, the most realistic and even the most honest in its refusal to draw out ideas beyond their moment of appearance. "Who cares tomorrow," Cioran writes, "about an idea we had entertained the day before?—After any night, we are no longer the same, and we cheat when we play out the farce of continuity.—The *fragment*, no doubt a disappointing genre, but the only honest one" (*DAQ* 166). *Extending our thinking across time is false to our temporal experience of thought appearing (and disappearing) in the moment, but even more false to our temporal experience of being.* Not only do we not care about yesterday's thought, but "*we* are no longer the same." Yesterday's thought belonged to someone else; it *was* someone else. Today's is someone different. To draw these two, and many others, together into an artificial narrative is, as Cioran says, to cheat—to create the fictitious identity of a single author in place of the multiplicitous soul that is the origin of a series of contradictory thoughts. A collection of aphorisms therefore, not only documents the process of their creation, but the *variety* of processes and disjunctions that are their source, and the journey that a single body has taken through that variety. Aphoristic writing reveals the internal divisions of the mind, created by the flow of time, rather than pretending to the unity of spirit that Socratic philosophy tortuously urges us to attain.

As a result, rather than emphasizing community and identity, as a dialogue does, aphoristic wisdom tends to separate its reader from his or her self and from the group of which he or she is a part. The ironic and often openly sarcastic aphorisms of the early masters of this form throw a cold light on various common social and political hypocrisies. Indeed, the deflation of currently acclaimed values and habits has long been the particular task of the aphorist, a task for which this genre—brief, witty, frank, and (when successful) trenchant—is particularly well-made. If aphorisms belabor their points, they sound preachy and contrived. If they give up their humor, they sound schoolmarmish. As a group, their very disconnection from one another prevents them from acquiring the aspect of a rival hypocrisy to the one they pester. Yet their antisystematic form can still contain a view of the world that can inform its reader in positive as

well as negative ways. The aphorism stands at the greatest distance from
that form of philosophy that attempts to depict a grand order to the universe and in so doing embodies the pessimistic attitude that freedom is to
be found only with such distance. So Cioran writes: "Aristotle, Aquinas,
Hegel—three enslavers of the mind. The worst form of despotism is the
system, in philosophy and in everything" (*TBB* 117).

3

MAXIMS, FRAGMENTS, POEMS

An extensive literature links the aphorism to the other *formes brèves* that
have appeared in philosophy and literature: not only those mentioned
above (the maxim and the fragment) but also the reflection, *pensée*, sentence, proverb, adage, remark, and, especially in literary criticism, the
prose poem.[3] While this literature is in agreement on some of the obvious
formal qualities of the aphorism (e.g., concision, wit, discontinuity), there
is, nonetheless, an important debate about the aphorism's origins and essential character. If, on the one hand, we consider the aphorism to be most
closely related to the maxim and the adage, then its history would have
to be a very long one, starting perhaps with the Bible and at least with certain Greek and Roman authors and continuing through the *Tacitisme* of
early modern writers to the *Maximes* of La Rochefoucauld and the other
moralistes (Fricke 1984, chap. 2; Moret 1997, chap. 1). While some of
the historical work done by defenders of this approach is very interesting,
it has been hampered by the lack of an image of pessimism with which
the aphorism could be connected. Thus, Phillippe Moret's excellent book
(*Tradition et Modernité de L'Aphorisme*) acknowledges that there is a no-
ticeable break between the premodern and modern aphorism, where the
latter (starting in the eighteenth century) focuses more on the subjectivity
of the author and throws into question the truths that the premodern version enunciated (Moret 1997, 393–99). But without a substantive philosophy to connect this change with, his account can only describe it in
terms of a stylistic evolution or as a kind of incipient postmodernism. At
the other historical extreme, it has been argued that the aphorism is best
understood as a largely contemporary phenomenon, either as an expression of Surrealism (Berranger 1988) or postmodernism generally (*TE*
11).[4] But while these critics also have important things to say about twen-

---

[3] See, e.g., Berranger 1988, Camprubí 1999, Fedler 1992, Fricke 1984, Helmich 1991,
Moncelet 1998, Moret 1997, Neumann 1976a and 1976b, Ortemann 1998, and Spicker
1997, in addition to those cited above.

[4] In her introduction to Cioran's *Temptation to Exist*, Susan Sontag wrote: "The starting

tieth-century philosophy, their framework simply cannot take meaningful account of earlier aphoristic writing, like that of Leopardi or Schopenhauer, which may be antisystematic but is hardly postmodern.

Closer to the mark, I think, are those commentators who have focused on the romantic concept of the "fragment" as developed by Novalis, the Schlegels, and Goethe (Spicker 1997, Neumann 1976a). Here, at least, the form of writing is tied to a philosophy that is distinctively modern (as opposed to classical or postmodern) and to an idea of subjectivity that explains why aphorisms often feel more like a personal expression of the author, even when they are phrased in highly abstract ways. But the pessimistic aphorism—the writing of those aphorists discussed in previous chapters—remains at some distance, I think, from the romantic fragment. For one thing, the fragmentary character of the fragment is intended as something provisional or temporary—the result of our fallen, temporal condition, but written in the hope that that condition can be cured. The fragment always looks *over* its own horizon, so to speak, to a prospective reunion with an imagined whole. The aphorism, by contrast, marks out boundaries and abides by them, self-contained. While it may lament the lack of sense or meaning in our everyday experiences, it refuses to compensate for that lack with reference to a natural or metaphysical totality. Still, were it not for the existence of important aphorists that predate romanticism, we might think of aphorisms as fragments that have lost their faith in a future completion and become self-subsistent in the present.

The self-containedness of aphorisms, however, can also be misunderstood. While individual aphorisms do not rely, in a direct argumentative way, on those that immediately precede or follow them, it is nonetheless wrong to consider them entirely apart from their presentational context. Aphorisms are almost always presented in a series or collection and their meaning often relies, at least in part, on the sequence of ideas or vistas presented therein, as well as the contradictions between them. Much violence can be done to aphoristic texts by assuming, as Arthur Danto did of Nietzsche, for example, that the individual items can be taken up more or less in any order (Danto 1965, 19). This is one further thing that distinguishes aphorisms from maxims and epigrams. These also often appear in collections, but they are meant to be quoted singly and the order in which they appear in a series may have little significance. That is to say, the discontinuity that a collection of aphorisms presents is not generic—it is not simply the space that appears between any two sentences, words,

point for this modern post-philosophic tradition of philosophizing is the awareness that the traditional forms of philosophical discourse have been broken. What remain as leading possibilities are mutilated, incomplete discourse (the aphorism, the note or jotting)."

or letters. Rather, the author of a collection of aphorisms may intend to guide us from point to point, as the designer of a trail might take us from vista to vista—intending as well that we should do the hard work of covering the distance from one spot to the next.

Aphorisms then, can reproduce for us the stations of a quest. They can, in recreating moments of experience, give us a sense for the path an individual mind has taken, even when that path is a contradictory one. But they can do so only, so to speak, with our consent. If we do not make an effort to reach a point of understanding with the text, it will remain lifeless. "Thoughts reduced to paper," Schopenhauer wrote, "are generally nothing more than the footprints of a man walking in the sand. It is true that we see the path he has taken; but to know what he saw on the way, we must use our own eyes" (*PP* 2:555). Part of that work, surely, involves coming to grips with the "contradictory" nature of the various perspectives that are presented, something only ascribable to the text as a whole, rather than to any single item.

Aphorism has also been considered a literary as well as a philosophical genre, even as a form of poetry (e.g., Fedler 1992, Moncelet 1998, Ortemann 1998). This is instructive because it helps to explain, simultaneously as it were, both what is distinctive about the aphorism and why its practitioners have so often been excluded from the canon of philosophy proper. Aphorisms are not just pieces of wisdom expressed in a sententious manner. They are subjective, but not merely so, not *simply* a report of an experience, like a journal entry. And more than the fragment, they aim at an aesthetic wholeness that reflects a vision of the world or some piece of it. In that sense, they do aspire to a certain kind of poetic achievement and, though they usually lack the sort of formal structure that we associate with poetry, it is not altogether a mistake to view them through such a lens. This, however, has also been a means of discrediting writers like Nietzsche or Cioran. Their writing, it is sometimes claimed, is *merely* literary rather than strictly philosophical. But this criticism mistakes the quest of the pessimistic aphorist to match the form of writing to its subject in the closest way possible for mere aestheticism. If, in taking on the characteristics of vision, subjectivity, discontinuity (and the other various elements discussed), aphoristic pessimism comes to resemble prose poetry, then it is because the time-bound existence that such writing depicts may strike us as poetic when aptly translated into written language. Perhaps this was the point Cioran had in mind when he wrote: "Even more than in the poem, it is in the aphorism that the word is god" (*DAQ* 165). Aphorisms do not aim to be "literary;" if it turns out that their truthfulness strikes us as beautiful, that is more than a coincidence—but other ears will hear their discontinuity as dissonance.

4

APHORISM AND MORTALITY

La Rochefoucauld's most famous work is universally known as *The Maxims*, but that is not its full title. The complete title—*Réflexions ou sentences et maximes morales* —can be taken to mean that what is presented in the book is a miscellany of styles that do not all fit under a single genre.[5] Many of the entries are indeed maxims in the way I have been using the term, but this cannot be said for the famous last entry, which is worth quoting at some length.

> I want to speak about this contempt for death that the pagans boast of deriving from their own strength, without the hope of a better life. There is a difference between steadfastly enduring death and having contempt for it. The first is quite ordinary, but I believe that the other is never sincere. Yet, so much has been written in the attempt to persuade us that death is no evil; and the weakest men, as well as the heroes, have provided a thousand famous examples to establish this opinion. However, I doubt that anybody with good sense ever believed it; and the difficulty in persuading others and oneself of it shows well-enough that this undertaking is not easy. One can have various objects of disgust in life, but one is never right to have contempt for death. Those very people who willingly give themselves to death do not count it as so little a thing, and, when it comes to them by a way other than the one they have chosen, they are frightened by it and reject it like others do. The inequality that we notice in the courage of an infinite number of valiant men comes from death's revealing itself differently to their imaginations, and appearing there more vividly at one time than at another. Thus it happens that after having had contempt for what they do not know, they finally fear what they do know. It is necessary to avoid imagining it in all of

[5] It is hard to judge the degree of variety La Rochefoucauld intends by the title since the word "*morales*" could either be taken to modify one, two, or (perhaps) even three of the substantives, with very different effects, e.g., *Reflections or Moral Aphorisms and Maxims*, or *Reflections or Aphorisms and Moral Maxims*. I translate "*sentence*" here as "aphorism" since the English "sentence" is the equivalent of the French "*phrase*;" "*sentence*" in French refers to a pithy saying and could also be translated as "maxim" were that not redundant here—and since La Rochefoucauld obviously means to indicate something *other* than maxims. (In a prefacing note to the first edition, he refers to the book in an abbreviated way as *Réflexions ou Maximes morales*; in a note to the fifth edition, he calls it simply *Réflexions morales*—however, in both of these notes, La Rochefoucauld writes in the voice of the publisher, rather than the author, and it is hard to know how much weight to give these abbreviations of the full title, which, after all, he devised.) Warner's introduction to the text contains a discussion of some of these issues (La Rochefoucauld 2001, vii–xvi).

its particulars if one does not want to believe that it is the greatest of all evils. The most clever and the most brave are those who find more honest pretexts to prevent themselves from considering it. But any man who knows how to see it as it is finds that it is a dreadful thing. The necessity of dying caused all the constancy of philosophers. They believed that one had to go with good grace where one could not prevent oneself from going; and, unable to make their lives eternal, there was nothing they did not do to make their reputations eternal, and to save from the shipwreck that which cannot be guaranteed. Let us content ourselves in order to bear it well, not to tell ourselves all we think about it; and let us hope for more from our temperament than from that weak reasoning which makes us believe that we can approach death with indifference. The glory of dying with resolve, the hope of being regretted, the desire to leave a fine reputation, the assurance of being freed from the miseries of life, and not having to depend anymore on the caprices of fortune, are remedies that one should not cast away. But one should also not believe that these remedies are infallible. . . . We flatter ourselves when we believe that death appears to be from close-up what we judged it to be from afar, and that our sentiments, which are only weaknesses, are of a steely enough quality not to suffer a blow from the roughest of all trials. It is also to know badly the effects of vanity (*l'amour-propre*), to think that it can help us to consider as nothing that which must necessarily destroy it; and reason, in which one believes one finds so many resources, is too weak in this encounter to persuade us of what we want. On the contrary, it is reason which betrays us most often, and, which, instead of inspiring us with the contempt for death, helps us discover what is frightful and terrible to it. All reason can do for us is to advise us to turn our eyes away from death in order to have them rest upon other objects. (La Rochefoucauld 2001, 93–94; translation modified)

This entry (about 75 percent of it is reproduced here) is too long to be a maxim, too structured to be a fragment, too self-contained to be an essay—and too perfect to be a mistake. If it is a "reflection," it is not simply a personal observation but one meant to be instructive for many readers. For La Rochefoucauld it is unusual in its length and emotional depth but it presages the aphoristic style later used by Schopenhauer, Nietzsche, and Cioran, among others. Perhaps this is the first pessimistic aphorism. It comprises so many pessimistic themes: the power of the glance to the horizon and the desire to avoid it, the omnipresence of death and its effect on life and philosophy, the weakness of reason and the palliative effect of illusion.

Coming at the end of the book (and its placement can hardly be an accident), this entry marks the final boundary, as it were, of La Rochefoucauld's vision. By the combination of placement and subject matter it calls attention to the fact that death is the ultimate and common horizon for all human beings. And La Rochefoucauld begins by disputing what he takes to be the classical assertion that we can look past this horizon— "one is never right" to believe that, he says. We can, and perhaps should, distract ourselves from it—but this presupposes that this vision is one that we all share. However little La Rochefoucauld's readers may have noticed the discontinuities present at other points (and which his style calls attention to), death (and the end of the book) are discontinuities they cannot ignore. In this aphorism, La Rochefoucauld comes to the end of his thoughts in every way, and contemplates that end.

At the same time, the passage notes that the experience of this vision is distinct and individual for every person, a result of "death's revealing itself differently to their imaginations, appearing there more vividly at one time than at another." Thus, even as he insists that our vision has a common object, which we can never fully avoid, he acknowledges that the problem it poses for us is individuated, and therefore our response to it must be similarly so. This leads him to criticize the "constancy" of the philosophers who, like the pagans it seems, tried to avoid the total destructiveness of death by eternalizing, as it were, some piece of themselves. But neither pagan pride nor philosophical reason, he believes, are appropriate responses. He suggests instead, in a manner very much like Leopardi's "Dialogue of Plotinus and Porphyry" (see chapter 2), that after confronting death, we allow ourselves to be distracted from it, whether by something great or small, it makes little difference. The most appropriate thing would be to maintain an internal division, "not to tell ourselves all we think about it," which sounds almost nonsensical unless we recall that internal discontinuity of thought is one of the things that the aphorism means to document and reproduce.

La Rochefoucauld's final entry thus contains, in the largest sense, the experience of looking at the ultimate horizon. It includes both the initial reaction of terror, but then also the effects of that fear on the mind, and the response that the mind can make to those effects—the digestion, as it were, of the initial vision. In surveying the possible reactions one can have, it is instructive without being prescriptive. If it is "moral," it is not so in any traditional sense, since it rejects the classical, Christian, and rationalist responses to death. Either La Rochefoucauld intends this reflection to be something other than moral, or its moral reflectiveness consists in the fact that it concerns a burden that every human must bear by dint of their common mortality and that it acknowledges the force of this mortality more directly than any of the other moral systems elaborated to date. While La Rochefoucauld's work antedates the emergence of pessimism as a fully developed style of thought, it is still fair to say that what is written here anticipates, in both form and content, the pessimistic ethic that was soon to appear in more detail in other writers. It is a confrontation with death and temporality that leads to a prescription for life issued not as a universal command but as an interpretation of a common experience.

The pessimistic aphorism confronts us with an unavoidable horizon. Such a limit on our thought is not a problem that admits of a solution, but an ontological circumstance of politics, large or small, that must be attended to. Collections of aphorisms are prone to misinterpretation because they are full of gaps; they invite us to project a structure of meaning onto their silences, as a distant horizon seems to call for something to fill the space between itself and the viewer. For the most part, this creative activity is what aphorisms, by raising our sight to a far boundary, are meant to stimulate. But sometimes, as La Rochefoucauld suggests here, we measure the distance to a horizon as a preliminary to turning away from it.

5

APHORISM AND IRONY

A tone of cool irony is a further element of the pessimistic aphorism, not universal but at least widespread (more so than in the maxim or the fragment). A concept is introduced as a truism, only to be revealed as a local prejudice. An author begins by using a word in a way that seems conventional, but then ends by giving it nearly the opposite sense. I have emphasized in the preceding chapters how the pessimists often trade on historical irony. The seeming progress of our civilization, to them, conceals a process that contradicts, and perhaps even cancels, this trajectory. But the irony of the aphoristic voice has different, if parallel, aims. Externally, one might say, it reflects the absurdity of existence that pessimism constantly points to. Internally, it reflects the antidogmatic approach to theorizing that pessimism attempts to exemplify.

A form of writing is not antisystematic just because it appears in short dollops, as Wittgenstein's *Tractatus* gives ample evidence. Nor is the antidogmatism in question here simply a matter of self-undermining, of appending an "I doubt it" to every paragraph. Rather, the irony in pessimistic aphorisms is an attempt to bridge the gulf between the absurdity of events as we experience them and the model of meaning embedded in our ordinary grammar. From Rousseau forward, it is a common theme of the pessimists (though of course hardly exclusive to them) that the structure of our language encourages us to filter our experiences through a lens of temporal causality that in turn creates a perception of a greater order to events than is actually the case. To undo this effect without resorting, on the one hand, to gibberish, or on the other, to a mere gesture of in-communicability requires a form of writing that allows the substance of an insight to appear while resisting its tendency to become a dogma or a counterdogma. This is what pessimistic irony, combined with the other elements of the aphoristic form, attempts to accomplish.

Cioran gives an example of this in his attempt to look to the limit of our historical experience per se, to a period he calls "posthistory":

> No more schools; on the other hand, courses in oblivion and unlearning to celebrate the virtues of inattention and the delights of amnesia. The disgust inspired by the sight of any book, frivolous or serious, will extend to all Knowledge, which will be referred to with embarrassment or dread as if it were an obscenity or a scourge. To bother with philosophy, to elaborate a system, to attach oneself to it and believe in it, will appear as an impiety, a provocation, and a betrayal, a criminal complicity with the past. . . . Each will try to model himself upon the vegetable world, to the detriment of the animals, which will be blamed for suggesting, in certain aspects, the figure or the exploits of man. (*DAQ* 59)

Here Cioran imagines an historical irony as large as history itself. The result of our learning will be to despise learning; the result of our civilization will be to despise civilization. Humanity will attempt to close the circle with the vegetative life. But the irony here is not merely historical. Cioran's tone suggests that he is not merely reporting on the future but offering a wry comment on the present and its obsessive Socratic faith in the power of knowledge to cure all ills.

And then, in a move characteristic of Cioran but also of many other pessimistic writers, he turns on his own conclusion:

> How are we to believe that [humanity] would not weary of bliss or that it would escape the lure of disaster, the temptation of playing, it too, a role? Boredom in the midst of paradise generated our first ancestor's appetite for the abyss which has won us the procession of centuries whose end we now have in view. That appetite, a veritable nostalgia for hell, would not fail to ravage the race following us and to make it the worthy heir of our misfortunes. Let us then renounce all prophecies. (*DAQ* 60)

Extreme as Cioran's initial vision is, it leads him, in a manner that feels inexorable, to consider the opposite. Having witnessed the end of history, he imagines, we will, in the next moment, witness its rebirth. Desires give birth to their opposites in a pattern that follows an ironic, rather than a causal, logic. The aphorism ends by renouncing the power of prophecy that it appeared, at first, to embody.

These embedded ironies, far from diminishing or canceling the stuff of Cioran's philosophy, in fact have the effect of generating the substance of his voice. One could claim that the two passages somehow annul each other, that the dialectic of pain and boredom that he sketches does not amount to anything. But the rejection of foresight that issues from this historical imagination ("Let us renounce all prophecies") is not a generic skepticism. It is rather a plea to limit ourselves, in our plans, to a real present and not throw ourselves into a historical narrativity that can only end badly, as the substance of the aphorism suggests, in one ditch or another. As I maintained in chapter 4, this denunciation of the idolatry of the future is a central element of Cioran's pessimism, but also of Unamuno's and Camus'. Like La Rochefoucauld, Cioran suggests here that there are some experiences of vision that ought to teach us not to want them.

6

ADMISSANS AND POLITICAL THEORY

6

APHORISMS AND POLITICAL THEORY

Political theory suffers from the continuing embarrassment of not having a regular, well-specified format. Machiavelli's *Prince*, Sophocles' *Antigone*, and Locke's *Second Treatise* are all staples of the field—but to try to distill formal rules of genre from such examples would be ludicrous. From time to time, some have attempted to legislate against this embarrassment, as Leo Strauss did when he declared that the "natural" form of political philosophy was the treatise. But such attempts always fail: if Strauss had limited his critical gaze to those who remained within this genre, his life-work would have been radically abbreviated. Nor did he, among his many essays and books, write anything that one would want to call a "treatise."

Can this condition of disorder be viewed as a strength? Wittgenstein, once again, gives us a useful metaphor. In his later works, Wittgenstein attacked the idea that language has a single, overarching purpose. Instead, he maintained, the diverse aims of human beings are lent to language itself: "Think of the tools in a tool-box: there is a hammer, pliers, a saw, a screw-driver, a rule, a glue-pot, glue, nails and screws.—The functions of words are as diverse as the functions of these objects." (1958, 11) In other words, it is useless to try to think of some one thing that all tools have in common. They are not all used for the same purpose; they are not all used in the same way. What they all have in common is that they are found in a toolbox, that is, they all come in handy from time to time. And not everyone fills their tool box with the same items. Some houses are made of wood, others of stone.

It could be claimed that the tools *do* have a common function (i.e., they all "fix things"), but this argument immediately runs into problems. On one level, the definition breaks down quickly over particular cases (what, exactly, does the ruler "fix?"). At another level, there is a more interesting problem: such a definition involves an implicit understanding of what it is for things to work properly, so that the tools can be said to set them right when they are out of whack. While an answer to this problem could be attempted, it would defeat the purpose of having a box of tools around. One keeps a well-stocked toolbox in the house precisely because one does *not* know what one will need it for (a toolbox is thus not any collection: it is not a coin collection or a mess kit). Nor, when a problem presents itself, will it always be obvious what the best course of action is. Sometimes, it will be clear that we desire to return to the status quo ante. Other times, however, a problem becomes an opportunity, not just for repair, but for improvement, or even replacement, of whatever is causing the problem. But whatever the case, having a well-stocked toolbox, with a variety of tools, will be helpful.

Political theory comes in such myriad forms not because it is confused about its nature, or because it seeks to offer a spurious variety of "choices," but because it is a set of resources that can be called upon in manifold circumstances for different tasks. There is no answer to the question, then, of whether political theory is most concerned, say, with the good life for the individual or the best regime for the state. It may be used for either or both (one can even try to insist that they are the same). But there will be no overall answer to such a question because the contents of the toolbox have no definitive unifying theme. And the *users* of such a box will be even more varied. One could never tell how a box of tools would be used simply by looking at the tools themselves; the same tool may be employed quite differently by different people. And it is only "in use," as Wittgenstein would say, that such tools have value or meaning. Thus, what to one person is a revolutionary manifesto may to another be simply a tedious sermon on obedience. Both claims have been made, for example, about Locke's *Second Treatise of Government*. Such interpretations could simply be wrong of course, as it is "wrong" to try to drive a nail with a screwdriver. But it is not always wrong to use a tool in a way its designer never intended.

Of course, as a family moves from house to house, some tools will be employed more regularly and some will sink to the bottom of the box, all but forgotten until some circumstance creates a need for them afresh. This is what leads to debates about the "nature" of political theory and the occasional desire, like Strauss's, to rule some things in and some out. But seen from this perspective, the claim that the treatise is the natural form of political theory makes as much sense as the claim that a screwdriver is the central, natural tool. Not only was such a tool unknown for many centuries of building, but it is no more or less important than a variety of others, depending on the circumstances.

Is political theory, then, a toolbox for fixing your polity? The problem with such a position is the same that Wittgenstein envisioned for the definition of language that says "every word in a language signifies something:" such an account says everything and nothing, tending strongly in the direction of the latter. To say that political theory is intended for the repair of the polity (as opposed to a person?) requires an understanding of what a healthy polity is, or at least of what would make it healthier. And there will be no universal answers to such questions: sometimes a polity needs better laws; other times, it may need better people; still other times, it may need a better past or future; and at all times, the definition of "better" will surely be contentious. Indeed, every generation has come upon the toolbox of political theory and wondered at how haphazardly it was stocked by generations previous. New genres were invented as new tools are—to address problems not previously faced.

The aphorism may be like that: invented in a certain time, for a certain purpose, stored away among other things, largely forgotten. But no tool is limited in its application by the intentions or circumstances of its inventor. Surely the paleolithic inventor of the hammer could have had no notion how it would be used even a hundred years hence, much less several thousand.

.   .   .   .   .

Still, it is perfectly reasonable to want to distinguish a well-made tool from a faulty one and to know in what circumstances it is intended to function. And since the head of a faulty or misapplied hammer may fly off at the critical moment and injure its user, such distinctions will surely be considered important. Likewise, it seems perfectly fair to ask how aphorisms are safely used and what purposes they have been known to serve.

Perhaps aphorisms are poorly suited to do what some books and treatises of political theory claim to do: create a well-ordered and detailed design for what good government would look like. As a percentage of the books that attempt to do this, the number that actually succeed is, of course, vanishingly small. But there is no point in denying that this was in fact the intent of these books' authors. The mistake only comes in asserting that this is the only thing that a work of political theory could aim at—as if whoever does not make rulers does not make tools. The aphorism aims at something else; perhaps it even achieves it more often than the treatise does.

I have given some sense of a purpose for aphorism when I described it as something that strikes us dead and gives us a look round the horizon. But how does this contribute to the repair of our polity or our person? Like a sextant or a compass, devised to aid the traveller, the aphorism does not by itself build anything, but it can help to orient us for all particular projects of building. By having us look toward the horizon, not just once, but many times, from many perspectives, aphorisms help us to know where we are and how we came to be here. This is (or ought to be) a necessary preliminary to any serious construction. Without such a preliminary, we will have no idea of the limitations of our situation, no sense of the restrictions within which we must work if we are really to build something here on the Earth and not, in Socrates' phrase, "in the air." We will be tempted, in other words, to build Towers of Babel, immense projects disdainful of the political laws of gravity. When such projects collapse, they can leave the builders worse off than when they started, buried under the debris of their hubris and injured by the fall from a great height. Aphorisms do not address themselves directly to the political blueprints of books and treatises, but to the spirit of the men and women who have to choose among these and inhabit them. They seek to educate that spirit to its own limitations. These are the limitations to the *site* of political building, the human condition.

.   .   .   .   .

Even if the above is correct, however, it is a mistake to view the purpose of a tool from the point of view of any one person who comes into possession of it. A look to the horizon will indeed be a lesson in modesty to someone whose head is in the clouds. At the same time, however, such a look may be an education in possibilities to one who looks only at the ground in front of him. This accounts, I think, for the differential reception that many of history's great aphorists have gotten from the general public as opposed to academic philosophers. If one lists the best-known aphorists (Pascal, Lichtenberg, La Rochefoucauld, Schopenhauer, Nietzsche, and Cioran, for example), one lists some of the most popular and widely read authors in the history of philosophy. This has always puzzled professionals, not least because their writing is so pessimistic. To most philosophers, these writers speak of human frailty, prejudice, and limitation. And this is certainly true. Nevertheless, the general reader has often found these same authors to be inspirational. And I would argue that it is one and the same thing that produces these differing results: the aphoristic form. What is a limitation to one with a lofty vision is a vast expansion of horizons to many others. For some readers, Nietzsche conjures up possibilities of experience of which they have hardly dreamed. Indeed, they find encouragement to expand their dreams well beyond their current horizon. Such readers do not make mistakes. If they do not notice as readily the limits that Nietzsche also places on experience, this says more about their initial starting point than anything else. To one person, a compass may be something that marks off definite boundaries, to another, it may be that which measures the great spaces that are available. Neither uses the compass incorrectly. Readers of aphorisms do not always have the purposes that an academic does. But if the aphorism has a broader range of application than the political treatise, that is neither a mark against its seriousness nor a criticism of its employment in political situations.

Sometimes a polity stands in need of better laws and institutions, even radically better ones. At other times, however, the fault lies not within our laws but within ourselves. I do not mean that these two questions are really separable. But an excessive focus on *systems* of politics and justice obscures the equally important locus of politics within the individual. Aphorisms do not attempt systematic repairs of the polity. They work, or fail to, person by person. A landscape architect may plan a trail so that it leads the trekker to a series of vistas in a particular order—some may mean more to a solitary walker than others. But the final vista is not the "point" or the "meaning" of the journey, only its conclusion. Every walker makes the journey his own on the path.

Aphoristic writing is an attempt to educate the spirit to its possibilities and its limitations. Whether such a task is an essential or marginal one is also not something that can be answered in advance. It is not for the toolmaker to dictate the order of tools in the toolbox. That is something that can only be done by the person who has need of them.

This point needs to be emphasized so that the metaphor of tools does not mislead us. It does not reflect a hidden utilitarianism or pragmatism of aphoristic thinking that ultimately weighs everything in terms of predetermined ends. It is just this sort of instrumentality against which many modern aphorists have complained. Of course, it can be maintained that all human action has a purpose. But this is equivalent to Freud's assertion that every dream is the fulfillment of a wish: in the absence of divine intervention, we must ascribe a human motivation to any action in order to understand it as human. This is not exactly a tautology, since it stands opposed to metaphysical or mechanistic accounts of human events, but it is also much less than a true explanation for anything. To liken aphorisms to tools, then, is not to accept that life creates problems for which rational discourse fashions solutions. Rather, there is another sort of purpose for philosophy that cannot be captured by this kind of means-end thinking. Indeed, aphorisms are often best at questioning the entire causal model of existence in which this kind of thinking is rooted. In taking the measure of the world's disorder, aphorisms show some readers the proper limits of our scientific urge to master the world, while showing others the possibilities of life that this model does not encompass.

It is the initial distance between the horizon of writer and reader that shapes the experience of reading aphorism, as a parallel distance shapes the experience of writing them. If aphorisms are prone to misinterpretation because of their discontinuity, this proliferation of horizons, this polylateralism, also provides many opportunities for contact between different perspectives. Even for readers from radically different forms of life, a book of aphorisms usually has *something* to offer, while more systematic works can be impenetrable to outsiders. It is this quality, perhaps, that has caused critics to remark on the seeming "fresh" or "modern" quality of someone like La Rochefoucauld, whose book is over four hundred years old. Is the work really timeless? Or is it just better-made to seem so?

Cioran: "Words die: fragments, not having lived, cannot die either" (*TBB* 168).

7

For centuries, the *Aphorisms* of Hippocrates created an association between this literary form and medicine. We should not be too eager to lose it. Pessimism, as I have said, is a sort of writing that aims somewhere in between the systematic universal and the mere health regimen. But it does have in common with the latter the concern for personal well-being and the idea that prescriptions should be suited to individual circumstances. Perhaps this is what Cioran had in mind when he said that the aphorist must have a bit of charlatanism in him. A *charlatan*, in French, is originally a sort of lay practitioner of medicine, someone whose services were available for purchase in the public square to address whatever concerns a passer-by might have (the ultimate origins of the word are disputed, but this much is not in doubt). It was only with the professionalization and privatization of medicine that a *charlatan* became a "mere charlatan," and then later, a "quack" or a "con man." Just as pessimism, originally understood as a diagnosis of and prescription for our life-circumstances has, under the assault of professional optimism, been made to seem an illegitimate, dangerous deceiver. If we can recover this nonmalign sense of a public, nonprofessional purveyor of medicine, we can have some idea of what an aphorist attempts to provide his readers. For philosophy too can become professional and private to the point where it is no longer concerned with the actual experiences of those purportedly in its care. If the aphorisms of the pessimists have been among the most popular of philosophical books, perhaps it is because they have not forgotten that purveyors of medicine, even bitter medicine, at least answer to a public need.

Chapter Eight

PESSIMISM AND FREEDOM

(THE PESSIMIST SPEAKS)

"ALL THE TRAGEDIES which we can imagine return in the end to the one and only tragedy: the passage of time." These words appear in a lesson-plan found in one of Simone Weil's notebooks (Weil 1978, 197). The next sentence is equally striking: "Time is also the origin of all forms of enslavement." Animals can be tortured, imprisoned, exploited, and killed, in horrific fashion, but they cannot be enslaved. They have no past or future to steal.

.　.　.　.　.

The motley cow. Our measurements of time are a chaos of conflicting histories. From the Babylonians, we derive the twenty-four-hour day; from the Hebrews, the seven-day week. The shape of the year was largely settled by the Caesars, but the numbering of the years by medieval popes. In English, the names of the days are Germanic or Norse, but the names of the months are from the Latin. Each element of our calendar, which feels seamless to us today, has a distinct and complicated past. Some of these histories are better known than others, but any of them could be very different. Our calendar, in short, is a mélange of cultural influences held together with string and wax and the occasional leap-second but presenting to us, nonetheless, an appearance of order and continuity. It is as if we are the inheritors of a diverse kingdom that we have been duped into believing is a dull nature preserve and therefore never visit.

.　.　.　.　.

> *An ancient cleaning woman, in answer to my "How's everything going?" answers without looking up: "Taking its course." This ultrabanal answer nearly brings me to tears.*
> —CIORAN, *TBB* 62

The question of how far people are genuinely at liberty to shape their own fate is not just a question of the resources at their disposal. To the extent that we feel embedded in a pattern of historical destiny in which we have no major role to play, our choices are narrowed, even for the richest, to the career-options we believe are endemic to our age—the freedom of a restaurant patron. The reason we sometimes feel the Greeks were freer than ourselves, even though incredibly poor by modern standards, is because they do not seem to have been bound by this kind of historical emplotment. "Taking its course" is the answer of someone enslaved by more than poverty.

.   .   .   .   .

One could imagine a perspective in which nothing in particular was reliable, in this world, but in which the world as a whole was comprehensible. Such a view might mimic many of the effects of pessimism without really embracing it. Augustine, for example, could be viewed in this way. Indeed, many Augustinians are today called "Christian pessimists." They consider that this world is fundamentally disordered, that it will always contain evil, and cannot be set right, except, perhaps, by God at the Last Judgment. Nonetheless, this terrible world can be viewed from elsewhere—its existence is part of a larger cosmology that also includes the heavenly city. Although particular evils cannot be fathomed, the phenomenon of evil as a whole can be understood. It *shall* be understood when one leaves the city of man for the city of God, either in this life, or the next. Thus Augustine mimics (indeed foreshadows) many of the conclusions of pessimism—but always with the escape hatch of another world, where the effects of time are not felt. Are the pessimists, then, Augustinians who have become agnostics? Not really. The *civitas dei* was more than a codicil to Augustine's theory; it was a firm and complex firmament, with many byways and elements, all of which had to be explained in detail. The earth, on the other hand, was a lump of sand, a place where complexity required no explanation because it was fundamentally unreal or unimportant, a place without depth or process. For true pessimists, the opposite is the case. And still the pessimists say more honestly than the Christians, "*All* is vanity."

.   .   .   .   .

The question is what kind of connection we will have toward the future: one of freedom or enslavement? Optimism subordinates the present to what is to come and thereby devalues it. Pessimism embodies a free relation to the future. In refraining from hope and prediction we make possible a concern that is not self-abasing and self-pitying. By not holding every moment hostage to its future import, we also make possible a genuinely friendly responsibility to ourselves and to others.

.   .   .   .   .

Of the discipline of inability. Beckett wrote *Waiting for Godot* in French for the "discipline," he said, of working in a foreign language. But was it the foreign language that disciplined him—or his own incompetence? What discipline would it have been, after all, if Beckett had been perfectly fluent in French? What he wanted was to be forced to write clearly, simply, without complexity, in the style we now call "Godot-like" and associate with modernity and its fragmented incomprehensibility. When we speak a language we do not know well, but wish to use correctly, we must speak carefully, simply, in short sentences. This is the discipline of inability.

What a crippling ability it is, on the other hand, to be fluent in a language. Nothing checks us; nothing warns us away from overcomplexity, from tangled thoughts, from twisted logic. Our fluency gives us the illusion of power, but really, it is just a long rope with which we hang ourselves eight times a day.

If we really spoke with a fluency that matched our level of understanding (even of our own language), then we would all talk in a Godot-like manner—a clipped, disjointed style where conversations travel but without direction and where insight, seemingly near, constantly escapes our grasp. This was Beckett's insight: every modern tongue is a foreign tongue, even to its most intimate users.

.   .   .   .   .

When we think of freedom abstractly, we are inclined to see ourselves pushing forward through time, but when we *experience* freedom, we know it precisely because these are the moments when past and future fall away: wanting to say something *and saying it*; wanting to be something *and being it*; wanting to love someone *and loving them*—these are the moments when we feel liberated, when, if we could, we would give up the future and extend the moment forever. Which, as far as we know, we can never do.

.   .   .   .   .

A: So it's an alternative narrative that you want? Or the absence of narrative? You're so equivocal!

B: My formulations cannot escape the equivocation in our experience of time. No moment could be meaningful to a human being without a thousand preceding narrative steps. No moment could be free for a human being without escaping those steps. So the best narratives are those that support and make visible how randomly we pass from moment to moment.

A: More equivocation!

. . . . .

Optimism makes us perpetual enemies of those future moments that do not meet our expectations, which means all future moments. It is when we expect nothing from the future that we are free to experience it as it will be, rather than as a disappointment.

. . . . .

Aristotle: the best thing for friends is to live together (*Ethics* 1171b32). But in what way? Cervantes: the best thing for friends is to travel together. We are always traveling anyway, the journey just makes it visible. Friendship is not based on a plan—like marriage. Nor does it presuppose a common endeavor, like citizenship. Nor is it based on a principle, like a system of justice. It's the pure association of free individuals, which will (or won't) survive whatever life throws at it. Quixote fails as a knight; Sancho fails as a governor. But in the course of an accident-filled quest, they succeed in creating a friendship, not an equal one, ended only by death.

. . . . .

Pessimism liberates us to the accidents of our lives. To conceive of freedom as hewing to a life-plan is to commit oneself to a self-enslavement and to disparage those elements of life that do not cohere or conform to it. Pessimism makes possible the liberation of every moment from every other, makes their value independent of one another; in other words, it makes freedom possible *now* rather than in an indefinitely postponed future. Expectations are an endless deferral of freedom.

. . . . .

Friendship is our best model of an arena that is meant to harbor randomness and chaos, while channeling it into a relatively stable association. If I knew at all times what to expect from my friends, their friendship would be valueless. We look to our friends to surprise us, even as we expect them to cope with our own surprises. And yet we have no guarantee that we can never overstep the bounds—we *can* destroy our friendships in a way that we can never break family ties. It can happen in a moment, in fact. But the transience of friendships is no mark against them, or at least, it does not deter us from pursuing them. Perhaps, indeed, their permanently endangered status is one of their attractions? And the possibility of friendship is also the possibility for a form of social association consistent with a pessimistic ethic.

Because friendship has no end, it is the least-bad setting for the act of exploration, the most likely tie to survive self-transformation. That a friendship could survive a change of every goal is unlikely, but at least *possible*.

.   .   .   .   .

And how else can we describe the tolerance that we may choose to practice with respect to our disordered souls except as friendliness toward the self? If we cannot be easy with our inconsistent selves, what hope do we have of associating with others?

.   .   .   .   .

How shall we strengthen humanity? By means of an exoskeleton or an endoskeleton? A fireproof room or a fireproof heart? Which is easier to bring on the road?

.   .   .   .   .

Pessimism is the philosophy that can never crown itself king. To be king, to be master of every circumstance—that is what pessimism teaches as unattainable. Whatever modesty they profess, whatever authority they disclaim, optimistic philosophies secretly find this impossible to accept, which is why pessimism has found it necessary to appear before them as a jester.

.   .   .   .   .

Pessimism is the democracy of moments.

.   .   .   .   .

We must accept the possibility that the habit of reading is a fad, long in duration, but now in its final stages—destined to be carried on in the future only by a few devotees. Horsemanship was, for over twenty centuries, an indispensable adult skill for the middle and upper classes in Europe and Asia, much more so than reading. And yet, within the space of a century, it has become merely an elite hobby. So may it be with reading. Computers will soon become so adept at spoken language and displaying information with icons that it is possible to imagine a generation arising that does not perceive written language to be necessary for the general public for day-to-day life—as a generation has already arisen that hardly knows how to read clocks, since time is everywhere displayed digitally. Our only hope is that the pleasures of reading, meager as they are in comparison to visual entertainment, will continue to seduce a regular few and prevent reading from becoming the technical skill of scientists and history professors. But that is a gamble with perilous odds, given the inconstancy of the human libido. Did not man and horse, after all, once seem as inseparable as . . . well, as man and woman *once* seemed?

.   .   .   .   .

I will believe the animals have an inner life worth respecting when I see one of them disrespect it, that is, when I see one commit suicide. Genuine vain, selfish suicide, mind you, and not "altruistic self-sacrifice" (so-called), to which any robot can be programmed.

.   .   .   .   .

> Man cannot decide between freedom and happiness. On one
> side, infinity and pain; on the other, security and mediocrity.
> —CIORAN, TS 112

But this is not a problem of indecisiveness. We cannot choose freedom or happiness for the same reason we cannot paint a picture that is all black or all white. A question of navigation.

.   .   .   .   .

History as food. The idea that all of history tells one story makes no more sense than the idea that all food makes one meal. History nourishes us, but those who claim to take it in at one swallow lie—if they could, they would burst. The urge to find a totality to history is not really a desire to gorge. It is a desire to fast. It is a desire to eat one grand meal and then to cease one's dependence on food. It is a desire never to hunger, never to thirst. Since hunger and thirst are often given as examples of primordial desire, we might even say that the urge to find a historical totality is a desire not to desire—a final flower of the ascetic ideal. Knowing the one meaning of all history would be the final victory over desire, over urge, over oneself. Nevermore would one have to seek outside oneself for meaning—all has been ingested and digested. Is this not perfect freedom? A sickening thought. Better to accept our hunger and swallow our pride, along with a nightly supper.

.   .   .   .   .

An old saying: some eat to live; others live to eat. The one who eats to live bears a resemblance to creatures up and down the great chain of being, where the one who lives to eat seems like none of them. But we also say (and believe) "*chacun a son goût.*" We consider taste to be an individual, personal matter. And our experience of a good taste is one of the most private, incommunicable experiences that we can imagine. So does she who lives to eat labor under a human passion or an animal one? And is our urge to share our meals the most intimate or the most futile gesture?

.   .   .   .   .

> *Don't be fair to me: I can do without everything but the tonic*
> *of injustice.*
> —Cioran, *TBB* 14

Discovery of truth marks a terrible end to speech. If we identify man as a seeker of truth, what task is left to him when truth is discovered? Is the ideal condition we seek one of speech or silence? For if we value speech for an end it draws nearer to us, then it must be that end we seek above all. And if the end of speech is truth, then the endpoint of our wishes must appear as a speechless truthful condition. But this feels like a desire to cease being human, to escape into a godhead, to leap out of time. Perhaps it is even a wish to die—certainly it is a wish to end our lives as we have known them and enter another state more perfect than this.

But perhaps there is another way to view the matter? There is, indeed, a time-honored way. It is to consider speech as the opposite of truth, that is, truth-as-endpoint. Speech can be seen as the opposite of ending—not beginning, but continuation. This means viewing the essence of speech as communication, hence, as concerning two minds, hence as dialogue. If we consider speech as dialogue, then we do not face this contradiction between means and end. Nor does this weaken a political defense of speech, since there are many reasons for requiring dialogue in politics (indeed, even as its essence). But all of this will rest on the question, without truth, what end has speech? Can dialogue itself be an end?

Freud says "every dream the fulfillment of a wish," meaning every dream could only exist because some part of us willed it to. Every dream, no matter how morbid, then, is an expression of life. Ultimately, all speech is in some sense voluntary, an expression of will, hence life. But unlike dreams, which even dogs have, speech is an attribute only of humans and expresses whatever (if anything) is distinctive of human life.

But I think that speech-as-dialogue is likely to mean a long life for humanity as well, longer certainly than speech-as-truth-seeker. For the former is not in a state of war with time as the latter is. For truth seeks to stop time, but the "truth" of time is that it stops for nothing. This is what Nietzsche meant about truth-seekers when he said their ultimate frustration was with time itself. Sooner or later, if humanity pursues the path of speech-as-truth, our frustration with time will reach millennial proportions, as it already has for many individuals. Final solutions arise when we view life as a problem solvable with sufficient application of reason.

.   .   .   .   .

History and prophecy. Prophecy means that the future can be seen, thought or read by something in the present—that the future inheres in something already here. This cannot be if there were a sharp ontological divide between present and future. Prophecy, of course, is distinct from prediction, a more mundane matter that is a probabilistic guess about the future based on the past. Prophets do not say, "Troy will probably be destroyed."

Historians, of course, share the certainty of prophets—only the tense of their pronouncements changes. They say "Troy was destroyed" with as much certainty as prophets say "Troy will be destroyed." And yet the techniques of seer and historian appear similar: both read a cryptic fragment, see a relic, or hear incomplete testimony—and then render a statement about events, one in the future tense, one in the past. Each requires the inherence of past or future in the present. Out of the incomplete testimony of the present, the prophet reads the future and the historian the past.

But surely the historian is a responsible investigator and the seer a charlatan, or at best, deluded? Time does flow in one direction and not the other, so the historian's assumption is correct and the prophet's faulty!

Can this last sentence be proved? Is it not a hypothesis: useful, but of very recent provenance? If the flow of time is so obvious a fact, why is the systematic study of history such a minor, modern discipline? Not that it was never studied outside the West or before the seventeenth century; but, in comparison, both within and outside the West, prophecy has been a very ancient, very widespread, very public activity, which even today is very reluctant to give up the ghost. It has had both intuitive (Tiresias) and technical (Roman entrail-readers) practitioners, been official and unofficial, professional and amateur.

Should not the good *historian* confirm that his assumption about time has not, in the course of civilization, been widely shared? Should she not wonder, then, at the historical oddity of the widespread belief today in this assumption? Of course—and most good historians are well aware of their assumptions.

But then, were not most good seers aware of *their* assumptions too?

. . . . .

All that is necessary is an illusion to carry us through seventy or so years of life. Then they can bury us—with our "goals" alongside us in our coffins, having served their purpose.

Did ancient peoples, who included objects along with the dead, perhaps understand this better? Who was it, anyway, that decided these objects were for the afterlife?

. . . . .

The test of really knowing the past is the desire to repeat its mistakes.

. . . . .

> *For twenty centuries the sum total of evil has not diminished*
> *in the world.*
> —CAMUS, *R* 303

Many would dispute this point, but consider: In the past few decades, we have succeeded in doubling the earth's population. To what end? Have we doubled the number of artists, scientists or statesmen? Not at all: we have doubled the number of the poor and wretched while all these other categories have been stable or declined. Was it a plot, then? A plot to increase the number of slaves for the powerful to exploit? Absurd: the need of the rich for slaves and victims (though real) has diminished every year through automation and computerization; insofar as they are conscious of these new billions, the ruling classes fear and loath them. They fear them for their potential to overwhelm and they loath them for the guilt they induce. Why has it happened, then? Why so many new lives? A vast meadow with a billion leaves of grass spread over it—each of them so starved for nutrients that they are never able to grow above a height of two inches.

In the end, as Camus well understood, all such calculations are worthless: life will not be condemned by a quanta of pain, or redeemed by a quanta of pleasure. But the industrial reproduction of suffering hardly serves as an advertisement for our era's advantages.

. . . . .

Our neurasthenia. The dissolution of identity, the collapse of the monarchy of the ego, all this seems eerily to be the fault of multiculturalism, postmodernism, and other contemporary philosophies that are said to be opposed to all forms of "order" (even, it is claimed, psychic order) as a tool of oppression.

But the supposed victims of multiple personality disorder do not seek disorder—they seek the preservation of order—and they seek such order primarily through the *segregation of memory*. It is as if they say, "There is too much pain for one mind to bear, I will leave it to several minds." Just the opposite of multiculturalism, which seeks to bring hidden memories to light, we have here the spectacle of a segregation willed not from hatred but from fear, a fear of being overwhelmed with oneself.

It is as if when all the memories were allowed to mingle they would form a narrative the conclusion of which was unbearable; but broken into little pieces, no matter how horrible, they can be borne. Thus it is really narrative, rather than the events it contains, that holds the horror. Not the isolated acts of sexual abuse, for example, (a common occurrence in the personal history of MPD patients) but the fact that it continued for months or years. Not the fact that it occurred for no reason, but the fact that there *was* a reason for it. It would be easier if they were the victims of "senseless" suffering, like that which results from a tornado. Indeed, this is what the illness does—it *makes* the pain into "senseless" suffering by destroying the narrative of which it is a part. Freud thought he could cure neurotics by offering them a narrative that explained their symptoms. But the victims here suffer *because* they possess such a narrative and it is in order to flee this coherence that they become "ill" with MPD. Psychic order is preserved at the cost of narrative coherence.

It is sometimes urged that the crimes of fascism or racism are so severe and strange that they must remain "senseless" to be properly feared and preserved. To attempt to "make sense" or "explain" these things is somehow to diminish them. There is certainly something to be said for this view—that these things must be regarded as no ordinary time. And yet, to the victims of MPD, it is *as a narrative whole* that evil is most evil. Is the Shoah better recalled as six million random acts of murder (is six million *comprehensibly* worse than, say, two hundred thousand?)? Or is it worse *as* a story (a manifold story, to be sure) of a planned extermination of a whole people? The horror, I think, is not lessened but increased by setting the story in the context of German and European history, showing the many sources of ideology, interest, and behavior that came together in the cataclysm—even if they are *ultimately* insufficient to explain it.

So then MPD *is* the characteristic illness of our age—but not so much for its theoretical trendiness as for its need to flee the horrors of narrative for the ordered world of limited suffering and an amnesia that is always on the move, blocking out whichever element of the past threatens, at that moment, to lend a terrible coherence to our lives. As humans live longer and the accuracy of our histories and memories improves, can we not expect this to be a more common ailment?

. . . . .

The Daily Progress. There once was a short-lived television series in which the hero receives, every day, without explanation, the following day's newspaper. He then has one day to prevent some awful tragedy that appears in the magic paper so that when the "real" paper appears, the following day, all is well. He does not, of course, attempt to redress the mass of human suffering that takes place around the world every day and is dutifully reported—but let that pass; it is hardly fair to tax our entertainments for their limited moral horizons when our philosophy is little better. No, what is remarkable about this program is that it exposed a fundamental article of the journalistic faith: that order is restored when each day's paper reports an incremental improvement on that which preceded it. It is quite wrong to see our papers as carping and negative, as conservative critics maintain. Indeed, it would be quite impossible for newspapers to exist and be profitable if they performed as their critics believe, that is, depressing us with a constant bewailing of our state. After a short time, no one would be able to bear them. Instead, every morning our papers deliver to us a subtle encouragement to persist, as our morning prayers once did (on this point, see Hegel). Not too much, of course; for if the promise was too great, its emptiness would soon become readily apparent. Rather, we are comforted every day by a report of the world's Daily Progress. The progress must be almost immeasurably small, to be sure, since, like a constant flurry of snow, it is recorded every day but never seems to accumulate. But no matter, in little ways, our papers assure us that it is certainly taking place. If there are scandals being uncovered, their very revelation implies our moral advance. If there are conflicts to be recorded, then our evenhandedness demonstrates their ultimate and inevitable solubility. If evil has appeared, it is at least far away and clearly the result of primitive forces who have yet to read our pristine pages. If it is close by, then its amelioration has already been undertaken. And if pure, dumb, blind, powerful, terrible tragedy strikes so close and so completely that it cannot be ignored—why, then, we are pierced, pierced to the heart for a good twenty minutes and so outraged that such a thing (so rare nowadays) could strike us that we instantly clamor for redress, or, if it appears to be a force of nature, at least a government commission.

No, to receive every day a newspaper that recorded a tragedy that touched us personally—that is a horror that our TV hero cannot bear and his viewers will not be satisfied until that condition is righted. Even if, were our papers written and read with half a heart and as much honesty, it would be no more than the truth . . .

. . . . .

To imagine that humanity only had to be set free from Platonism in order to flourish! The faith of hack revolutionaries everywhere.

. . . . .

Every great science has ended as a scientific failure but as a successful philosophy. Aristotelianism, Stoicism, Thomism—all came to dominate the West's way of thinking as a "science," that is, as an explanation of the universe and its workings. And long after each has lost its adherents as any kind of science, each still has strong advocates as a "philosophy." The way of life that each favored is still defended as a reasonable policy, long after the image of nature that each held is banished from public discourse. Each, in its time, took the name of Science itself, and would not tolerate that there be other notions of science. Even today, Science only tolerates the idea of an "Aristotelian science" or a "Stoic science" as an historical designation of an ancient practice with scientific pretensions. "Really," our scientists say, "what they did was not science at all but some preliminary fumbling."

And will it be any different in the future? What will they call our Science then? "Positivistic science," perhaps? "Baconian science?" And will it still have its advocates as a philosophy, as a way of life, long after our expert universe-studiers have discarded it? Undoubtedly some will still recommend its method of experiment, its anthropocentric attitude toward nature, its inquiry-by-manipulation, its clear-eyed materialism. All this, no doubt, will have much to recommend it, even after the metatheoretical assumptions that ground Positivist science are shown to be as baseless as those that grounded Stoic science. Is not the leading edge of this phenomenon already in view? Already physicists and philosophers of science as a group disbelieve in positivism, though for the moment they lack an alternative. Even now, positivism is at its strongest as a philosophy of life, among the economists, sociologists, engineers, and their allies in advertising and marketing.

Every successful science ends as a failure in scientific terms but as a success in philosophical ones. Someday Baconism will be ably argued by an energetic cadre of university professors. And to most everyone it will seem as quaintly appealing as Aristotelianism.

.   .   .   .   .

Hegel claimed that the Romans' true contribution to world culture was satire, by which he meant the destruction in thought of all that was built up before. Satire represented the witty dismantling of principles that others held dear, with nothing left in their place. Perhaps pessimism, then, is no more than a satire on earlier philosophies—a kind of cackling at their misfortunes. But there is a Hegelian answer to be made here, though Hegel himself would not have appreciated it. Thus Sartre: "There may be more beautiful times. But this one is ours."

.   .   .   .   .

Pessimism expects nothing. But this is not nihilism. Nihilism would be not *wanting* anything. Extreme nihilism? *Wanting nothing.*

.   .   .   .   .

Time is money. Augustine famously remarked that time is a concept we use easily but are unable to explain. That we use money every day, that we easily measure it and trace its flows at many levels is likewise not evidence for our understanding it. Indeed, even the simplest questions about money result in the kind of paradoxes that bedevil the philosophy of time. What *is* money? Does it measure something objective or subjective? Is it something real and natural or artificial and imaginary? This list of questions could be endlessly ramified—perhaps to the point where we would all be prepared to confess that we did not understand money at all. But soon enough the routine transactions of everyday life would comfort us with the illusion of control they provide. We might say, pragmatically, "We know all we need to about money. . . ."

But though Augustine was wrong about many things, he was certainly right not to be satisfied with this kind of response. For there is one thing at least that we should like to know about time and money. We should like to know whether we are controlling them (as our everyday transactions lead us to believe) or whether they are controlling us. There have been cultures that have done without money just as there have been cultures with a minimal sense of time (not coincidentally they are often the same). Even if we determine that we cannot or will not choose such a condition, we ought at least to know whether it is a gain or a loss to live as we do. Or more precisely, we should want to know how it is a gain and how a loss. But here again we confront the basic question: in what currency shall we measure such gains and losses?

. . . . .

Pascal and Nietzsche both describe time as the root of human unhappiness, but in opposite ways. For Nietzsche it is the *past* that crushes us with its obstinacy and weight, an "it was" that can never be changed, can never be made one whit more beautiful than it is. For Pascal, it is the *future* that prevents us from being truly happy: "The future alone is our end. So we never live, but we hope to live; and as we are always preparing to be happy, it is inevitable we should never be so" (*Pensées* 172). Different concepts of time? Not at all. For Pascal, to be happy would be to be completely at rest (though he also calls this death), not to seek, not to yearn, but to rest in a perfect repose. But humans cannot possess this because they ceaselessly move, ceaselessly seek, and, hence, are inevitably unhappy. For Nietzsche, on the other hand, unhappiness would be: to be trapped in yourself, exactly as you are forever (the insight of Sartre's *Huis Clos*). The future at least offers the possibility of change, growth, et cetera. The past is a prison.

. . . . .

Would we really be satisfied to understand space as the opposite of "spacelessness?" Philosophers of time have confused matters by comparing "Time" to "Eternity," which is conceived as timelessness, an eternal present, an everlasting "now." Time is without an opposite. We would like to grasp time as the opposite of something, so we make up that something, timelessness, in order to give a name to time. But this is a subterfuge. Or we backpedal and say, "Time is that within which difference appears," as if every image had to be painted on some canvas. We must try instead to grasp time without the prop of "eternity." If we should not grasp time by imagining its absence, what then should we do? Imagine its *intensification*?

Dreams must be our closest analog. We should not compare linear time to timelessness, but rather to a multiplicity of times. We cannot really compare color to the absence of color, no matter how hard we try. We are really always comparing one color with another, a shade of black, white, or grey. So it is with time. Individual colors may have opposites, and so may particular times, but "color" has no opposite. And neither does time.

Perhaps at bottom we have been using the wrong mathematical analogies. We have thought "time" names a line or a curve, when actually it names a *set*. We contrast red with blue, not with "redlessness." It should be the same with time: our linear time with others. And then "Time" names the set of all times as Color names the set of all colors.

·   ·   ·   ·   ·

It is a familiar claim that without a belief in truth "we can't go on." We would never get out of our beds in the morning, it is maintained, without some belief in the reality of things. In fact, it is the notion of *time* that we cannot do without. What we need to act, above all, is a belief in the existence of a future, that is, that our acts might *lead to something*. What the something is is not important. It might be world revolution or a cup of coffee (my personal motivation for leaving bed every morning). The substance is irrelevant; but goals can only exist *in the future*, in the not-yet, in time. I simply can't see how a verification of reality is involved in my anticipation of my morning coffee, only memory and hope.

And if our memories and hopes proved *false*? An absurd objection— they certainly *are* always false, or at least imperfectly true; they work none the worse for that.

·   ·   ·   ·   ·

Eating of the fruit of the Tree of Knowledge was not a one-time affair. Rather we have continuously devoured the contents of this tree, one branch at a time. It is what sustains us, fallen into time as we are, from the eternal present of Eden, where no sustenance was necessary. If we were to complete our meal of knowledge—if we were to "explain" consciousness fully, for example—that would mean that we had eaten the last piece of fruit from the tree that has fed us for thousands of years. If we did not choke to death on that last bite, we would surely starve, that is, endure a slow and painful death for want of nourishment.

And what of the Tree of Life? It stands beckoning, but a few yards away. Why not turn to it? But *could* we stomach a new food if our diet has been the unalloyed consumption of the other fruit for centuries? It is unlikely that we would be able to *digest* it. It would have no flavor for us—we would retch it up and die all the more miserably, like a shipwrecked sailor surrounded by sea water. Perhaps we should begin to adapt our diet to this new fare now, while we still have time, while our guts are still strong?

·   ·   ·   ·   ·

To go on a quest, as has often been observed, one must cut one's ties to home. Pessimism is a kind of freedom from home. It is a freedom from having to discipline yourself so that your every act is ordered and predictable. It is a freedom to dissent in a society where every kind of optimism (even the supposedly radical, such as communism) is a kind of assent to what you have been taught. It is a freedom to cut yourself loose from a project that everyone insists you participate in.

Pessimism cuts us free of an optimism that is demanded of us. Pessimism cuts us out of a social activity we were enrolled in without our assent. Not the least of its freedoms is the freedom to report on the modern project.

. . . . .

When, sometime in the next century, historians of philosophy attempt to understand the recently completed century as a whole, they will be astonished. How, they will ask, in this century of massacres that stand out even against those of previous centuries, was it possible for professional philosophy to maintain an air, not so much of optimism, but of utter detachment? The spectacle resembles nothing so much as fourteenth-century scholasticism, which debated how many angels could dance on a pinhead as the Black Death killed nearly a third of Europe. Was it not this contrast, rather than the "refutations" of Descartes and Hobbes, that brought about an end to scholasticism? Is the Trolley Problem a pinhead problem?

. . . . .

A: Even granting that the universe is morally disordered, this is no objection to the *goal* of morally ordering it? Nothing you say speaks against the desirability of such a goal—and a good deal speaks for it. So the traditional practice of moral philosophy must at least be tolerable?

B: Indeed so. And I, for one, am prepared to tolerate it. But the point applies equally: we must demand toleration as well for that philosophy that does *not* expect to find or succeed in creating such an order, that seeks to find the best mode of life in the absence of such an order. Surely we are entitled, at this late date, to take the failure and cruelty of all attempts to construct or find such an order, along with the massive human catastrophes of the last century, as evidence that it is permissible to philosophize without postulating such orders. Or are we to be chastised for our failure to continue to *hope* in such matters? Would we chastise those who fail to continue hoping for proof of telepathy and witchcraft, after thousands of years of believing and hoping for such evidence have proved empty?

. . . . .

There is much debate these days about how the brain "causes" consciousness, most of it horribly misguided. Setting aside, for the moment, the question of whether causality exists at all as currently conceived, the main problem is that these scientists and philosophers, though they dissect and model many brains, seek to explain consciousness as if it were produced by *one* brain—or rather by one brain at a time. But this is completely absurd. It is like asserting that the throat "causes" language. At one level, of course, this is true—but one could dissect a thousand throats, know the movement of every muscle, even know how all the sounds were produced, and still have no idea what language was, what it meant, or how it came about. Brains cause consciousness in the way that throats cause speech—they are necessary but relatively minor conditions. Speech is a human achievement built up over centuries of effort, making use of our ability to make sounds. Similarly, consciousness is an achievement, not something that flashed across Adam's mind one day in a freak of nature, but an ability that is socially nurtured and developed. Even today consciousness does not "snap on" in the heads of our infants, but is rather drilled into them through the stimulation of other conscious minds.

But before we congratulate ourselves on our accomplishments, we might want to ask ourselves *what* it was that drove us to develop this capacity for suffering, alienation, and misery? Was it our innate nobility, our drive for achievement? But these are effects rather than causes. . . . What was it then that drove our monkey ancestors into intensive consultations with their fellows?

.   .   .   .   .

There is no time, only temporality. Today physicists accept the fundamental relativity of time because of Einstein. But philosophers, who could easily have deduced it earlier, do not.

Even such banal statements as "time flows" or "time passes" are already temporalizations, as becomes obvious once one tries to specify the statements any further. At what rate does time "pass"? At one second per second? Or "like a river"?

.   .   .   .   .

There must have been a first thought, a thought of thoughts, so to speak, a thought that made all other thoughts possible, or at least did not impede them. But what was it?

Surely not "Let there be thought!" Such an abstraction must have been light-years beyond a creature that had never thought before. And yet the first thought must indeed have had something about it that enabled thought to continue, something that allowed thinking to go on. It must have been a thought that indicated, somehow, the value of thinking, something that gave a reason to go on thinking—since, at that point, having never thought before, to *not* go on thinking would surely have been a feasible, sensible option.

Perhaps the first thought was "things could be otherwise." Not in English, of course. Not in any language, written, spoken, or thought that we could today possibly recognize. If articulated, it might have sounded no more complicated than "Hmmm," yet, I think, it might well have been translatable to something like "things could be otherwise."

The candidacy of this phrase becomes more plausible if we consider what could possibly have driven an animal to think. We know from our study of evolution that animals tend to be fairly well-adapted to their environment. They face daily challenges, of course. They are threatened by other animals and by the other, inanimate elements of nature. But this is just part of their environment. And whether their lives are long or short, "eventful" or placid, they generally do a pretty good job of contributing to the continuance of their species. Even when their species is dying out, there is not much for the individual animal to take notice of. Ordinary deaths are merely happening at a higher-than-normal rate. Death and deprivation, then, are nothing unusual to the animal and certainly do not require thought in order to be dealt with—neither does "pain" (in whatever way it makes sense to talk about that condition with regard to animals). "Suffering," whether in the form of a lack of resources or the attack of predators, is an ordinary part of animal life. It is as common for fleas as it is for frogs or higher mammals. So there is no reason to think that these conditions "must" cause higher animals to think anymore than they cause fleas to think. Not in their ordinary amounts, anyhow.

But what if we imagine, not ordinary animal suffering, but a pain so intense and prolonged that we can only call it "unnatural." Ordinary animal suffering has a regular place in animal life and is perfectly well dealt with by instincts. But what if there were a pain that continued long beyond its normal span? A pain that trapped the animal, made it squirm, made it wrestle with itself, made it try to hide from existence, until finally, unable to escape physically from the "pain," it finally found a mental escape in the thought (a grunt really) "things could be otherwise." Not as a generalization about life or thought, but as a brute desire to be *anywhere* but at that one particular place where it is at that moment. Nietzsche imagined that such a pain came from out-and-out torture. Rousseau might have said it was the pain of jealousy. But the point is the same.

One sees the power of this thought: although it is not a generalization but a very particular wish, it certainly *contains* a generalization—even several. In the word "things" it grasps the particulars of existence into the general concept of "existence," of life as a whole, hence as something to be thought about. Many writers have observed that language rests on generalization. Having a different word for every single thing would be no language at all—nothing could be communicated. It is only when a word can stand for more than one instance that it becomes a usable word. The generalization about existence is only one such—but it is, in some sense, the primordial one. In indicating the generalizability of existence, it enables more particular generalizations, so to speak. More words, that is, about things.

Then in the phrase "could be" we have a generalization about time. "Could be" indicates that there is some difference between "now" and "not-now": and this is something that the animal never needed to grasp, not until it was subjected to inordinate pain, when it wanted to be somewhen other than "now." The full distinction between past and future remains, if you will, in the future for this animal. But that between present and not-present, which already encompasses the idea of time, is there at the start.

Finally "otherwise," which is really just the opposite of "things." It means "not-things," "not-existence." It is this which makes the whole thought worthwhile. It provides, as I maintained was necessary, the motivation to go on thinking. For it indicates escape from the pain. Hegel said that negation was of the essence of thinking. The first thought is the originating case of this. The wish that things be otherwise is the wish that they be "not-this." And this first thought is most plausibly brought on by an experience so dreadful and out of the ordinary that the animal's instincts (which are quite accustomed to pain and suffering) cannot cope with it.

"Things could be otherwise" thus meets the two tests I proposed for the first thought. It *enables* further thought by happening upon the generalizations of existence and time. These are the basic tools that allow thought to continue. And this thought also points to the *value* of thought with its attempt at negation, which holds out the prospect of an end of suffering.

Of course, many animals must have simply expired under the brunt of this pain before one or several thought to think their way out of this death with a thought-death. For that is another way to understand this first thought—as a death-wish. The animal wants the pain to stop. But it knows not time. It cannot separate the pain from existence. It wants to perish of the "pain-now." Since its first thought is of existence as a whole and its first wish to depart from it, we can only call this thought (in our modern language) a death-wish. The discovery (or the creation) of time is thus linked to the wish to depart from existence, from the "things-now," from life. At the end of the sentence, we might say, the human, no longer an animal, knows time. It knows that to depart from the things-now is not necessarily to die. But not at the beginning. There the animal only wants to depart from the only existence there is.

And so we say that humanity only began to live when it wanted to die.

. . . . .

The inability to keep the past alive is the truly reactionary feature.
—ORTEGA Y GASSET 1961, 49

Here Ortega puts his finger on something that is often misunderstood. True reverence for the past is not the same thing as wishing for its return. To feel the past as part of oneself is to know that it is alive, ever-changing in relation to the self that necessarily alters as it passes through time. It is only those who have no real connection to the past who can view it as something unchanging, because it is something outside them. It is only these who can worship the past as an icon, rather than loving it as a person—or rather, as the people that it was.

. . . . .

A pessimistic population would not be quiescent or cynical. To one another, they might appear skeptical, as competitors at a debate appear skeptical. They know that the ideas of others must have weaknesses that time will reveal. But in fact they are investigators, each in search of a new direction that might claim a day, or a week, or a span of years, and of compatriots with whom to explore that path. A mobile army of meddlers, métiers, anthropomorphizers, in short, a sum of human relationships that, viewed from the proper distance, appears as solid as a fleet of ships, or a hornets' nest.

. . . . .

Hope. Kafka's response to the suggestion that there was no hope: "Oh yes, there is hope, infinite hope—but not for us." A Platonic thought perhaps: for what else did Plato express in his *Republic* but the hope that a perfect human life could be achieved? But not by us—we, who have been raised imperfectly, have no hope of achieving it. It would require raising children "from the ground up."

Many do blame their parents for an inability to enjoy life. And why? Because we are bombarded with the optimistic idea, from our first to our last breath, that such enjoyment is our right, our nature and, indeed, within our grasp if only our "problems," "wants," "needs," "desires," "interests," or whatever term you like, could be satisfied. And so we constantly seek the proper mix of stimulants and entertainments in a vain desire to make this so. But why should we think that there is an innate human ability to enjoy life? Would it not make much more sense to think of such an ability as a rare gift, like Seurat's gift of drawing?

And yet, such an ability *could* perhaps be learned, at least to some degree. If all cannot be the artists of joy, perhaps they could be its draftsmen.

. . . . .

A pessimist believes:

    a) that there is no *formula* for producing freedom and happiness in this world
    b) that there is no other world where there is such a formula
    c) that time is linear

A fatalist believes (a) and (c) are true.
A skeptic believes (a) and (b) are only provisionally true.
A nihilist would derive satisfaction from this state of affairs.
A Dionysian pessimist believes (c) is only provisionally true.

. . . . .

The shipwrecked. They are without that which carried them through. They are without that which carried them through a void which is death to them. They are surrounded by the void. They do not know why they live still. They do not know whether they are near or far from home. They do not know why what carried them through no longer suffices. They are at rest but not at home. Without purpose they reflect on the shattered remains of what carried them through. Each plank, deserving or not, receives a severe and unnatural attention that it never received as a floorboard or cabinet. Only as a wreck can they appreciate that which carried them through. They were passengers, pilots even, not shipbuilders.

Will they build another ship? But they already know that which carried them through would not survive. What can they learn from its shards? Why rebuild it?

And if they conceived and built something else to carry them through? What then? Where would they sail? Home? Which way would that be? Where they started? Where the old ships are? Ithaca?

Ithaca is just an island of the shipwrecked to them now.

AFTERWORD

IN *Freedom and Necessity*, the economic historian Joan Robinson wrote, "Anyone who writes a book, however gloomy its message may be, is necessarily an optimist. If the pessimists really believed what they were saying there would be no point in saying it" (1970, 124). This, I suppose, will be a common response to the foregoing; certainly, many others have repeated it. Even for those inclined to be sympathetic to what I have written, there will be the urge to find some kind of happy conclusion to it all, so that one will be able to say, in the end, it's not "really" pessimistic. To any reader now feeling this temptation (generous toward me though it may be), I have but one word to say: *Resist*.

The stance Robinson offers is nothing more than an intellectual dodge; the last refuge, one might say, of an optimistic scoundrel. It amounts to saying that *whatever* a pessimist may suggest, in the very act of suggesting it, he defeats himself. But this charge of performative contradiction is just one more way in which the pessimist is refused a hearing. For on this logic, the content of what is said is irrelevant, since it is known in advance to be self-defeating. It is on account of such reasoning that the pessimists have not, over the centuries, been heard very well or very frequently, however cogent their arguments may have been. Rousseau already anticipated this response when he wrote: "People may some day say: This avowed enemy of the sciences and arts nevertheless wrote and published plays." But, he continued, the joke is not on him but on those "People;" in time it is they who will look foolish: "and I admit that that discourse will be a most bitter satire, not on myself, but on my century" (Rousseau 1986, 111).

The goals of this book have been two: first, to reorient the history of European political theory in the last three centuries so that pessimism becomes one of its principal themes; second, to rearticulate that pessimism in such a way that its inherent appeal becomes more visible to twenty-first-century readers. I would be satisfied if readers felt I made some progress toward either of these aims, though of course I would be more pleased if they felt both had been accomplished. In some sense, of course, the two are linked. Part of the reason for pessimism's having been left out of standard histories, as I repeat now for the last time, is that its rendering as a feeling or mood has made its appeal as a philosophy nearly invisible. But the pessimistic spirit, as with any serious account of the fundamental problems of life, is much more than a sentiment. It is an orientation toward those problems marked out by a profound sensitivity to our time-bound condition and to the limitations such a condition imposes.

Within this orientation, there is, of course, room for conflicting and even contrasting views on some questions. But, if my efforts in this book have amounted to anything, the family resemblance between these writers, which I spoke of in chapter 1, will by now be eminently visible to the reader.

For far too long, the alternative to modern liberalism that is embodied in Continental philosophy has been conceptualized around the axis of Hegel and Marx, with postmodernism an appendage that appears, root-less, in response to Nietzsche. But viewed from a broader perspective, the history of Western political thought since the Renaissance is better un-derstood as a conflict between an optimism that has branches in both lib-eralism and the descendants of Hegel, on the one hand, and, on the other hand, a pessimism that comprises the larger part of Continental theory (with occasional Anglo-American representatives that I have been unable to discuss here, for example, Twain, Carlyle, Santayana). While it would be foolish to say that this split was in any sense required by the adoption of linear time as the modern standard, it nonetheless seems clear that it was the broader cultural change in time-consciousness that made the ap-pearance of both modes of modern philosophy possible and that created the context for their conflict.

Is this conflict a necessary one? That is profoundly hard to say. For the most part, this book has ignored that literature about time and identity that has long preoccupied a small corner of Anglo-American philosophy with denying the reality of time (and thus, in a sense, depriving the prob-lem of identity of its problem). I do not apologize for this but refer my readers to a fine essay by Jorge Luis Borges, which, after adopting such theories to the point of total identification concludes:

> To deny temporal succession, to deny the self . . . appear to be acts of des-peration and are secret consolations. Our destiny is not terrifying because it is unreal; it is terrifying because it is irreversible and iron-bound. Time is the substance of which I am made. Time is a river that sweeps me along, but I am the river; it is a tiger that mangles me, but I am the tiger; it is a fire that consumes me, but I am the fire. The world, unfortunately, is real; I, unfor-tunately, am Borges. (1999, 332)

Equally unfortunately, I am not Borges and thus feel compelled to beg for-giveness for prose the length and clumsiness of which he would no doubt have condemned as criminal. At least, however, he would have agreed that the problems temporality creates for humanity are real problems and ought to be central to any examination of ethics or politics. While we can certainly imagine alternative structures of temporality that are neither op-timistic nor pessimistic in the modern senses of these terms, mere con-ceptualizations will not liberate us from the social, cultural, and political structures we inhabit, all of which were drawn up within the modern horizon of temporality. Nor can we really know, without inhabiting them, that alternative structures of temporality would be in any sense more liberating.

Optimistic philosophies, liberal or otherwise, have largely assumed that our temporal condition is an unproblematic framework for progress and have conceived obstacles to liberty in material or social terms. Since Rousseau, however, the pessimistic tradition has drawn attention to the burden of time as the crucial problem in human affairs. Temporality creates barriers to freedom and happiness that political institutions devoted to managing, say, scarcity, sociability, domination, or faction, do not consciously address. Both optimistic political theory and modern political institutions have, for the most part, been oblivious to these barriers with the result that citizens of modern states face inevitable disappointment when their lives do not measure up to what contemporary political rhetoric tells them is possible. This disappointment then generates resentment as the search for a responsible party leads to a kind of competitive victimization in which all can participate.

Pessimism, by contrast, has outlined a set of attitudes and practices that are meant to fortify the individual and cope with these limitations. It admits limits to, not defeat of, human aspirations. Indeed, in the very openness and indeterminacy of human history, the pessimists, or at least the anti-misanthropes among them, have seen the possibility of a distinct form of human freedom, one that envisages life as a quest amidst the unknown, undiscovered country of the future. Questing figures both real (Columbus) and imaginary (Don Quixote) have repeatedly served as exemplars for this kind of life. The freedom they embody can only appear on a landscape (or seascape) of radical indeterminacy. This indeterminacy may contain enormous dangers, but not every episode in Quixote's story ends with a beating. There are also occurrences that Cervantes terms "undreamed of," which represent welcome expansions of the human field of experience. It is this exploration and expansion that makes pessimistic freedom something worth pursuing.

To say this is not to disparage or take lightly modern political liberties. It is, however, to point out that the value of such liberties has often been given with reference to a larger progressive historical frame. This is true even for such ostensibly liberal theories like those of Kant, Mill, and Dewey. While such frames are no longer openly credited in contemporary liberal theory, they are often restored or relied upon sotto voce—the belief in the possibility of moral (and material) progress motivates more current theorizing than is frankly acknowledged. Thus even as the plausibility of totalizing Hegelian histories has receded, contemporary Western political discourse has remained unnecessarily bound within the narrow confines of liberal optimism. So long as pessimism goes unheard, the alternatives to this discourse (like ancient virtue or civic republicanism) will seem outlandish because they are, one way or another, so alien to our time. But pessimism is as modern as its rivals. The art of living it proposes is, if anything, more suited to our era than the liberal habits it proposes to replace. Indeed, if there is to be any defense of Western political norms in the provisional terms suited to our situation, it is the account of pessimistic freedom to which their value can best be tied. That is, rather than deriving the value of our political liberties from their capacity to allow individuals to pursue a hollow idol of the future, we should defend them in terms of their contribution to the democracy of moments.

· · · · ·

Pessimism is not so much postmodernist as it is postimpressionist. Impressionism exposed the "fiction" of straight lines, pure black, and large fields of constant color. Intolerant of this fictionality, it insisted on the "natural" absence of line, mixture of color, and quantum of light in every true image. Now, postimpressionism accepted this impressionist lesson but desired nonetheless to paint objects with solidity, line, and the appearance of definition. Only now these elements were *understood* to be fictions, creations, impositions. The absence of structure in the natural world, which the impressionist both discovered and worshipped, was taken as an obstacle, a *worthy* obstacle, which painting, and human life itself had to tackle. Thus postimpressionist painting reverts to the human, to the constructed, to the indoor, in its subjects—besides returning in form to the depiction of objects and masses, as opposed to surfaces and colors. The impressionists painted humans, but they always understood them as a piece of nature. Likewise, postimpressionists painted nature, but always emphasized how it was a function of man—either humans in general or the artist in particular.

Similarly, pessimism accepts the lesson of philosophical impressionism (whether its source is Heraclitus or Nietzsche): that the world contains no natural order to be depicted by philosophy. Like Seurat or Cezanne, we expect nothing of the world, not even that it will sit still long enough to be painted or grasped as a whole. Nonetheless, we may still desire to take this obstacle and work on it until we achieve something to our satisfaction. Think how little the postimpressionist artist could hope to accomplish as compared with those of the Renaissance or Reformation. The latter could imagine that their work was in harmony with, or depicted, some universal law of nature or of God. The former could only see his little rectangular canvas as a tiny pocket of fictitious order adrift on the chaos of the Universe. The pessimist faces the same challenge in politics. To make

something stable in the universe means to take account of the natural tu-
multuousness of the universe and the self and nonetheless to effect a transformation worth remembering—rather than attempting to merely read
off the shape of pregiven order. Success in such an effort can only be provisional; respecting the provisional is the sacrifice that pessimism requires
of modern man.

.   .   .   .   .

It is sometimes said that pragmatism is the defining feature of American
philosophy. There may be a distinctly American strain of pragmatism, but
pragmatism itself—if it is taken to mean the assumption that the problems of human social life and personal psychology are amenable to solution by human means—is typical of most European philosophy, at least
since Bacon. This is so much the case that it has often been the strategy
of attack against the pessimists—the only dissenters from this general
pragmatism—to say that they are not philosophers but rather *bellelet-
trists* or mystics or novelists or "wits": anything but philosophers.[1]

As I argued in chapter 1, the pessimists' antipragmatism rejects the idea
that history is a riddle. Nor is human existence a question or problem
waiting to be solved. Human existence just is—it has no predicate. There
is no sphinx who would grow impatient if humans simply turned their
minds away from philosophy, away from the sun and chose to stare eternally instead into "Egyptian darkness" (as Locke called it). Darkness and
light there are. But the one is not Egyptian and the other Greek. We are
each given one human life with no promise as to how much light or darkness it may contain. Nor is there any promise that turning ourselves toward the light *or* the darkness will make us free and happy. Freedom and
happiness exist, occasionally they are even visible—*but they do not exist
as the "solution" to a "problem" any more than do the sun and moon.*
The coexistence of freedom and happiness is like the appearance of the
sun and moon in the same portion of the sky, and effected by similar
means. How many eclipses have been created by philosophy? When Leopardi wrote, "As much as you or any other, I desire the good of my species
in general; but I cannot hope for it in any way," he captured how concern
for others is, if anything, strengthened by an absence of beneficent expectations (*OM* 185). The pessimists have been consistent critics of pity

---

[1] Optimism is also said to be particularly at home in America. But I would wager that this
too is an effect of an interpretive lens that has not been keen to focus on pessimism. It may
be that, in the future, armed with pessimism as a conceptual and historical category, we may
see more clearly the pessimistic side of American intellectual history and perhaps Melville
or Twain will appear to be an American Cervantes. For the moment, these must remain
speculations.

because it degrades our concern for others by ignoring the individuality of suffering and subsuming it into a compensatory narrative. And just for this reason, it seems to me, they have been *more* attuned to, and concerned to document, the multiple forms of distress that afflict us.

Perhaps some readers will grant that I have gone some distance toward outlining philosophical pessimism as an historical phenomenon but deny that any contemporary debates are thereby affected. We are, they might contend, beyond such simplistic dichotomies as optimism and pessimism today. Is this really the case? I doubt it very much. While claims about progress in history are perhaps more muted today than in the past, they are far from absent. Indeed, an implicit idea of moral progress underlies much of the critical history that is written today, in which the past is brought to the bar and condemned under a guise of scholarly objectivity. But even this scholarly phenomenon is simply a minor part of something larger that Nietzsche sought to identify by linking optimism with the figure of Socrates. "[F]or who could mistake the *optimistic* element in the nature of dialectic, which celebrates a triumph with every conclusion?" (*BT* 14). Platonic philosophy's faith in the power of reason is itself inherently optimistic in the sense that every well-founded conclusion is thought to drive the darkness from yet another corner of the universe. Rationalism *is* optimism—if by "rationalism" we mean, not any use of reason, but a faith that reason is the core capacity of humanity and, in a marvelous coincidence, the fundamental structure of the universe as well. One does not need to look far to see this faith retained in many corners of modern philosophy (especially but not only in liberalism) that otherwise disdain Platonic solutions. Pessimism, then, is not "against" reason or philosophy; indeed, it claims both of these honorifics for itself. It simply does not view philosophy as a technique for sweeping darkness from the universe and replacing it with light. Its goal, instead, is to teach us how to live with what we cannot eradicate, the limitations of death and time with which the universe saddles us. From this perspective, optimistic rationalism remains rife in contemporary philosophy, not to mention society at large, in the form of an ever-more-powerful faith in science.

. . . . .

It may frustrate some readers that, in this book, I have not taken either of two possible courses. I have not, on the one hand, assessed the claims of the cultural, metaphysical, and existential pessimists against one another and declared some, or one, to be superior as philosophical reasoning. But nor have I, as a historian of ideas might have done, simply reported the development of writings around a theme without reference to their inherent persuasiveness or plausibility. Instead, I have tried to chart the middle course that I think is distinctive to a political theorist in this sort of situation: my ambition has been to reanimate and reimagine a preexisting, if little-noticed, tradition of thought. I have been interested first in identifying that which the pessimists all share, rather than that which differentiates them from one another. Covering so many writers in a relatively brief treatment, I have tried to present the position of each sympathetically while identifying the horizon of understanding within which they stand. Or perhaps it would be better to say, I have tried to use these authors as points of reference in building up an understanding of the pessimistic perspective as a whole. Like any tradition of thought, pessimism is nothing more than a series of authors held together, in the eyes of an audience, by guiding themes. It does not stand or fall on the viability of any one writer's arguments—but the viability of the tradition itself can ultimately rest on nothing other than the light it sheds on questions of central concern to our species. To me, it is unquestionable that pessimism, as the only tradition that honestly eschews both progress and circularity as guiding temporal frames, is well above such a threshold. Indeed, it may offer us resources for coping with our "disenchanted," "hyperreal," "postmodern" condition (the terms are not mine, of course) that can be found nowhere else. But even if I have not spelled out such contributions here, I will remain satisfied if I have at least made pessimism *visible* and *audible* as a political theory, and thus added it to a toolbox from which others might draw. So long as pessimism was merely a psychological condition, it could not play this role.

Another sort of reader (a rather different sort, I imagine) might bring the following kind of objection: in tracing the history of pessimism in a more-or-less chronological fashion, this book falls prey to the very time-slavishness that it supposedly decries. Moreover, both pessimism and the optimism that it opposes move within a modern conception of time that is increasingly obsolete. The true alternative to consider is the nonlinear time of postmodernism, as exampled in contemporary film and literature, and the philosophy about them (such as that of Henri Bergson and Gilles Deleuze), that does not obey traditional temporal conventions, ancient or modern. Here I have to say that I think this perspective is less well-developed than its proponents would like to believe. Though I am highly sympathetic to the aesthetic aims of the sort of art in question, it cannot yet be considered to have broken with linear time-conventions in a fundamental way. Most of these works could, I believe, be easily shown to rely on such conventions—they often get their kick precisely by forcing an audience to translate a discombobulated narrative into a conventional one (think of movies such as *Pulp Fiction, Memento,* and *Amores Perros*). While this is not the place to pursue such an argument in detail, my point is that the idea of escape from modernity's linear time, while not impossible, is far more challenging than such art and theory would like us to believe. It is not simply a question of nonlinear styles of presentation or imagination.

To do without linear time in a serious way would require us to put away our calendars—not so much to deny them, but simply to not take them seriously, to not find them helpful in the organization of life. *Ignoring* our calendars, our clocks, and our other time-pieces would be, I think, infinitely more difficult than simply *denying* them. While such a world is within the capacity of our imagination, it is near the very limits of it. Linear time may not be the absolute cognitive a priori that Kant and Schopenhauer imagined it to be, but it has certainly shown itself to have an extraordinary historical durability. Doing without it would mean looking past one of the most fundamental horizons of our understanding. Indeed, it would require a fundamentally different kind of looking. Postmodernism, to date, has done little more than suggest the possibility of this— it is very far from instantiating that possibility in anything real. The linear view of time, centuries in the making and deeply embodied in every cranny of our culture and habits of thought, will not be shrugged off with a simple gesture, no matter how radical. The revolutions of the heavens were displaced by clock and calendar. If these in turn are to be displaced, we hardly have an inkling of what techniques or perspectives could do so. For a temple to be erected, Nietzsche wrote, a temple must be destroyed. But also the reverse: modern temporality cannot be overthrown without being replaced, but no alternative calendar (or anticalendar) has yet shown itself capable of successfully reorganizing our world. Parisian revolutionaries in 1848 fired on the clock-towers of the city *"contre l'heure / pour arrêter le jour"*; but they had no alternative temporality to offer. So their revolution only succeeded in exchanging one monarch for another.

In any case, if we are now more open to the possibility of such a change in time-consciousness than we have been in the past, it seems clear that it is pessimism that has laid the groundwork for it. And while I would in no way discourage exploration in this direction, I cannot say that such exploration has yet made much . . . progress. In the *meantime*, which may be forever, and to return to our point of departure with Camus,

> The important thing, as Abbé Galiani said to Mme. d'Epinay, is not to be cured, but to live with one's ailments. (*MS* 38)

BIBLIOGRAPHY

Abelson, Philip H. 1985. *Enough of Pessimism*. Washington: American Association for the Advancement of Science.

Adorno, Theodor W. 1973. *Negative Dialectics*. New York: Continuum.

Affeldt, Steven G. 1999. "The Force of Freedom: Rousseau on Forcing to Be Free." *Political Theory* 27:3:299–333.

Appel, Frederick. 1999. *Nietzsche Contra Democracy*. Ithaca: Cornell University Press.

Aquinas, Thomas. 1981 [1948]. *Summa Theologica*. Westminster, Md.: Christian Classics.

Aristotle. 1985. *Nichomachean Ethics*. Indianapolis: Hackett.

———. 1941. "Physics," in *The Basic Works of Aristotle*. New York: Random House, 218–394.

Augustine. 1960. *The Confessions of St. Augustine*. New York: Doubleday.

Avila Crespo, Remedios. 1989. "Pesimismo y Filosofia en A. Schopenhauer." *Pensamiento* 45:177:57–75.

Bailey, Joe. 1988. *Pessimism*. London: Routledge.

Basu, S. 1990. "In a Crazy Time, The Crazy Come Out Well—Machiavelli and the Cosmology of his Day." *History of Political Thought* 11:2:213–39.

Becker, Alois. 1971. "Arthur Schopenhauer—Sigmund Freud." *Schopenhauer-Jahrbuch* 52:114–56.

Bennett, Oliver. 2001. *Cultural Pessimism: Narratives of Decline in the Postmodern World*. Edinburgh: Edinburgh University Press.

Bergson, Henri. 1907. *L'évolution créatrice*. Paris: Press Universitaires de France.

Berkowitz, Peter. 1995. *Nietzsche: The Ethics of an Immoralist*. Cambridge, Mass.: Harvard University Press.

Berranger, Marie-Paule. 1988. *Dépaysement de L'aphorisme*. Paris: Librairie José Corti.

Bilsker, Richard. 1997. "Freud and Schopenhauer: Consciousness, the Unconscious, and the Drive towards Death." *Idealistic Studies* 27:1–2:79–90.

Blondel, Eric. 1991. *Nietzsche: The Body and Culture*. Stanford: Stanford University Press.

Blumenberg, Hans. 1974. "On a Lineage of the Idea of Progress." *Social Research* 41:1:5–27.

———. 1983. *The Legitimacy of the Modern Age*. Cambridge, Mass.: The MIT Press.

Bonaparte, Marie. 1952. *Chronos, Eros, Thanatos*. Paris: Presses Universitaires de France.

Borges, Jorge Luis. 1962. *Ficciones*. New York: Grove, Weidenfeld.

———. 1999. *Selected Non-Fictions*. New York: Viking Press.

Borst, Arno. 1993. *The Ordering of Time: From the Ancient Computus to the Modern Computer*. Chicago: University of Chicago Press.

Bradley, F. H. 1930. *Aphorisms*. Oxford: Clarendon Press.

Brinton, Crane. 1965 [1941]. *Nietzsche*. New York: Harper and Row.

Brobjer, Thomas H. 2000. "To Philosophize with a Hammer: An Interpretation." *Nietzsche-Studien* 28:38–41.

Brockhaus, Richard. 1991. *Pulling up the Ladder: The Metaphysical Roots of Wittgenstein's Tractatus Logico-philosophicus*. LaSalle, Ill.: Open Court.

Brown, Wendy. 1995. *States of Injury: Power and Freedom in Late Modernity*. Princeton: Princeton University Press.

Bury, J. B. 1923. *The Idea of Progress*. New York: Macmillan.

Butler, Judith. 1990. *Gender Trouble: Feminism and the Subversion of Identity*. New York: Routledge.

———. 1997. *The Psychic Life of Power: Theories in Subjection*. Stanford: Stanford University Press.

Cahn, Zilla Gabrielle. 1998. *Suicide in French Thought from Montesquieu to Cioran*. New York: Peter Lang.

Camprubí, Carles Besa. 1999. "Formes Brèves: Maxime, Aphorisme, Proverbe." *Rivista di letterature moderne e comparate* 52:1:1–15.

Camus, Albert. 1960. *Resistance, Rebellion, and Death*. New York: Alfred A. Knopf.

———. 1991. *The Rebel: An Essay on Man in Revolt*. New York: Vintage Books.

———. 1991. *The Myth of Sisyphus and Other Essays*. New York: Vintage Books.

Čapek, Milič, ed. 1976. *The Concepts of Space and Time: Their Structure and Development*. Boston: D. Reidel Publishing.

Cartwright, David E. 1998. "Nietzsche's Use and Abuse of Schopenhauer's Moral Philosophy for Life." In *Willing and Nothingness: Schopenhauer as Nietzsche's Educator*, ed. Christopher Janaway. Oxford: Clarendon Press, 116–50.

Cauchi, Francesca. 1991. "Nietzsche and Pessimism: The Metaphysic Hypostatised." *History of European Ideas* 13:3:253–67.

Cavell, Stanley. 1988. *In Quest of the Ordinary: Lines of Skepticism and Romanticism*. Chicago: University of Chicago Press.

Chambers, Clarke A. 1958. "The Belief in Progress in Twentieth-Century America." *Journal of the History of Ideas* 19:2:197–224.

Cioran, E. M. 1968. *The Temptation to Exist*. Chicago: Quadrangle Books.

———. 1970. *The Fall into Time*. Chicago: Quadrangle Books.

———. 1974. *The New Gods*. Chicago: Quadrangle Books.

———. 1975. *A Short History of Decay*. New York: Viking Press.

———. 1983. *Drawn and Quartered*. New York: Seaver Books.

———. 1987. *History and Utopia*. New York: Seaver Books.

———. 1992. *Anathemas and Admirations*. London: Quartet Books.

———. 1992. *On the Heights of Despair*. Chicago: University of Chicago Press.

———. 1993. *The Trouble With Being Born*. London: Quartet Books.

———. 1995. *Tears and Saints*. Chicago: University of Chicago Press.

———. 1995. *Oeuvres*. Paris: Éditions Gallimard.

———. 1999. *All Gall Is Divided*. New York: Arcade Publishing.

Cervantes, Miguel de. 1981. *Don Quixote*. New York: W. W. Norton and Co.

———. 2001. *El ingenioso hidalgo don Quijote de la Mancha*. Newark, Del.: European Classics.

Cladis, Mark. 1995. "Tragedy and Theodicy: A Meditation on Rousseau and Moral Evil." *Journal of Religion* 75:2:181–99.

Clark, Maudemarie. 1990. *Nietzsche on Truth and Philosophy*. Cambridge: Cambridge University Press.

———. 1998. "On Knowledge, Truth and Value: Nietzsche's Debt to Schopenhauer and the Development of His Empiricism." In *Willing and Nothingness: Schopenhauer as Nietzsche's Educator*, ed. Christopher Janaway. Oxford: Clarendon Press, 37–78.

Clarke, J. J. 1970. "Sunt Lacrimae Rerum: A Study in the Logic of Pessimism." *Philosophy* 45:193–209.

Clegg, Jerry. 1980. "Freud and the Issue of Pessimism." *Schopenhauer-Jahrbuch* 61:37–50.

Connolly, William. 1991. *Identity/Difference: Democratic Negotiations of a Political Paradox*. Ithaca: Cornell University Press.

Dale, Peter Allan. 1989. *In Pursuit of a Scientific Culture: Science, Art, and Society in the Victorian Age*. Madison: University of Wisconsin Press.

Danto, Arthur C. 1965. *Nietzsche as Philosopher: An Original Study*. New York: Macmillan.

Deleuze, Gilles. 1983 [1962]. *Nietzsche and Philosophy*. New York: Columbia University Press.

Derrida, Jacques. 1967. *L'écriture et la difference*. Paris: Éditions du Seuil.

———. 1978. *Writing and Difference*. Chicago: University of Chicago Press.

———. 1978. *Spurs: Nietzsche's Styles*. Chicago: University of Chicago Press.

———. 2001. "A Discussion with Jacques Derrida." *Theory and Event* 5:1. http://muse.jhu.edu/journals/theory_and_event/v005/5.1derrida.html.

Dienstag, Joshua Foa. 1997. *"Dancing In Chains": Narrative and Memory in Political Theory*. Stanford: Stanford University Press.

———. 1999. "The Pessimistic Spirit." *Philosophy and Social Criticism* 25:1:71–95.

———. 2001. "Nietzsche's Dionysian Pessimism." *American Political Science Review* 95:4:923–37.

———. 2004. "Tragedy, Pessimism, Nietzsche." *New Literary History* 35:1:83–101.

Dohrn-van Rossum, Gerhard. 1996. *History of the Hour: Clocks and Modern Temporal Orders*. Chicago: University of Chicago Press.

Drassinower, Abraham. 2003. *Freud's Theory of Culture: Eros, Loss and Politics*. New York: Rowman and Littlefield.

Dumm, Thomas L. 1998. "Resignation." *Critical Inquiry* 25:56–76.

———. 1999. *A Politics of the Ordinary*. New York: New York University Press.

Eagleton, Terry. 2003. *Sweet Violence: The Idea of the Tragic*. Oxford: Blackwell.

Epicurus. 1964. *Letters, Principal Doctrines, and Vatican Sayings*. New York: Macmillan Publishing Company.

Euben, J. Peter. 1990. *The Tragedy of Political Theory: The Road Not Taken*. Princeton: Princeton University Press.

Fedler, Stephan. 1992. *Der Aphorismus: Begriffsspiel zwischen Philosophie und Poesie*. Stuttgart: Verlag fur Wissenschaft und Forschung.

Ferruci Carlo, ed. 1989. *Leopardi e il Pensiero Moderno*. Milano: Giangiacomo Feltrinelli Editore.

Fink, Arthur-Hermann. 1934. *Maxime und Fragment: Grenzmöglichkeiten einer Kunstform—Zur Morphologie des Aphorismus*. Munich: Max Hueber Verlag.

Fitzgerald, F. Scott. 1991 [1925]. *The Great Gatsby*. New York: Scribner Classics.

Foucault, Michel. 1986. *The Care of the Self: The History of Sexuality, Volume 3*. New York: Random House.

Freud, Sigmund. 1953. *The Standard Edition of the Complete Psychological Works of Sigmund Freud*, 24 vols. London: Hogarth Press.

———. 1959. *Collected Papers*, 5 vols. New York: Basic Books.

———. 1960. *The Ego and the Id*. New York: W. W. Norton and Co.

———. 1961a. *Beyond the Pleasure Principle*. New York: W. W. Norton and Co.

———. 1961b. *Civilization and Its Discontents*. New York: W. W. Norton and Co.

———. 1961c. *The Future of an Illusion*. New York: W. W. Norton and Co.

———. 1965. *The Interpretation of Dreams*. New York: Avon Books.

Fricke, Harald. 1984. *Aphorismus*. Stuttgart: J. B. Metzlersche Verlagsbuchhandlung.

Fuentes, Carlos. 2003. "Tilt" [A review of *Don Quixote* in a new translation]. *New York Times*, November 2, 2003.

Gillespie, Michael Allen. 2000. "Nietzsche and the Anthropology of Nihilism." *Nietzsche-Studien* 28:141–55.

Gooding-Williams, Robert. 2001. *Nietzsche's Dionysian Modernism*. Stanford: Stanford University Press.

Gottfried, Paul. 1975. "Arthur Schopenhauer as A Critic of History." *Journal of the History of Ideas* 36:2:331–38.

Greene, Brian. 2004. "The Time We Thought We Knew." *New York Times*, January 1, 2004.

Guyer, Paul. 1999. "Schopenhauer, Kant and the Methods of Philosophy." In *The Cambridge Companion to Schopenhauer*, ed. Christopher Janaway. Cambridge: Cambridge University Press.

Hadot, Pierre. 1995. *Philosophy as a Way of Life: Spiritual Exercises from Socrates to Foucault*. Oxford: Blackwell Publishers.

Hallett, Garth. 1977. *A Companion to Wittgenstein's "Philosophical Investigations."* Cornell: Cornell University Press.

Hamblen, Emily S. 1911. *Friedrich Nietzsche and His New Gospel*. Boston: The Gorham Press.

Harries, Karsten. 1991. "Questioning the Question of the Worth of Life." *Journal of Philosophy* 88:11:684–90.

Hartmann, Eduard von. 1923 [1869]. *Philosophie des Unbewussten*. Leipzig: Alfred Kröner.

———. 1876. *Geammelte Studien und Aufsätze*. Berlin: Carl Duncker's Verlag.

———. 1895. *The Sexes Compared and Other Essays*. New York: Macmillan.

———. 1931. *Philosophy of the Unconscious*. London: Kegan Paul.

———. 1992 [1880]. *Zur Geschichte und Begründung des Pessimismus*. Eschborn: Verlag Dietmar Klotz.

Hegel, G.W.F. 1975. *Aesthetics: Lectures on Fine Art*. Oxford: Oxford University Press.

Heidegger, Martin. 1977. *The Question Concerning Technology and Other Essays*. New York: Harper and Row.

Helmich, Werner. 1991. *Der moderne französische Aphorismus: Innovation und Gattungsreflexion*. Tübingen: Max Niemeyer Verlag.

Herman, Arthur. 1997. *The Idea of Decline in Western History*. New York: The Free Press.

Higgins, Kathleen. 1998. "Schopenhauer and Nietzsche: Temperament and Temporality." In *Willing and Nothingness: Schopenhauer as Nietzsche's Educator*, ed. Christopher Janaway. Oxford: Clarendon Press, 151–77.

Hollinrake, Roger. 1982. *Nietzsche, Wagner and the Philosophy of Pessimism*. London: Allen and Unwin.

Honig, Bonnie. 1993. *Political Theory and the Displacement of Politics*. Ithaca: Cornell University Press.

Hübscher, Arthur. 1989. *The Philosophy of Schopenhauer in Its Intellectual Context: Thinker Against the Tide*. Lewiston, N.Y.: The Edwin Mellen Press.

Hulliung, Mark. 1994. *The Autocritique of the Enlightenment: Rousseau and the Philosophes*. Cambridge, Mass.: Harvard University Press.

Isaac, Jeffrey C. 1992. *Arendt, Camus, and Modern Rebellion*. New Haven: Yale University Press.

Israel, Jonathon I. 2001. *Radical Enlightenment: Philosophy and the Making of Modernity 1650–1750*. Oxford: Oxford University Press.

James, William. 1896. *Is Life Worth Living?* Philadelphia: S. Burns Weston.

———. 1912. *On Some of Life's Ideals*. New York: Henry Holt.

Janaway, Christopher. 1998. "Schopenhauer as Nietzsche's Educator." In *Willing and Nothingness: Schopenhauer as Nietzsche's Educator*, ed. Christopher Janaway. Oxford: Clarendon Press, 13–36.

Jarrety, Michel. 1999. *La morale dans l'écriture: Camus Char Cioran*. Paris: Press Universitaires de France.

Kateb, George. 1992. *The Inner Ocean: Individualism and Democratic Culture*. Ithaca: Cornell University Press.

Kaufmann, Walter. 1974 [1955]. *Nietzsche: Philosopher, Psychologist, Antichrist*, 4th ed. Princeton: Princeton University Press.

Kerényi, Carl. 1976. *Dionysos: Archetypal Image of Indestructible Life*. Princeton: Princeton University Press.

Kirk, G. S., J. E. Raven, and M. Schofield. 1983 [1957]. *The Presocratic Philosophers*. Cambridge: Cambridge University Press.

Klossowski, Pierre. 1997 [1969]. *Nietzsche and the Vicious Circle*. Chicago: University of Chicago Press.

Kofman, Sarah. 1983. *Nietzsche et la métaphore*. Paris: Editions Galilée.

Koselleck, Reinhart. 1985. *Futures Past: On the Semantics of Historical Time*. Cambridge, Mass.: The MIT Press.

Kumar, Krishan. 1978. *Prophecy and Progress*. London: Allan Lane.

Kundera, Milan. 1996. *Slowness*. New York: HarperCollins.

Lafond, Jean. 1984. *Les Formes Brèves de la Prose et Le Discours Discontinu (XVIe–XVIIe Siècles)*. Paris: Librairie Philosophique J. Vrin.

Laignel-Lavastine, Alexandra. 2002. *Cioran, Eliade, Ionesco: L'oubli du fascisme*. Paris: Presses Universitaires de France.

La Rochefoucauld. 2001. *The Maxims*. South Bend, Ind.: St. Augustine's Press.

Lasch, Christopher. 1991. *The True and Only Heaven: Progress and Its Critics*. New York: W. W. Norton.

Leibniz, G. W. 1985 [1710]. *Theodicy*. LaSalle, Ill.: Open Court.

Leiter, Brian. 1994. "Perspectivism in Nietzsche's '*Genealogy of Morals*.'" In *Nietz-*

sche, Genealogy, Morality, ed. Richard Schact. Berkeley: University of California Press, 334–57.

Leopardi, Giacomo. 1983. *The Moral Essays (Operette Morali)*. New York: Columbia University Press.

———. 1997. *Selected Poems*, trans. Eamonn Grennan. Princeton: Princeton University Press.

———. 2004. *Thoughts (Pensieri)*. London: Hesperus Press.

Lichtenberg, Georg Christoph. 1990. *Aphorisms*. London: Penguin.

Löwith, Karl. 1949. *Meaning in History: The Theological Implications of the Philosophy of History*. Chicago: University of Chicago Press.

Machiavelli, Niccolò. 1970. *The Discourses*. London: Penguin.

Magee, Bryan. 1997. *The Philosophy of Schopenhauer*. Oxford: Oxford University Press.

Marcuse, Herbert. 1955. *Eros and Civilization: A Philosophical Inquiry into Freud*. Boston: The Beacon Press.

Migotti, Mark. 1995. "Schopenhauer's Pessimism and the Unconditioned Good." *Journal of the History of Philosophy* 33:4:643–60.

Momigliano, Arnaldo. 1966. "Time in Ancient Historiography" *History and Theory, Beiheft 6, History and the Concept of Time*. Wesleyan: Wesleyan University Press.

Moncelet, Christian, ed. 1998. *Désir D'Aphorismes*. Clermont-Ferrand: Association des Publications de la Faculté des Lettres et Sciences Humaines de Clermont-Ferrand.

Montaigne, Michel de. 1958. *The Complete Essays of Montaigne*. Stanford: Stanford University Press.

Montesquieu, Baron de. 1949. *The Spirit of the Laws*. New York: Hafner.

Moret, Phillipe. 1997. *Tradition et Modernité de L'Aphorisme: Cioran, Reverdy, Scutenaire, Jourdan, Chazal*. Geneva: Librairie Droz.

Murray, Peter Durno. 1999. *Nietzsche's Affirmative Morality: A Revaluation Based in the Dionysian World-View*. Berlin: Walter de Gruyter.

Nehamas, Alexander. 1985. *Nietzsche: Life as Literature*. Cambridge, Mass.: Harvard University Press.

———. 1998. *The Art of Living: Socratic Reflections from Plato to Foucault*. Berkeley: University of California Press.

Neiman, Susan. 2002. *Evil in Modern Thought: An Alternative History of Philosophy*. Princeton: Princeton University Press.

Neumann, Gerhard, ed. 1976a. *Der Aphorismus: Zur Geschichte, Zu Den Formen und Möglichkeiten Einer Literarischen Gattung*. Darmstadt: Wissenschaftliche Buchgesellschaft.

———. 1976b. *Ideenparadiese: Untersuchungen Zur Aphoristik Von Lichtenberg, Novalis, Friedrich Schlegel und Goethe*. Munich: Wilhelm Fink Verlag.

Nietzsche, Friedrich W. 1962. *Philosophy in the Tragic Age of the Greeks*. Washington: Regnery Gateway.

———. 1966a. *Beyond Good and Evil*. New York: Random House.

———. 1966b. *Thus Spoke Zarathustra*. New York: Random House.

———. 1967a. *On the Genealogy of Morals and Ecce Homo*. New York: Random House.

———. 1967b. *The Birth Of Tragedy and The Case of Wagner*. New York: Random House.

———. 1967c. *The Will to Power*. New York: Random House.

———. 1967ff. *Werke Kritische Gesamtausgabe*, ed. by Giorgio Colli and Mazzino Montinari. Berlin: Walter de Gruyter.

———. 1968. *Twilight of the Idols and The Anti-Christ*. New York: Penguin.

———. 1974. *The Gay Science*. New York: Random House.

———. 1982. *Daybreak*. Cambridge: Cambridge University Press.

———. 1984. *Untimely Meditations*. Cambridge: Cambridge University Press.

———. 1986. *Human, All-Too-Human*. Cambridge: Cambridge University Press.

———. 1989. *Friedrich Nietzsche on Rhetoric and Language*, ed. Sander L. Gilman, Carole Blair, David J. Parent. Oxford: Oxford University Press.

Nussbaum, Martha. 1991. "The Transfigurations of Intoxication: Nietzsche, Schopenhauer, and Dionysus." *Arion* 1:2:75–111.

———. 1994. *The Therapy of Desire: Theory and Practice in Hellenistic Ethics*. Princeton: Princeton University Press.

Oakeshott, Michael. 1975. *On Human Conduct*. Oxford: The Clarendon Press.

Opstelten, J. C. 1952. *Sophocles and Greek Pessimism*. Amsterdam: North-Holland.

Origo, Iris. 1999 [1953]. *Leopardi: A Study in Solitude*. New York: Books and Co. and Helen Marx Books.

Orlie, Melissa A. 1997. *Living Ethically, Acting Politically*. Ithaca: Cornell University Press.

Ortega y Gasset, José. 1961. *Meditations on Quixote*. New York: W. W. Norton.

Ortemann, Marie-Jeanne, ed. 1998. *Fragment(s), Fragmentation, Aphorisme poétique*. Nantes: Centre de Recherches sure Les Identites Nationales et L'Interculturalite.

Parfait, Nicole. 2001. *Cioran ou le défi de l'être*. Paris: Éditions Desjonquères.

Pauen, Michael. 1997. *Pessimismus: Geschichtsphilosophie, Metaphysik und Moderne von Nietzsche bis Spengler*. Berlin: Akademie Verlag.

Philonenko, Alexis. 1980. *Schopenhauer: Une philosophie de la Tragedie*. Paris: Librairie Philosophique J. Vrin.

———. 1984. *Jean-Jacques Rousseau et la Pensée du Malheur*, 3 vols. Paris: Librairie Philosophique J. Vrin.

Pigault-Lebrun, Ch[arles]. 1789. *Le pessimiste ou L'homme mécontent de tout: comédie en un acte et en vers*. Paris: Chez Cailleau and fils.

Plato. 1997. *Complete Works*, ed. John M. Cooper. Indianapolis: Hackett.

Pocock, J.G.A. 1975. *The Machiavellian Moment: Florentine Political Thought and the Atlantic Republican Tradition*. Princeton: Princeton University Press.

Poole, Reginald. 1918. *Medieval Reckonings of Time*. London: Society for Promoting Christian Knowledge.

Poole, Robert. 1998. *Time's Alteration: Calendar reform in Early Modern England*. London: The UCL Press.

Postrel, Virginia. 1998. *The Future and Its Enemies: The Growing Conflict over Creativity, Enterprise and Progress*. New York: The Free Press.

Poulet, Georges. 1956. *Studies in Human Time*. Baltimore: The Johns Hopkins University Press.

Ricoeur, Paul. 1970. *Freud and Philosophy: An Essay on Interpretation*. New Haven: Yale University Press.

Rieff, Philip. 1961. *Freud: The Mind of the Moralist*. New York: Doubleday.

Robinson, Joan. 1970. *Freedom and Necessity: An Introduction to the Study of Society*. New York: Pantheon Books.

Rockefeller, Steven C. 1991. *John Dewey: Religious Faith and Democratic Humanism*. New York: Columbia University Press.

Rorty, Richard. 1989. *Contingency, Irony and Solidarity*. Cambridge: Cambridge University Press.

Rousseau, Jean-Jacques. 1960. *Politics and The Arts: Letter to M. d'Alembert on the Theatre*. Cornell: Cornell University Press.

———. 1968. *The Social Contract*. New York: Penguin.

———. 1979. *Émile, or On Education*. New York: Basic Books.

———. 1986. *Discourses and the Essay on the Origin of Languages*, ed. Victor Gourevitch. New York: Harper and Row.

———. 1990. *Essai sur l'origine des langues*, ed. Jean Starobinski. Paris: Éditions Gallimard.

———. 1994. *Émile et Sophie, ou Les Solitaires*. Paris: Éditions Payot and Rivages.

———. 2000. *Collected Writings of Rousseau, Volume 8: The Reveries of the Solitary Walker and other writings*, ed. Christopher Kelly. Hanover, N.H.: University Press of New England.

Russell, Bertrand. 1945. *A History of Western Philosophy*. New York: Simon and Schuster.

Salomé, Lou [Andreas-]. 1988. *Nietzsche*. Redding Ridge, Conn.: Black Swan Books.

Saltus, Edgar Evertson. 1885. *The Philosophy of Disenchantment*. New York: Belford Company.

Sambursky, S. 1956. *The Physical World of the Greeks*. London: Routledge and Kegan Paul.

———. 1959. *Physics of the Stoics*. London: Routledge and Kegan Paul.

Samuel, Alan E. 1972. *Greek and Roman Chronology: Calendars and Years in Classical Antiquity*. München: C. H. Beck'sche Verlagsbuchhandlung.

Schopenhauer, Arthur. 1966. *The World as Will and Representation*, 2 vols. New York: Dover.

———. 1970. *Essays and Aphorisms*. London: Penguin. [Duplicates material in Schopenhauer 1974 with some preferable translations.]

———. 1972. *Sämtliche Werke*, 7 vols. Wiesbaden: Brodhaus.

———. 1974. *Parerga and Paralipomena*, 2 vols. Oxford: Oxford University Press.

Simmel, Georg. 1986 [1907]. *Schopenhauer and Nietzsche*. Urbana: University of Illinois Press.

Soll, Ivan. 1988. "Pessimism and the Tragic View of Life: Reconsiderations of Nietzsche's 'Birth of Tragedy.'" In *Reading Nietzsche*, ed. Kathleen M. Higgins and Robert C. Solomon. Oxford: Oxford University Press, 104–31.

———. 1998. "Schopenhauer, Nietzsche and the Redemption of Life through

Art." In *Willing and Nothingness: Schopenhauer as Nietzsche's Educator*, ed. Christopher Janaway. Oxford: Clarendon Press, 79–115.

Sophocles. 1982. *The Three Theban Plays*. New York: Penguin.

Spacks, Patricia Meyer. 1995. *Boredom: The Literary History of a State of Mind*. Chicago: University of Chicago Press.

Spicker, Friedemann. 1997. *Der Aphorismus: Begriff und Gattung von der Mitte des 18. Jahrhunderts bis 1912*. Berlin: Walter de Gruyter.

Stambaugh, Joan. 1972. *Nietzsche's Thought of Eternal Return*. Baltimore: Johns Hopkins University Press.

———. 1987. *The Problem of Time in Nietzsche*. Lewisburg, Maine: Bucknell University Press.

Starobinski, Jean. 1964. "Introduction" to *Discours Sur l'Origine et les Fondements de l'Inégalité*. In Jean-Jacques Rousseau, *Oeuvres completes*. Paris: Éditions Gallimard.

———. 1988. *Jean-Jacques Rousseau: Transparency and Obstruction*. Chicago: University of Chicago Press.

Steiner, George. 1961. *The Death of Tragedy*. London: Faber and Faber.

Stephens, Carlene. 2002. *On Time: How America Has Learned to Live by the Clock*. New York: Little, Brown.

Strong, Tracy. 1988 [1975]. *Friedrich Nietzsche and the Politics of Transfiguration*. Berkeley: University of California Press.

———. 1994. *Jean-Jacques Rousseau: The Politics of the Ordinary*. Thousand Oaks, Calif.: Sage Press.

Sully, James. 1891. *Pessimism: A History and a Criticism*. New York: D. Appleton.

Tallis, Raymond. 1999. *Enemies of Hope: A Critique of Contemporary Pessimism: Irrationalism, Anti-Humanism and Counter-Enlightenment*. New York: St. Martin's.

Theile, Leslie. 1990. *Friedrich Nietzsche and the Politics of the Soul: A Study of Heroic Individualism*. Princeton: Princeton University Press.

Toulmin, Stephen, and June Goodfield. 1965. *The Discovery of Time*. London: Hutchinson.

Turetzky, Philip. 1998. *Time*. London: Routledge.

Unamuno, Miguel de. 1967. *Our Lord Don Quixote*. Princeton: Princeton University Press.

———. 1972. *The Tragic Sense of Life in Men and Nations*. Princeton: Princeton University Press.

Vattimo, Gianni. 2001. *Nietzsche: An Introduction*. Stanford: Stanford University Press.

Villa, Dana. 1991. *Socratic Citizenship*. Princeton: Princeton University Press.

Virilio, Paul. 1986. *Speed and Politics: An Essay on Dromology*. New York: Semiotext(e).

Voltaire. 1992 [1759]. *Candide*. New York: Alfred A. Knopf.

Voytko, Victoria. 1994. *Recurrence and Teleology in Stoic Physics*. Ph. D. Diss. Charlottesville: University of Virginia.

Vyverberg, Henry. 1958. *Historical Pessimism in the French Enlightenment*. Cambridge, Mass.: Harvard University Press.

Warren, Mark. 1988. *Nietzsche and Political Thought*. Cambridge, Mass.: The MIT Press.

Weil, Simone. 1978. *Lectures on Philosophy*. Cambridge: Cambridge University Press.

Whitrow, G. J. 1972. *What Is Time?* London: Thames and Hudson.

Wittgenstein, Ludwig. 1958. *Philosophical Investigations*. New York: Macmillan.

———. 1969. *On Certainty*. New York: Harper and Row.

Young, Christopher, and Andrew Brook. 1994. "Schopenhauer and Freud." *International Journal of Psycho-Analysis* 75:1:101–18.

Young, Julian. 1987. *Willing and Unwilling: A Study in the Philosophy of Arthur Schopenhauer*. Boston: Martinus Nijhoff.

INDEX

absurdity of existence: Camus' concept of, 33, 124, 128–32; Cioran's concept of, 128; as pessimistic reaction to the human condition, 32–36; quixotic ethic as Unamuno's response to, 151–54; rebellion as Camus' response to, 148–56

Adams, Henry, 45n

Adorno, Theodor: as exemplar of pessimism, 5; manner of presentation of philosophy, significance of, 227–28; permanent decline of the human condition, belief in, 18; pessimism and political participation, 41n; tyranny of reason, concern regarding, 29

Aeschylus, 167

Anaximander, 168, 192, 199

aphorism: function, writing, and impact of, 226–27; irony and, 236–38; meaning of, xii, 226; mortality and, 233–36; other forms of expression, linkage to, 230–32; pessimism and, xii, 44–45, 121, 227–30, 243; political theory, employment for, 238–43

Aquinas, Saint Thomas, 20, 230

architecture, 185

Arendt, Hannah: birth, human ability to appreciate, 40; Camus and, 149n; as close associate of pessimism, 6; pessimism and political participation, 41n

Aristotle: Cioran's criticism of, 230; friends, the best thing for, 247; political regimes, inventory of, 10; time and historical patterns, view of, 9–10; and tragedy as offering purification, 169

art: functions of for Nietzsche, 182–85; genius in, 108–10; of living, Nietzsche's conception of, 8, 164–65, 188; politics and, Camus' vision of, 149–53, 157; postimpressionism, 268–69; Quixote and, 152

Assorted Opinions and Maxims (Nietzsche), 196

"Attempt at a Self-Criticism" (Nietzsche), 166

Augustine of Hippo, Saint: and evil as the absence of good, 93; and linear account of time, 12–13, 15; and pessimism, foreshadowing of, 245; and Rousseau, question of influence on, 52n; and time, inability to explain, 256

auto-critique of the Enlightenment, 29

Bailey, Joe, 6n

Becker, Alois, 86n.10

Beckett, Samuel, 30, 246

Benjamin, Walter, 6

Bennett, Oliver, 6n

Bergson, Henri, 228n.2, 229, 271

Beyond the Pleasure Principle (Freud), 86, 91, 93

Bilsker, Richard, 86n.8

Birth of Tragedy, The (Nietzsche), 166–68, 170–73, 178–79, 188, 194

Bizet, Alexandre-César-Léopold, 183–85

Blumenberg, Hans, 11–12n.12

Bonaparte, Marie, 95n.21

boredom: Cioran on, 32, 139–40; fashion, self-disguising of to ward off, 66; Leopardi on, 30–32; for metaphysical pessimists, 98–101; Schopenhauer on, 31

Borges, Jorge Luis, 266

Bradley, F. H., 228

Brobjer, Thomas, 181n.35

Brown, Wendy, 192n

Buddhism, 38, 84

Bury, J. B., 6n

calendar: Gregorian reform of, 14–15; ignoring the, difficulty of, 272. *See also* history; time

Camus, Albert: and the absurd, concept of, 33, 124, 128–32; Cioran and, 120n.4; "dandyism," critique of, 156–57; Don Juan, discussion of, 142–43; on *Don Quixote*/Don Quixote, 202; and the ethic of quantity, 142–44; on evil, 252; as exemplar of pessimism, 5; as existential pessimist, 43, 118–23; the future as a transcendental value, 42; humanistic ethic of, 122, 131–32, 155; and ironic history of rebellious thought, 135; life, affirmation of, 37, 272; living in the

Camus, Albert (*continued*)
  moment as a response to the pessimistic
  diagnosis, 141–44; Myth of Sisyphus,
  the challenge of, 36–37; Nietzsche and,
  157; pessimism and discouragement, rejection of association of, 3, 45; pessimism and political participation, 41;
  political activism as a response to the
  pessimistic diagnosis, 123, 144–45,
  148–57; reason and creation, opposition
  of, 34; reference to the future to authorize the present, concerns regarding,
  136; Sisyphus as happy, conclusion that
  we must imagine, 221; suicide, argument
  regarding, 128–31
Carmen (Bizet), 183–84
Cartwright, David E., 175n.26
Case of Wagner, The (Nietzsche), 183–84
Cauchi, Francesca, 165n.11
Cavell, Stanley, 79n
Cervantes, Miguel de: friends, the best
  thing for, 247; narrative, focus on, 210–
  13; the pessimists' affinity for, 201–5;
  politics of, 204–5n.4; the practice of
  pessimism illustrated by Quixote, 44,
  194, 219–24; Quixote as political educator, 213–17; Quixote's madness, 217–
  19; reintroduction of premodern values
  into the modern world, lampooning of,
  206; time, Don Quixote's struggle with,
  207–9. *See also* Quixote, Don
Cezanne, Paul, 268
Chambers, Clarke A., 6n
Chestov, Léon, 130
Christianity: Augustinians as "Christian
  pessimists," 245; Catholicism of Unamuno, 127n.10; change in western time-
  consciousness and, 11–12, 15; eluding
  by, 129; reform of the calendar and, 14–
  15; Rousseau's view of time and, 52n;
  time-keeping in monasteries, 12–13n.14
Christo, 198n.50
Chrysippus, 10
Cioran, E. M.: absurd, concept of, 128; on
  aphorism, 226, 229, 232, 243; aphoristic writing of, 232, 234, 241; banality,
  impact of, 244; boredom, problem of,
  32, 139–40; Camus and, 120n.4;
  "dandyism" of, 156–57; on *Don
  Quixote*/Don Quixote, 202; ecstasy, the
  ethic of, 140–41; as exemplar of pes-

simism, xii, 5; as existential pessimist,
  43, 118–23; fascism, question of early
  association with prewar, 118–19n.2,
  144n; freedom and happiness, man cannot decide between, 249; on happiness,
  118; the idolatry of tomorrow, 42, 135–
  36; misanthropic ethic of, 122, 155; pessimism of, 132–39; pessimistic irony, use
  of, 237–38; politics and the horrors of
  the twentieth century, energetic effort to
  hide from, 157n; posthistory, the nightmare of, 147n, 237; on Schopenhauer,
  121; suicide, argument regarding, 128,
  137–39; systematic philosophy as
  despotism, 230; "tonic of injustice,"
  250; withdrawal from life advocated
  by, 144–48
Civilization and Its Discontents (Freud),
  86, 112–16
Clark, Maudemarie, 173n.23
Clegg, Jerry, 86n.10
clocks, appearance of mechanical, 12–14
Columbus, Christopher: boredom, action
  as a means to avoid, 30–31; freedom,
  seeking of by embracing risk, 77; pessimistic freedom as exemplified by, 41;
  public consequences of the voyages of,
  82
Combat (Camus), 123n.8, 155
Connolly, William, 196
consciousness: brains as cause of, 259–60;
  of death, 21–22, 40; happiness and, tension between, 35–36; of history, 42–43
  (*see also* history); Rousseau's view of
  human capacity for, 23–24; Schopenhauer's view of, 86–91, 125; self (*see*
  self-consciousness); time (*see* time); Unamuno's understanding of, 124–25; unfortunate qualities of, 24
Cooper, Anthony Ashley (Lord Shaftesbury), 20n.27
Critique of Pure Reason (Kant), 87–88
cultural pessimism, 42–43; historical irony,
  55–63; humanism and misanthropy,
  choice between, 82–83; the ironies of
  modern life, 63–72; Leopardi's as alternative to Rousseau, 50–51; problems of,
  alternative responses to, 72–83; reason,
  limits of, 55; Rousseau as patriarch of,
  49–50; time, the burdens of, 51–55
cynics and cynicism: individual life rather

than state structure, focus on, 8; pessimism, relation to, 4

Danto, Arthur, 231
death: aphorism and, 233–36; centrality of for metaphysical pessimists, 101–6; consciousness of, 21–22, 40; problematic of for Camus, 128–32; problematic of for Unamuno, 125–28. *See also* suicide
Deleuze, Gilles, 271
Democritus, 167
Derrida, Jacques, 5n, 228
Dewey, John, xi, 17–18
"Dialogue of an Almanac-Peddler and a Passer-by, The" (Leopardi), 79–80
"Dialogue of Fashion and Death" (Leopardi), 21–22, 65–66
"Dialogue of Nature and a Soul" (Leopardi), 38
"Dialogue of Nature and the Soul," 77–78
"Dialogue of Plotinus and Porphyry" (Leopardi), 78–79
"Dialogue Between Torquato Tasso and his Guardian Spirit" (Leopardi), 53
Dionysian pessimism, 44; artistic pathos of, 182–85; as an art of living, 188; beliefs of, 264; critiques of contemporary pessimisms, 173–80; Don Quixote as exemplification of (*see* Quixote, Don); the future of, 195–200; Greek pessimism and, 166–73, 194; Nietsche's description of, 40, 161; Nietzsche as a pessimist, 161–67; origin of the term, 163; pessimism as a terror that liberates, 178; as a quest looking toward becoming and the future, 187–95; as a strong pessimism that destroys and builds, 180–87
Dionysus, 169–70
Dohrn-van Rossum, Gerhard, 12–13
Don Juan, 142–43
Don Quixote (Cervantes), 117, 194, 201–2, 205–6. *See also* Quixote, Don
Dostoevsky, Fyodor, 6, 183–84, 186
drama. *See* theater
Drassinower, Abraham, 91, 93n.16, 106n.30
Du Bois, W.E.B., 45n
Dumm, Thomas, 19n.25

Ecartèlement (Cioran), 133
Ecce Homo (Nietzsche), 172, 215

Einstein, Albert, 21n, 260
"Elegy to Birds, An" (Leopardi), 80–81
eluding. See *l'esquive*
Émile (Rousseau), 74–75
Émile et Sophie (Rousseau), 75
Enlightenment, the: auto-critique of, 29; progress of human reason celebrated by, 55
Epicureanism: individual life rather than state structure, focus on, 8; pessimism, distinguished from, 8; pessimism, parallels with, xi
Epicurus, 93n.17, 146
Essay on the Origin of Languages (Rousseau), 59–60
eternal recurrence, 181n.35, 190–92, 198
Euben, J. Peter, 19n.24
eudemonology, 107, 111–12, 114
Euripides, 167
evil, 252–54
existence, the absurdity of. *See* absurdity of existence
existential pessimism, 43–44, 118–24, 156–57; boredom and living the moment, 139–44; Camus' political activism, 144–45, 148–57; Cioran's, 132–39; Cioran's withdrawal from life, 144–48; the pessimistic rebel, 148–56; time, consciousness, and the absurd in Unamuno and Camus, 124–32

Fall into Time, The (Cioran), 133–34, 137
fascism: Camus on the plague of, 148; Cioran and, 118–19n.2, 144n
fashion: death, dialogue with, 21–22, 65–66; illusions produced by, 65–66
food, as history, 249–50
Foucault, Michel: as cultural pessimist, 44; as exemplar of pessimism, 5; Hadot and, 164–65n.9; pessimism and political participation, 41n; philosophy as a technique of the self, 8
"Fragments for the History of Philosophy" (Schopenhauer), 89
freedom: art and rebellion as Camus' route to, 149–51; Cioran's conception of, 146–48; Dienstag on, 248–49; experience of, 246–47; for Freud, 115; happiness and, tension between, 35–36, 63, 71; Leopardi's seeking of as a response to the problems uncovered by pessimism,

freedom (*continued*)
77–78, 81–82; modern life and the illusion of, 63, 66, 69–72; pessimistic (*see* pessimistic freedom); questions of, 244–45; Quixote and Unamuno's vision of, 151–53; Schopenhauer's position on, 111–12

Freud, Sigmund: boredom as point of departure from Schopenhauer, 100–101; death, centrality of for, 22, 101, 104–6; dialogue on religion paralleling that of Schopenhauer, 103n; dreams as an act of will, 250; as exemplar of metaphysical pessimism, 43, 85–86; as exemplar of pessimism, 5; grand structural approach to philosophy of, 119; the human condition, response to, 107, 112–15; humanistic ethic of, 115–17; human purpose and the reality of the universe, tension between, 33; illusions replaced by reason, implications of, 27; Kant, echoes of in, 95n.20; metaphysics of, 97n.23; the pleasure principle, 93–95, 101; psychotherapy, task of, 92, 106, 114; the reality principle, 95, 100–101, 112; unconscious, evidence of the existence of, 97n.22; the unconscious and time, gap between as fundamental cause of unhappiness, 91; unhappiness in human life, 92–97

Friedrich Nietzsche and His New Gospel (Hamblen), 162n.2
friendship, 247–48
Fuentes, Carlos, 206n
Future of an Illusion, The (Freud), 103n, 106
Futures Past (Koselleck), 11
futurity. *See* spontaneity

Gadamer, Hans-Georg, 227
Gast, Peter, 180n
Gay Science, The (Nietzsche), 179–80, 190–91, 203, 204n.3, 222
Genealogy of Morals, On the (Nietzsche), 108n.33
General Will, 74n.19, 90
Gillespie, Michael Allen, 191n.42
Goethe, Johann Wolfgang von, 231
Gooding-Williams, Robert, 188n.39, 193n
Gottfried, Paul, 85n.4
Greek pessimism, 166–73, 194

Greene, Graham, 127n.10
Gregorian calendar reform, 14–15
Guyer, Paul, 87n

Hadot, Pierre, 8, 164, 165n.9
Hamblen, Emily, 162n.2
happiness: the cultural pessimists on, 66–69; freedom and, tension between, 35–36, 63, 71; Freud's route to the possibility of, 113–14; Leopardi's position regarding, 78; possibility of for Schopenhauer, 112; reason and, 26–28; time-consciousness and, 23; outside of time for Rousseau, 51–52. *See also* unhappiness
Hardenberg, Friedrich von, 231
Hartmann, Eduard von: madness, speaking with the voice of, 192n; Nietzsche's criticism of, 37n.34, 162–63, 173–76, 188; Schopenhauer, interpretation of using the Hegelian Idea, 175n.27
Havel, Václav, 156n
Hegel, G.W.F.: artistic genius, theory of shared with Schopenhauer, 109n.35; Cioran's criticism of, 134, 230; historical utopianism of, xi; morning prayers, impact of, 254; negation as the essence of thinking, 262; question-answer vision in philosophy of history of, 34; satire, Romans' contribution of, 256; Schopenhauer's scorn for, 85
Heidegger, Martin: Camus' interest in, 124; fascism, question of early association with, 119n.2; foreshadowing of by Schopenhauer, 88, 90; as metaphysical pessimist, 44; reason, dangers of, 29–30
Heights of Despair, On the (Cioran), 132–33, 134n.14, 140–41
Heraclitus, 84, 168, 268
Herman, Arthur, 4n
Higgins, Kathleen, 179n
Hippocrates, 243
Historical Pessimism in the French Enlightenment (Vyverberg), 6n
history: ancient view of cyclical, 9–11; cultural pessimism and consciousness of, 42–43; emergence of modern concepts of, 14–16; existential pessimism and, 43; as food, 249–50; the future as the idolatry of tomorrow, 135–37; the irony of, 25–32; the irony of for cultural pes-

simists, 55–63; the irony of for existential pessimists, 135–36; modern view of linear, 10–12; pessimism as looking differently at, 5; prophecy and, 251–52. *See also* time

History of the Hour (Dohrn-van Rossum), 12

"History of the Human Race" (Leopardi), 26–28, 56–57

Hobbes, Thomas, 18n.23, 35

Hollingdale, R. J., 17n.20

Hollinrake, Roger, 162n.2

Holocaust, the, 253

Horkheimer, Max, 18, 29

hour-glasses, 13–14

Human, All-Too-Human (Nietzsche), 177

human condition, the: absurdity of existence as pessimistic reaction to (*see* absurdity of existence); optimism/pessimism denoted by position regarding, 17–18; pessimism and, xi–xii; pessimism as nonprogressive, linear view of, 18

humanistic ethic of pessimism: of Camus, 122, 131–32, 155; of Freud, 115–17; of Leopardi, 82–83; misanthropic ethic, distinguished from, 157–58; of Unamuno, 122, 155

In Search of Lost Time (Proust), 150

insomnia, 140

Interpretation of Dreams, The (Freud), 94

Ionesco, Eugène, 120n.4

irony: aphorism and, 236–38; historical, 25–32, 55–63, 135–36

Isaac, Jeffrey C., 149n

Is Life Worth Living? (James), 36–37n.32

James, William, 36–37n.32

Janaway, Christopher, 166n.13

Jansenism, 52n

Jarrety, Michel, 120n.5

Jaspers, Karl, 130

Jünger, Ernst, 118n.2

Kafka, Franz, 39, 263

Kant, Immanuel: epistemology of, 54n; freedom, idea of, 111; Freud, definition of consciousness and, 95n.20; progressive liberalism of, xi; Schopenhauer, influence on, 84, 87–89

Kaufmann, Walter, 166n.13

Kerényi, Carl, 169n.18

Kierkegaard, Søren, 124, 129

Koselleck, Reinhart, 11, 12n.12

Laignel-Lavastine, Alexandra, 118–19n.2

language: the discipline of inability in using, 246; Rousseau on the development of, 58–61

La Rochefoucauld, François de: aphoristic writing of, 241; fresh/modern quality of the writing of, 243; history of the aphorism, place in, 230; pessimistic ethic, anticipation of in possibly the first pessimistic aphorism, 233–36; as precursor of pessimism, 6, 49

Lasch, Christopher, 5n

laughter, in Leopardi's response to the ironies of life, 80–81

Leibniz, G. W., 9n.7

Leopardi, Giacomo: on the absurdity of existence, 36; aphoristic writing of, 231; boredom, effects of, 30–32, 140; concern for others by pessimists, 269; cultural pessimism, as exemplar of, 42, 50–51; death, centrality of, 21–22; on *Don Quixote*/Don Quixote, 201–2; as exemplar of pessimism, xii, 5; fashion, deceptions presented by, 65–66; human distress, expectation of, 34; humanistic ethic of, 82–83; life, affirmation of, 37–38, 40–41; modern life, the delusions of, 63–68, 70–72; Nietzsche's praise of, 44n, 162–63; pleasure, time and the inability to experience, 97; poetry of, 55n.9; problems of pessimism, strategy for coping with, 72, 76–83; reason, destructiveness of, 26–28; reason, development of and the ironies of history, 55–58, 60n; Rousseau and, 50, 53–54, 58; time, the burdens of, 53–55

l'esquive (eluding), 129–32, 134

Letter to M. D'Alembert on the Theatre (Rousseau), 64, 68, 73, 82

liberalism: justice as achievable object, assumption of, 35; optimism of, 18, 267–68; pessimism as critical of progressive, xi

Lichtenburg, Georg Christoph: aphoristic writing of, 241; hour-glasses, meaning associated with, 14; "pessimismus," usage of the term, 9n.7; as precursor of pessimism, 6

Locke, John: consciousness as the capacity for "reflection," 23; "Egyptian darkness" of the turn away from philosophy, 269; progressive liberalism of, xi; *Second Treatise*, format of, 238; *Second Treatise*, mixed response to, 239
Löwith, Karl, 11n.12

Machiavelli, Niccolo: format of the *Prince*, 238; fortune, power of, 71; historical time, interest in, 49; Rousseau, comparison to, 74n.20
Magee, Bryan, 85n.5
Man of La Mancha, 202–3
Mann, Thomas, 6
Marcuse, Herbert, 86n.9
Marx, Karl, 17
Marxism, 129
Melville, Herman, 45n, 269n
metaphysical pessimism, 43, 84–86, 115–17; the boredom of conscious life, 98–101; death, centrality of, 101–6; influence of predecessors on, 97; remedies for the human condition, 106–15; time and human consciousness, problem posed by, 86–91; unhappiness as the reality of human life, 92–98
Migotti, Mark, 175n.26
Mill, John Stuart, xi, 4, 17
Misanthrope, The (Molière), 82
misanthropic ethic of pessimism: of Cioran, 122, 155; humanistic ethic, distinguished from, 157–58; of Rousseau, 82–83; of Schopenhauer, 116–17
modernity: the cultural pessimists' responses to, 72–82; ironies of for cultural pessimists, 63–72; pessimism as a child of, 8–16; time-consciousness as the distinguishing element of, 9–16
Molière, Jean-Baptiste, 68–69, 82
Momigliano, Arnaldo, 11
money, 256–57
Montaigne, Michel de, 5–6, 16, 49
Montesquieu, Charles-Louis de Secondat, 49
Moral Essays (Leopardi), 30, 52–54, 56, 63–64, 76–81
Moret, Phillippe, 230
multiple personality disorder, 253–54
Mumford, Lewis, 5, 45n
Murray, Peter Durno, 191n.42, 194n

Myth of Sisyphus, The (Camus), 36, 121, 123–24, 129–30, 141–43, 148–49

Nehamas, Alexander, 166n.13
Neiman, Susan, 19n.24, 191n.43
newspapers, 254–55
Newton, Isaac, 13n.16
Nietzsche, Friedrich: aphoristic writing of, 231–32, 234, 241; "art of living" as a criteria substituting for ethics, 8, 164–65; Camus and, 157; Cervantes and, 211–12; Dionysian pessimism (*see* Dionysian pessimism); *Don Quixote*/Don Quixote, affinity with, 44, 194, 197, 201–4, 219, 222–25; eternal recurrence, 181n.35, 190–92, 198; grand structural approach to philosophy, discrediting of, 119; Hartmann, criticisms of, 37n.34, 162–63, 173–76, 188; Leopardi and, 44n, 50, 162–63; life, affirmation of, 37, 39–40; metaphysics, origin of, 41–42; pain that instigated the first thought, 261; Pascal, contrasted with, 257; as a pessimist, xii, 3, 5, 161–66; postimpressionism, source of, 268; propositions of pessimism, response to, 19; Quixote, comparison of Zarathustra to, 223–24; resignation, denial of pessimist's need for, 197–200; Rousseau and, 44n, 162; Schopenhauer and, 44, 108n.33, 162–63, 165–69, 173, 175–80, 225; Socrates, optimistic philosophy of, 34, 270; temples: to erect one, another must be destroyed, 272; time, humans and cows compared regarding their sense of, 20; time's effects on the human soul, 55; on truth-seekers, 251; Zarathustra, self-identification as continuation of, 215
Nietzsche, Wagner and the Philosophy of Pessimism (Hollinrake), 162n.2
nihilism: pessimism, relation to, 4–5, 186, 256; pessimism and, Nietzsche's perception of, 163; Schopenhauer's pessimism and, 176–79
No Exit (Sartre), 30
Novalis. *See* Hardenberg, Friedrich von
Nussbaum, Martha, 8, 165n.11

Oakeshott, Michael, 220
O'Hara, Frank, 226

optimism: account of the human condition as definitive of, 17–18; metaphysics and, 41–42; pessimism as opposed to a modern, xi; reason as a source of power over the world, belief in, 34; time, disappointment and resentment generated by obliviousness to, 267

Ortega y Gasset, José: Cervantes' focus on narrative, reason for, 211; Dionysian pessimism found in Quixote, 225; on *Don Quixote*/Don Quixote, 201–2, 204, 213, 221, 223; as exemplar of pessimism, 5; the past, relation to, 263; Unamuno, disagreement with over Cervantes, 204n.4

Panza, Sancho: government by, 205, 214–17; Quixote's education of, 213–15; story left unfinished by, 208–9

Parerga and Paralipomena (Schopenhauer), 103–4, 107

Parfait, Nicole, 157n

Pascal, Blaise: aphoristic writing of, 241; modernism of, 52n; Nietzsche, contrasted with, 257; as precursor of pessimism, 6, 49

Penal Colony, The (Kafka), 39

perfectibility, 58–62

performative contradiction, charge of, 265

pessimism: absurdity of existence (*see* absurdity of existence); account of the human condition as definitive of, 17–18; American, 45n; antipragmatism of, 269; as antisystematic philosophy, 7–8; aphorism and (*see* aphorism); beliefs of, 264; burden of time and, 19–25 (*see also* time); cultural (*see* cultural pessimism); decline, not equivalent to theories of, 18; Dionysian (*see* Dionysian pessimism); disposition rather than theory, perception as, 3–4, 17; existential (*see* existential pessimism); freedom associated with (*see* pessimistic freedom); the irony of history, 25–32; life, resignation and the range of responses to the question of, 36–41; metaphysical (*see* metaphysical pessimism); as a modern phenomenon, 8–9, 16; negative assumptions regarding, ix–x; nihilism and (*see* nihilism); political potential of (*see* pessimistic politics); postimpressionism of, 268–69;

propositions of, 19–41; responses to the diagnoses of (*see* responses to the pessimistic diagnosis); self-contradiction, charge of, 54n; time and (*see* time); as a tradition/school of thought, xii–xiii, 3, 5–8, 43–44, 121–22, 156, 270–71; types of, 42–44, 132n, 156–58 (*see also* cultural pessimism; existential pessimism; metaphysical pessimism); widespread use of the term, beginning of, 9

pessimistic freedom: articulation of a concept of, 41; Dienstag on, 248–49; experience of, 246–47; questing figures as exemplars for, 267 (*see also* Columbus, Christopher; Quixote, Don); questions of, 244–45. See also freedom

pessimistic politics, 123–24, 145; of Camus, 123, 144–45, 148–57; challenge of, 268–69; as a critique of modern political orders, 5; Freud's indication of the way toward, 115; government of Sancho Panza, 205, 214–17; Nietzsche's, 196–97; participation in, 41; Unamuno's, 123, 144

Philonenko, Alexis, 49n.2, 73n, 84n.2

philosophy: as failed science, 255–56; "Is life worth living?" as fundamental question of, 36–37; Leopardi on, 67–68, 71; non-system-building, 8; political (*see* political philosophy/theory); school of thought, identification of, 7; twentieth-century detachment of, 259

Philosophy in the Tragic Age of the Greeks (Nietzsche), 168

Philosophy as a Way of Life (Hadot), 8

Pindar, 203

pity, 58–59n.11

Plague, The (Camus), 148

Plato: assumption that reason would provide happiness, 34; dialogic form of, 121; dialogues as "aporetic," 228; knowledge and happiness as coterminous, 26–27; optimistic philosophy of, 171–72, 270; perfect human life, hope for others to achieve, 263; systematic, ordering philosophy of, 167; time, views on, 9–10n.8

Pocock, J.G.A., 11, 14–15

political philosophy/theory: aphorism as tool for, 238–43; pessimism, reasons for rejection from the canon of, 3–5, 7–8, political philosophy/theory (*continued*) 265; post-Renaissance, conflict between optimism and pessimism as best characterization of, 266, 270; starting point for, mutual contradictoriness of freedom and happiness as, 36; temporality, problems created by as central for, 266–67 (*see also* time)

politics, pessimistic. *See* pessimistic politics

Polybius, 10

population of the earth, puzzle posed by, 252

postimpressionism, 268–69

postmodernism, 271–72

Poulet, George, 12n.12

pragmatism, 18, 34–35, 269

Précis (Cioran), 134n.15

pre-Socratics, pessimism of, 167–69. *See also* Greek pessimism

progress: contemporary grasp of time/history and the idea of, 5; contemporary Western discourse continues to depend on, 267–68; as a modern idea, 16; pessimism as negation, not opposite, of theories of, 18; pessimist position regarding, 25; as reported in the newspaper, 254–55; transmuted/refracted into its opposite, Rousseau's view of, 28–29

prophecy, 251–52

Proust, Marcel, 150, 211

Pythagoras, 9, 88

questing. *See* Columbus, Christopher; Quixote, Don

"Question Concerning Technology, The" (Heidegger), 29

Quixote, Don: death, constant presence of, 22; as inspiration, 225; madness, the narrative quest creates the appearance of, 217–19; narrative exemplars, values contained in, 210–13; Nietzsche's questing pessimist, as example of, 44, 194, 197, 203–5, 222–24; pessimistic ethic, embodiment of, 117; pessimistic freedom exemplified by, 41; pessimists, parallels with, xi; pessimists' interest in, 201–2; as political educator, 213–17; the practice of pessimism, illustration of, 219–24; time, struggle with, 207–9; Unamuno's vision of, 136, 151–52, 157;

windmills, charging at, 209; Zarathustra, comparison to, 223–24

quixotic ethics, 151–55, 157

Rand, Ayn, 199

reading, 248–49

reason: historical irony for cultural pessimists and, 55–63; ironic results of obtaining, 27–30; life and, conflict between, 125–28; limits of for the cultural pessimist, 55; unhappiness arising from, 23–24, 26–28. *See also* consciousness

Rebel, The (Camus), 120n.4, 122–24, 130–31, 134–35, 148–51, 153–55

Réflexions ou sentences et maximes morals (La Rochefoucauld), 233–34

resignation: Cioran's advocacy of, 144–48; Nietzsche's contention regarding, 166; Nietzsche's denial that pessimism must lead to, 197–200; as possible response to life, 38–40; Rousseau's advocacy of, 37, 82–83, 107; Schopenhauer's advocacy of, 37–39, 82, 106–12, 145; usage of the term, 19n.25

responses to the pessimistic diagnosis: Camus' living in the moment/ethic of quantity, 141–44; Camus' rebel and artist, political activity and, 148–56; Cioran's boredom and the ethic of ecstasy, 139–41; Cioran's withdrawal from life, 144–48; Leopardi's embrace of self-directed activity, 76–83; Nietzsche's "art of living," 8, 164–65; Nietzsche's denial of pessimist's need for resignation, 197–200; Rousseau's resignation from life, 37, 72–76, 82–83, 107; Schopenhauer's resignation from life, 37–39, 82, 106–12, 145; Unamuno's quixotic ethic, 151–54, 157

ressentiment, 110n, 192n

Reveries of the Solitary Walker (Rousseau), 51–52, 58

Ricoeur, Paul, 86n.9

Rieff, Philip, 103n

Robinson, Joan, 265

Rodin, Auguste, 184n

Rohde, Erwin, 169n.18

Romania's Transfiguration (Cioran), 141n

romanticism, 179–80

Rousseau, Jean-Jacques: animal/savage

condition and conscious/reasoning beings, distinction between, 20, 52; consciousness and reflection, capacity for, 23–24; cultural pessimism, as exemplar of, 42, 49–50; freedom, idea of, 111–12; language, development of, 58–61; Leopardi and, 50, 53–54, 58; Machiavelli, comparison to, 74n.20; misanthropic ethic of, 82–83; on modern freedom, 69–70; modern life, the delusions of, 64–72; moral degeneration of human species as basis for pessimism of, 18; Nietzsche's criticism of, 44n, 162; pain that instigated the first thought, 261; perfectibility, faculty of, 58–62; performative contradiction, response to charge of, 265; permanent decline of the human condition, belief in, 18; pessimism, as exemplar of, 5; pleasure, time and the inability to experience, 97; pleasure as a negative condition, 93n.17; problems of pessimism, strategy for coping with, 72–78, 82–83; reason, development of and decline in moral character, 28–29, 55; reason and Nature, opposition of, 33–35; reflection, capacity for and human development as historical irony, 58–63; resignation from life, advocacy of, 37, 72–76, 82–83; Schopenhauer, parallels to and influence on, 87–88, 90, 94n.18; suffering, time-consciousness as leading to, 25; the theatre, critique of, 64–65; time, problems posed by, 51–53, 125; time-consciousness, emergence into as advance in human development, 21

Saint-Just, Louis-Antoine-Léon de, 131
Santayana, George, 45n
Sartre, Jean-Paul, 6, 30, 256
satire, 256
Schlegel, August Wilhelm von, 170n.19, 231
Schlegel, Friedrich von, 231
Schopenhauer, Arthur: on the absurdity of existence, 36; the animal as present incarnate, 20; aphoristic writing of, 231, 234, 241; artistic genius, theory of, 108–10; boredom in human life, 30–31, 98–100, 140; change and suffering as a function of time-consciousness, 22–23; death, centrality of, 101–6; on Don Quixote/Don Quixote, 201; downward historical trend, not a believer in permanent, 18; epistemology, derivation from Kant, 54n; as exemplar of metaphysical pessimism, 43, 84–86; as exemplar of pessimism, xii, 5; the future, acknowledgment of the power of the past but not of, 193; grand structural approach to philosophy of, 119; human life as a mistake, 33; humans as equilibria-seekers for, 93n.17; interpreting written thoughts, task of, 232; Kant, influence of, 84, 87–89; Leopardi and, 50; linear time as an illusion, 21; misanthropic ethic of, 116–17; Nietzsche and, 44, 108n.33, 162–63, 165–69, 173, 175–80, 225; as pessimist in both psychological and philosophical senses, 4, 17; propositions of pessimism, response to, 19; resignation from life, advocacy of, 37–39, 82, 106–12, 145; Rousseau, parallels to and influence of, 87–88, 90, 94n.18; suffering, and the incomplete pessimism of, 191–92; time in human consciousness, centrality and problematic of, 86–91, 125; time's effects on the human soul, 55; unhappiness in human life, 92–98; the vanity of existence, 98–100; will, evidence of the existence of, 97n.22; Wittgenstein, relation to, 89n

Schopenhauer as Educator (Nietzsche), 177, 225

Second Discourse (Rousseau), 52, 58–59, 61–62, 68–70, 73

self, the: pessimism and, xi–xii; philosophies of, distinction between pessimism and, 8–9; sexuality and, 189–90

self-consciousness: association with time-consciousness, 20–21; boredom and, 30–32; and time for Schopenhauer, 86–91

Seurat, Georges, 264, 268
sexuality, 189–90, 196n.47
Shaftesbury, Lord. See Cooper, Anthony Ashley
shipwrecked, the, 264
Shoah, the, 253

Short History of Decay, A (Cioran), 120, 134–35, 138–39
Simmel, Georg, 175n.26
skeptics and skepticism, 4–5, 8
Social Contract, The (Rousseau), 74–76
socialism, optimism of, 18
Socrates: Greek tragedy, destruction of, 167; Leopardi's critique of, 67; optimistic philosophy of, 34–35, 170–72, 270
Soll, Ivan, 175n.26, 179n
Sontag, Susan, 230–31n.4
Sophocles, 167, 238
Spacks, Patricia Meyer, 30n
speech, truth and, 250–51
speed, modern emphasis on, 65n
Spinoza, Baruch, 90n.14
spontaneity, as a pessimist response to the question of life and suffering, 40–41
Stambaugh, Joan, 193n
Starkie, Walter, 49n.3
Starobinski, Jean, 49n.2, 52n
Steiner, George, 169n.17
stoicism: cyclical view of time, 9; as a guide to existence, not a set of moral duties, 111; immunity of mental powers from the effects of time, belief in as point of departure from pessimism, 71–72; individual life rather than state structure, focus on, 8; Nietzsche on, 190; pessimism, parallels with, xi; pessimism distinguished from, 8
Strauss, Leo, 238–39
Strong, Tracy, 167n, 186n, 196
suffering: Christian or tragic meaning of, Nietzsche's conception of the choice between, 194–95; desire to escape, question of, 37, 39; development of as historical irony for Leopardi, 57–58; Dionysian, 169–71; eternal recurrence as taking pleasure in destruction that causes, 190–91; as instigation of the first thought, 261–62; metaphysical pessimism and, 43; pragmatic assumption that answers are available to deliver us from, 34–35; Schopenhauer's withdrawal as alternative to Nietzsche's affirmation of, 191; time-consciousness as leading to, 23–25; uselessness and aimlessness of, 34

suicide: if an animal were to commit, 249; Camus' position on, 128–31; Cioran's position on, 128, 137–39; Leopardi's position on life and, 78–79, 103; philosophical problem, as the one truly serious, 36–37; Schopenhauer's position on, 102–3

Tacitus, 10n.9
Tallis, Raymond, 4n
Tears and Saints (Cioran), 134n.14, 140–41
Temptation to Exist, The (Cioran), 144n
theater: Camus' embrace of, 142–43, 149, 152–53; *Carmen,* 183–84; Greek tragedy, 167, 169–71, 185; Greek tragedy, Apollonian element of, 170n.20, 172n; Rousseau's comparison of ancient and modern, 68; Rousseau's critique of, 64–65, 143
Therapy of Desire, The (Nussbaum), 8
thought, the initial, 260–63
Thus Spoke Zarathustra (Nietzsche), 174n, 192–93, 195, 211–12, 223–24
time: ancient view of, 9–10; burdens of, 19–25, 51–55, 125; consciousness and, Schopenhauer's view of, 86–91; consciousness of, 9–16, 20–21, 39; Don Quixote's struggle with, 207–9; the Gregorian calendar reform, 14–15; historians and, 251–52; hour-glasses, use of, 13–14; knowledge and, 258; knowledge of/destruction resulting from the passage of, tension between, 54n; mechanical clocks, appearance of, 12–14; metaphysical pessimism and, 43; modern unhappiness predicated on the unidirectionality of, 67; money and, 256–57; nonlinear of postmodernism, 271–72; opposite of, lack of, 257–58; pessimism as looking differently at, 5; pessimism as a nonprogressive, linear account of, 16; problems posed by, 125–26, 266–67; Rousseau's view of reason/morals and, 29; as threat and promise for pessimists, xi–xii
Tragic Sense of Life in Men and Nations, The (Unamuno), 120–21, 124–27
Transfiguration of Romania, The (Cioran), 118n.2

Trouble with Being Born, The (Cioran), 137, 140
Twain, Mark, 45n, 269n
Twilight of the Idols (Nietzsche), 180–81, 189–90

Unamuno, Miguel de: "baneful consequences" of opposing views, objection to attacking, x; consciousness, unfortunate qualities of, 24; contradictions, living in and by, 130; on *Don Quixote/* Don Quixote, 201, 204n.4; as exemplar of pessimism, 5; as existential pessimist, 43, 118–23; the future, dismissal of, 136; humanistic ethic of, 122, 155; life, affirmation of, 37–38; political activism of, 123, 144; quixotic ethics as response to diagnosis of pessimism, 151–54, 157; reason and life, conflict between, 124–28; religious views of, 127n.10
unhappiness: the aimlessness of suffering and pessimism's concern with, 33–34; in human life for metaphysical pessimists, 92–98; pessimism as unrelated to, 17; prevalence of for existential pessimists, 122. *See also* happiness

vanity of existence, for Schopenhauer, 98–100
Varro, 14n.17
Vattimo, Gianni, 193n
Vauvenargues, Luc de Clapiers de, 49
Villa, Dana, 41n

Voltaire, 9n.7
Vyverberg, Henry, 6n, 49n.1

Wagner, Richard, 179–80, 182n
Waiting for Godot (Beckett), 30, 246
Warren, Mark, 165n.10
Weber, Max, 5
Weil, Simone, 6, 244
What Makes a Life Significant? (James), 37n.32
White, Hayden, 211n
Whitrow, G. J., 12
Williams, Raymond, 6n
Will to Power, The (Nietzsche), 164n.8
withdrawal from life. *See* resignation
Wittgenstein, Ludwig: as close associate of pessimism, 6; "family resemblance," notion of, 7; language, description of, 89n; style of in the *Tractatus*, 236; tool box, notion of, 238–40
World as Will and Representation, The (Schopenhauer), 84n.2, 87–89, 90n.13, 94, 108–11

Young, Julian, 85n.7

Zappa, Frank, 156n
Zarathustra, comparison to Quixote, 223–24

Bierce, Ambrose: "Death is not the end. There remains the litigation over the estate."